A. Robinson

Scenarios for Risk Management and Global Investment Strategies

For other titles in the Wiley Finance Series
please see www.wiley.com/finance

Scenarios for Risk Management and Global Investment Strategies

Rachel E. S. Ziemba

and

William T. Ziemba

John Wiley & Sons, Ltd

Other Wiley Editorial Offices

John Wiley & Sons Inc., 111 River Street, Hoboken, NJ 07030, USA

Jossey-Bass, 989 Market Street, San Francisco, CA 94103-1741, USA

Wiley-VCH Verlag GmbH, Boschstr. 12, D-69469 Weinheim, Germany

John Wiley & Sons Australia Ltd, 42 McDougall Street, Milton, Queensland 4064, Australia

John Wiley & Sons (Asia) Pte Ltd, 2 Clementi Loop #02-01, Jin Xing Distripark, Singapore 129809

John Wiley & Sons Canada Ltd, 6045 Freemont Blvd, Mississauga, Ontario, L5R 4J3, Canada

Wiley also publishes its books in a variety of electronic formats. Some content that appears
in print may not be available in electronic books.

Anniversary Logo Design: Richard J. Pacifico

Library of Congress Cataloging-in-Publication Data

Ziemba, Rachel.
  Scenarios for risk management and global investment strategies / Rachel
E. S. Ziemba and William T. Ziemba.
    p. cm. – (Wiley finance series)
  Includes bibliographical references and index.
  ISBN 978-0-470-31924-6 (cloth)
  1. Investments, Foreign. 2. Risk management. 3. International finance.
4. Investment analysis. I. Ziemba, W. T. II. Title.
  HG4538.Z57 2007
  332.67'3 – dc22

                                   2007026413

British Library Cataloguing in Publication Data

A catalogue record for this book is available from the British Library

ISBN 978-0-470-31924-6 (HB)

Typeset in 10/12 Times by Laserwords Private Limited, Chennai, India
Printed and bound in Great Britain by Antony Rowe Ltd, Chippenham, Wiltshire
This book is printed on acid-free paper responsibly manufactured from sustainable forestry
in which at least two trees are planted for each one used for paper production.

Dedicated to Sandra L. Schwartz,
our third family member without whose help
this book would not have been finished.

Contents

Acknowledgements

We owe a great debt to Paul Wilmott for starting his wonderful magazine *Wilmott*. Since the magazine's launch in September 2002, Bill has had a regular column with Rachel guest writing her own or joint columns. Paul also kindly gave us access to the beautiful artwork of the magazine for use in this book.

Special thanks go to Dan Tudball, executive editor of *Wilmott* for his help in turning our draft columns into professional articles in the magazine. Liam Larkin who does the artwork for the magazine was very helpful in not only producing the original columns but in providing them for our use in producing this book.

Thanks go to Emily Pears and the Wiley staff for providing us the opportunity to revisit this material in this book and for producing this volume.

Thanks also to Ren Ruoen and Bjarni Kristjansson for assisting with research material in Chapters 16 and Chapter 19, respectively. Special thanks to David Luenberger and Edward O. Thorp for helpful comments.

Rachel would like to thank a number of colleagues and mentors at Oxford University, the Canadian International Development Agency (CIDA), the International Development Research Center (IDRC) and Roubini Global Economics for supporting work that inspired many of the items in this book, as well as participants at talks at the University of Cyprus, Renmin University of China, Oxford University, University of Victoria and IDRC where some of the ideas were first aired. In particular Kalypso Nicolaidis, Ngaire Woods, Brent Herbert-Copley, Rohinton Medhora, Andrés Rius and Martha Melesse provided feedback and guidance on work that was incorporated into this book. IDRC funded my research project on Currency Devaluations in Developing Countries on which parts of Chapters 17 and 18 are based. Although I joined Roubini Global Economics after the bulk of this book was completed, my work with Nouriel Roubini and Brad Setser has helped me understand new aspects of risks to the global economy.

I do not have space to list here the many friends and family members who supported this work, either by reading drafts, helping to arrange meetings, providing places to stay or encouraging my ideas. Two friends stand out: Rutha Astravas, who added a new angle to my research agenda in Argentina and Lindsay Wise, who convinced me to just come to Egypt in the fall of 2003 to check out some 'currency shenanigans', which provided me with the material for my first *Wilmott* column and much more.

Bill thanks the various organizations and universities who invited him to give talks on these subjects over the years and his coauthors who are cited in the text.

Our third family member, Sandra Schwartz, has not only produced this book and the columns but has been a research colleague and sounding board on all the topics. Much of the quality of this book is due to her efforts. Without her this book would not have been possible. All mistakes are the responsibility of the authors.

Preface

This book discusses scenarios for risk management and developing global investment strategies. We are guided by the use of careful analysis to generate prospective scenarios. Simply put, what are the chances that various future events will occur over time? How should these events and their chances influence investment decisions? Assessing all possible outcomes is fundamental to risk management, financial engineering and investment strategies. We believe that a careful consideration of future scenarios will lead to better investment decisions and avoid financial disasters. The book presents tools and case studies for analyzing a wide variety of investment strategies, building scenarios to optimize returns.

We discuss a variety of topics and provide various case studies relevant for hedge fund, insurance, pension fund and other investment professionals and amateur investors. We place a special emphasis on strategies used by the greatest investors to gain their high returns. To do so, we analyze hedge fund concepts and performance including major fund disasters. These disasters have basic common characteristics, which we call the recipe for disaster. This negative outcome materializes when one overbets, that is, has too many positions relative to one's capital (including capital that can reliably be called upon in times of need) and one is not diversified. By not diversified we do not mean that we are mean-variance diversified in average times. Rather diversification in all the possible scenarios is crucial. This means that low probability scenarios cannot, as is typically done, be assigned probability zero, that is disregarded. Also, and very crucially, scenario dependent correlation matrices are needed, so that one knows how assets correlate in a scenario that actually occurs. Simulations of past average correlations, which are typically done even with stress testing, are insufficient for full protection. For example, it is known that equity correlations rise and equity/bond correlations fall with a decline in equity prices. However, when one is in a crash mode, then equity prices are falling but bond prices are generally rising so that the bond/stock correlation is negative. Indeed historically, the bond/stock correlation is frequently negative even though most of the time this correlation is positive. Chapter 21 provides an example of these scenario dependent correlation matrices used in a model that has been used across Austria since 2000 for the Siemen's Austria pension plan. Pension plans are less levered or not levered at all as compared to hedge funds.

If one violates (1) that is, one overbets, and (2) one is not diversified in all plausible scenarios then two things can happen. In such cases, one can be lucky and avoid a bad scenario, racking up excess profits and receiving large fees. Indeed many hedge funds and traders typically do this as there are huge rewards for making such profits and an adverse outcome is statistically less likely. In fact, even if traders know about the dangers of (1) and (2), it may be optimal for them to just up the bets to make more fees assuming that a bad scenario will not occur or if it occurs, it is so far in the distant future that previous profits and fees will exceed the disastrous negative results. However, if one is over bet and not diversified and a bad scenario hits, then one can lose a large percent of ones wealth. We discuss such disastrous outcomes in Chapters 11–13 using the case studies of hedge fund disasters of LongTerm Capital Management (LTCM), Niederhoffer and Amaranth Advisors. For LTCM the bad scenario was subtle, namely *investor confidence*. They were greatly over-bet but reasonably well diversified except in this confidence failure when all the correlations rose so that they lost in all their investments. Option volatilities rose, bond yields rose and this led to their 95 %, $ 4 billion loss in August and September 1998. LTCM was loaded with talent but their risk control based on value at risk plus simulations was insufficient to protect them. At the end of 1997, they returned $ 2.8 billion to investors hoping to boost their returns. The non-availability of liquidity, after returning money to their investors, was crucial as disaster unfolded after Russia's currency devaluation. The October 1997 imported crash caused a 7 % fall on the 27th and a 3 % fall in the S&P futures on the morning of the 28th which caused the Niederhoffer fund to fail. Their positions were just too many and not diversified, namely, a massive number of short S&P500 futures puts. Regrettably, the market returned to its initial value by the end of the week and the puts went to zero a few weeks later. So the 10 % fall on Monday and Tuesday was recovered by Friday. But one must have enough capital at all times. Amaranth, discussed in Chapter 13, has common elements: a trader way overbet in one market, natural gas, and lost $ 6 billion when the gas prices fell from $ 7 to $ 5. Of course, natural gas prices fluctuated wildly in the past few years, ranging from $ 2 to $ 11, so such a drop is not surprising.

We have organized the book in four sections. Part I focusses on the Kelly criterion which is used by many great investors to achieve great returns. The Kelly or capital growth criterion is the maximization of long run asymptotic wealth and the minimization of the time to sufficiently large goals. This is equivalent to maximizing the expected logarithm of final wealth period by period. Thus if you plan forever, the Kelly investor will not only get the most final wealth but get all the wealth. In the short run, with its almost zero Arrow-Pratt risk aversion, log is the most risky utility function one would ever want to use. If the data is uncertain, it is very easy to overbet. Also, even in the long but not infinite run, one can still lose a lot of money with the Kelly criterion. A simulation shows that over 700 independent bets, all with a substantial advantage, that most of the time the Kelly criterion will generate very high final wealth. But a small percent of the time, a sequence of bad scenarios coupled with the large bets the Kelly criterion rec-ommends, leads to enormous losses. Hence, one should use the criterion carefully. Great investors such as Keynes in the 1920s–40s and Warren Buffett of Berkshire Hathaway have acted as if they were Kelly bettors. Ed Thorp and Bill Benter have used the Kelly criterion along with investment strategies with positive means to make hundreds of millions in hedge fund investment vehicles. We propose a modification of the Sharpe ratio to evaluate great investors. The Sharpe ratio, which is based on normal distributions, penalizes large *gains* as well as losses. Our measure is based solely on losses. Investors with high mean returns and low monthly losses score well on this measure. Berkshire Hathaway improves with this measure to about 0.90 but the Ford Foundation, Harvard, the Quantum Fund (George Soros) and the Windsor fund do not. Still Ford and Harvard beat Berkshire Hathaway slightly because Berkshire Hathaway had too many losses. The second best known investor is Thorp at 13.8 for his Princeton-Newport hedge fund with only three monthly losses in 240 months in 1969–88. Renaissance Medallion, at 26.4, is even higher, see pages 295–8. Part I ends with a discussion of the top US university endowments including Yale which had excellent returns, about 16 % for the past twenty years. Harvard has a similarly good record. They do this with very careful analysis in their own internal trading plus good relationships with excellent outside private placement, real assets such as real estate and timber and hedge funds. The proportion of typical exchange traded equities and bonds has declined to be only a small part of the portfolio. The behaviour of great investors is explained by breaking down investors into five distinct camps as discussed in Chapter 6.

Part II of the book discusses hedge fund investment strategies. There are two areas covered: a detailed discussion of a typical successful convergence trade; and a discussion of how traders lose money in derivatives and then three case studies of hedge fund disasters. Chapter 9 discusses hedge fund strategy types and then describes the Nikkei put warrant risk arbitrage of 1990. The Japanese stock market in 1989 was overvalued but held up with low interest rates. Nikkei put warrants (three year puts) appeared in Canadian and later US markets. The Canadian puts traded for prices substantially above fair value based on historical volatility. Hence, a risk arbitrage trade was to short the Canadian overpriced warrants while simultaneously hedging by buying fairly priced US puts. The both sides do not constitute an arbitrage as the two sides were not the exact same product but one that was close. Then one waits until the two sides converge within a transaction band. A second successful trade with both puts on the same (the American stock exchange) was based simply on the size of the contract. This trade, similar to the small firm advantage effect, was to buy cheap puts worth half a Nikkei and to short 2.5 times as many expensive puts worth 0.2 of a Nikkei, then in about a month, the prices converged. These types of trades are very good for hedge funds but are not without various risks. Chapter 10 discusses ways traders lose money trading derivatives. These ways remind one of what not to do to try to have successful trading. Then Chapters 11–13 discuss in turn the Long Term Capital failure in 1998, an imported fear driven crash in 1997 that sunk the Niederhoffer fund, and the 2006 Amaranth natural gas disaster. These failures all involve over betting and not being diversified in all scenarios.

Part III presents studies of various emerging economies which begin the process of explicitly acknowledging uncertain income paths and evaluating the risks and vulnerabilities to assess investments. These studies or *snapshots* lay out the elements necessary for good scenario building for investment. The studies are wide ranging from emerging economies of the Middle East, North Africa, China, and Argentina. Collectively these assess key macro and micro trends in emerging economies and emerging areas within developed economies, with a focus on identifying growth trends and investment risks. They address risks of exchange rates, political conditions and the institutional environment. There is a particular focus on the impact of currency regime choice and the political economy of liberalization. These case studies illustrate risks and opportunities of these dynamic economies, including their receptiveness to foreign investment, the prospects for equity and (to a lesser degree) fixed-income investment, the impact of new trade agreements and the effects of political changes and institutions.

Chapter 14 assesses the impacts of Egypt's decision to float its currency and how its attempts to attract foreign direct investment foretell investment prospects. Chapters 15 and 16 assess macroeconomic growth in China and the trends of its equity markets, respectively. We present scenarios for macroeconomic growth, possible changes in China's exchange rate regime and likely trajectory of Chinese stock markets, focusing on opportunities for investors. Chapter 17 discusses Argentina, focusing on its economic recovery following the currency crisis of 2001–2. It details how Argentina benefitted from strong external demand for its commodity exports, particularly as the devaluation made them more competitively priced. The last half of Part III, Chapters 18–20, concerns three regions in or integrated with the EU at various levels of development. They range from a new EU member (Cyprus), a very open economy, that has seemed very vulnerable in the last year (Iceland), being viewed as a bellwether for emerging markets, but increasingly tied to the EU by trade and investment and the challenges faced by a less developed region within the EU (Sicily). Chapter 18 focuses on Cyprus, putting its high human capital and favorable terms of trade into the context of trade in the Mediterranean region. It also assesses European and US interaction with the southern Mediterranean. Chapter 19 discusses Iceland's vulnerabilities, in particular whether its rising interest rates can control capital outflows and assesses the likelihood of a crash in either its equity market or other asset classes. Finally, Chapter 20, focusing on Sicily, one of the poorest regions of Italy, asks what could jumpstart growth in slower growth areas within the EU where transportation, infrastructure and institutions may be weaker.

Part IV presents the stochastic programming or constrained scenario optimization approach to risk control and optimal investment decision making for various financial institutions such as bank trading departments, insurance companies, pension fund and hedge as well as high net worth individuals or family businesses.

Fixed mix strategies where one sells high and buys low have attractive features. However, in Chapter 21 we show how stochastic programming policies will generally beat fix mix. That is because the SP approach optimally uses the information that unfolds over time to determine better decisions in all periods. This outperformance is substantial in sample but unfortunately is usually much less out of sample because the random input data are structurally different from those in sample so the stochastic programming model loses some of its advantage adapting to the information available in the scenario tree. Also the performance of the fixed mix approach improves because the asset mix is updated at each stage.

Chapter 21 then discusses the InnoALM model for the Siemens Austria pension fund, whose most innovative feature is the use of scenario dependent correlation matrices. Historical evidence shows that correlations across equity classes rise as one moves from normal to high volatility and then to crash times. Meanwhile, the stock bond correlations fall and in crash are negative. Hence, if one does not use scenario dependent correlations such as by using average correlations as most people do, you simply cannot get these negative correlations. The multiple correlation matrix approach appears crucial for correctly modeling multi-period investment problems. Tests on plausible data show the superiority of the approach. But one is reminded from the discussion in Chapter 4 that the optimal portfolio weights in period one are very sensitive to the mean return estimates. For example, a change from 12 % (the 100 year average equity return) to 9 % dramatically changes the equity weights from 100 % to 30 %. However, the sensitivity in later periods in much lower.

In Chapter 22 we show that it is possible and likely that scenarios will occur that are beyond the range of all past data. And that such rare events, to which most modelers assign a zero probability, are increasing in number in recent years. What is important is to use scenarios that cover the board of various possible, if unlikely, occurrences.

Chapter 23 discusses the bond-stock crash prediction model which WTZ discovered in 1989 in his crash study group at the Yamaichi research Institute in Tokyo. Simply put, when the difference between the long bond and the equity earnings yield (the reciprocal of the price-earnings ratio) is too high, the chance of a crash in equity prices is almost surely to occur. We discovered the model by studying the US October 1987 crash. In that case, the model went into the danger zone in April 1987 and the crash occurred in October, six months later. The model was 12/12 in predicting crashes (a 10 % or more fall within one year from the current equity price) during 1948–1988 in Japan. There were twenty 10 %+ declines during these forty years so eight occurred for other reasons. The measure also called the 1990 crash in Japan and the 2000/1 and 2002 crashes in the US S&P500 markets. Chapter 23 also discusses presidential election effects. A major one is that equity returns are, on average, much higher in the last two years of presidential four year terms. Also, historically, small cap returns have been higher with Democrats especially out of the small caps best month January. Chapter 24 is more technical and discusses statistical and mathematical ways to generate scenarios. One approach is through vector auto-regressive econometric modeling. Such models are estimated by generalized least squares using Zellner's seemingly unrelated approach since the various equations are tied together through a covariance matrix of the errors. Once such a model is estimated one can generate a multiperiod scenario tree.

Another approach through a hierarchy of stochastic differential equation models, that is, short term interest rates affect inflation which in turn affects long term real interest rates, which affect currencies, which affect stock prices, etc. Towers Perrin has successfully used such a model called CAP:Link in various pension fund and insurance company applications across the world. The system provides scenarios for a variety of assets.

Many hedge funds employ long-short investment strategies that tend to neutralize most of the market risk. One strategy is to go long mean return stocks and short low mean return stocks. A factor model can be used to rank stocks based on their fundamentals. Chapter 25 shows such a model for the Japanese first section stocks. Using past monthly data, the 1000+ stocks are ranked from 1, 2 . . . using 30 fundamental factors. The most important predictor of the estimated model is future expected earnings divided by the current price. This is a forward looking price/earnings ratio. Other valuable predictors are current price to book, the usual price earnings ratio based on reported past earnings, small cap and various mean reversion variables. The CAPM beta is not one of the top predictors. The model is then able to, for example, determine the best 50, 100, . . . 500 etc stock portfolios and revise them monthly. The model worked well and was used by Yamaichi Securities in Tokyo. A similar model was developed for Buchanan Partners, a London hedge fund which used the model to predict stocks to go long or short in warrant arbitrage and other strategies.

Chapter 26 discusses mathematical approaches to generate scenarios. One approach is through moment matching which can be used, for example, to aggregate a larger set of scenarios into a smaller set with the same means, variances, covariances, etc up to say the first four moments. Or it can be used to sample from a given distribution. The approach originated in the Russell Yasuda model in 1991 and was further extended by Høyland and Wallace. While moment matching works well it frequently leads to strange distributions. An alternative approach as in Hochreiter and Pflug is to model the scenarios as a multidimensional facility location problem. One minimizes the Wasserstein distance measure from the true distribution. The approach yields a few scenarios to model the distribution and works well in practice.

Finally Chapter 27 discusses how one can plan for possible disasters that might impact the market such as hurricane Katrina as well as stock market corrections.

Appendix A discusses William Poundstone's book on the Kelly criterion, and briefly describes the work in Nassim Taleb's *Fooled by Randomness* and David Swensen's book about personal investing.

All the chapters in this book have appeared in *Wilmott* magazine. The columns begin with the first issue of the magazine in September 2002. We have edited all the chapters for consistency, updates and other necessary changes. Rachel wrote her columns (Chapters 14, 17, 18 and 20) and the joint ones (Chapters 8, 13, 15, 16, and 19) independent of her current employment with Roubini Global Economics in New York and previous work with the Canadian International Development Agency and the International Development Research Centre, although these experiences clearly influence the work, as noted in the acknowledgments. All mistakes and opinions are our own.

July 31, 2007
Rachel E. S. Ziemba   William T. Ziemba
New York   Vancouver

About the authors

Rachel E. S. Ziemba has a AB in History from the University of Chicago and an MPhil in International Relations from St. Antony's College, Oxford University where her thesis concerned the politics of dollarization in developing economies. She has traveled widely and has worked for the Canadian International Development Agency (CIDA) in Egypt, and the International Development Research Centre (IDRC) in Ottawa, Canada. At Roubini Global Economics (www.rgemonitor.com) in New York she is currently doing research on various global macroeconomic issues including emerging markets, the management of oil wealth and geo-strategic risks to the global economy. She has written and given talks on various political economy and international development topics including currency politics, emerging economies and geostrategic issues.

William T. Ziemba is the Alumni Professor of Financial Modeling and Stochastic Optimization (Emeritus) at the Sauder School of Business, University of British Columbia, Vancouver, Canada. He is a well published and known academic around the world with books, research articles and talks on a wide range of topics related to investments and other areas. He trades and consults through William T. Ziemba Investment Management Inc. and Dr Z Investments, Inc. and for a very private institutional wealth management syndicate and a select group of hedge funds. He has held visiting professorships at MIT, Chicago, Berkeley, UCLA and Cambridge, LSE, Oxford and the Reading ICMA Centre in the UK. He has or currently consults for Buchanan Partners and RAB Capital in London, the Frank Russell Company, Morgan Stanley, Canyon Capital Advisors, Credit Suisse First Boston and Edward O Thorp and Associates in the US, Yamaichi Research Institute in Japan, Siemens Innovest and Gruppo Uni Credit in Europe and Market Research in Nassau. A list of his books and other activities and publications is on the website www.williamtziemba.com.

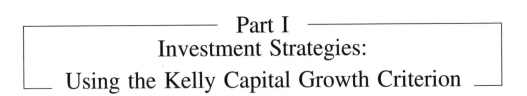

Part I
Investment Strategies:
Using the Kelly Capital Growth Criterion

1

Take a chance

Gambling and investment practices are not so far removed from one another

There is a fine line between the public's and the law's distinction between investing and legalized gambling. Stocks and bonds, bank accounts and real estate are traditional investments. Poker, blackjack, lotteries and horseracing are popular gambling games. Gold and silver, commodity and financial futures and stock and index options are somewhat in between but are generally thought to be on the investment side of the line. English spread betting is a good example where legal bets can be made without tax liability on sports events and financial investments such as stock index futures. The higher transaction costs are compensated by the absence of taxes. See Tables 1.1 and 1.3.

Gambling and Investment practices are not so far removed from one another

In all of these situations, one is making decisions whose outcome has some degree of uncertainty. The outcome may also depend upon the actions of others. For example, consider buying shares of Qualcom. The stock is one of the few high flying US internet and high tech stocks did not completely crash in 2000. The stock was around 100 in December 2000 versus a high of 200 in January 2000. The company has signed deals with the Chinese government and others for their pioneering wireless technology. Despite its 90 plus price earnings ratio, its future prospects looked excellent. While its niche in digital wireless communication is fairly unique and future demand growth looks outstanding, others could possibly market successful and cheaper alternatives or the marketing deals could unravel. What looks good now has frequently turned into disaster in the current technology market place since enormous growth is needed in the future to justify today's high prices. Qualcom has continued to grow but at a slower rate and its stock price fell to a third of its December 2000 value in mid 2002. Such is typical price experience of high PE stocks.

Economic effects that manifest themselves into general market trends are important also in a stock's price. Most stocks are going up in a rising market and vice versa. Indeed in the most popular stock market pricing theory – the so-called capital asset market equilibrium beta model – securities are compared via their relative price movement up or down and at what rate when the general market average (e.g. S&P500 index) rises or falls. Over time, stocks have greatly outperformed bonds, T-bills, inflation and gold. For example, $1 invested in 1802 in gold was only worth $14.38 in 1997, similar to the CPI inflation at $14.67. T-bills made, $4455, bonds $13 975 and stocks were a whopping $8.8 million and

Table 1.1 Essentials of Investment and Gambling

INVESTING	LEVERAGED INVESTING	GAMBLING
Bank accounts and term deposits Gold and silver Mutual funds Real estate Stocks and bonds	Commodity and financial futures Options Spread betting Hedge funds	Blackjack Dice games Horseracing Jai Alai Lotteries Roulette Sports Betting
• Positive sum game usually • SLOW – 'buy and hold' • To preserve your capital • Gains usually exceed transaction costs for the average person • Path dependence is not extremely crucial	• ZERO SUM game • Many winners and many losers • Low transactions costs • Risk control is important • Path dependence is crucial	• Negative sum game, average person LOSES • FAST play • Entertainment • High transactions costs • Winners share net pool: house cannot lose if payoffs are parimutuel, percent of play • Edge on each play: each play is either won or lost; house cannot lose except in fixed odds cases where they do not diversify

Table 1.2 Average continuously compounded yearly rates of return, 1802–2001. *Source*: Siegel (2002)

	Average edge, percent
Gold	1.4
CPI	1.4
T-bills	4.3
Bonds	4.9
Stocks	8.3

the gains are pretty steady over time; see Table 1.2. In purchasing power $1 in 1802 is about $15 in 2002, see Siegel (2002).

So for success in stocks, one has two crucial elements: general uncertainty about the economy and the product's acceptance and the effect of competition.

An analogous situation is found in a gambling context such as sports betting on the Super Bowl. The general uncertainty affects the outcome of the game whereas the competition from other players shows up in higher or lower odds.

What then is the difference between investing and gambling? In investing one buys some item, be it a stock, a bar of platinum or a waterfront house, pays the commission to the

Table 1.3 Aspects of Several Gambling/Investment Situations with Winning Systems

	Average Edge	Probability of Winning	Wagers	Does the Wager Affect the Odds?
Blackjack	1.5 %	45–55 %	Large	No
Financial Futures	10 %+	2–98 %	Extremely Large	Yes
Horseracing	10 %+	2–98 %	Medium to Large	Yes
Lotteries	25 %+	Less than 1 %	Very Small	Yes

seller and goes, off possibly for a long time. Nothing prevents all participants from gaining. In fact they usually do. The essence of an investment is this: it is possible for *every* person buying the item to gain and it is generally expected that most people will in fact reap profits.

More interesting and profitable is the construction of hedges involving combinations of long and short risky situations where one makes a moderate profit most of the time with little risk. This is the basis of some successful hedge fund and bank trading department strategies, as we will discuss in later chapters.

The situation is different with a gambling game. There is usually a house or some type of negative or zero sum game, be it a casino, racetrack management or provincial lottery that takes predetermined (minimum or average) commission. On the surface, it seems that the house cannot lose except in rare instances and certainly not in the aggregate. Surprisingly, lottery organizations around the world make many conceptual mistakes in game design that lead to situations in which winning player strategies exist and we will discuss some of these in a later column. How about the players? On average, they must lose since the house always makes its commission. So all players *cannot* win. Some may win but many or most will lose. In fact estimates show that very few persons (about one in a hundred) actually make profits in gambling over extended periods of time. Most people talk about their wins and are much more quiet about their losses. As my colleague Mr B says, they want 'bragging rights'. For most people, gambling is a form of entertainment and although they would like to win, their losses seem to be adequately compensated by the enjoyment of the play. The game also does not take very long. When it is played, the management takes its commission and distributes the prizes or winnings in a quick and orderly fashion. Then the game is repeated.

A gambling situation can be of two types. In fixed payment games the players wager against the house. In any particular play, the house and the player either win or lose. What one wins the other loses so both parties have risk. However, by having an edge and by diversifying over many players, the house remains profitable. But the players cannot do this. In pari-mutuel games, the house is passive and takes a fixed piece of the action. The rest is then split among the winners. In this way the house cannot lose and takes no risk.

In these games, the players are really wagering against each other. In both types of gambling the average player loses. Some players may win, but the players as a group have a net loss. The vigorish (transactions costs) is essentially the payment for the pleasure of playing. It is an important result in the mathematics of gambling that, faced with a sequence of unfavorable games, no gambling system can be devised that will yield a profit on average after one, two, three or any number of plays. You simple cannot change an unfavorable (negative expected value) game into a favorable game with a clever mathematical betting scheme.

THE COLOCATION OF MONEY AND MATH

Be especially wary of advice of the doubling up strategies: Martingales, pyramids, etc. While such systems may allow you to make small profits most of the time, the gigantic losses you suffer once in a while yield losses in the long run.

The most useful result that we have for unfavorable games is that if you want to maximize your chances of achieving a goal before falling to some lower wealth level, you should use **bold play**. With bold play you do not let the casino defeat you by grinding out small profits from you along the way. Rather, you bet amounts that get you to your goal as soon as possible.

Consider roulette, which is an unfavorable game with an edge of minus 2/28 or minus 5.26. Assuming that you are not able to predict the numbers that will occur any better than random, then you should bet on only one number with a wager that if you win you will either reach your goal or a wealth level from which you can reach it on one or more subsequent plays. If your fortune is $ 10 and your goal is $ 1000, then it is optimal to bet the entire $ 10 on only one number. If you lose you are out. If you win you have $ 360 (with the 35-1 payoff) and then you bet $ 19, which takes you to $ 1006 if you win and $ 341 if you lose. Upon losing you would bet the smallest amount – $ 19 again – so that if you win you reach your goal of $ 1000, etc. This bold play strategy always gives you the highest chance of achieving your goal.

On the other hand, as in the case of roulette, the casino has the edge and your goal is to reach some higher level of wealth before falling to a lower level with as high a probability as possible, then 'timid play' is optimal. With timid play, you wager small amounts to make sure some small sample random result does not hurt you. Then, after a moderate number of plays you are virtually sure of winning. This is precisely what casinos do. With even a small edge, all they need to do to be practically guaranteed of large and steady profits is to diversify the wagers so that the percentage wagered by each gambler is small. With crowded casinos, this is usually easy to accomplish. A simple example of this idea, non-diversification, shows up in many if not most or all financial disasters as we will discuss in later chapters.

CHANGING A GAMBLE INTO AN INVESTMENT

The point of all this is that if you are to have any chance at all of winning, you must develop a playing strategy so that at least some of the time, and preferably most or all the time, when you are betting you are getting on average more than a dollar for each dollar wagered. We call this changing a gamble into an investment. This is possible in roulette, see Tom Bass' *The Eudomonic Pie*. Also, for the simpler game of the wheel of fortune, see Ed Thorp's article in the March 1982 issue of *Gambling Times*.

This section of the book discusses topics in the mathematics of gambling and investment. The basic goal is to turn gambles into investments with the development of good playing strategies so that one can wager intelligently. The strategy development follows general principles but is somewhat different for each situation. The wagering or money management concepts apply to all games. The difference in application depends upon the edge and the probability of winning. The size of the wager depends on the edge but much more so on the probability of winning if one takes a long run rate of growth of profit approach, as discussed in Chapter 2. We will look at situations where the player has an edge and develop playing strategies to exploit that edge. These are situations where, on average, the player can win using a workable system. The analyses will utilize concepts from modern financial economics investment theory and related mathematical optimization, psychological, statistical and computer techniques and apply them to the gambling situations to yield profitable systems. This frequently involves the identification of a security market imperfection, anomaly or partially predictable prices. Naturally in gambling situations all players cannot win so the potential gain will depend upon how good the system is, how well it is played and how many are using it or other profitable systems. Also, most crucially, on the risk control system in use. Nor will every game have a useful favorable system where one can make profits on average. Baccarat or Chemin de Fer is one such example. However, virtually every financial market will have strategies that lead to wining investment situations. Chapter 3 discusses lottery betting on unpopular numbers. Chapter 4 discusses the good and bad properties of the Kelly criterion. Chapter 5 discusses how to modify the Kelly fraction to stay above a wealth path with high probability.

There are two aspects of the analysis of each situation: when should one bet and how much should be bet? These may be referred to as strategy development and money management. They are equally important. While the strategy development aspect is fairly well understood by many, the money management (risk control) element is more subtle and it is such errors that lead to financial disasters. Chapter 2 discusses the basic theory of gambling/investing over time using the capital growth/Kelly and fractional Kelly betting systems and apply this to futures trading. Chapters 11–13 discuss hedge funds and focus on strategy development and risk control failures such as Niederhoffer in 1997, Long Term Capital Management in 1998 and Amaranth in 2006 and models of lottery, horse race and other betting situations, pension, insurance company and individual investment planning over time.

I have been fortunate to have worked and consulted with seven individuals who have used these ideas in three separate areas: 'market neutral' hedge funds, private futures trading hedge funds and racetrack betting to turn essentially zero into more that $300 million plus. One, Jim Simons of the Renaissance Hedge Fund made $1.4 billion in 2005 and $1.6 billion in 2006. All seven, while different in many ways, began with a gambling focus and retain this in their trading. They are true investors with heavy emphasis on computerized mathematical investing and risk control. They understand down side risk well. They are even more focused on not losing their capital than on having more winnings. They have their losses but rarely do they overbet or not diversify enough to have a major blow out like the three hedge fund disasters discussed in Chapters 11–13.

2
The capital growth theory of investment

How do we grow the wealth as fast as possible

The use of log utility dates at least to the letters of Daniel Bernoulli in 1738. The idea that additional wealth is worth less and less as it increases and thus utility tails off proportional to the level of wealth is very reasonable to many students of investment. On the surface, this utility function seems safe for invest- ing. However, I shall argue that log is the most risky utility function one should ever consider using and it is most dangerous. However, if used properly in situations where it is appropriate, it has wonderful properties. For long term investors who make many short term decisions, it yields the highest long run levels of wealth. This is called Kelly betting in honor of Kelly's 1956 paper that introduced this type of betting. In finance, it is usually called the Capital Growth Theory.[1]

Consider the example described in Table 2.1. There are five possible invest- ments and if we bet on any of them, we always have a 14 % advantage. The dif- ference between them is that some have a higher chance of winning and, for some, this chance is smaller. For the latter, we receive higher odds if we win than for the former. But we always receive $ 1.14 for each $ 1 bet on average. Hence we have a favorable game. The optimal expected log utility bet with one asset (here we either win or lose the bet) equals the edge divided by the odds.[2] So for the 1-1 odds bet, the wager is 14 % of one's fortune and at 5-1 it's only 2.8 %. We bet more when the chance that we will lose our bet is smaller. Also we bet more when the edge is higher. The bet is linear in the edge so doubling the edge doubles the optimal bet. However, the bet is non-linear in

---

[1] For readers who would like a technical survey of capital growth theory, see Hakansson and Ziemba (1995), MacLean and Ziemba (2006), and Thorp (2006).

[2] For one or two assets with fixed odds, take derivatives and solve for the optimal wagers; for multi-asset bets under constraints; and when portfolio choices affect returns (odds), one must solve a nonlinear program which, possibly, is non-convex.

Table 2.1   The Investments. *Source*: Ziemba and Hausch (1986)

Probability of Winning	Odds	Probability of Being Chosen in the Simulation at at Each Decision Point	Optimal Kelly Bets Fraction of Current Wealth
0.57	1-1	0.1	0.14
0.38	2-1	0.3	0.07
0.285	3-1	0.3	0.047
0.228	4-1	0.2	0.035
0.19	5-1	0.1	0.028

Table 2.2   Statistics of the Simulation. *Source*: Ziemba and Hausch (1986)

Final Wealth Strategy	Min	Max	Mean	Median	Number of times the final wealth out of 1000 trials was				
					>500	>1000	>10 000	>50 000	>100 000
Kelly	18	483 883	48 135	17 269	916	870	598	302	166
Half Kelly	145	111 770	13 069	8 043	990	954	480	30	1

the chance of losing our money, which is reinvested so the size of the wager depends more on the chance of losing and less on the edge.

The simulation results shown in Table 2.2 assume that the investor's initial wealth is $ 1000 and that there are 700 investment decision points. The simulation was repeated 1000 times. The numbers in Table 2.2 are the number of times out of the possible 1000 that each particular goal was reached. The first line is with log or Kelly betting, The second line is half Kelly betting. That is you compute the optimal Kelly wager but then blend it 50-50 with cash. We discuss later various Kelly fractions and how to utilize them wisely but for now, we will just focus on half Kelly. The α-fractional Kelly wager is equivalent to the optimal bet obtained from using the concave risk averse, negative power utility function, $-w^{-\beta}$, where $\alpha = \frac{1}{1-\beta}$. For half Kelly ($\alpha = 1/2$), $\beta = -1$ and the utility function is $w^{-1} = \frac{1}{w}$. Here the marginal increase in wealth drops off as w^2, which is more conservative than log's w. Log utility is the case $\beta \to -\infty$, $\alpha = 1$ and cash is $\beta \to -\infty$, $\alpha = 0$.

A major advantage of log utility betting is the 166 in the last column. In fully 16.6 % of the 1000 cases in the simulation, the final wealth is more than 10 times as much as the initial wealth. Also in 302 cases, the final wealth is more than 50 times the initial wealth. This huge growth in final wealth for log is not shared by the half Kelly strategies, which have only 1 and 30, respectively, for their 50 and 100 time growth levels. Indeed, log provides an enormous growth rate but at a price, namely a very high volatility of wealth levels. That is, the final wealth is very likely to be higher than with other strategies, but the ride will be very bumpy. The maximum, mean, and median statistics in Table 2.2 illustrate the enormous gains that log utility strategies usually provide.

Let's now focus on bad outcomes. The first column provides the following remarkable fact: one can make 700 independent bets of which the chance of winning each one is at least 19 % and usually is much more, having a 14 % advantage on each bet and still turn $ 1000 into $ 18, a loss of more than 98 %. Even with half Kelly, the minimum return over the 1000 simulations was $ 145, a loss of 85.5 %. Half Kelly has a 99 % chance of not losing more

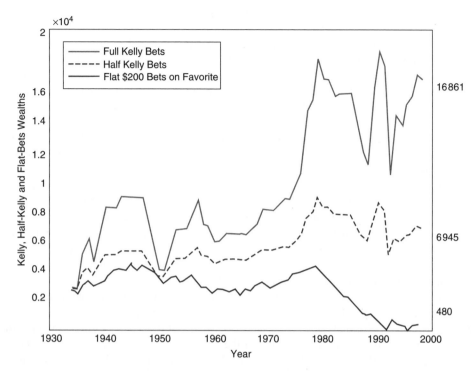

Figure 2.1 Wealth level histories from place and show betting on the Kentucky Derby, 1934–1998 with the Dr Z system utilizing a 4.00 dosage index filter rule with full and half Kelly wagering from $200 flat bets on the favorite using an initial wealth of $2500. *Source*: Bain, Hausch and Ziemba (2006)

than half the wealth versus only 91.6% for Kelly. The chance of not being ahead is almost three times as large for full versus half Kelly. Hence to protect ourselves from bad scenario outcomes, we need to lower our bets and diversify across many independent investments. This is explored more fully in the context of hedge funds in various chapters in this book.

Figure 2.1 provides a visual representation of the type of information in Table 2.2 displaying typical behavior of full Kelly versus half Kelly wagering in a real situation. These are bets on the Kentucky Derby from 1934 to 1998 using an inefficient market system where probabilities from a simple market (win) are used in a more complex market (place and show) coupled with a breeding filter rule [dosage filter 4.00] to eliminate horses who do not have enough stamina. You bet on horses that have the stamina to finish first, second or third who are underbet to come in second or better or third or better relative to their true chances estimated from their odds to win.

The full Kelly log bettor has the most total wealth at the horizon but has the most bumpy ride: $2500 becomes $16861. The half Kelly bettor ends up with much less, $6945 but has a much smoother ride. The system did provide out of sample profits. A comparison with random betting proxied by betting on the favorite in the race, shows how tough it is to win at horseracing with the 16% track take plus breakage (rounding payoffs down to the nearest 20 cents per $2 bet) at Churchill Downs. Betting on the favorite turns $2500 into $480. Random betting has even lower final wealth at the horizon since favorites are underbet.

BLACKJACK

The difference between full and fractional Kelly investing and the resulting size of the optimal investment bets is illustrated via a tradeoff of growth versus security. This is akin to the static mean versus variance so often used in portfolio management and yields two dimensional graphs that aid in the investment decision making process. This can be illustrated by the game of blackjack where fractional Kelly strategies have been used by professional players.

The game of blackjack or 21 evolved from several related card games in the 19th century. It became fashionable during World War I and now has enormous popularity, and is played by millions of people in casinos around the world. Billions of dollars are lost each year by people playing the game in Las Vegas alone. A small number of professionals and advanced amateurs, using various methods such as card counting, are able to beat the game. The object is to reach, or be close to, twenty-one with two or more cards. Scores above twenty-one are said to bust or lose. Cards two to ten are worth their face value: Jacks, Queens and Kings are worth ten points and Aces are worth one or eleven at the player's choice. The game is called blackjack because an ace and a ten-valued card was paid three for two and an additional bonus accrued if the two cards were the Ace of Spades and the Jack of Spades or Clubs. While this extra bonus has been dropped by current casinos, the name has stuck. Dealers normally play a fixed strategy of drawing cards until the total reaches seventeen or more at which point they stop. A variation is when a soft seventeen (an ace with cards totaling six) is hit. It is better for the player if the dealer stands on soft seventeen. The house has an edge of 1–10 % against typical players. The strategy of mimicking the dealer loses about 8 % because the player must hit first and busts about 28 % of the time ($0.28^2 \approx 0.08$). However, in Las Vegas the average player loses only about 1.5 % per play.

The edge for a successful card counter varies from about -5 % to $+10$ % depending upon the favorability of the deck. By wagering more in favorable situations and less or nothing when the deck is unfavorable, an average weighted edge is about 2 %. An approximation to provide insight into the long-run behavior of a player's fortune is to assume that the game is a Bernoulli trial with a probability of success $p = 0.51$ and probability of loss $q = 1 - p = 0.49$.

Figure 2.2 shows the relative growth rate $\pi ln(1 + p)(1 - \pi)ln(1 - \pi)$ versus the fraction of the investor's wealth wagered, π. The security curves show the bounds on the true probability of doubling or quadrupling before halving. This is maximized by the Kelly log bet $\pi^* = p - q = 0.02$. The growth rate is lower for smaller and for larger bets than the Kelly bet. Superimposed on this graph is also the probability that the investor doubles or quadruples the initial wealth before losing half of this initial wealth. Since the growth rate and the security are both decreasing for $\pi > \pi^*$,, it follows that it is never advisable to wager more than π^*. Also it can be shown (see the end of Chapter 4) that the growth rate of a bet that is exactly twice the Kelly bet, namely $2\pi^* = 0.04$, is zero plus the risk-free rate of interest. Figure 2.2 illustrates this. Hence log betting is the most aggressive investing that one should ever consider. The root of hedge fund disasters is frequently caused by bets above π^* when they should have bets that are π^* or less, especially when parameter uncertainty is considered. However, one may wish to trade off lower growth for more security using a fractional Kelly strategy. This growth tradeoff is further illustrated in Table 2.3. For example, a drop from $\pi^* = 0.02$ to 0.01 for a 0.5 fractional Kelly strategy, decreases the growth rate by 25 %, but increases the chance of doubling before halving from 67 % to 89 %.

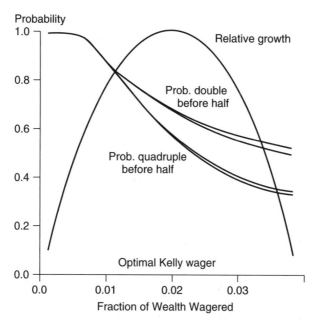

Figure 2.2 Probability of doubling and quadrupling before halving and relative growth rates versus fraction of wealth wagered for Blackjack (2% advantage, $p = 0.51$ and $q = 0.49$). *Source*: McLean and Ziemba (1999)

Table 2.3 Growth Rates Versus Probability of Doubling Before Halving for Blackjack. *Source*: MacLean and Ziemba (1999)

	0.1		0.999		0.19
	0.2		0.998		0.36
Range	0.3		0.98		0.51
for	0.4	Safer	0.94	Less Growth	0.64
Blackjack	0.5		0.89		0.75
Teams	0.6	Riskier	0.83	More Growth	0.84
	0.7		0.78		0.91
	0.8		0.74		0.96
	0.9		0.70		0.99
	1.0	Kelly	0.67		1.00
	1.5		0.56		0.75
Overkill →	2.0		0.50		0.00
Too Risky					

COMMODITY TRADING: INVESTING IN THE TURN OF THE YEAR EFFECT WITH INDEX FUTURES

Repeated investments in commodity trades are well modeled by the capital growth theory with modifications for margin, daily mark-to-the-market account variation and other practical details. An interesting example is the turn-of-the-year effect in US small capitalized stocks

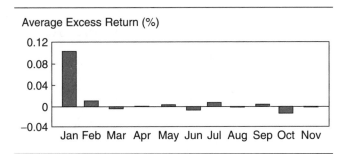

Figure 2.3 Average excess returns of smallest minus largest decile of US stocks, 1926–93.
Source: Ibbotson Associates

in January. Figure 2.3 shows the mean excess return of the smallest minus largest decile US
stocks over the 68 years from 1926 to 1993 by month. In eleven of the months the advantage
is small or negative, however, there was a large advantage in January. The 10.36 % mean
difference provides a strong advantage with high reliability since there was a small stock
advantage in 63 of the 68 years.

One way to invest in this anomaly is to hold long positions in a small stock index and
short positions in large stock indices because the transaction costs (commission plus market
impact) are less than a tenth of that of trading the corresponding basket of securities. An
example from Clark and Ziemba (1987), using data from 1976/77 to 1986/87, follows.
During the time of this study, the March Value Line index was a geometric average of
the prices of about 1700 securities and emphasizes the small stocks while the S&P500 is
a value weighted index of 500 large stocks. This means by the arithmetic-geometric mean
inequality that the geometric mean decays about $\frac{1}{2}$ % a month. This does not affect our trade
much. But four very talented Wharton PhD students, now well-known finance professors,
forgot about this and entered the trade months before and got wiped out by Fischer Black
of Goldman Sachs who understood this and took the other side. They lost about 3 % on this
negative drift. See Ritter (1996).

The VL/S&P spread is long in small stocks and short in big stocks at the end of the year.
Each point change in the index spread is worth $ 500. The spread is entered in mid December
before futures anticipation bids up the lightly traded Value Line index. On average, the
December 15 to (−1) day gain on the spread, that is the futures anticipation, was 0.57
points. By January 15, the largest average gains are over and the risks increase. On average,
the spread dropped 0.92 points in this period with a high variance. The projected gain from a
successful trade was 0–5 points and averaged 2.85 points or $ 1342.50 per spread, assuming
a commission of $1.5 \times \$ 55$.

The average standard deviation of the VL/S&P spread was about 3.0. With a mean of
2.85 the following is an approximate return distribution for the trade

Gain	7	6	5	4	3	2	1	0	−1
Probability	0.007	0.024	0.0700	0.146	0.217	0.229	0.171	0.091	0.045

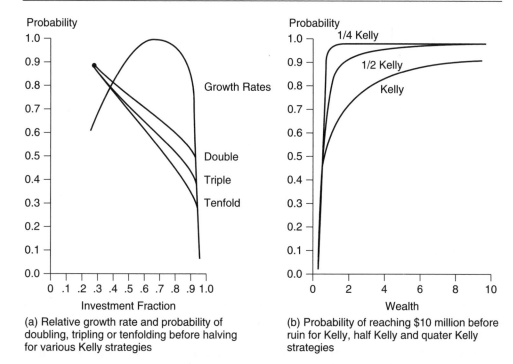

(a) Relative growth rate and probability of doubling, tripling or tenfolding before halving for various Kelly strategies

(b) Probability of reaching $10 million before ruin for Kelly, half Kelly and quater Kelly strategies

Figure 2.4 Turn of the year effect

The optimal Kelly investment based on this return distribution is 74 % of one's fortune! Such high wagers are typical for profitable situations with a small estimated probability of loss. Given the uncertainty of the estimates involved and the volatility and margin requirements of the exchanges, a much smaller wager is suggested.

Figure 2.4(a) displays the probability of doubling, tripling, and increasing one's fortune ten-fold before losing half of it, as well as the growth rates, for various fractional Kelly strategies. At fractional strategies of 25 % or less, the probability of tenfolding one's fortune before halving it exceeds 90 % with a growth rate in excess of 50 % of the maximal growth rate. Figure 2.4(b) gives the probability of reaching the distant goal of $ 10 million before ruining for Kelly, half Kelly and quarter Kelly strategies with wealth levels in the range of $ 0–10 million. The results indicate that the quarter Kelly strategy seems very safe with a 99 % chance of achieving this goal. The markets in 2006 have become much more dangerous than in the period of this study, so an even lower Kelly fraction is suggested.

These concepts were used in a $ 100 000 speculative account by a Canadian investment management company. Five VL/S&P spreads were purchased to approximate a slightly less than 25 % fractional Kelly strategy. Watching the market carefully, these were bought on December 17, 1986 at a spread of −22.18 which was very close to the minimum that the spread traded at around December 15. The spread continued to gain and the position was cashed out at −16.47 on January 14 for a gain of 5.55 points per contract or

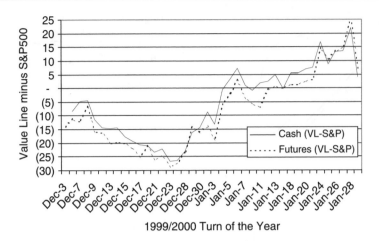

1999/2000 Turn of the Year

Figure 2.5   ValueLine500 minus S&P500 value-adjusted spread for cash and March futures for the turn-of-the-year, 1999/2000. *Source*: Rendon and Ziemba (2007)

$ 14 278.50 after transactions costs. Additional discussion of many of the issues in this section appears in Clark and Ziemba (1987), which was updated Ziemba (1994) and again by Hensel and Ziemba (2000) and again by Rendon and Ziemba (2007). Throughout the 1980s and up to the mid 1990s the data were consistent with the past substantial small cap advantage, see Hensel and Ziemba (2000) who provide year by year daily data plots of the VL/S&P500 spreads, up to 1999/2000. Since then the trade has been more risky and the volume very low, but the trade won in December in all years from 1995/96 to 2004/05.

Figure 2.5 is a typical trade for 1999/2000 showing the futures and cash spreads. The dotted line is the futures spread and the dark line is the cash spread. In this case you could enter at a discount in mid December. The trade gained but observe that you had to cash out in mid January at a discount.

Table 2.4 shows the results when the ValueLine and S&P500 were both worth $ 500 a point for 1982/83 to 1995/2000. Table 2.5 updates the results to 2005 when the ValueLine was worth $ 100 and the S&P500 $ 250 a point from 1998/99 to 2004/05 respectively.

There were gains in the second half of December (15–31) and from December 15 to January 15. The advantage is still there especially in the December period but the volume in recent years was so low that the trade is too risky to do. Historically, WTZ played this for 14 years from 1982/83 to 1995/96 winning each year. These 14 winning years are shown in Table 2.4. Teaching the trade to Morgan Stanley and lower volume prompted retirement from this trade. The January effect is still alive at least in the futures markets in December but the low volume makes it too risky to trade. Spreads using the Russell 2000 small cap index will have more liquidity than the Value Line. There the trade still works if done carefully with the gains essentially only in the December 15 to 31 period. See Table 2.6 for the 1993/94 to 2004/05 results. Figure 2.6(a) shows a typical year, 2004/05, with essentially no gains in December and losses in January. Figure 2.6(b) shows large gains in 2000/01. Again, the dotted line is the futures spread and the dark line is the cash spread. See Rendon and Ziemba (2007) and Keim and Ziemba (2000) for more of the spread plots.

Table 2.4 Results from VL500/S&P500 March futures spread trades in index points on various buy/sell dates for the 18 turn-of-the-years 1982/83 to 1999/2000 trades. *Source*: Rendon and Ziemba (2007)

TOY	Difference Dec 15 to (−1)	Difference (−1) to Jan 15	Difference Jan 15 to end Jan	Trade Gain Dec 15 to Jan 15	Trade Weights S&P vs. VL
1982/1983	1.50	3.05	0.65	4.55	.5v.5
1983/1984	(0.70)	4.00	(4.90)	3.30	.5v.5
1984/1985	1.10	3.55	2.90	4.65	.5v.5
1985/1986	3.15	0.45	(2.60)	3.60	.5v.5
1986/1987	2.75	(0.30)	(9.85)	2.45	.5v.5
1987/1988	8.15	(0.90)	(0.25)	7.25	.5v.5
1988/1989	3.50	(2.95)	(1.70)	0.55	.5v.5
1989/1990	(0.50)	1.85	(1.45)	1.35	.5v.5
1990/1991	1.70	3.60	3.20	5.30	.5v.5
1991/1992	(7.15)	10.20	13.80	3.05	.5v.5
1992/1993	5.45	6.55	4.05	12.00	.5v.5
1993/1994	4.65	–	1.15	4.65	.5v.5
1994/1995	6.15	(1.65)	(8.50)	4.50	.5v.5
1995/1996	6.00	(3.75)	(9.70)	2.25	.5v.5
1996/1997	4.35	(15.90)	(10.75)	(11.55)	.5v.5
1997/1998	10.70	(6.50)	(12.30)	4.20	.5v.5
1997/1998	1.01	(6.40)	(6.42)	(5.39)	.64v.36
1998/1999	0.91	2.17	(28.19)	3.08	.60v.40
1999/2000	6.09	14.00	7.33	20.08	.59v.41
Average					
1982–1998	3.18	0.08	(2.27)	3.26	
Std Dev	4.10	5.90	6.89	4.74	
t stat	0.78	0.01	(0.33)	0.69	
Average					
1998–2000**	2.67	3.26	(9.09)	5.93	
Std Dev	2.96	10.24	17.91	12.97	
t stat	0.90	0.32	(0.51)	0.46	

Table 2.5 Results from VL 100/S&P500 March futures spread trades in index points on various buy/sell dates for the 8 turns-of-the-years 1997/98 to 2004/05. *Source*: Rendon and Ziemba (2007)

TOY	Difference Dec 15 to (−1)	Difference (−1) to Jan 15	Difference Jan 15 to end Jan	Trade Gain Dec 15 to Jan 15	Trade Weights S&P vs. VL
1998/1999	0.35	1.15	(11.26)	1.50	.23v.77
1999/2000	2.29	5.26	2.76	7.55	.22v.78
2000/2001	8.68	15.81	7.72	24.49	.24v.76
2001/2002	6.00	(2.13)	4.62	3.87	.29v.71
2002/2003	0.66	(0.11)	0.50	0.54	.32v.68
2003/2004	1.45	7.16	(0.87)	8.61	.36v.64
2004/2005	4.42	(11.20)	6.31	(6.78)	.37v.63
Average	3.41	2.28	1.40	5.68	
Std Dev	3.10	8.41	6.36	9.73	
t stat	1.10	0.27	0.22	0.58	

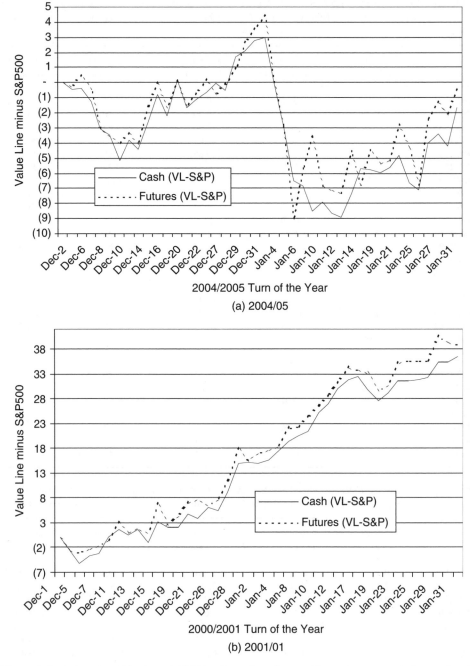

(a) 2004/05

(b) 2001/01

Figure 2.6 Value Line 100 minus S&P500 value-adjusted spread for cash and March futures for the turns-of-the-years 2004/05 and 2000/01

Table 2.6   Results from Russell 2000/S&P500 March futures spread trades in index points on various buy/sell dates for the 11 turns-of-the-years 1993/94 to 2004/2005. *Source*: Rendon and Ziemba (2007)

TOY	Difference Dec 15 to (−1)	Difference (−1) to Jan 15	Difference Jan 15 to end Jan	Trade Gain Dec 15 to Jan 15	Trade Weights S&P vs. R2
1993/1994	4.23	(2.22)	1.84	2.01	.52v.48
1994/1995	5.84	(3.93)	(5.49)	1.91	.52v.48
1995/1996	5.28	(7.68)	(2.96)	(2.39)	.51v.49
1996/1997	(1.63)	(6.02)	(7.20)	(7.65)	.51v.49
1997/1998	7.43	(8.47)	(6.52)	(1.04)	.53v.47
1998/1999	9.74	2.78	(15.33)	12.51	.59v.41
1999/2000	27.66	9.17	12.30	36.83	.61v.39
2000/2001	27.10	8.07	8.98	35.17	.59v.41
2001/2002	7.84	(3.29)	5.15	4.55	.45v.55
2002/2003	(0.93)	(6.27)	5.72	(7.20)	.47v.53
2003/2004	1.06	17.69	(4.30)	18.76	.51v.49
2004/2005	(0.34)	(19.02)	8.12	(19.36)	.52v.48
Average	7.77	(1.60)	0.03	6.17	
Std Dev	9.86	9.72	8.24	16.96	
t stat	0.79	(0.16)	0.00	0.36	
without 2000 and 2001					
Average	3.85	(3.64)	(2.10)	0.21	
Std Dev	4.05	9.35	7.24	10.69	
t stat	0.95	(0.39)	(0.29)	0.02	

The next two chapters discuss three topics: investing using unpopular numbers in lotto games with very low probabilities of success but where the expected returns are very large (this illustrates how bets can be very tiny); good and bad properties of the Kelly log strategy and why this led me to work with Len MacLean on a through study of fractional Kelly strategies and futures and commodity trading, and how large undiversified positions can lead to disasters as it has for numerous hedge funds and bank trading departments.

3
Betting on unpopular lotto numbers using the Kelly criterion

Using the Kelly criterion for betting on favorable (unpopular) numbers in lotto games – even with a substantial edge and very large payoffs if we win – the bets are extremely tiny because the chance of losing most or all of our money is high.

Lotteries predate the birth of Jesus. They have been used by various organizations, governments and individuals to make enormous profits because of the greed and hopes of the players who wish to turn dollars into millions. The Sistine Chapel in the Vatican, including Michelangelo's ceiling, was partially funded by lotteries. So was the British Museum. Major

Ivy League universities in the US such as Harvard used lotteries to fund themselves in their early years. Former US president Thomas Jefferson used a lottery to pay off his debts when he was 83. Abuses occur from time to time and government control is typically the norm. Lotteries were banned in the US for over a hundred years from the early 1800s and resurfaced in 1964. In the UK, the dark period was 1826–1994. Since then there has been enormous growth in lottery games in the US, Canada, the UK and other countries. Current lottery sales in the UK are about five billion pounds per year. Sales of the main 6/49 lotto game average about 80 million pounds a week. The lottery operator takes about 5 % of lotto sales for its remuneration, 5 % goes to retailers, 12 % goes to the government in taxes, and another 28 % goes to various good causes, as do unclaimed prizes.

One might conclude that the expected payback to the Lotto player is 50 % of his or her stake. However, the regulations allow a further 5 % of regular sales to be diverted to a Super Draw fund. Furthermore we must allow for the probability that the jackpot is not won. Eighty of 567 jackpots to the end of May 2001 had not been won. This means that the expected payback in a regular draw is not much more than 40 %. This is still enough to get people to play. With such low paybacks it is very difficult to win at these games and the chances of winning any prize at all, even the small ones, is low.

Table 3.1 describes the various types of lottery games in terms of the chance of winning and the payoff if you win. Lottery organizations have machines to pick the numbers that yield random number draws. Those who claim that they can predict the numbers that will occur cannot really do so. There are no such things as hot and cold numbers or numbers that are friends. Schemes to combine numbers to increase your chance of winning are mathematically fallacious. For statistical tests on these points, see Ziemba et al (1986). One possible way to beat pari-mutuel lotto games is to wager on unpopular numbers or, more

Table 3.1   Types of Lottery Games

		Complete Luck	Skill Involved
Payoff if you win	**Complete Luck**	Scratch Lottery Games No hope whatsoever in analyzing such games. **Payoff:** Fixed payment *Impossible to beat*	Example: Pay $1 for a chance to pick all winners of football games on Saturday. From those who have all correct selections, one name is chosen at random and awarded $100 000. **Payoff:** Fixed payment *Possibly beatable*
	Skill Involved	6/49 6/48 6/44 6/39 6/36 6/40 5/40 7/53 Lotto Games have some skill elements by picking unpopular numbers. **Payoff:** Pari-mutuel *Possibly beatable*	Sports Pool Games in UK, Mexico, Australia, France, etc Legalized Sports Betting in Nevada Horseracing Blackjack **Payoff:** Varies, can be pari-mutuel or have fixed price per dollar wagered. *Definitely beatable*

precisely, unpopular combinations.[1] In lotto games players select a small set of numbers from a given list. The prizes are shared by those with the same numbers as those selected in the random drawing. The lottery organization bears no risk in a pure pari-mutuel system and takes its profits before the prizes are shared. I have studied the 6/49 game played in Canada and several other countries.[2]

Combinations like 1, 2, 3, 4, 5, 6 tend to be extraordinarily popular: in most lotto games, there would be thousands of jackpot winners if this combination were drawn. Numbers ending in eight and especially nine and zero as well as high numbers (32+, the non-birthday choices) tend to be unpopular. Professor Herman Chernoff found that similar numbers were unpopular in a different lotto game in Massachusetts. The game Chernoff studied had four digit numbers from 0000 to 9999. He found advantages from many of those with 8, 9, 0 in them. Random numbers have an expected loss of about 55%. However, six-tuples of unpopular numbers have an edge with expected returns exceeding their cost by about 65%. For example, the combination 10, 29, 30, 32, 39, 40 is worth about $1.507 while the combination 3, 5, 13, 15, 28, 33 of popular numbers is worth only about $0.154. Hence there is a factor of about ten between the best and worst combinations. The expected value rises and approaches $2.25 per dollar wagered when there are carryovers (that is when the jackpot is accumulating because it has not been won). Most sets of unpopular numbers are

---

[1] Another is to look for lottery design errors. As a consultant on lottery design for the past twenty years, I have seen plenty of these. My work has been largely to get these bugs out before the games go to market and to minimize the damage when one escapes the lottery commissions' analysis. Design errors are often associated with departures from the pure parimutuel method, for example guaranteeing the value of smaller prizes at too high a level and not having the games checked by an expert.

[2] See Ziemba et al (1986), *Dr Z's Lotto 6/49 Guidebook*. While parts of the guidebook are dated, the concepts, conclusions, and most of the text provide a good treatment of such games. For those who want more theory, see MacLean and Ziemba (1999, 2006).

worth $2 per dollar or more when there is a large carryover. Random numbers, such as those from lucky dip and quick pick, and popular numbers are worth more with carryovers but never have an advantage. However, investors (such as Chernoff's students) may still lose because of mean reversion (the unpopular numbers tend to become less unpopular over time) and gamblers' ruin (the investor has used up his available resources before winning). These same two phenomena show up in the financial markets repeatedly.

Table 3.2 provides an estimate of the most unpopular numbers in Canada in 1984, 1986 and 1996. The same numbers tend to be the most unpopular over time but their advantage becomes less and less over time. Similarly, as stock market anomalies like the January effect or weekend effect have lessened over time. However, the advantages are still good enough to create a mathematical advantage in the Canadian and UK lottos.

Strategy Hint #1: When a new lotto game is offered, the best advantage is usually right at the start. This point applies to any type of bet or financial market.

Strategy Hint #2: Games with more separate events, on each of which you can have an advantage, are more easily beatable. The total advantage is the product of individual advantages. Lotto 6/49 has 6; a game with 9 is easier to beat and one with 3 harder to beat.

But can an investor really win with high confidence by playing these unpopular numbers? And if so, how long will it take? To investigate this, consider the following experiment shown in Table 3.3.

Table 3.2   Unpopular numbers in the canadian

| Rank | 1984 | | 1986 | | 1996 | |
	Number	% More Unpopular Than Average	Number	% More Unpopular Than Average	Number	% More Unpopular Than Average
1	39	34.3	40	26.7	40	13.8
2	40	34.0	39	22.9	39	12.0
3	30	33.0	20	20.5	48	11.2
4	20	26.8	30	18.1	20	9.6
5	41	18.8	41	16.8	45	9.1
6	10	17.9	38	16.7	41	9.0
7	42	16.1	42	16.4	46	9.0
8	38	15.0	46	15.3	38	8.3
9	46	12.5	29	14.9	42	7.4
10	48	11.5	49	14.9	37	6.9
11	45	9.9	48	14.0	29	6.3
12	49	9.2	32	13.0	30	6.2
13	1	8.4	10	11.6	36	5.1
14			47	10.5	44	4.5
15			1	8.2	47	4.0
16			37	6.3	32	3.1
17			28	6.3	35	2.9
18			34	6.2	34	2.9
19			45	3.2	28	2.5

Table 3.3 Lotto game experimental data

Prizes	Probability of Winning	Mean Time to Win	Prize	Case A Contribution to Expected Value	Prize	Case B Contribution to Expected Value
Jackpot	1/13,983,816	134,460 y	$ 6 M	42.9	$ 10 M	71.5
Bonus, 5/6+	1/2,330,636	22,410 y	0.8 M	34.3	1.2 M	51.5
5/6	1/55,492	533 y 29 w	5,000	9.0	10,000	18.0
4/6	1/1,032	9 y 48 w	150	14.5	250	24.2
3/6	1/57	28 w	10	17.6	10	17.5
				118.1		182.7
Edge				18.1 %		82.7 %
Optimal Kelly Bet				0.0000011		0.0000065
Optimal Number of Tickets				11		65

Purchased per Draw with $ 10 M Bankroll

*Mean time in years and weeks to win if you buy one ticket in each of two draws per week

5/6+ is 5 of 6 right and the 7th number is the last one, that is 6 of 7. *Source*: MacLean and Ziemba (1999)

Case A assumes unpopular number six-tuples are chosen and there is a medium sized carryover. Case B assumes that there is a large carryover and that the numbers played are the most unpopular combinations. Carryovers (called rollovers in the UK) build up the jackpot until it is won. In Canada, carryovers build until the jackpot is won. In the UK 6/49 game, rollovers are capped at three. If there are no jackpot winners then, the jackpot funds not paid out are added to the existing fund for the second tier prize (bonus) and then shared by the various winners. In all the draws so far, the rollover has never reached this fourth rollover. Betting increases as the carryover builds since the potential jackpot rises.[3] These cases are favorable to the unpopular numbers hypothesis; among other things they correspond to the Canadian and UK games in which the winnings are paid up front (not over twenty or more years as in the US) and tax free (unlike in the US). The combination of tax free winnings plus being paid in cash makes the Canadian and UK prizes worth about three times those in the US. The optimal Kelly wagers are extremely small. The reason for this is that the bulk of the expected value is from prizes that occur with less than one in a million probability. A wealth level of $ 1 million is needed in Case A to justify $ 1 ticket. The corresponding wealth in Case B is over $ 150 000. Figures 3.1(a) and 3.1(b) provide the chance that the investor will double, quadruple or increase tenfold this fortune before it is halved using Kelly and fractional Kelly strategies for Cases A and B respectively. These chances are in the 40–60 % and 55–80 % ranges for Cases A and B, respectively. With fractional Kelly strategies in the range of 0.00000004 and 0.00000025 or less of the investor's initial wealth, the chance of increasing one's initial fortune tenfold before halving it is 95 % or more with Cases A and B respectively. However, it takes an average of 294 billion and 55 billion years respectively to achieve this goal assuming there are 100 draws per year as there are in the Canadian 6/49 and UK 6-49.

---

[3] An estimate of the number of tickets sold versus the carryover in millions is proportional to the carryover to the power 0.811. Hence, the growth is close to 1:1 linear. See Ziemba et al (1986).

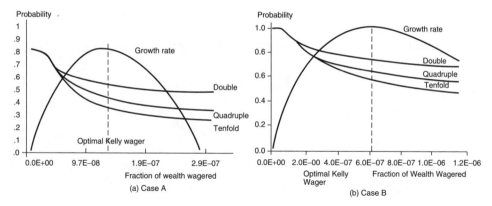

Figure 3.1 Probability of doubling, quadrupling and tenfolding before halving, lotto 6/49. *Source*: MacLean and Ziemba (1999)

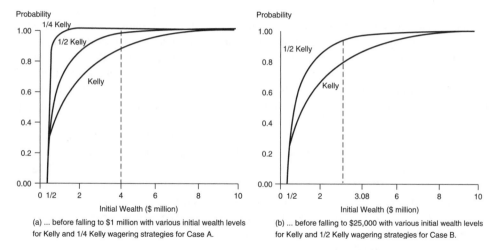

Figure 3.2 Probability of reaching the goal of $ 10 million under various conditions. *Source*: MacLean and Ziemba (1999)

Figures 3.2(a) and 3.2(b) give the probability of reaching $ 10 million before falling to $ 1 million and $ 25 000 for various initial wealth for cases A and B, respectively, with full, half and quarter Kelly wagering strategies. The results indicate that the investor can have a 95 % plus probability of achieving the $ 10 million goal from a reasonable initial wealth level with the quarter Kelly strategy for cases A and B. Unfortunately the mean time to reach this goal this is 914 million years for case A and 482 million years for case B. For case A with full Kelly it takes 22 million years on average and 384 million years with half Kelly for case A. For case B it takes 2.5 and 19.3 million years for full and half Kelly, respectively. It takes a lot less time, but still millions of years on average to merely double one's fortune: namely 2.6, 4.6 and 82.3 million years for full, half and quarter Kelly, respectively for case A and 0.792, 2.6 and 12.7 for case B. We may then conclude that millionaires can enhance their dynasties' long-run wealth provided their wagers are sufficiently small and made only when carryovers are sufficiently large (in lotto games around the world). There are quite a few that could be played.

What about a non-millionaire wishing to become one? The aspiring investor must pool funds until $150 000 is available for case B and $1 million for case A to optimally justify buying only one $1 ticket per draw. Such a tactic is legal in Canada and in fact is highly encouraged by the lottery corporation which supplies legal forms for such an arrangement.

Also in the UK, Camelot will supply model *agreement* forms for syndicates to use, specifying who must pay what, how much, and when, and how any prizes will be split. This is potentially very important for the treatment of inheritance tax with large prizes. The situation is modeled in Figure 3.3. Our aspiring millionaire puts up $100 000 along with nine others for the $1 million bankroll and when they reach $10 million each share is worth $1 million. The syndicate must play full Kelly and has a chance of success of nearly 50 assuming that the members agree to disband if they lose half their stake. Participants do not need to put up the whole $100 000 at the start. The cash outflow is easy to fund, namely 10 cents per draw per participant. To have a 50 % chance of reaching the $1 million goal, each participant (and their heirs) must have $50 000 at risk. It will take 22 million years, on average, to achieve the goal.

The situation is improved for case B players. First, the bankroll needed is about $154 000 since 65 tickets are purchased per draw for a $10 million wealth level. Suppose our aspiring nouveau riche is satisfied with $500 000 and is willing to put all but $25 000/2 or $12 500 of the $154 000 at risk. With one partner he can play half Kelly strategy and buy one ticket per case B type draw. Figure 3.2(b) indicates that the probability of success is about 0.95. With initial wealth of $308 000 and full Kelly it would take million years on average to achieve this goal. With half Kelly it would take, on average, 2.7 million years and with quarter Kelly it would take 300 million years.

The conclusion is that except for millionaires and pooled syndicates, it is not possible to use the unpopular numbers in a scientific way to beat the lotto and have high confidence of becoming rich; these aspiring millionaires will also most likely be residing in a cemetery when their distant heirs finally reach the goal.

What did we learn from this exercise?

1. Lotto games are in principle beatable but the Kelly and fractional Kelly wagers are so small that it takes virtually forever to have high confidence of winning. Of course, you could win earlier or even on the first draw and you do have a positive mean on all bets. Ziemba et al (1986) have shown that the largest jackpots contain about 47 % of the nineteen most unpopular numbers in 1986 shown in Table 3.1(b) versus 17 % unpopular numbers in the smallest jackpots. Hence, if you play, emphasizing unpopular numbers is a valuable strategy to employ. But frequently numbers other than the unpopular ones are drawn. So the strategy of focussing on three or four unpopular numbers and then randomly selecting the next two numbers might work. Gadgets to choose such numbers

are easy to devise. But you need deep pockets here and even then you might ruin. The best six numbers, see Table 3.2 once won a $ 10 million unshared jackpot in Florida. Could you bet more? Sorry: log is the most one should ever bet.

2. The Kelly and fractional Kelly wagering schemes are very useful in practice but the size of the wagers will vary from very tiny to enormous bets. My best advice: never over bet; it will eventually lead to trouble unless it is controlled somehow and that is hard to do!

4
Good and bad properties of the Kelly criterion

If your outlook is well extended, the Kelly criterion is the approach best suited to generating a fortune.

In this chapter we discuss the good and bad properties of the Kelly expected log capital growth criterion and in the process lead into the next chapters on hedge funds by discussing two of the great hedge fund traders who ran the unofficial hedge funds. If your horizon is long enough then the Kelly criterion is the road, however bumpy, to the most wealth at the end and the fastest path to a given rather large fortune.

It is known that the great investor Warren Buffett's Berkshire Hathaway actually has had a growth path quite similar to full Kelly betting. Figure 4.1 shows this performance from 1985 to 2000 in comparison with other great funds. Buffett also had a great record from 1977 to 1985 turning 100 into 1429.87, and

Mr Keynes believed God to be a large chicken, the Reverend surmised

65 852.40 in April 2000 and about 109 900 on December 2006.

Keynes was another Kelly type bettor. His record running King's College, Cambridge's Chest Fund is shown in Figure 4.2 versus the British market index for 1927 to 1945, data from Chua and Woodward (1983). Notice how much Keynes lost the first few years; obviously his academic brilliance and the recognition that he was facing a rather tough market kept him in this job. In total his geometric mean return beat the index by 10.01 %. Keynes was an aggressive investor with a capital asset pricing model beta of 1.78 versus the benchmark United Kingdom market return, a Sharpe ratio of 0.385, geometric mean returns of 9.12 % per year versus −0.89 % for the benchmark. Keynes had a yearly standard deviation of 29.28 % versus 12.55 % for the benchmark. These returns do not include Keynes' (or the benchmark's) dividends and interest, which he used to pay the college expenses. These were about 3 % per year. Kelly cowboys have their great returns and losses and embarrassments. Not covering a grain contract in time led to Keynes taking delivery and filling up the famous chapel. Fortunately it was big enough to fit in the grain and store it safely until it could be sold; see the cartoon. Keynes' investment behavior, according to Ziemba (2003)

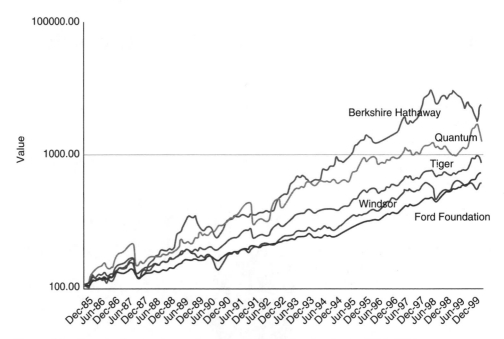

Figure 4.1 Growth of assets, log scale, various high performing funds, 1985–2000. *Source*: Ziemba (2003)

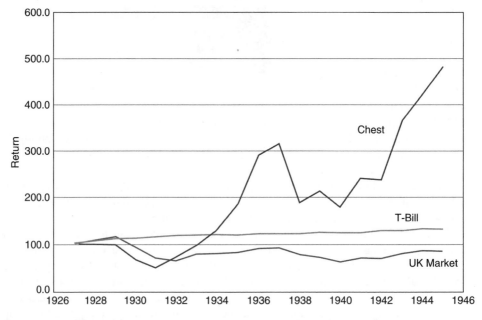

Figure 4.2 Graph of the performance of the Chest Fund, 1927–1945

was equivalent to 80 % Kelly and 20 % cash so he would use the negative power utility function $-w^{-0.25}$. Year by year returns of the Chest Fund are shown in Table 9.3.

Keynes emphasized three principles of successful investments in his 1933 report:

1. a careful selection of a few investments (or a few types of investment) having regard to their cheapness in relation to their probable actual and potential intrinsic value over a period of years ahead and in relation to alternative investments at the time;
2. a steadfast holding of these in fairly large units through thick and thin, perhaps for several years until either they have fulfilled their promise or it is evident that they were purchased on a mistake; and
3. a balanced investment position, i.e., a variety of risks in spite of individual holdings being large, and if possible, opposed risks.

He really was a lot like Buffett with an emphasis on value, large holdings and patience.

In November 1919, Keynes was appointed second bursar. Up to this time King's College investments were only in fixed income trustee securities plus their own land and buildings. By June 1920 Keynes convinced the college to start a separate fund containing stocks, currency and commodity futures. Keynes became first bursar in 1924 and held this post which had final authority on investment decisions until his death in 1945.

And Keynes did not believe in market timing as he said:

> We have not proved able to take much advantage of a general systematic movement out of and into ordinary shares as a whole at different phases of the trade cycle. As a result of these experiences I am clear that the idea of wholesale shifts is for various reasons impracticable and indeed undesirable. Most of those who attempt this sell too early and buy too late, and do both too often, incurring heavy expenses and developing too unsettled and speculative a state of mind, which, if it is widespread, has besides the grave social disadvantage of aggravating the scale of the fluctuations.

The main disadvantages result because the Kelly strategy is very aggressive with huge bets that become larger and larger as the situations are most attractive: recall that the optimal Kelly bet is the mean edge divided by the odds of winning. As I repeatedly argue. the mean counts by far the most. There is about a 20–2:1 ratio of expected utility loss from similar sized errors of means, variances and covariances, respectively. See Table 4.1 and Figure 4.3, and Kallberg and Ziemba (1984) and Chopra and Ziemba (1993) for details. Returning to Buffett who gets the mean right, better than almost all, notice that the other funds he outperformed are not shabby ones at all. Indeed they are George Soros' Quantum, John Neff's Windsor, Julian Robertson's Tiger and the Ford Foundation, all of whom had great records as measured by the Sharpe ratio. Buffett made 32.07 % per year net from July 1977 to March 2000 versus 16.71 % for the S&P500. Wow! Those of us who like wealth prefer Warren's path but his higher standard deviation path (mostly winnings) leads to a lower Sharpe (normal distribution based) measure; see Siegel et al (2001). Chapter 7 proposes a modification of the Sharpe ratio to not penalize gains. This improves Buffett's evaluation.

Since Buffett and Keynes are full or close to full Kelly bettors their means must be even more accurate. With their very low risk tolerances, the errors in the mean are 100+ times as important as the co-variance errors.

Table 4.1 Average Ratio of Certainty Equivalent Loss for Errors in Means, Variances and Covariances. *Source*: Chopra and Ziemba (1993)

Risk Tolerance	Errors in Means vs Covariances	Errors in Means vs Variances	Errors in Variances vs Covariances
25	5.38	3.22	1.67
50	22.50	10.98	2.05
75	56.84	21.42	2.68
	↓	↓	↓
	20	10	2
	Error Mean	Error Var	Error Covar
	20	2	1

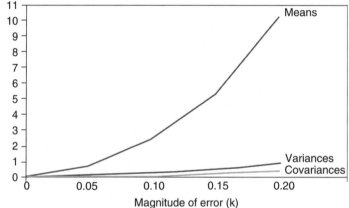

Figure 4.3 Mean Percentage Cash Equivalent Loss Due to Errors in Inputs

Kelly has essentially zero risk aversion since its Arrow-Pratt risk aversion index is

$$-u''(w)/u'(w) = 1/w,$$

which is essentially zero. Hence it never pays to bet more than the Kelly strategy because then risk increases (lower security) and growth decreases so is stochastically dominated. As you bet more and more above the Kelly bet, its properties become worse and worse. When you bet exactly twice the Kelly bet, then the growth rate is zero plus the risk free rate; see the proof at the end of this chapter.

If you bet more than double the Kelly criterion, then you will have a negative growth rate. With derivative positions one's bet changes continuously so a set of positions amounting to a small bet can turn into a large bet very quickly with market moves. Long Term Capital is a prime example of this overbetting leading to disaster but the phenomenon occurs all the time all over the world. Overbetting plus a bad scenario leads invariably to disaster.

Thus you must either bet Kelly or less. We call betting less than Kelly fractional Kelly, which is simply a blend of Kelly and cash. Consider the negative power utility function $\delta \omega^\delta$ for $\delta < 0$. This utility function is concave and when $\delta \to 0$ it converges to log utility. As δ gets larger negatively, the investor is less aggressive since his Arrow-Pratt risk aversion is also higher. For a given δ and $\alpha = 1/(1 - \delta)$ between 0 and 1, will provide the same portfolio when α is invested in the Kelly portfolio and $1 - \alpha$ is invested in cash.

This result is correct for lognormal investments and approximately correct for other distributed assets; see MacLean, Ziemba and Li (2005). For example, half Kelly is $\delta = -1$ and quarter Kelly is $\delta = -3$. So if you want a less aggressive path than Kelly pick an appropriate δ. Chapter 5 discusses a way to pick δ continuously in time so that wealth will stay above a desired wealth growth path with high given probability; see Figure 5.1.

Let's now list these and other important Kelly criterion properties, updated from MacLean, Ziemba and Blazenko (1992) and MacLean and Ziemba (1999).

Good Maximizing ElogX asymptotically maximizes the rate of asset growth. See Breiman (1961), Algoet and Cover (1988).

Good The expected time to reach a preassigned goal is asymptotically as X increases least with a strategy maximizing $Elog X_N$. See Breiman (1961), Algoet and Cover (1988), Browne (1997a).

Good Maximizing median logX. See Ethier (1987).

Bad False Property: If maximizing $Elog X_N$ almost certainly leads to a better outcome then the expected utility of its outcome exceeds that of any other rule provided N is sufficiently large. *Counter Example:* $u(x) = x, 1/2 < p < 1$, Bernoulli trials $f = 1$ maximizes $EU(x)$ but $f = 2p - 1 < 1$ maximizes $Elog X_N$. See Samuelson (1971), Thorp (1975, 2006).

Good The ElogX bettor never risks ruin. See Hakansson and Miller (1975).

Bad If the $Elog X_N$ bettor wins then loses or loses then wins with coin tosses, he is behind. The order of win and loss is immaterial for one, two, . . . , sets of trials since $(1 + \gamma)(1 - \gamma)X_0 = (1 - \gamma^2)X_0 < X_0$. This is not true for favourable games.

Good The absolute amount bet is monotone in wealth. $(\delta Elog X)/\delta W_0 > 0$.

Bad The bets are extremely large when the wager is favorable and the risk is very low. For single investment worlds, the optimal wager is proportional to the edge divided by the odds. Hence for low risk situations and corresponding low odds, the wager can be extremely large. For one such example, see Ziemba and Hausch (1986: 159–160). There, in the inaugural 1984 Breeders' Cup Classic $\$3$ million race, the optimal fractional wager on the 3–5 shot Slew of Gold was 64 %. (See also the 74 % future bet on the January effect in Chapter 2. Thorp and I actually made this place and show bet and won with a low fractional Kelly wager. Slew finished third but the second place horse Gate Dancer was disqualified and placed third. Luck (a good scenario) is also nice to have in betting markets. Wild Again won this race; the first great victory by the masterful jockey Pat Day.

Bad One overinvests when the problem data is uncertain. Investing more than the optimal capital growth wager is dominated in a growth-security sense. Hence, if the problem data provides probabilities, edges and odds that may be in error, then the suggested wager will be too large.

Bad The total amount wagered swamps the winnings – that is, there is much churning. Ethier and Tavare (1983) and Griffin (1985) show that the Expected Gain/E Bet is arbitrarily small and converges to zero in a Bernoulli game where one wins the expected fraction p of games.

Bad The unweighted average rate of return converges to half the arithmetic rate of return As with the bad property above this indicates that you do not seem to win as much as you expect. See Ethier and Tavaré (1983) and Griffin (1985).

Bad Betting double the optimal Kelly bet reduces the growth rate of wealth to zero plus the risk free rate. See Stutzer (1998) and Janecek (1999) and the next page for proofs.

Bad Given iid coin tossing with $p > 1/2$, for every $L < 1$ there is a strategy with the following properties: (1) with probability $> L$ it beats Kelly on all but a finite number of tosses, hence it eventually gets ahead and stays there forever with probability $> L$; (2) it differs from Kelly on **every** trial. If $(1/2)^{1/2} > p > 1/2$ betting more than the Kelly strategy (in coin tossing) puts you ahead with probability $p > 1/2$ after the first trial. But betting less that the Kelly strategy puts you ahead after 2 trials with probability $2pq + q^2 = 1 - p^2 > 1/2$. See Finkelstein and Whitley (1981) and Thorp (2007).

Good The ElogX bettor has an optimal myopic policy. He does not have to consider prior nor subsequent investment opportunities. This is a crucially important result for practical use. Hakansson (1972) proved that the myopic policy obtains for dependent investments with the log utility function. For independent investments and power utility a myopic policy is optimal, see Mossin (1968).

Good The chance that an ElogX wagerer will be ahead of any other wagerer after the first play is at least 50 %. See Bell and Cover (1980).

Good Simulation studies show that the ElogX bettor's fortune pulls way ahead of other strategies wealth for reasonable-sized samples. The key again is risk. See Ziemba and Hausch (1986). General formulas are in Aucamp (1993).

Good If you wish to have higher security by trading it off for lower growth, then use a negative power utility function or fractional Kelly strategy. See MacLean, Sanegre, Zhao and Ziemba (2004) who show how to compute the coefficent to stay above a growth path with given probability. See Figure 5.1 for the idea and the examples in Chapter 5.

Bad Despite its superior long-run growth properties, it is possible to have very poor return outcome. For example, making 700 wagers all of which have a 14 % advantage, the least of which had a 19 % chance of winning can turn $ 1000 into $ 18. But with full Kelly 16.6 % of the time $ 1000 turns into at least $ 100 000, see Ziemba and Hausch (1996). Half Kelly does not help much as $ 1000 can become $ 145 and the growth is much lower with only $ 100 000 plus final wealth 0.1 % of the time.

Bad It can take a long time for a Kelly bettor to dominate an essentially different strategy. In fact this time may be without limit. Suppose $\mu_\alpha = 20\,\%$, $\mu_\beta = 10\,\%$, $\sigma_\alpha = \sigma_\beta = 10\,\%$. Then in five years A is ahead of B with 95\,% confidence. But if $\sigma_\alpha = 20$, $\sigma_\beta = 10\,\%$ with the same means, it takes 157 years for A to beat B with 95\,% confidence. In coin tossing suppose game A has an edge of 1.0\,% and game B 1.1\,%. It takes two million trials to have an 84\,% chance that game A dominates game B, see Thorp (2006).

Chapters 6 and 7 discuss the use of full and fractional Kelly and other strategies for hedge funds.

APPENDIX

Proof that betting exactly double the Kelly criterion amount leads to a growth rate equal to the risk free rate. This result is due to Thorp (1997), Stutzer (1998) and Janacek (1998). This simple proof in continuous time is due to Harry Markowitz.

$$g_p = E_p - \tfrac{1}{2} V_p$$

E_p, V_p, g_p are the portfolio expected return, variance and expected log, respectively. In the CAPM

$$E_p = r_o + (E_M - r_0)X$$
$$V_p = \sigma_M^2 X^2$$

where X is the portfolio weight and r_0 is the risk free rate. Collecting terms and setting the derivative of g_p to zero yields

$$X = (E_M - r_0)/\sigma_M^2$$

which is the optimal Kelly bet with optimal growth rate

$$g^* = r_0 + (E_M - r_0)^2 - \tfrac{1}{2}[(E_M r_0)/\sigma_M^2]^2 \sigma_M^2$$
$$= r_0 + (E_M - r_0)^2/\sigma_M^2 - \tfrac{1}{2}(E_M - r_0)^2/\sigma_M^2$$
$$= r_0 + \tfrac{1}{2}[(E - M - r))/\sigma_M]^2.$$

Substituting double Kelly, namely $Y = 2X$ for X above into

$$g_p = r_0 + (E_M - r_0)Y - \tfrac{1}{2}\sigma_M^2 Y^2$$

and simplifying yields

$$g_0 - r_0 = 2(E_M - r_0)^2/\sigma_M^2 - \tfrac{4}{2}(E_M - r_0)^2/\sigma_M^2 = 0.$$

Hence $g_0 = r_0$ when $Y = 2S$.

The CAPM assumption is not needed. For a more general proof and illustration, see Thorp (2006).

5

Calculating the optimal Kelly fraction

Lets find the optimal Kelly fraction to keep us above a given growth path with high probability

In this Chapter I discuss how to calculate the optimal Kelly fraction to grow wealth as fast as possible in the long run but to stay above a wealth growth path at particular intervals with high probability in the short run. This approach provides one way to scientifically cut down the size of one's bet to raise security levels while still maintaining high growth levels.

Most applications of fractional Kelly capital growth strategies pick the fraction in an ad hoc way. MacLean, Ziemba and Li (2005) show that growth and security tradeoffs are effective for general return distributions in the sense that growth is monotone decreasing in security. But with general return distributions, this tradeoff is not necessarily efficient in the sense of Markowitz (generalized growth playing the role of mean and security the role of variance). However, if the investment returns are lognormal, the tradeoff is efficient. MacLean, Ziemba and Li also develop an investment strategy where the investor sets upper and lower targets and rebalances when those targets are achieved. Empirical tests in MacLean, Sanegre, Zhao and Ziemba (MSZZ) (2004) show the advantage of this approach.

A solution of a version of the problem of how to pick an optimal Kelly function was provided in MSZZ (2004). To stay above a wealth path using a Kelly strategy is very difficult since the more attractive the investment opportunity, the larger the bet size and hence the larger the chance of falling below the path. Figure 5.1 illustrates this.

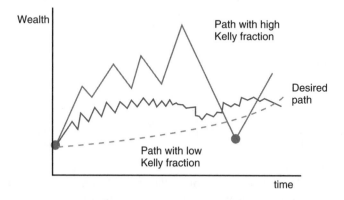

Figure 5.1   Kelly fractions and path achievement

HOW TO STAY ABOVE A GIVEN WEALTH PATH

MSZZ use a continuous time lognormally distributed asset model to calculate the Kelly fraction at various points in time to stay above an exogenously specified wealth path with a given probability. They provide an algorithm for this. The idea is illustrated using the following application to the fundamental problem of asset allocation over time, namely,

Table 5.1 Yearly Wealth Relatives on Assets Relative to Cash (%)

Parameter	Stocks	Bonds	Cash
Mean: μ	108.75	103.75	100
Standard deviation: σ	12.36	5.97	0
Correlation: ρ		0.32	

Table 5.2 Rates of Return Scenarios

Scenarios	Stocks	Bonds	Cash	Probability
1	95.00	101.50	100	0.25
2	106.50	110.00	100	0.25
3	108.50	96.50	100	0.25
4	125.00	107.00	100	0.25

the determination of optimal fractions over time in cash, bonds and stocks. The data in Table 5.1 are yearly asset returns for the S&P500, the Salomon Brothers Bond index and US T-bills for 1980–1990 with data from Data Resources, Inc. Cash returns are set to one in each period and the mean returns for other assets are adjusted for this shift. The standard deviation for cash is small and is set to 0 for convenience.

A simple grid was constructed from the assumed lognormal distribution for stocks and bonds by partitioning $\Re^2$ at the centroid along the principal axes. A sample point was selected from each quadrant to approximate the parameter values. The planning horizon is $T = 3$, with 64 scenarios each with probability 1/64 using the data in Table 5.2. The problems are solved with the VaR constraint (Table 5.3) and then for comparison, with the stronger drawdown constraint (Table 5.4).

VaR Control with $w^* = a$

The model is

$$\max_{X} \left\{ E \sum_{t=1}^{3} \ln(R(t)^{\top} X(t)) \middle| \Pr \left[\sum_{t=1}^{3} \ln(R(t)^{\top} X(t)) \geqslant 3 \ln a \right] \geqslant 1 - \alpha \right\}.$$

With initial wealth $W(0) = 1$, the value at risk is a^3. The optimal investment decisions and optimal growth rate for several values of a, the secured average annual growth rate and $1 - \alpha$, the security level, are shown in Table 5.3. The heuristic described in MSZZ was used to determine A, the set of scenarios for the security constraint. Since only a single constraint was active at each stage the solution is optimal.

- The mean return structure for stocks is favorable in this example, as is typical over long horizons.[1] hence the aggressive Kelly strategy is to invest all the capital in stock most of the time.

---

[1] See, e.g. Keim and Ziemba (2000), Dimson et al (2006), Constantinides (2002) and Siegel (2002).

Table 5.3   Growth with Secured Rate

Secured Growth Rate a	Secured Level $1 - \alpha$	Period 1 S	Period 1 B	Period 1 C	Period 2 S	Period 2 B	Period 2 C	Period 3 S	Period 3 B	Period 3 C	Optimal Growth Rate (%)
0.95	0	1	0	0	1	0	0	1	0	0	23.7
	0.85	1	0	0	1	0	0	1	0	0	23.7
	0.9	1	0	0	1	0	0	1	0	0	23.7
	0.95	1	0	0	1	0	0	1	0	0	23.7
	0.99	1	0	0	0.492	0.508	0	0.492	0.508	0	19.6
0.97	0	1	0	0	1	0	0	1	0	0	23.7
	0.85	1	0	0	1	0	0	1	0	0	23.7
	0.9	1	0	0	1	0	0	1	0	0	23.7
	0.95	1	0	0	1	0	0	1	0	0	23.7
	0.99	1	0	0	0.333	0.667	0	0.333	0.667	0	18.2
0.99	0	1	0	0	1	0	0	1	0	0	23.7
	0.85	1	0	0	1	0	0	1	0	0	23.7
	0.9	1	0	0	1	0	0	1	0	0	23.7
	0.95	1	0	0	0.867	0.133	0	0.867	0.133	0	19.4
	0.99	0.456	0.544	0	0.27	0.73	0	0.27	0.73	0	12.7
0.995	0	1	0	0	1	0	0	1	0	0	23.7
	0.85	1	0	0	0.996	0.004	0	0.996	0.004	0	23.7
	0.9	1	0	0	0.996	0.004	0	0.996	0.004	0	23.7
	0.95	1	0	0	0.511	0.489	0	0.442	0.558	0	19.4
	0.99	0.27	0.73	0	0.219	0.59	0.191	0.218	0.59	0.192	12.7
0.999	0	1	0	0	1	0	0	1	0	0	23.7
	0.85	1	0	0	0.956	0.044	0	0.956	0.044	0	23.4
	0.9	1	0	0	0.956	0.044	0	0.956	0.044	0	23.4
	0.95	1	0	0	0.381	0.619	0	0.51	0.49	0	19.1
	0.99	0.27	0.73	0	0.008	0.02	0.972	0.008	0.02	0.972	5.27

- When security requirements are high some capital is in bonds.
- As the security requirements increase the fraction invested in bonds increases.
- The three-period investment decisions are more conservative as the horizon approaches.

Secured Annual Drawdown: b

The VaR condition only controls the loss at the horizon. At intermediate times the investor could experience substantial loss, and face bankruptcy. A more stringent risk control constraint, drawdown, considers the loss in each period using the model

$$\max_X \left\{ E \sum_{t=1}^{3} \ln(R(t)^\top X(t)) \,\middle|\, \Pr\left[\ln(R(t)^\top X(t)) \geqslant \ln b, t = 1, 2, 3\right] \geqslant 1 - \alpha \right\}.$$

Table 5.4   Growth with Secured Maximum Drawdown

Draw-down b	Secured Level $1-\alpha$	Period 1			Period 2			Period 3			Optimal Growth Rate (%)
		S	B	C	S	B	C	S	B	C	
0.96	0	1	0	0	1	0	0	1	0	0	23.7
	50	1	0	0	1	0	0	0.846	0.154	0	23.1
	75	1	0	0	0.846	0.154	0	0.846	0.154	0	23.1
	100	0.846	0.154	0	0.846	0.154	0	0.846	0.154	0	21.9
0.97	0	1	0	0	1	0	0	1	0	0	23.7
	50	1	0	0	1	0	0	0.692	0.308	0	22.5
	75	1	0	0	0.692	0.308	0	0.692	0.308	0	21.3
	100	0.692	0.308	0	0.692	0.308	0	0.692	0.308	0	20.1
0.98	0	1	0	0	1	0	0	1	0	0	23.7
	50	1	0	0	1	0	0	0.538	0.462	0	21.2
	75	1	0	0	0.538	0.462	0	0.538	0.462	0	18.6
	100	0.538	0.462	0	0.538	0.462		0.538	0.462	0	16.1
0.99	0	1	0	0	1	0	0	1	0	0	23.7
	50	1	0	0	1	0	0	0.385	0.615	0	21.2
	75	1	0	0	0.385	0.615	0	0.385	0.615	0	18.6
	100	0.385	0.615	0	0.385	0.615	0	0.385	0.615	0	16.1
0.999	0	1	0	0	1	0	0	1	0	0	23.7
	50	1	0	0	1	0	0	0.105	0.284	0.611	17.7
	75	1	0	0	0.105	0.284	0.611	0.105	0.284	0.611	11.8
	100	0.105	0.284	0.611	0.105	0.284	0.611	0.105	0.284	0.611	5.84

This constraint follows from the arithmetic random walk $\ln W(t)$,

$$\Pr[W(t+1) \geqslant bW(t), t = 0, 1, 2] = \Pr[\ln W(t+1) - \ln W(t) \geqslant \ln b, t = 0, 1, 2]$$
$$= \Pr[\ln R(t)^{\top} X(t) \geqslant \ln b, t = 1, 2, 3].$$

The optimal investment decisions and growth rate for several values of b, the drawdown and $1 - \alpha$, the security level are shown in Table 5.4.

- The heuristic in MSZZ is used in determining scenarios in the solution.
- The security levels are different since constraints are active at different probability levels in this discretized problem.
- As with the VaR constraint, investment in the bonds and cash increases as the drawdown rate and/or the security level increases.
- The strategy is more conservative as the horizon approaches.
- For similar requirements (compare $a = 0.97$, $1 - \alpha = 0.85$ and $b = 0.97$, $1 - \alpha = 0.75$), the drawdown condition is more stringent, with the Kelly strategy (all stock) optimal for VaR constraint, but the drawdown constraint requires substantial investment in bonds in the second and third periods.

- In general, consideration of drawdown requires a heavier investment in secure assets and at an earlier time point. It is not a feature of this aggregate example, but both the VaR and drawdown constraints are insensitive to large losses, which occur with small probability.
- Control of that effect would require the lower partial mean violations condition or a model with a convex risk measure that penalizes more and more as larger constraint violations occur, see, e.g. the InnoALM model in Chapter 21.
- The models lead to hair trigger type behavior, very sensitive to small changes in mean values (as discussed in Chapters 4 and 21; see also Figure 6.6.

6
The great investors, their methods and how we evaluate them: Theory

If you are going to beat the market you better believe that you can beat the market with careful study

The next three chapters discuss how great investors succeed. This is an enormous topic but we think our principles and results apply reasonably broadly. Winning has two parts: getting an edge and then betting well. The former simply means that investments have an advantage so $1 invested returns on average more than $1. The latter involves not overbetting, and truly diversifying in all scenarios in a disciplined, wealth enhancing way.

This chapter begins with a categorization of the efficient market camps which inform how various people try to get an edge. Some feel that one cannot get an edge. This becomes then a self fulfilling prophecy and those who hold this belief, of course, are not in our list of great or even good investors. Many great investors are Kelly or fractional Kelly bettors who focus on not losing. This chapter discusses the records of some great investors and concludes with a suggested method to evaluate them. In Chapter 7 we evaluate the records of some great investors in more depth. Chapter 8 discusses the methods of the great university

endowment managers such as David Swensen of Yale as well as the managers of the Harvard, Princeton and Stanford endowments. In the appendix, we review some recent investment books that relate to great investing including more on the Kelly capital growth criterion.

THE VARIOUS EFFICIENT/INEFFICIENT MARKET CAMPS: CAN YOU BEAT THE STOCK MARKET?

Why Buffett wants to endow university chairs in efficient market theory

Market participants can be divided into five groups. There are other ways to do such a categorization but this way is useful for our purpose of isolating and studying great investors and naturally evolves from the academic study of the efficiency of financial markets.

The Five Groups are:

1. Efficient markets (E)
2. Risk premium (RP)
3. Genius (G)
4. Hog wash (H)
5. Markets are beatable (A)

The first group are those who believe in efficient markets (E). They believe that current prices are fair and correct except possibly for transactions costs. These transaction costs, which include commissions, bid-ask spread, and price pressures, can be very large.[1]

The leader of this school which had dominated academic journals, jobs, fame, etc in the 1960s to the 1980s was Gene Fama of the University of Chicago. A brilliant researcher, Fama is also a tape recorder: you can turn him on or off, you can fast forward or rewind him or change his volume, but you cannot change his views no matter what evidence you provide; he will refute it forcibly.

This group provided many useful concepts such as the capital asset pricing model of Sharpe (1964), Lintner (1965) and Mossin (1966) which provided a theoretical justification for index funds which are the efficient market camp's favored investment mode. They still beat about 75 % of active managers. Since all the managers comprise the market, that's 50 % of them beaten by the index. Transactions and other costs eliminate another 25 %. Let's consider the arguments adapted from Ziemba and Schwartz (1991):

Why professional fund managers cannot beat the market averages

The evidence is that professional managers all over the world have a hard time beating the market averages. In a given year, only about 25 % to 40 % of managers actually beat a buy-and-hold strategy of holding the index. Over longer periods, say 5–10 years, the percentage is even lower. There are a number of reasons for this.

- The market averages stay fully invested at all times, never missing market moves nor paying commissions for stock changes and market timing.
- When funds get behind the index, they often make hasty moves to try to catch up and, more often than not, this puts them further behind.
- Portfolio managers have a tendency to window dress at reporting times, adding to turnover and commissions.
- Since the managers collectively more or less are the market (with individual investors forming less and less of the market each year) the indices, on average, beat half of the fund managers. Then with commissions, fees, and these other reasons, only the 25 % to 40 % typically beat the market averages (which does quite well with a lot less work).
- The fund managers take fees; the averages work for free.

---

[1] A BARRA study by Andy Rudd some years ago showed that these costs averaged 4.6 % one-way for a $ 50 000 institutional investor sale. This is if you use a naive market order for the full transaction rather than limit orders or smaller market orders. Thorp, in a private communication, told us that he traded about $ 60 billion in statistical arbitrage from 1992–2002 in lot sizes of 20k to 100k and found that the mean transaction cost was about 1 cent per share and the market impact was about 4.5 cents per share for shares averaging about $ 30. So the one-way costs were about $ 0.18.

- The fund managers' goals may get in the way of the fund's best interests. This is the so-called agency problem.
- Portfolio managers tend to follow each other's moves. They tend to move the market which gains the full amount, and they can easily be a little behind.

We have the following four reasons why the high commissions of active trading often lead to poorer performance than the market indices.

1. Commissions are higher in active portfolios because the turnover is greater.
2. The bid-ask spreads are larger for many smaller international securities that an active manager would buy.
3. Exchange taxes can be as large as 1% on both buys and sells.
4. Active managers usually hold a small number of large positions so they have market impact on getting in and out.

Index funds have grown and grown. Dimension Fund Advisors formed by Fama's students manages over $ 25 billion and others such as Barclays in San Francisco manage over $ 100 billion. This is done with low fees in an efficient manner. The indices for these passive funds have grown to include small cap, foreign investments and a variety of exchange traded funds as well as the traditional market index, the S&P500.

As an example, Table 6.1 gives such results for 1988 for 167 funds based in Hong Kong with investments in various parts of the world. Only 48, or 28.7%, actually beat the benchmark indices. ASEAN equity funds did do well, averaging 41.4% returns versus the market's 27.7%, and 11 of the 13 funds beat this measure. But Japanese equity funds did

Table 6.1 Sector Median Returns of Hong Kong Based Funds Compared with Market Average, January 1 to November 30, 1988. *Source*: Ziemba and Schwartz (1991)

Class of Fund	Median Return, %	Reference Market Average	% Change	Number of Funds Outperforming Market Average
Japanese equity funds	19.1	TSE Index	34.9	4 of 30
Hong Kong equity funds	24.4	Hang Seng index	20.8	9 of 15
Australian equity funds	23.1	All-Ordinaries index	43.3	1 of 11
Singapore/Malaysian equity funds	25.8	FT Actuaries Singapore	25.9	3 of 7
Asean equity funds	41.4	FT Actuaries HK & Singapore	27.7	11 of 13
Far East equity funds	22.1	FT Actuaries Pacific	35.1	3 of 20
US equity funds	7.6	S&P Composite	14.0	5 of 25
British equity funds	6.8	FT All Shares Index	10.9	4 of 19
European equity funds	13.0	FT Actuaries Europe	13.9	7 of 15
International managed funds	9.4	FT Actuaries World	23.1	0 of 6
British gilt funds	1.0	FT All Stock Bond index	5.0	1 of 6
			(28.7%)	48 of 167

not fare so well. Indeed only 4 out of 30 funds beat the TSE index of 34.9 % and their average return was 19.1 %, more than 15 points below the Topix.

Over time the hard efficient market line has softened into a Risk Premium (RP) camp. They feel that markets are basically efficient but one can realize extra return by bearing additional risk. They strongly argue that, if returns are above average, the risk must be there somewhere; you simply cannot get higher returns without bearing additional risk they argue. For example, beating the market index S&P500 is possible but not when risk adjusted by the CAPM. They measure risk by Beta, which must be greater than one to receive higher than market returns. That is, the portfolio risk is higher than the market risk. But they allow other risk factors such as small cap and low book to price. But they do not believe in full blown 20–30 factor models such as described in Chapter 25. Fama and his disciples moved here in the 1990s. This camp now dominates the top US academic journals and the jobs in academic finance departments at the best schools in the US and Europe.

The third camp is called Genius (G). These are superior investors who are brilliant or geniuses but you cannot determine in advance who they are. Paul Samuelson has championed this argument. Samuelson feels that these investors do exist but it is useless to try to find them as in the search for them you will find 19 duds for every star. This view is very close to the Merton-Samuelson criticism of the Kelly criterion: that is, even with an advantage, it is possible to lose a lot of your wealth (see Table 2.2). The evidence though is that you can determine them ex ante and to some extent they have persistent superior performance, see Fung et al (2006) and Jagannathan et al (2006). Soros did this in futures trading with superior timing and choice of futures to bet on: this is in the traders are *made not born* philosophy. This camp will isolate members of other camps such as in (A) or (H).

The fourth camp is as strict in its views as camps (E) and (RP). This group feels that the efficient market view, which originated in and is perpetuated by the academic world, is hogwash (H). In fact the leading proponent of this view and one with whom it views is hard to argue as he is right at the top of the list of the world's richest persons is Warren Buffett, who wants to give university chairs in efficient markets to further improve his own very successful trading. An early member of this group, the great economist John Maynard Keynes was an academic. We see also that although they may never have heard of the Kelly criterion, this camp does seem to use it implicitly with large bets on favorable investments.

This group feels that by evaluating companies and buying them when their value is greater than their price, you can easily beat the market by taking a long term view. They find these stocks and hold them forever. They find a few such stocks that they understand well and get involved in managing them or they simply buy them and make them subsidiaries with the previous owners running the business. They forget about diversification because they try to buy only winners. They also bet on insurance when the odds are greatly in their favor. They well understand tail risk which they only take at huge advantages to themselves when the bet is small relative to their wealth levels. They are thus great put sellers.

The last group are those who think that markets are beatable (A) through behavioral biases, security market anomalies using computerized superior betting techniques. They construct risk arbitrage situations with positive expectation. They research the strategy well and follow it for long periods of time repeating the advantage many times. They feel that factor models are useful most but not all of the time and show that beta is not one of the most important variables to predict stock prices. They use very focused, disciplined, well researched strategies with superior execution and risk control. Many of them use Kelly or fractional Kelly strategies. All of them extensively use computers. They focus on not losing,

Three great investors: Warren Buffett, Paul Samuelson and Ed Thorp

and they rarely have blowouts. Members of (A) include Ed Thorp (Princeton Newport and later funds), Bill Benter (the Hong Kong racing guru), Blair Hull, Harry McPike, Jim Simons (Renaissance hedge fund), Jeff Yass (Susquehanna Group), David Swensen, Nikolai Battoo (a private trader with unique criterion applications) and me. Blowouts occur more in hedge funds that do not focus on not losing and true diversification and over-bet; when a bad scenario hits them, they get wiped out, such as LTCM, Niederhofer, and Amaranth; see Chapters 11–13; and the June 2007 Bear Stearns hedge fund blowout bond blow up; see our forthcoming column in Wilmott that discusses this typical hedge fund blowup and the wider August 2007 sub-prime world wide equity, banking and bond market crisis. My idea of using scenario dependent correlation matrices, see Chapter 21 is very important here.

HOW DO INVESTORS AND CONSULTANTS DO IN ALL THESE CASES?

All investors can be multimillionaires but the centimillionaires are in (G), (H) and (A) like the eight listed before me in (A) and Buffett. These people make more money for their clients than themselves but the amount they make for themselves is a huge amount: of course these people eat their own cooking, that is, they are clients themselves with a large amount of their money in the funds they manage. An exception is someone who founded an (RP) or (E) company kept most of the shares and made an enormous amount of fees for themselves irrespective of the investment performance given to the clients because the sheer volume of assets they have gathered under management is so large. I was fortunate to work/consult with seven of these and was also the main consultant to the Frank Russell Research Department for nine years which is perhaps the leading conservative RP implementor. (A) people earn money by winning and taking a percent of the profits, Thorp returned 15.8 % net with $ 200 million under management; fees $ 8 million/year (1969–88). (E) and (RP) people earn money from fees by collecting assets through superior marketing and sticky investment decisions.

Many great investors use Kelly betting including most in camp (A). There are compelling reasons for this discussed in previous chapters. For long and mathematical survey papers, see MacLean and Ziemba (2006) and Thorp (2006). But there are critics and chief among them are Nobel prize winners Bob Merton and Paul Samuelson. Their argument is that successful investing requires a lot of luck and it is hard to separate luck from skill. Therefore while many Kelly investors will make huge gains, a few will have huge losses. Indeed they are correct. A good way to explain this is via the simulation Donald Hausch and I did; see the experiment in Chapter 2, Tables 2.1 and 2.2. The simulation of 700 bets was performed 1000 times.[2] The successful traders combine the pure theory with good risk control as well.

In support of Kelly, notice that 166 times out of the 1000 simulated wealth paths, the investor has more than 100 times initial wealth with full Kelly. But this great outcome occurs only once with half Kelly. However the probability of being ahead is higher with half Kelly, 87.0 vs 95.4. A negative observation, and related to the Merton-Samuelson criticism, is that the minimum wealth is only 18. So you can make 700 independent bets, each with a 14 % edge and the result is that you still lose over 98 % of your fortune with bad scenarios. Luenberger (1993) shows that, theoretically, if your utility function is based solely on the tail losses, then the optimal strategy is to tradeoff expected log and variance of log (like a static mean variance analysis).

Let's now look at the records of wealth over time of some great investors and then discuss a way I propose to evaluate them. Recall Figures 4.1 high performing funds and 4.2 the record of the Chest Fund. Of these wealth records, the smoothest, nicest ones are Thorp's (Figure 6.2) with a downside symmetric Sharpe ratio of 13.8 (the highest known to the authors), Benter's (Figure 6.1) and mine (Figure 6.3, of course at a lower level of total gains, but ... with my own and clients money I am making progress) of camp A, Keynes, and Buffett of camp H and Soros (Quantum) of camp G and Ford of camp RP. Ford gains the least but has a very smooth wealth path. By law they must pay out 5 % of their wealth in gifts each year. Their expenses are about 0.3 % so their goal, which they have been quite successful in achieving, is to make 5.3 % in real terms. So they have less wealth but a high Sharpe ratio. Ziemba (2003) argues that Keynes is a negative power $-w^{-0.25}$ (80 % Kelly,

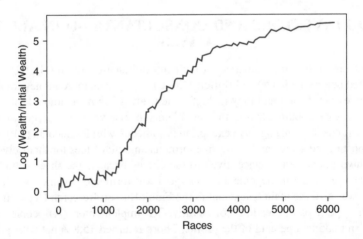

Figure 6.1 The record of Bill Benter, the world's greatest racetrack, a well known fractional Kelly bettor. *Source*: Ziemba (2005)

---

[2] See also the empirical paper by Bicksler and Thorp (1973) where they calculate the probability that investors will be ahead after given numbers of favorable bets. Their conclusions are consistent with those in the Hausch and Ziemba study discussed here.

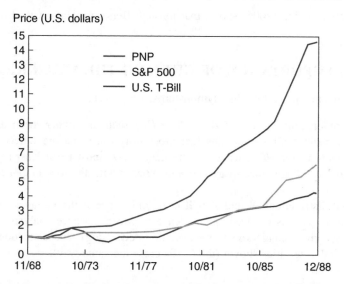

Figure 6.2 The record of Princeton Newport Partners, LP, cumulative results, Nov 1969–Dec 1998 (Thorp). *Source*: Ziemba (2003)

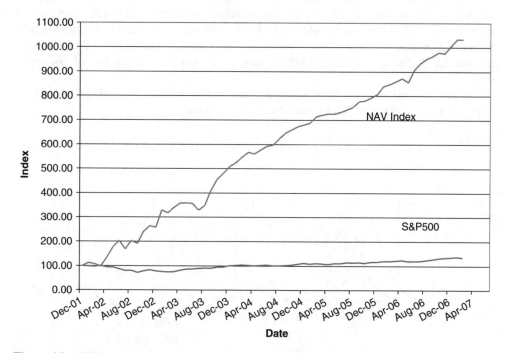

Figure 6.3 WTZ's futures account at Vision, L.P., New York and Chicago, January 1, 2002 to May 4, 2007

20 % cash) bettor. Thorp (2006) shows that through Berkshire Hathaway, Buffett is a full Kelly bettor.

THE IMPORTANCE OF GETTING THE MEAN RIGHT

The mean dominates if the two distributions cross only once.

Theorem: Hanoch and Levy (1969) If $X \sim F(\cdot)$ with the higher mean and $Y \sim G(\cdot)$ have cumulative distribution functions that cross only once, but are otherwise arbitrary, then F dominates G for **all** concave u. The mean of F must be at least as large as the mean of G to have dominance. Variance and other moments are unimportant. Only the means count.

With normal distributions X and Y will cross only once if the variance of X does not exceed that of Y. That is the basic equivalence of Mean-Variance analysis and Expected Utility Analysis via second order (concave, non-decreasing) stochastic dominance. See Figure 6.4 with the densities shown (the CDFs cross the same way).

Errors in means, variances and covariances: empirical

Replace the true mean μ_i by the observed mean $\mu_i(1 + kZ_i)$ where Z_i is distributed $N \sim (0, 1)$ with scale factor $k = 0.05$ to 0.20, being the size of the error. Similarly, replace the true variances and covariances by the observed variances $\sigma_i^2(1 + kZ_i)$ and covariances $\sigma_{ij}(1 + kZ_i)$. We use monthly data from 1980–89 on ten DJIA securities which include Alcoa, Boeing, Coke, Dupont and Sears. See Chopra-Ziemba (1993) which updates and extends Kallberg and Ziemba (1984) and studies the important effect of risk aversion.

The certainty equivalent, CE, of a portfolio with utility function u equals u^{-1} (expected utility of a risky portfolio). This comes from the equation:

$$u(CE) = E_\xi u(\xi'x) \Rightarrow CE = u^{-1}[E_\xi u(\xi x).]$$

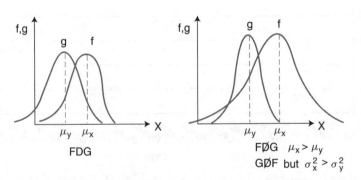

Figure 6.4   The main theorem of mean-variance analysis

Assuming exponential utility and normal distributions yields exact formulae to calculate all quantities in the certainty equivalent loss

$$(CEL) = \left\{ \frac{CE_{opt} - CE_{approx}}{CE_{opt}} \right\} 100$$

Observe that the mean-variance problem is

$$\text{mean} \left(\frac{\text{risk aversion}}{2} \right) \text{variance.}$$

Table 4.1 and Figure 4.3 show that the errors in means are about 20 times errors in covariances in terms of CEL value and the variances are twice as important as the covariances. So roughly, there is a 20:2:1 ratio in the importance of these errors. Also, this is risk aversion dependent with $T_R = (R_A/2)100$ being the risk tolerance. So for high risk tolerance, that is low risk aversion, the errors in the means are even greater. Hence for utility functions like log of Kelly with essentially zero risk aversion, the errors in the mean can be 100 times as important as the errors in the other parameters. So Kelly bettors should never overbet. See Table 4.1.

Conclusion: spend your money getting good mean estimates and use historical variances and covariances

Chopra (1993) shows that a similar relationship holds regarding turnover but it is less dramatic than for the cash equivalents, see Figure 6.5.

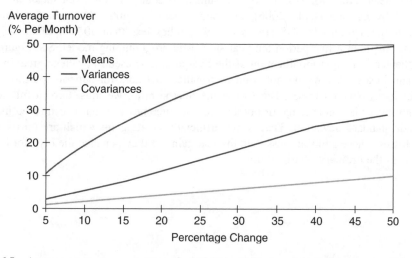

Figure 6.5   Average turnover: percentage of portfolio sold (or bought) relative to preceding allocation. *Source*: Chopra (1993)

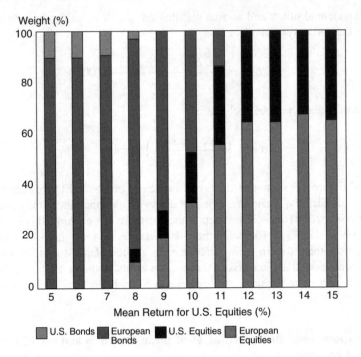

Figure 6.6 Optimal asset weights at stage 1 for varying levels of US equity means in a multiperiod stochastic programming pension fund model for Siemens Austria. *Source*: Geyer and Ziemba (2007)

The results here apply to essentially all models. You must get the means right to win!

If the mean return for US stocks is assumed to equal the long run mean of 12 % as estimated by Dimson et al. (2006), the model yields an optimal weight for equities of 100 %. A mean return for US stocks of 9 % implies less than 30 % optimal weight for equities. This is in a five period ten year stochastic programming model. See Figure 6.6.

In Chapter 7, a slight modification of the Sharpe ratio is used to evaluate great investors. The main idea is that we do not want to penalize investors for superior performance so we will focus only on losses. But to use the Sharpe ratio, we must have a full standard deviation over the whole range of possible return outcomes and that is estimated using the downside standard deviation. That is, we artificially create gains which are mirror images of the losses. These gains are less than the real gains so they penalize the investor less than if one uses the ordinary Sharpe ratio.

7

The Great Investors, a way to evaluate them

To fairly evaluate great investors you cannot penalize them for gains only for their losses

It is widely argued that Warren Buffett is the world's greatest investor with more than $40 billion in his personal stake in the $120 plus billion Berkshire Hathaway fund. Indeed, my Wilmott columnist colleague, Ed Thorp, upon meeting Buffett for the first time in 1969, said to his wife: we had dinner tonight with the man who someday will be the world's richest. He was right, now only Bill Gates has more wealth than Buffett and Buffett had led Gates for a few months in the early 1990s. Ed was also wise enough

to buy Berkshire Hathaway shares in the $100 area which have gone up 1000-fold in the past 37 years. Berkshire stock was $15 in 1965 when the partnership began. Berkshire Hathaway operates like a closed end mutual fund with a net asset value which can be proxied by its book value and a correct net asset value obtained by adding up all its assets minus its liabilities and a market price.

According to *Morningstar*, the late March 2006 price of $90000 for the A shares and $3000 for the B shares (1/30 of an A share) is exceeded by a fair value of $121560 or $4052. So if *Morningstar* is correct, Berkshire Hathaway sells at a discount. As of December 2006, the shares are up over 20% from March to $109900 and $3660, respectively. If you want to do your own analysis of the net asset value refer to the Berkshire Hathaway annual reports. They are fascinating reading. Buying one share of the B's provides the reports and a ticket to the annual meeting. While I bought later than Thorp, it has been a good investment for me too. Table 7.1 gives long term insight and shows that in the forty-one years from 1965 to 2005, the book value increased in all but one year (2001) when it fell 6.2%. There was an average gain of 22.02% geometric mean versus 10.47% for the S&P500.[1] Meanwhile the S&P500 fell in ten of those forty-one years. Figure 4.1 plots the rate of return in wealth

---

[1] Martin and Puthenpurackal (2007) analyzed the Berkshire Hathaway results from 1980–2003. Berkshire Hathaway beat the S&P500 in 20 out of 24 years by an average of 12.24% per year. They concluded that: the results are not luck, nor are they explained by high risk taking, Warren Buffett has superior stock-picking skills that allows him to identify undervalued securities and thus obtain risk-adjusted positive abnormal profits which were 11.38% per year using a benchmark of value weighted returns on all stocks provided by the Center for Security Prices of the University of Chicago universe. Moreover, Berkshire purchases yield significant positive movements in future stock prices.

Table 7.1   Increase in per share book value of Berkshire Hathaway versus returns on the S&P500 with dividends included, 1965–2005, in percent

Year	BH	S&P500	Diff	Year	BH	S&P500	Diff
1965	23.8	10.0	13.8	1985	48.2	31.6	16.6
1966	20.3	(11.7)	32.0	1986	26.1	18.6	7.5
1967	11.0	30.9	(19.9)	1987	19.5	5.1	14.4
1968	19.0	11.0	8.0	1988	20.1	16.6	3.5
1969	16.2	(8.4)	24.6	1989	44.4	31.7	12.7
1970	12.0	3.9	8.1	1990	7.4	(3.1)	10.5
1971	16.4	14.6	1.8	1991	39.6	30.5	9.1
1972	21.7	18.9	2.8	1992	20.3	7.6	12.7
1973	4.7	(14.8)	19.5	1993	14.3	10.1	4.2
1974	5.5	(26.4)	31.9	1994	13.9	1.3	12.6
1975	21.9	37.2	(15.3)	1995	43.1	37.6	5.5
1976	59.3	23.6	35.7	1996	31.8	23.0	8.8
1977	31.9	(7.4)	39.3	1997	34.1	33.4	.7
1978	24.0	6.4	17.6	1998	48.3	28.6	19.7
1979	35.7	18.2	17.5	1999	.5	21.0	(20.5)
1980	19.3	32.3	(13.0)	2000	6.5	(9.1)	15.6
1981	31.4	(5.0)	36.4	2001	(6.2)	(11.9)	5.7
1982	40.0	21.4	18.6	2002	10.0	(22.1)	32.1
1983	32.3	22.4	9.9	2003	21.0	28.7	(7.7)
1984	13.6	6.1	7.5	2004	10.5	10.9	(0.04)
				2005	6.4	4.9	1.5

Overall Gain	305,134	5,583	
Arithmetic Mean	22.02	10.47	12.07
Geometric Mean	21.50	10.30	11.20
(to 2004)			

Source: Berkshire Hathaway 2005 Annual Report, Hagstrom (2004) and Ziemba (2005). Data are for calendar years except 1965 and 1966, year ended 9/30; 1967, 15 months ended 12/31. Starting in 1979, accounting rules required insurance companies to value the equity securities they hold at market rather than at the lower of cost or market, which was previously the requirement. In this table, Berkshire's results through 1978 have been restated to conform to the changed rules.

The S&P500 numbers are pre-tax whereas the Berkshire numbers are after-tax. If a corporation such as Berkshire were simply to have owned the S&P500 and accrued the appropriate taxes, its results would have lagged the S&P500 in years when that index showed a positive return, but would have exceeded the S&P in years when the index showed a negative return. Over the years, the tax costs would have caused the aggregate lag to be substantial.

growth terms of Berkshire Hathaway and a number of other funds from December 1985 to April 2000. Larry Siegel of the Ford Foundation gave me the monthly data for these funds which are aggregated into the yearly data in Table 7.2 and in statistical terms in Table 7.3. Crucial is the summary at the top of the three panels in Table 7.3 which lists the losses by month, quarter and year.

Observe that the great Buffett had 58 losing months out of 172 and 15 quarters out of 57 with losses. All the other funds had roughly similar records. In contrast, Ed Thorp, albeit working with a much smaller base than these funds, had no losing quarters and only three losing months in close to 240 months during 1969-88 with his hedge fund Princeton-Newport.

Table 7.2 Yearly return data of the funds in the sample in percent. *Source*: Ziemba (2005)

Date	Windsor	Berkshire Hathaway	Quantum	Tiger	Ford Found	Harvard	S&P500 Total	US Trea	US T-bills	US Infl
Yearly data, 14 years										
Neg years	2	2	1	0	1	1	1	2	0	0
Dec-86	20.27	14.17	42.12	26.83	18.09	22.16	18.47	15.14	6.16	1.13
Dec-87	1.23	4.61	14.13	7.28	5.20	12.46	5.23	2.90	5.47	4.41
Dec-88	28.69	59.32	10.13	15.76	10.42	12.68	16.81	6.10	6.35	4.42
Dec-89	15.02	84.57	35.21	24.72	22.15	15.99	31.49	13.29	8.37	4.65
Dec-90	−15.50	−23.05	23.80	5.57	1.96	−1.01	−3.17	9.73	7.81	6.11
Dec-91	28.55	35.58	50.58	37.59	22.92	15.73	30.55	15.46	5.60	3.06
Dec-92	16.50	29.83	6.37	8.42	5.26	4.88	7.67	7.19	3.51	2.90
Dec-93	19.37	38.94	33.03	24.91	13.07	21.73	9.99	11.24	2.90	2.75
Dec-94	−0.15	24.96	3.94	1.71	−1.96	3.71	1.31	−5.14	3.90	2.67
Dec-95	30.15	57.35	38.98	34.34	26.47	24.99	37.43	16.80	5.60	2.54
Dec-96	26.36	6.23	−1.50	8.03	15.39	26.47	23.07	2.10	5.21	3.32
Dec-97	21.98	34.90	17.09	18.79	19.11	20.91	33.36	8.38	5.26	1.70
Dec-98	0.81	52.17	12.46	11.21	21.39	12.14	28.58	10.21	4.86	1.61
Dec-99	11.57	−19.86	34.68	27.44	27.59	23.78	21.04	−1.77	4.68	2.68

The Sharpe ratio

$$S = \frac{\overline{R} - R_F}{\sigma}.$$

where $\overline{R}$ is the portfolio mean return, R_F is the risk free asset return and σ is the standard deviation of the portfolio's returns. This can be based on monthly, quarterly or yearly data and use arithmetic or geometric returns.

During this 14+ year period, the Ford Foundation had a Sharpe ratio of 0.970 versus Berkshire Hathaway's 0.773 and the S&P500's 0.797, despite the fact that the Ford Foundation's geometric mean rate of return of 14.29 % was below the S&P500's 16.80 % and well below the 22.67 % for Berkshire Hathaway.

Much of modern finance portfolio theory uses arithmetic returns since it is one period static theory. This includes Markowitz mean-variance analysis and the Sharpe-Lintner-Mossin capital asset pricing model and the Sharpe ratio. We know that for multiperiod investments this produces biases because of the arithmetic-geometric mean inequality. For example, if one has returns of +50 % and −50 % in two periods, then the arithmetic mean is zero which does not correctly reflect the fact that 100 became 150 and then 75. The geometric mean, the correct measure to use, is −13.7 %. For investment returns in the 10–15 % range, the arithmetic returns are about 2 % above the geometric returns. But for higher returns this approximation is not accurate. Hence, geometric means as well as more typical arithmetic means are used in this paper. Lo (2002) points out that care must be used in Sharpe ratio estimations when the investment returns are not independent identically distributed (iid), which they are for the investors discussed here. For dependent but stationary returns he derives a correction of the Sharpe ratios that deflates artificially high values back to correct values using an estimation of the correlation of serial returns. See

Table 7.3 Fund return data: yearly means and standard deviations (in percent) and Sharpe ratios for various high yielding funds versus the S&P500, Treasuries, T-bills and inflation using monthly and quarterly and yearly data with arithmetic and geometric means, December 1985 to April 2000. *Source*: Ziemba (2005)

	Windsor	Berkshire Hathaway	Quantum	Tiger	Ford Found	Harvard	S&P500 Total	US Trea	US T-bills	US Infl
Monthly data, 172 months										
Neg months	61	58	53	56	44	na	56	54	0	13
arith mean, mon	1.17	2.15	1.77	2.02	1.19	na	1.45	0.63	0.44	0.26
st dev, mon	4.70	7.66	7.42	6.24	2.68	na	4.41	1.32	0.12	0.21
Sharpe, mon	0.157	0.223	0.180	0.54	0.80	na	0.230	0.145	0.000	−0.827
arith mean	14.10	25.77	21.25	24.27	14.29	na	17.44	7.57	5.27	3.14
st dev	16.27	26.54	25.70	21.62	9.30	na	15.28	4.58	0.43	0.74
Sharpe, yr	0.543	0.773	0.622	0.879	0.970	na	0.797	0.504	0.000	−2.865
geomean, mon	1.06	1.87	1.48	1.83	1.16	na	1.35	0.62	0.44	0.26
geo st dev,mon	4.70	7.67	7.42	6.25	2.69	na	4.41	1.32	0.12	0.21
Sharpe, mon	0.133	0.186	0.140	0.222	0.267	na	0.208	0.139	0.000	−0.828
geo mean, yr	12.76	22.38	17.76	21.92	13.86	na	16.25	7.47	5.27	3.14
geo st dev, yr	16.27	26.56	25.72	21.63	9.30	na	15.28	4.58	0.43	0.74
Sharpe, yr	0.460	0.644	0.486	0.770	0.924	na	0.719	0.482	0.000	−2.868
Quarterly data, 57 quarters										
Neg quarters	14	15	16	11	11	11	10	15	0	1
mean, qtly	3.55	6.70	5.70	4.35	3.68	3.86	4.48	1.93	1.32	0.79
st dev, qtly	8.01	14.75	12.67	7.70	4.72	4.72	7.52	2.67	0.36	0.49
mean, yr	14.20	26.81	22.79	17.42	14.71	15.44	17.91	7.73	5.29	3.16
st dev, yr	16.03	29.50	25.33	15.40	9.43	9.45	15.05	5.34	0.73	0.97
Sharpe, yr	0.556	0.729	0.691	0.788	0.999	1.074	0.839	0.456	0.000	−2.188
geomean, qtly	3.23	5.67	4.94	4.07	3.57	3.75	4.20	1.90	1.32	0.79
geo st dev,qtly	8.02	14.79	12.69	7.70	4.72	4.73	7.53	2.67	0.36	0.49
geo mean, yr	12.90	22.67	19.78	16.28	14.29	15.01	16.80	7.59	5.29	3.16
geo st dev, yr	16.04	29.58	25.38	15.41	9.43	9.45	15.06	5.34	0.73	0.97
Sharpe, yr	0.475	0.588	0.571	0.713	0.954	1.029	0.764	0.431	0.000	−2.190
Yearly Data, 14 years										
Neg years	2	2	1	0	1	1	1	2	0	0
mean,	14.63	28.55	22.93	18.04	14.79	15.47	18.70	7.97	5.40	3.14
st dev,	13.55	30.34	16.17	11.40	9.38	8.52	12.88	6.59	1.50	1.35
Sharpe, yrly	0.681	0.763	1.084	1.109	1.001	1.181	1.033	0.390	0.000	−1.673
geom mean	13.83	24.99	21.94	17.54	14.43	15.17	18.04	7.78	5.39	3.13
st dev	13.58	30.57	16.20	11.41	9.39	8.53	12.90	6.59	1.50	1.35
Sharpe	0.621	0.641	1.022	1.064	0.962	1.146	0.981	0.362	0.000	−1.672

also Miller and Gehr (2005) and Knight and Satchell (2005) who derive exact statistical properties of the Sharpe ratio with normal and lognormal assets, respectively. The Sharpe ratios are almost always lower when geometric means are used rather than arithmetic means with the difference between these two measures a function of return volatility. However, the basic conclusions we have here such as the relative ranking of the various funds, are the same for the arithmetic and geometric means. See Tables 7.5 and 7.6 for further details.

We want to penalize superior managers such as Warren Buffett for losing but not for winning and get a fairer Sharpe ratio than the ordinary one which penalizes gains equally as losses and thus poorly ranks investors with high returns that are volatile.

So define the downside risk as

$$\sigma_{x_-}^2 = \frac{\sum_{i=1}^n (x_i - \overline{x})_-^2}{n - 1},$$

where our benchmark $\overline{x}$ is zero, i is the index on the n months in the sample and the x_i taken are those below $\overline{x}$, namely those m of the n months with losses. This is the downside variance measured from zero, not the mean, so it is more precisely the downside risk. To get the total variance we use twice the downside variance namely $2\sigma_{x_-}^2$ so that Buffett gets only the symmetric gains added not his actual gains. Using $2\sigma_{x_-}^2$, the usual Sharpe ratio with monthly data and arithmetic returns becomes the downside symmetric Sharpe ratio (DSSR)

$$DSSR = \frac{\overline{R} - R_F}{\sqrt{2}\sigma_{x_-}}.$$

Table 7.4 shows that this measure moves Berkshire Hathaway higher to 0.917 but not up to the level of the Ford Foundation and not higher because of some rather high monthly losses. Berkshire Hathaway did gain in the switch from ordinary Sharpe to downside symmetric Sharpe while all the other funds fell. Ford is now 0.920 and Tiger 0.865. When annualized, these Berkshire Hathaway's monthly losses are over 64 % versus under 27 % for the Ford Foundation.

Figure 7.1 shows these rather fat tails on the upside and downside of Berkshire Hathaway versus the much less volatile Ford Foundation returns. When Berkshire Hathaway had a losing month it averaged −5.36 % versus +2.15 % for all months including these negative ones. Meanwhile, Ford lost −2.44 % and gained, on average, 1.19 %. Figure 7.2 shows the histogram of quarterly returns for all funds including Harvard for which monthly data was

Table 7.4 Comparison of ordinary and symmetric downside Sharpe yearly performance measures, monthly data and arithmetic means. *Source*: Ziemba (2005)

	Ordinary	Downside
Ford Foundation	0.970	0.920
Tiger Fund	0.879	0.865
S&P500	0.797	0.696
Berkshire Hathaway	0.773	0.917
Quantum	0.622	0.458
Windsor	0.543	0.495

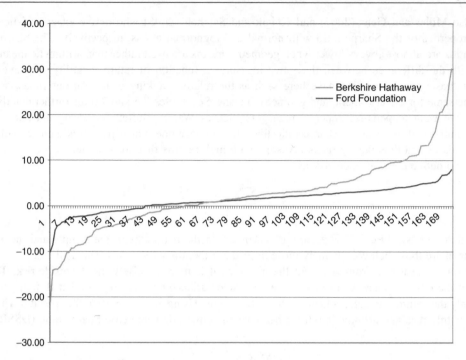

Figure 7.1   Berkshire Hathaway versus Ford Foundation, monthly return distributions, January 1977 to April 2000. *Source*: Ziemba (2005)

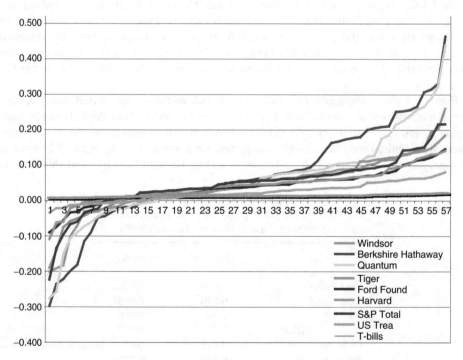

Figure 7.2   Return distributions of all the funds, quarterly return distributions, December 1985 to March 2000. *Source*: Ziemba (2005)

Table 7.5 Yearly Sharpe and symmetric downside Sharpe ratios computed from quarterly return data using arithmetic and geometric means and standard deviations (in percent), December 1985 to April 2000. *Source*: Ziemba (2005)

	Windsor	Berkshire Hathaway	Quantum	Tiger	Ford Found	Harvard	S&P Total	Trea
qtly data, 57 quarters								
neg qts	14	15	16	11	10	11	10	15
mean, neg	−6.69	−10.50	−7.77	−6.26	−3.59	−2.81	−6.92	−1.35
mean, qtly	3.55	6.70	5.70	4.35	3.68	3.86	4.48	1.93
ds st dev, qtly	10.52	14.00	12.09	8.18	4.44	5.12	9.89	1.35
mean, yr	14.20	26.81	22.79	17.42	14.71	15.44	17.91	7.73
ds st dev, yr	21.04	28.00	24.17	16.35	8.89	10.24	19.78	2.70
ds Sharpe	0.424	0.769	0.724	0.742	1.060	0.991	0.638	0.903
geomean, qtly	3.23	5.67	4.94	4.07	3.57	3.75	4.20	1.90
ds geo st dev,qtly	10.20	13.49	11.80	7.71	3.91	4.99	9.34	1.28
geo mean, yr	12.90	22.67	19.78	16.28	14.29	15.01	16.80	7.59
ds geo st dev, yr	20.41	26.97	23.60	15.43	7.83	9.97	18.68	2.56
ds Sharpe	0.373	0.644	0.614	0.712	1.150	0.975	0.616	0.900

not available. This figure shows that the distributions of all the funds lie between those of Berkshire Hathaway, Harvard and Ford.

Using the quarterly data, the Harvard endowment has a record almost as good as the Ford Foundation, see Tables 7.5 and 7.6. Berkshire Hathaway made the most money but took more risk; so, by both the Sharpe and the downside Sharpe measures, the Ford Foundation and the Harvard endowment had superior rewards.

I first used this symmetric downside Sharpe ratio measure in Ziemba and Schwartz (1991) to compare the results of superior investment in Japanese small capitalized stocks during the late 1980's. The choice of $\bar{x} = 0$ is convenient and has a good interpretation. But other $\bar{x}$'s are possible and might be useful in other applications. This measure is closely related to the Sortino ratio (see Sortino & van der Meer, 1991 & Sortino and Price, 1994) which considers downside risk only. That measure does not have the two sided interpretation of my measure and the $\sqrt{2}$ does not appear and it is not a Sharpe ratio modification. The notion of focusing on downside risk is popular these days as it represents real risk better. I started using it in asset-liability models in the 1970s; see Kallberg, White and Ziemba (1982) and Kusy and Ziemba (1986) for early applications. Others such as Roy (1952), Markowitz (1959), Mao (1970), Bawa (1975, 1977), Bawa and Lindenberg (1977), Fishburn (1977), Harlow and Rao (1989), and Harlow (1991) have used downside risk measures in portfolio theories alternative to those of Markowitz and Sharpe based on mean-variance and related analyses. In the models we measure risk as the downside non-attainment of investment target goals which can be deterministic such as wealth growth over time or stochastic such as the non-attachment of a portfolio of weighted benchmark returns. See Chapter 21 for an application of this to the Siemens Austria pension fund.

Calculating the ordinary Sharpe ratio and the downside symmetric Sharpe ratio using quarterly or yearly data does not change the results much. However, this smoothes the data since individual monthly losses are combined with gains to have lower volatility. The

Table 7.6 Summary of the means, both arithmetic and geometric (in percent), and the Sharpe and symmetric downside Sharpe ratios for the monthly quarterly and yearly data all annualized, December 1985 to April 2000. *Source*: Ziemba (2005)

	Windsor	Berkshire Hathaway	Quantum	Tiger	Ford Found	Harvard	S&P Total	Trea
mean (arith, mon)	14.10	25.77	21.25	24.27	14.29	na	17.44	7.57
Sharpe (arith, mon)	0.543	0.773	0.622	0.879	0.970	na	0.797	0.504
ds Sharpe (arith, mon)	0.495	0.917	0.458	0.865	0.920	na	0.696	0.631
mean (geom, mon)	12.76	22.38	17.76	21.92	13.86	na	16.25	7.47
Sharpe (geom, mon)	0.460	0.644	0.486	0.770	0.924	na	0.719	0.482
ds Sharpe (geom, mon)	0.420	0.765	0.358	0.758	0.876	na	0.628	1.053
mean (arith, qtly)	14.20	26.81	22.79	17.42	14.71	15.44	17.91	7.73
Sharpe (arith, qtly)	0.556	0.729	0.691	0.788	0.999	1.074	0.839	0.456
ds Sharpe (arith, qtly)	0.424	0.769	0.724	0.742	1.060	0.991	0.638	0.903
mean (geom, qtly)	12.90	22.67	19.78	16.28	14.29	15.01	16.80	7.59
Sharpe (geom, qlty)	0.475	0.588	0.571	0.713	0.954	1.029	0.764	0.431
ds Sharpe (geom, qtly)	0.373	0.644	0.614	0.712	1.150	0.975	0.616	0.900
mean (arith, yrly)	14.63	28.55	22.93	18.04	14.79	15.47	18.70	7.97
Sharpe (arith, yrly)	0.681	0.763	1.084	1.109	1.001	1.181	1.033	0.390
mean (geom, yrly)	13.83	24.99	21.94	17.54	14.43	15.17	18.04	7.78
Sharpe (geom, yrly)	0.621	0.641	1.022	1.064	0.962	1.146	0.981	0.362

yearly data is closer to normally distributed returns so the symmetric downside and ordinary Sharpe measures yield similar rankings. Tables 7.2 and 7.5 shows the yearly returns for the various funds and their Sharpe ratios computed using arithmetic and geometric means and the yearly data. There is insufficient data to compute the downside Sharpe ratios based on yearly data. The Ford Foundation had only one losing year (-1.96%). Berkshire Hathaway had two losing years with losses of -23.1% and -19.9%. The Ford Foundation had a higher Sharpe ratio than Berkshire Hathaway but was exceeded by the Tiger and Quantum funds and the S&P500. Table 7.6 summarizes the annualized results using monthly, quarterly and yearly data. The Ford Foundation had the highest symmetric downside Sharpe ratio followed by Harvard and both exceeded Berkshire Hathaway and the other funds.

As Siegel privately acknowledges, some of the Ford Foundation's high Sharpe ratio results are due to using an artificially smoothed standard deviation. The private equity allocation does not have real market prices, so notational valuations do not reflect actual volatility. This is also true of the Harvard and Yale endowments which are discussed in Chapter 8.

The means, standard deviations and Sharpe (1966, 1994) ratios of these six funds, based on monthly, quarterly and yearly net arithmetic and geometric total return data are shown in Table 7.3. Also shown here is data from the Harvard endowment (quarterly) plus that of US Treasuries, T-bills and US inflation and the number of negative months and quarters. The top panel of Table 7.3 shows the data of Figure 4.1 which illustrates the large mean returns of Berkshire Hathaway and the Tiger Fund's and that the Ford Foundation's standard deviation was about a third of Berkshire's. The Ford Foundation actually trailed the S&P500 mean return. Observe that the much lower monthly and quarterly Sharpe ratios are compared to the annualized values based on monthly, quarterly and yearly data.

By the Sharpe ratio, the Harvard endowment and the Ford Foundation had the best performance, followed by the Tiger Fund then the S&P500 total return index, Berkshire Hathaway Quantum, Windsor and US Treasuries. The basic conclusions are the same with monthly or quarterly data and with arithmetic and geometric means. Because of data smoothing, the Sharpe ratios with yearly data usually exceed those with quarterly data which in turn exceed the monthly calculations.

The reason for this ranking is that though the Ford Foundation and the Harvard endowment had less growth, they also had much less variability. Indeed, these funds have different purposes, different investors, different portfolio managers, and different fees, so such differences are not surprising.

Clifford, Kroner and Siegel (2001) have similar calculations for a larger group of funds. They also show that starting from July 1977 to March 2000, Berkshire Hathaway's Sharpe ratio was 0.850 versus Ford's 0.765 and the S&P500 was 0.676. The geometric mean returns were 32.07 % (Buffett), 14.88 % (Ford), and 16.71 % (S&P500). See also Siegel, Kroner and Clifford (2001) for additional calculations and discussion.

The geometric mean helps mitigate the autocorrelated and time varying mean and other statistical properties of returns that are not iid.

Figure 7.3 shows that the Harvard Investment Company, that great school's endowment, had essentially the same wealth record over time as the Ford Foundation. This is based on quarterly data which is all I have on Harvard. Harvard beats Ford by the ordinary Sharpe ratio but Ford is superior by the symmetric downside risk measure. We discuss in Chapter 8 the Harvard asset allocation along with Yale's and other top university endowments.

The symmetric downside Sharpe ratio measure is ad hoc as all performance measures are and adds to the debate on this subject.

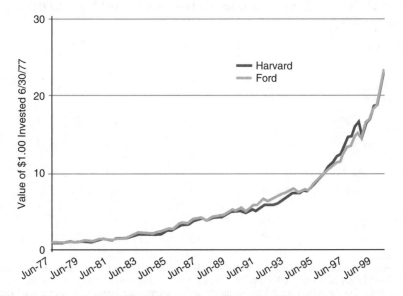

Figure 7.3 Ford Foundation and Harvard Investment Corporation Returns, quarterly data, June 1977 to March 2000

Hodges (1998), see also the discussion in Ziemba (2003), proposed a generalized Sharpe measure where some of the paradoxes that the Sharpe measure leads to are eliminated. It uses a constant absolute risk return exponential utility function and general return distributions. When the returns are normally distributed, this is the usual Sharpe ratio since that portfolio problem is equivalent to a mean-variance model. A better utility function is the constant relative risk aversion negative power; see the additional discussion in Ziemba (2003). Leland (1999) shows how to modify β's when there are fat tails into more correct β's in a CAPM framework.

Goetzmann et al (2002) and Spurgin (2001) show how the Sharpe ratio may be manipulated using option strategies to obtain what looks like a superior record to obtain more funds to manage. Managers sell calls to cut off upside variance and use the proceeds to buy puts to cut off downside variance leading to higher Sharpe ratios because of the reduced portfolio variance. These options transactions may actually lead to poorer investment performance in final wealth terms even with their higher Sharpe ratios. For example, Tompkins, Ziemba and Hodges (2003) show how on average the calls sold and the puts purchased on the S&P500 both had negative expected values from 1985–2002.

I have not tried to establish when the symmetric downside risk Sharpe ratio might give misleading results in real investment situations nor to establish its mathematical and statistical properties except for noting that it is consistent with an investor with utility based on the negative of the disutility of losses. It is a simple way to avoid penalizing superior performance so that a fairer performance can be evaluated.[2] Another way will have to be found to measure and establish the superiority of Warren Buffett. One likely candidate is related to the Kelly way of evaluating investments which simply considers at compounded wealth over a long period of time which we know in the limit is attained by the log bettor which Buffett seems to be. This is, of course, the geometric mean. After 40+ years, most of us believe that Buffett is in the skill not luck category; after all $ 15 a share in 1965 became $ 109 900 in December 2006, but since he is a log bettor only more time will tell. For studies of dynamic Sharpe ratios, see Cvitanić, Lazrak and Wang (2004) and Nielsen and Vassalou (2004).

---

[2] Another interesting idea is to penalize for losses but give credit for gains, continuously across the return axis. This is explored in Zakamouline (2007) who discusses the relationships with other papers in the literature such as Hodges (1998). But the results are not as conclusive as one might have hoped with such a good idea. Indeed, when applied to Medallion Renaissance data, these measures, like the Sharpe ratio, fail to show the true brilliance of their performance record which is shown clearly by the DSSR, see pages 295–8.

8
The methods and results of managing top US university endowments

The great university endowments are effectively successful hedge funds

High-ranked private universities like Harvard, Yale, Princeton and Stanford are attracting more funds to maintain their scholarly output, to attract and retain the best scholars and students – especially as some specialties become more expensive. Tuitions are climbing but even those revenues do not cover costs and the gap continues to widen. The current patterns of higher than inflation tuition increases are not enough. How are they filling this gap and how well will they continue to do so with increasing need for human and capital investment? A key asset is the university endowment. The endowments of these four great schools and many others in the top 25 (in terms of endowment value) have had extremely high returns. The strategies explain the high returns of these endowments and whether they provide lessons for other investors are explored here.

The finance and economics departments of these universities are filled with faculty that believe in efficient markets, so it is not to them that the superior returns are attributable since they would basically suggest investment in passive index funds or active RP closet index funds trying to get a little alpha. According to the classification of investors discussed in Chapter 7, it is a mixture of A (markets are beatable with careful research) H (hogwash), G (genius) and RP (risk premium) by some excellent endowment managers that produce these results. These endowments are run like hedge funds with some trading in the fund by its internal managers with much outsourced to superior managers in a wide variety of areas and asset classes. Outside sourcing costs about twice as much in fees so internal management good return for a substantial amount of the fund is desirable.

The consistent returns are impressive. A lot of attention has been focused on the returns of Yale's endowment, which under the management of David Swensen, has had high returns averaging 16 % for the past 21 years and 17.2 % net for the ten years ending June 30, 2006 growing the endowment from $4.0 to $18.0 billion. This compares with a benchmark of about 10 %. The correlations between the real assets in Yale's portfolio and Yale's other classes range from about −0.04 with foreign equity and 0.29 with the absolute return asset class. During the year ending June 30, 2006 the net returns were 22.9 %, the second best return of the 25 largest US college funds, trailing only MIT's 23 % return (on its $8.4 billion endowment). MIT's high returns in 2005/6 are part of its recovery after losing $1.4 on bad technology bets three years ago. See Table 8.1. Table 8.2 which lists the 15 largest US endowments per student shows that Princeton, Yale and Harvard greatly outdistance the others and are double MIT, Cal Tech and Stanford. Yale's endowment, adding in contributions and netting off university deployed funds, increased by $2.8 billion in 2005/06 to $18 billion, the second largest in the US following Harvard's $29.2 billion. Stanford, the third largest endowment at $15.2 billion, returned 19.4 % and Harvard 16.7 %. These funds greatly outpaced the S&P500 index, which returned only 8.6 %. Investing abroad, a

Table 8.1 The top 25 US university endowment funds, performance 2003–4, 2004–5, 2005–6. *Source*: Adapted from Bloomberg (2005)

	Institution	Size, $ bil 30-Jun-05	Size, $ bil 30-Jun-06	Return, % 2003–04	Return, % 2004–05	Return, % 2005–06
1	Harvard University	25.90	29.20	21.10	19.20	
2	Yale University	15.20	18.00	19.40	22.30	22.90
3	Stanford University	12.40	15.20	18.00	19.50	19.40
4	University of Texas	11.60	15.50	20.10	13.60	
5	Princeton University	11.20	13.00	16.50	17.00	
6	MIT	6.70	8.40	18.10	17.60	23.00
7	University of California	5.20	9.99	14.70	10.30	
8	Texas A & M University	5.00	5.94	21.00	9.70	
9	University of Michigan	4.90	4.96	20.70	19.10	
10	Columbia University	4.90	5.70	16.90	17.70	
11	U of Pennsylvania	4.40		16.90	8.50	
12	Washington U (St. Louis)	4.40	5.30	18.20	10.00	
13	Emory University	4.40	4.75	14.60	6.80	
14	Northwestern University	4.20	4.92	19.20	15.10	
15	University of Notre Dame	4.10	4.80	20.30	19.10	
16	University of Chicago	4.10	4.50	16.60	18.10	
17	Cornell University	3.90	4.30	16.10	13.60	
18	Duke University	3.80	4.20	18.00	18.10	20.20
19	Rice University	3.60		17.20	13.60	
20	Dartmouth College	2.70	3.52	18.60	14.40	
21	University of Virginia	2.60		12.70	14.30	
22	Vanderbilt University	2.60		16.90	17.90	
23	U of Southern California	2.30	3.04	16.90	17.80	
24	Johns Hopkins University	2.00		15.30	9.60	
25	Brown University	1.90	2.30	16.30	13.30	
	Notre Dame					19.40
	average					16.30

strategy which along with private placements has provided good returns for the endowments, returned 27.2 % for European and Australian stocks, see Forsyth (2006).

Harvard gained 16.1 % annualized in the decade to June 2005, beating the median US university endowment by 3.6 %. They had superior bond returns and alternative investments from hedge funds, timber probably to be in a position to profit from trading carbon rights, land and other real assets. Harvard's 16.7 % in fiscal 2005 was its lowest in three years with its new management and was the result of interest rates rises causing the bond positions of Harvard's previous management team to lose 2.3 %. In previous years, the bond positions were high return assets such as 20.3 % in fiscal 2005.

In this chapter, we focus on at what is known about the investment strategy of Yale, the second largest and fastest growing endowment for the past several years. Swensen, who has managed the fund since 1985, received his PhD in economics from Yale in 1979 then spent six years with Lehman Brothers in New York before coming back to run Yale's endowment. He is widely credited with developing the Yale model which is essentially a multi-strategy

Table 8.2 Top 15 Endowments per Student. *Source*: Wikipedia (2006)

Rank	Institution	Endowment per Student
1.	Princeton University	1 678 406
2.	Yale University	1 567 535
3.	Harvard University	1 476 313
4.	Grinnell College	893 666
5.	Baylor College of Medicine	891 825
6.	Pomona College	837 825
7.	MIT	823 426
8.	Swarthmore College	789 735
9.	Williams College	748 146
10.	Rice University	723 909
11.	Stanford University	714 622
12.	Caltech	701 004
13.	Amherst College	698 469
14.	Wellesley College	557 347
15.	Berea College	553 778

hedge fund in which the various strategies are largely independent but include private equity and other non-traditional asset classes. Yale's superior endowment performance was $ 8.5 billion above its benchmarks and $ 9.1 billion above the average of a broad universe of college and university endowments. Swensen (2000) discusses his institutional investor approach and Swensen (2005) gives advice to small individual investors. He argues that small investors are wise to consider exchange traded funds largely because you can focus on the sector you want and they have lower taxes and other expenses. Large investors can try for superior returns with similar asset classes as Yale.

Yale defines six asset classes based on their differential expected response to economic conditions. They are weighted in the portfolio according to risk adjusted returns and correlations so as to provide the highest expected return for a given level of risk.

Yale was the first institutional investor to follow absolute return strategies as a separate asset class, The initial target allocation in July 1990 was 15 % but currently has increased to 25 %, well above the educational institutional average of 18.6 % reflecting the growing importance of this strategy in hedge funds. Absolute return investments exploit market inefficiencies to generate high long-term real returns (that is, category A). The portfolio is divided about equally into corporate event-driven strategies like mergers, spin-offs and bankruptcy restructuring and value-driven strategies, which involve hedged positions in assets or securities that are estimated to differ from underlying economic value. The returns are largely uncorrelated to overall market returns with an expected real return of 6.0 % and standard deviation levels of 10.0 % for event-driven strategies and 15.0 % for value-driven strategies. However, over the past decade, the portfolio exceeded expectations, returning 12.9 % per year essentially independent of the domestic stock and bond markets.

To align the interests of investors and investment managers, the absolute return accounts are structured with performance related incentive fees, hurdle rates, and clawback provisions. As well, the managers invest a significant portion of their net worth along with Yale to avoid principal agent pitfalls. See Kouwenberg and Ziemba (2007) who show the theoretical

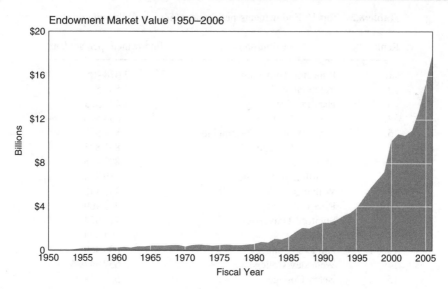

Figure 8.1   Investment growth of Yale's endowment versus inflation, 1950–2006. *Source*: YEC, 2006

optimality of such *eat your own cooking* strategies where the hedge fund manager has a
large amount, preferably at least 30 %, of their own money in the fund.

The increased growth of the endowment has enabled further spending. In 1990 the endowment paid for 12 % of Yale's operating revenues. In 2006 it was 34 %. The growth in Yale's
endowment since 1950 has strongly outpaced inflation. Figure 8.1 illustrates this trend from
1950 to 2006. The distinguished Yale economist Robert Shiller (2006) argues that Swensen
has helped the university more than any other person but remains curious as to how he
achieved these excellent returns consistently. The answer we think is a careful analysis
using our strategies A especially with some H a little G and a little RP in areas where
advantages are hard to find. The success is based on good research, careful execution, long
standing excellent relationships and superior risk control.

The Yale endowment contains thousands of bequests with a variety of designated purposes
and restrictions. Approximately four-fifths are true endowments, the remaining one-fifth represent quasi-endowment, monies that the Yale Corporation can invest in the endowment.
Donors frequently specify a particular purpose for gifts, creating endowments to fund professorships, teaching, and lectureships (23 %), scholarships, fellowships, and prizes (18 %),
maintenance (4 %), books (3 %), and miscellaneous specific purposes (25 %). The remaining
funds (27 %) are unrestricted. Thirty-four percent of the endowment benefits the overall university as a whole, with remaining funds earmarked for specific units, including the Faculty
of Arts and Sciences (31 %), the professional schools (22 %), the library (7 %). Figure 8.2
shows the endowment fund allocation and the Yale University revenue budget in fiscal
year 2006.

Endowment funds are commingled in an investment pool and valued much like a large
hedge fund. Gifts of cash, securities, or property are valued and exchanged for units that represent a claim on a portion of the entire investment portfolio. Other major sources of revenues
were grants and contracts of $ 507 million (29 %), medical services of $ 277 million (16 %),
net tuition, room, and board of $ 234 million (13 %), gifts of $ 76 million (4 %), other investment income of $ 24 million (1 %), and other income and transfers of $ 83 million (5 %).

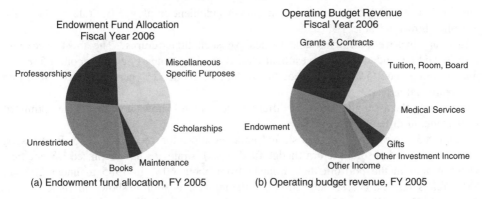

Endowment Fund Allocation
Fiscal Year 2006

Operating Budget Revenue
Fiscal Year 2006

(a) Endowment fund allocation, FY 2005   (b) Operating budget revenue, FY 2005

Figure 8.2   Yale Allocations. *Source*: YEC, 2006

In the last decade, spending from the endowment grew from $ 149 million to $ 567 million, an annual growth rate of 14 % while the proportion of contributions to total revenue expanded from 15 % of total revenues in fiscal 1995 to 32 % in fiscal 2005 of the Yale's $ 1768 million operating income. Spending was expected to be about $ 613 million, or 33 % of projected revenues in 2006. Thus spending and investment policies have supported both high levels of cash flow to the operating budget while preserving endowment purchasing power for future generations.

Yale's endowment fund was among the first institutional investors to participate in private equity, making its first commitment to leveraged buyouts in 1973 and to venture capital in 1976. They invest through partnerships managed by private equity firms, including venture capitalists Greylock, Kleiner Perkins, Sequoia, and Sutter Hill, and buyout specialists Bain Capital, Berkshire Partners, Clayton Dubilier & Rice, and Madison Dearborn Partners. From 1973–2006, private equity has generated an annual return of 30.6 % while the annual return from 1996–2006 was 34.4 % which included an astounding 168.5 % in fiscal 2000, when the University made $ 2.1 billion on its private equity investments. Real assets returned 20.5 % from 1996–2006, some 6.5 % above the real assets benchmark.

Yale's portfolio is managed using a combination of portfolio theory and informed market judgment. But there is much of strategic approach A in their thinking; they believe they can win through their managers and with careful research and good risk control they do provide superior returns. Using statistical techniques to combine expected returns, variances, and covariances of investment assets, Yale employs mean-variance analysis to estimate expected risk and return profiles of various asset allocation alternatives and to test sensitivity of results to changes in input assumptions. Their investment decisions seem in line with our strong belief that getting the mean right (theory and patience) is the most important aspect of portfolio management.

Since investment management involves art as well as science, qualitative assessments play an important role in portfolio decisions. Asset class definitions are subjective, requiring precise categories which may be fuzzy. Expected returns and correlations are difficult to forecast. Historical data must be merged with structural changes to compensate for anomalous periods. Quantitative measures have difficulty incorporating factors such as market liquidity or the influence of significant, low-probability scenarios. Despite the operational challenges, the mean-variance analysis is important in the asset allocation process. The combination of quantitative analysis and market judgment employed by Yale produces the portfolio shown in Table 8.3:

How are these endowments able to achieve such high returns? The most successful have looked beyond standard investment classes such as bonds (yielding about 4.5 %), T-bills (yielding about 5 %) and US equities (returning about 12 % per year since 1900) into non-traditional assets.

Comparing the asset allocations of different endowments shows how they have optimized investments in different asset classes.

Figure 8.3 shows how Yale has shifted its asset allocation mix since 1985. Real assets, private equity and absolute return (hedge fund types), strategies have replaced US equities, whose weight in the portfolio has dropped from about 60 % in 1985 to under 20 % in 2005. Yale's June 2005 asset allocation and the target allocation is shown in Table 8.3 and Figure 8.3. The declining role of US equity and US bonds in Yale's portfolio is particularly noticeable. This trend continued in 2006.[1]

Harvard's endowment asset allocation as of June 2004 was in 12 basic asset classes; see Table 8.4. Of these, bonds (domestic, foreign and inflation-indexed) were 22 % of the portfolio with another 5 % in high yield securities. Equities (domestic, foreign, and emerging

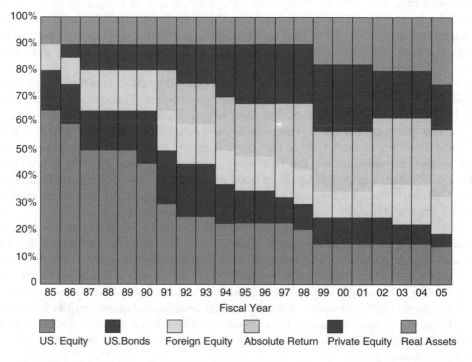

Prior to 1999, Real Assets included only real estate. Oil and gas and timber were classified as Private Equity

Figure 8.3 Yale policy asset allocation targets, 1985–2005. *Source*: YEC, 2005

[1] Yale's approach has paid off with superior risk-adjusted returns. Others have much to learn from their approach. For example, the giant $ 300 billion Norwegian government pension fund which invests the country's oil revenues is shifting to a 40 % bond-60 % equity mix (up from 40 % equity) and has had returns averaging only 6.5 % since 1997. The fund is considering investing in real estate and private equity and hedge funds.

Table 8.3 Asset classes, Yale current (June 2006) and target compared with institutional average plus Princeton (2005). *Source*: YEC, 2006 and Mulvey (2007)

Asset Class	Yale's %	Yale's Target, %	Princeton (2005)	Institutional Mean, % (2005)
Absolute Return	23.3	25.0	25.0	18.6
Domestic Equity	11.6	12.0	15.0	29.1
Fixed Income	3.8	4.0	10.0	14.3
Foreign Equity	14.6	15.0	17.0	20.0
Private Equity	16.4	17.0	15.0	6.4
Real Assets	27.8	27.0	18.0	8.4
Cash	2.5	0.0	0.0	3.3

Table 8.4 Asset allocation of Harvard endowment to June 2004. *Source*: Barron's, February 1, 2005

Harvard's Holdings By Sector	Annual Returns 1-Year, %	10-Year, %	Weight In Endowment, %
Domestic Equities	22.8	17.8	15
Foreign Equities	36.1	8.5	10
Emerging Markets	6.6	9.7	5
Private Equity	20.8	31.5	13
Hedge Funds	15.7	n.a	12
High Yield	12.4	9.7	5
Commodities	19.7	10.9	13
Real Estate	16.0	15.0	10
Domestic Bonds	9.2	14.9	11
Foreign Bonds	17.4	16.9	5
Inflation-indexed Bonds	4.2	n.a.	6
Total Endowment	21.1	15.9	105 %*
			*includes slight leverage

markets) were 30 %, well below standard 60 – 40 pension fund mixes. Holdings of hedge funds were 12 %, commodities, 13 % and real estate 10 %. The fund was levered 5 % with borrowing. The big winning asset class was a 13 % allocation to private equity which returned an impressive 31.5 % annualized for the 10 years. Balanced returns across all the asset classes with no losing areas and only three below 10 % growth provided for the 21.1 % yearly return in 2004 and the 15.9 % for the 10 years to June 2004.

The Stanford endowment, see Stanford Management Company (2006), is run similarly to Harvard and Yale with almost as good results. The endowment is also a multi-strategy hedge fund with more than $ 10 billion in assets. From 1995 to 2004 the endowment grew $ 2.6 into $ 10 billion and returned 15.1 % per year, placing them in the top 5 % of university endowments. Venture capital is their strongest area with the closeness of Silicon Valley to the campus and the faculty. They also give a significant allocation to real estate. Indeed, they own much of the land and buildings adjacent to the campus which also gives them flexibility to also offer properties to important professors. From July 1,

2001 to June 30, 2004, Stanford's endowment had a 7.8% annualized return but the rate of return has increased significantly since then, moving it towards the top of the university endowment list.

Stanford's target allocation is lower than some of the others in fixed income (5%), about the same in equity and private equity (17%) and greater exposure in equities 28% (14% domestic and 14% foreign), and absolute return or hedge fund type investments 25% and real assets 25%.

Another thing (which we have found for great investors worldwide) is a great distaste for losses. Indeed Warren Buffett has two rules for investment success: Rule 1 – do not lose money; Rule 2 – do not forget Rule 1. Yale does scenario testing across thousands of possible outcomes and ends up with a superior portfolio with good mean returns and low downside risk. The same is true for the portion of the portfolio managed by outside investment firms. They are carefully selected and monitored. The experience has been that they have been able to have long standing relationships with good managers. Hiring them early in their career before achieving their best results and avoiding termination after poor results has helped. Fees are kept in check relative to performance.

Good returns are harder and harder to obtain as more and more endowments follow similar strategies. At Harvard, the legendary head of the Harvard Investment company, Jack Meyer, had a terrific record. But superior managers expect and demand high compensation. For outside managers, this is no problem as it is a built-in standard expense so no one at the university can object. For example, Jim Simon's Renaissance hedge fund charges a 5% flat management fee plus 44% of the profits which is a huge set of fees. But his performance net of these fees in the 35% range year by year means he has as many clients as he wants. Actually even with their high fees, it is better to stock the fund with his own and employees' money. Indeed, only about six outside investors remain and some large players had their money returned to them. The fund had about $5 billion in 2006. His new stock fund, targeting $100 billion in assets, is up to about $65 billion in April 2007.

Harvard had a system to reward superior internal managers. Two bond traders received an incentive of 10% of their excess returns over their benchmarks. That sounds cheap and is well below standard hedge fund fees which average 2% flat plus 20% of the net new profits, see Kouwenberg and Ziemba (2007). But from Table 8.4 you see that the bond index returned about 5% and they returned about 15% so the 10% fee of the 10% outperformance, their 1% fee was enormous for these two traders. In fiscal 2003, these two managers, Maurice Samuels and David Mittleman earned a total of $69.2 million. That size of payoff angered some professors and alumni which in the end led Meyer and some 30 of his staff, including the entire fixed income trading group, to leave Harvard and start their own firm, Convexity Capital Management, LP, which has $500 million of Harvard's endowment. Meyer's $7.2 million salary and bonus in his highest paid year and $6 million in his last year, fiscal 2005, was less of an issue.

But the $69.2 million paid to internal managers seemed excessive. Also the remoteness of the managers in a Boston office away from the Cambridge campus did not help. The new head of the Harvard Management company, Mohamed El-Erian, has very big shoes to fill. His pay and those of this staff is well below that of Meyer's team. El-Erian was part of Bill Gross' Pimco Newport Beach bond shop, the world's largest and most important fixed income manager. He will teach at the Harvard Business School and his most important colleague will teach in statistics to try to interact more into the campus (as Swensen has done so well at Yale). He views the challenges as:

In addition to stretched valuations in several market segments, the outlook for high returns is being adversely impacted by three inter-related developments: first, the large-scale migration of endowments and foundations to similar asset allocations; second, indications that other institutional investors, including large public and private pension funds, are following; and third, limits on the availability of appropriate investment management capacity . . . We have gone back to first principles on a number of issues, asking the basic question of how to design an organization that can continue to deliver superior returns over time in a rapidly changing investment environment . . . These issues are intrinsically complex. As such, we are drawing on the broader Harvard community for insights and discussions. The initiative is still in its early stages and, as such, we have more questions than answers.

The first fiscal year of his tenure (2005/06) shows some positive signs, although it was a rebuilding year and the departure of the fixed income team in September led a significant portion of funds to be invested in indices to match the market. This restructuring may have been a factor that contributed to Harvard's lower returns of 16.7 % (Harvard Magazine, 2006[2]). El-Erian lowered the bond allocation from 21 to 13 % and he plans to increase foreign investments, buyout funds in private equity, real estate and commodities. He also had to rely more on indexing (30 %) as he rebuilt the investment group. In contrast, Yale's allocation to fixed-income in 2006 was only 3.8 %.

Table 8.5 shows the 20 year growth in endowment values. Yale's gain was 10.85 % and Harvard's 10.02 %. Michigan, which was 9th in Table 8.1 was the best by a substantial margin over the 20 years. Duke, Virginia and Notre Dame all beat the top four. These values are misleading as universities have had different spending policies out of their endowments as well as varying levels of success in attracting gifts. Many universities are increasingly launching large campaigns to grow their endowments. In May 2006, Columbia introduced a campaign to grow their $ 5.2 billion endowment by $ 4 billion over seven years, which is now the largest university capital campaign, but one that other universities are likely to try to surpass. Columbia has already received a $ 400 million donation earmarked for student support rather than the traditional use: named buildings. Yale's 20-year actual endowment return was 16.0 % which is at or near the 20-year top.

Yale's endowment committee believes that active management efforts in less efficiently priced, less liquid instruments such as real estate, leveraged buyouts, and especially venture capital can provide greater rewards. This means that these assets have much greater variability of returns, see Table 8.6 and Figure 8.4. They believe that hard work and intelligence reap rich rewards in an environment where superior information and deal flow provides an *edge*.

Selecting top managers in private markets leads to a much greater reward than identifying top managers in public markets. Yale has also found that identifying superior managers in the relatively inefficiently priced private markets proves less challenging than in the efficiently priced marketable securities markets. They also attempt to identify opportunities in the far less efficient private equity market.

During the decade to 2005, Yale's bond portfolio, had a 0.7 % per annum return over the benchmark. In the same period, the private equity positions gained 39.5 % per annum versus 21.9 % for the pool of private equity managers compiled by Cambridge Associates. While both the bond portfolio and private equity portfolio benefited from superior active

---

[2] http://www.harvardmagazine.com/on-line/110665.html.

Table 8.5 Institutions by 20 year endowment growth. *Source*: Wikipedia (2006)

Rank Order	Name	Total Growth 2005–1986, %	Annual Growth 2005–1986, %	Endowment in 2005$ (000)	Endowment in 1986$ (000)
1.	University of Michigan	1861	14.88	4 931 000	251 517
2.	Duke University	955	11.78	3 826 000	362 706
3.	University of Virginia	846	11.23	3 219 000	340 387
4.	University of Notre Dame	838	11.19	3 650 000	388 965
5.	Yale	775	10.85	15 225 000	1 739 460
6.	Stanford	712	10.47	12 205 000	1 502 583
7.	University of Pennsylvania	709	10.45	4 370 000	540 084
8.	Univ of Southern California	659	10.13	2 746 000	361 784
9.	Harvard	642	10.02	25 474 000	3 435 013
10.	M.I.T.	591	9.66	6 712 000	971 346
11.	Northwestern	494	8.91	4 215 000	709 236
12.	Vanderbilt	489	8.86	2 628 000	446 458
13.	Emory	487	8.85	4 376 000	745 188
14.	Princeton	479	8.78	11 207 000	1 934 010
15.	Dartmouth	468	8.69	2 714 000	477 774
16.	Cornell	461	8.62	3 777 000	673 848
17.	University of Chicago	416	8.20	4 138 000	802 500
18.	Case Western Reserve	393	7.98	1 516 000	307 250
19.	Rice	378	7.82	3 611 000	755 782
20.	University of Texas	359	7.62	11 611 000	2 530 730

Table 8.6 Dispersion of Active Management Returns Source: YEC, 2005.

Asset Class	1st Quartile, %	Median, %	3rd Quartile, %	Range, %
US Fixed Income	7.2	6.9	6.7	0.5
US Large Cap Equity	11.3	10.4	9.4	2.0
US Large Cap Equity	15.3	13.2	10.5	4.7
International Equity	9.7	8.2	5.7	4.0
Absolute Return	15.6	12.5	8.5	7.1
Real Estate	17.6	12.0	8.4	9.3
Leveraged Buyouts	13.3	8.0	−0.4	13.7
Venture Capital	28.7	−1.4	−14.5	43.2

Asset returns by quartile, ten years ending June 30, 2005

management, the absolute contribution in dollars from superior results in the inefficient world of private equity far exceeded the contribution from superior results in the efficient world of government bonds. Yale does not like low yielding fixed income securities and unlike Harvard is not involved in fixed income derivatives to try to achieve higher returns.

Yale's venture capital managers have been very successful. In the 1970s and 1980s, they invested in several start-ups that in the end helped define the technology industry, including Compaq Computer, Oracle, Genentech, Dell Computer, and Amgen. Then the 1990s they invested in Amazon.com, Yahoo, Cisco Systems, Red Hat, and Juniper Networks. Yale's $ 300 000 investment in Google generated $ 75 million when the company went public in

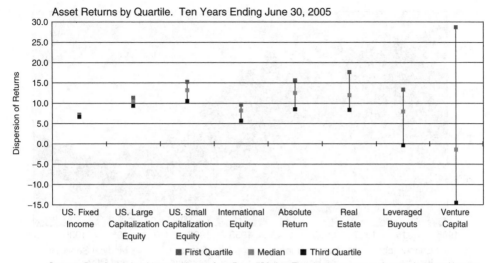

Figure 8.4   Alternative Asset Returns Exhibit Significant Dispersion. *Source*: YEC, 2005

2004. Yale's leveraged buyout investments including Snapple Beverage, AutoZone, Lexmark International, Kinko's, Carter's, and Domino's Pizza also created consistently high returns. They have also been investing internationally in private equity with leveraged buyouts in Europe and venture capital participation in Asia providing potential gains though with the increased risks of investing in emerging countries with less well-established laws and markets.

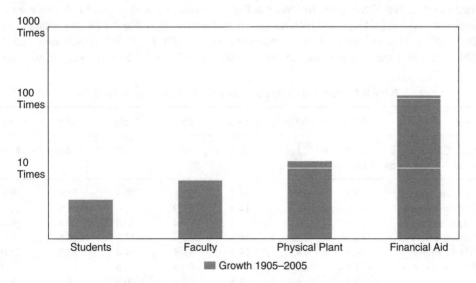

Figure 8.5   Yale growth, 1905–2005. *Source*: YEC, 2006

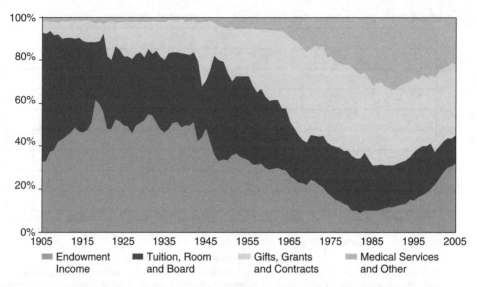

Figure 8.6 University Revenue by Source 1905–2005. *Source*: YEC, 2006

Where do Swensen and the other top university endowment managers rate compared to other great investors such as Warren Buffett, George Soros, John Maynard Keynes, Ed Thorp, Nikolai Battoo, Jeff Yass, Bill Benter, Harry McPike, Blair Hull, the Ford Foundation, the Harvard endowment, etc? Swensen's 16 % net over 20 years is almost identical to Thorp's 15.8 % over 20 years (1969–88) but with more money and much more scrutiny.

Figure 8.7 shows that Swensen and his team of inside and outside managers have consistently beaten his benchmarks in the ten years from 1996–2006. However, Swensen's monthly losses are much greater than Thorp's so his downside symmetric Sharpe ratio is well below Thorp's 13.8. In addition, much of Swensen's portfolio is in assets that are hard to value. David Swensen, like Warren Buffett, would argue that monthly losses are not important as he is looking for long term growth and not losing. Table 8.7 has the results from 2000–2006. This includes the very impressive 19.4 % (2004), 22.3 % (2005) and 22.9 % (2006) and also the lack of losses in 2000–2006. The 41.0 % in 2000 is likely from a few

Table 8.7 Yale's endowment returns in %, fiscal year 2000–2006

Year	2006	2005	2004	2003	2002	2001	2000
Yale % Return	22.9	22.3	19.4	8.8	0.7	9.2	41.0
Asset Allocation, as of June 30, in %							
Absolute returns	23.3	25.7	26.1	25.1	26.5	22.9	19.5
Domestic equity	11.6	14.1	14.8	14.9	15.4	15.5	14.2
Fixed income	3.8	4.9	7.4	7.4	10.0	9.8	9.4
Foreign equity	14.6	13.7	14.8	14.6	12.8	10.6	9.0
Private equity	16.4	14.8	14.5	14.9	14.4	18.2	25.0
Real assets	27.8	25.0	18.8	20.9	20.5	16.8	14.9
Cash	2.5	1.9	3.5	2.1	0.3	6.2	8.1

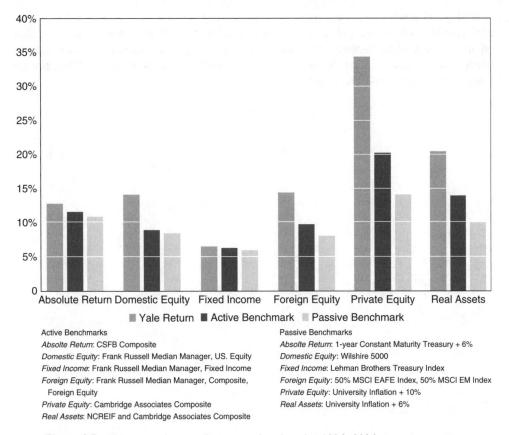

Figure 8.7 Yale asset class results trounce benchmarks, 1996–2006. *Source*: YEC, 2006

tech bubble home runs (above the 25 % allocation to provide equity in 2000). We do not have the data for a full analysis but certainly Swensen's Yale record is outstanding and a very good example of category A financial market managers. He is definitely a great investor.

Swensen, in summing up his success, says he thinks that investing is a simple business, which comes down to two principles. First, equities are best for the long run. With a portfolio like Yale's, with a time horizon measured in centuries, it is far better to have equities in your portfolio than bonds or cash. Indeed Figure 23.7 shows this. Swensen's definition of equities extends beyond exchange traded shares encompassing any asset whose base value has an upside potential. The second principle, well argued throughout this book, is diversification. Swensen was influenced by his teacher, the late Nobel Laureate Yale Economics Professor James Tobin, who said "don't put all your eggs in one basket."

In 1985 when Swensen inherited the portfolio it had 40 % bonds and 10 % each in six other assets. In restructuring the portfolio he had asset allocation, market timing and security selection as useful tools. He focuses on asset allocation and uses a volatility pumping fixed mix approach balancing back to the target allocations periodically. For example, after the 1987 crash, he was buying when others were selling. Swensen learned this from the

CAPM – and much better than most who just learned about index funds. He focuses on equity assets outside the public markets that are more inefficient than exchange traded equities. The CAPM suggests that stock selection except for added risk is not easy to master nor is market timing. Some of Swensen's assets are illiquid such as IPOs, private placements, forestry and hedge funds.

Part II
Investment Strategies: Hedge Funds

9
Hedge fund concepts and a typical convergence trade: Nikkei put warrant risk arbitrage

A difference of opinion: the Japanese stock market cannot fall (Japanese) vs the prices are way too high so the market will crash (others)

In this, the first of five chapters focusing on hedge funds, general strategies, types of funds and a successful trade are discussed. Chapter 10 discusses ways to lose money in derivatives and Chapters 11–13 focus on hedge fund disasters, their prevention and related risk control.

Hedge funds are pooled investments that attempt to obtain superior returns for their mostly wealthy investors. The general partner runs the fund and collects fees to compensate for expenses, management fee and superior performance. Typically, the general partner is an investor in the fund. This is called *eating your own cooking*. Standard fees are 1 to 2 % for expenses and a performance fee of 20 % of the net new profits (above a high water mark). On occasion, funds return fees not earned after a period of time but this is more rare. The top funds are in a strong bargaining position with investors desperate for good steady returns. Renaissance's $ 6.7 billion Medallion Fund performance fees are 44 % plus a 5 % management fee. Despite high fees, Medallion has gained 36 % net per year since its inception in 1988. The $ 10 billion Caxton Global has netted investors over 25 % per year since 1986. In 2003 they raised the expense fee from 2 % to 3 % and the incentive from 20 % to 25 %. Both of these funds are closed to new investors. In 2003, Medallion reduced its size to $ 5 billion by returning $ 1.7 billion to investors to help increase its returns which have been dropping because of too much money relative to opportunities. This can be a dangerous practice if leverage is increased as Long Term Capital Management did in 1998 (as discussed in Chapter 11).

Investment by the general partner in the fund tends to give investors added confidence in that the incentive is to perform well and dampening the incentive of the manager to take excessive risks which helps the general partner as well as the investors. In addition it is convenient for the general partner to store fees collected month by month or quarter by quarter in the fund. Still a hedge fund can be considered to be a call option on the profits associated with managing other people's money since the fee structure gives the general partner the incentive to take risks that lead to profits that lead to large fees and no negative fees with losses except on their own money invested. In the last two decades, the hedge fund industry has grown explosively. The first official hedge fund was established in 1949. But unofficial hedge funds have existed for much longer. By the late 1980's, the number of funds had increased to about 100. In 1997 there were more than 1200 hedge funds, managing a total of more than $200 billion. In September 2006, they held about $1.3 trillion in assets. The January 2007 issue of *Bloomberg Markets* lists the best hedge funds as of September 2006 with Goldman Sachs at $295 billion. The assets are 28.4 % long-short, 13.4 % event driven, 10.9 % macro, 7.8 % fixed income, 5.1 % sector, 4.5 % distressed securities, 4.2 % emerging markets and 25.7 % other strategies.

In addition to official hedge funds that are regulated in various countries, there also are numerous variants that act like hedge funds including bank trading departments, treasury departments of corporations, high net work individuals, partnerships and the like. While official hedge funds are growing rapidly and have substantial size, the unofficial kind have much more money under management. Though the number and size of hedge funds are still small compared to mutual fund industry, their growth reflects the importance of alternative investments for institutional investors and wealthy individuals. In addition, hedge funds frequently exert an influence on financial markets that is much greater than their size. An important example is the collapse of the Long-Term Capital Management hedge fund in 1998, which jeopardized several large financial institutions and was considered a threat to the world economy by the US Federal Reserve. Hence, the study of risk taking in the hedge fund industry is relevant for the financial system as a whole.

The name *hedge fund* is misleading since a hedge fund is basically a vehicle to trade a pool of money from a number of investors in various financial markets. Some hedge funds actually use hedging such as those using long short or convergence trades. Others, the *macro funds*, use strategies that take directional bets on currencies, stock indices, etc. A list of ten distinct types of hedge funds appears in Table 9.1.

Since 1995, a number of academic studies have tried to estimate the returns and risks of investing in hedge funds (Fung & Hsieh, 1997, Brown, Goetzman & Ibbotson, 1999, Ackerman, McEnally & Ravenscraft, 1999, Liang, 1998, Agarwal & Naik 1999 and Amin & Kat, 2001). Obtaining data for empirical studies has been difficult, as hedge funds are not required to report their returns to the public. As a result, each study typically investigates a subset of the total hedge fund universe, depending on which data happened to be available. These are good academic data bases at the University of Massachusetts (contact Tom Schneeweis) and at the London Business School (contact Narayan Naik).

In general, the empirical studies seem to agree on one very important point: hedge funds significantly improve the tradeoff between risk and return, when added to a traditional portfolio of bonds, mutual funds and stock indices. This is due to the fact that some hedge funds have relatively little exposure to sources of general market risk. Except for Ackerman, McEnally and Ravenscraft (1999), the studies also find that individual hedge funds

Table 9.1 Selected Types of Pure Hedge Fund Strategy Categories, Modified from Agarwal and Naik (1999)

---

1. Market Neutral Strategies

- *Fixed Income Arbitrage* long and short bond positions via cash or derivatives markets in government, corporate and/or asset-backed securities. The risk varies depending on duration, credit exposure and the degree of leverage.
- *Event Driven* a strategy that attempts to benefit from mispricing arising in different events such as merger arbitrage, restructurings, etc. Positions are taken in undervalued securities anticipated to rise in value due to events such as mergers, reorganizations, or takeovers. The main risk is non-realization of the event.
- *Equity Convergence Hedge* investing in equity or equity derivative instruments whose net exposure (gross long minus short) is low. The manager may invest globally, or have a more defined geographic, industry or capitalization focus. The risk primarily pertains to the specific risk of the long and short positions.
- *Restructuring – buying and occasionally shorting securities of companies under Chapter 11 and/or ones which are undergoing some form of reorganization* the securities range from senior secured debt to common stock. The liquidation of financially distressed companies is the main source of risk.
- *Event Arbitrage* purchasing securities of a company being acquired and shorting that of the acquiring company. this risk relates to the ***deal*** risk rather than market risk.
- *Capital Structure Arbitrage* buying and selling different securities of the same issuer (e.g. convertibles/common stock) attempting to obtain low volatility returns by exploiting the relative mispricing of these securities.

2. Directional Strategies

- *Macro* an attempt to capitalize on country, regional and/or economic change affecting securities, commodities, interest rates and currency rates. Asset allocation can be aggressive, using leverage and derivatives. The method and degree of hedging can vary significantly.
- *Long* a ***growth***, ***value***, or other model approach to investing in equities with no shorting or hedging to minimize market risk. These funds mainly invest in emerging markets where there may be restrictions on short sales.
- *Long Bias* similar to equity convergence but a net long exposure.
- *Short* selling short over-valued securities and attempting to repurchase them in the future at a lower price.

---

provide better risk-adjusted performance (after fees) than a broadly diversified stock index, usually the S&P500.

There is little persistence in hedge fund performance: winners may easily become losers (Brown, Goetzman & Ibbotson 1999, Liang 1998, Agarwal & Naik 2000, Amin and Kat, 2001). However, Jagannathan, Malakhov and Novikhov (2006) find some persistence in their data sets. Although the hedge fund industry as a whole provides good opportunities for investors, some successful hedge fund managers tend to lose their magic now and then. A well-known and noteworthy example of a winner that turned into a loser is Long Term Capital Management (Edwards 1999, Jorion 1999, Ross, 1999 and Ziemba, 1999 and Chapter 11). Julian Robertson's Tiger and George Soros's Quantum funds effectively closed in 2000 after bad results following many years of high returns. Quantum lost about $ 5 billion of its $ 13 billion size shorting the Nasdaq too soon. Had they started shorting about two months later in April 2000, they could possibly have made ten times this amount. Timing and mean returns once again are the key elements of successful investing making good risk control essential for hedge funds. In addition, the real risk in hedge funds that are highly levered through borrowing or derivatives is frequently greatly understated by the monthly or quarterly reporting periods and by risk measures such as the standard deviation or the Sharpe ratio which are based on normality, which readers this book know is inadequate to measure the fat tails of real markets.

The theoretical literature about hedge funds is growing. The references contain a partial bibliography on risk control and trading strategies and their evaluation. Typically, papers focus on:

1. the optimal fee structure for investment funds: Heinkel and Stoughton (1994), Maug and Naik (1995) and Dybvig, Farnsworth and Carpenter (2000);
2. exploiting arbitrage opportunities with restrictions on short selling: Liu and Longstaff (2000) and Loewenstein and Willard (2000); and
3. applying option pricing to calculate the value of the incentive-fees paid to hedge fund managers: Goetzmann, Ingersoll and Ross (1998) and Kowenberg and Ziemba (2006).

Heinkel and Stoughton (1994), Maug and Naik (1995) and Dybvig, Farnsworth and Carpenter (2000) investigate the relationship between fee contracts and fund management. These papers apply the principal-agent framework developed by Ross (1973) in order to derive the optimal management contract from the point of view of the investor.

Liu and Longstaff (2000) and Loewenstein and Willard (2000) investigate the equilibrium impact of investors that exploit arbitrage opportunities (hedge fund managers). In the model of Loewenstein and Willard (2000) hedge fund managers provide liquidity to instutional investors who face uncertain cash withdrawals. Liu and Longstaff (2000) investigate a market with a pure arbitrage opportunity and hedge fund managers that face restrictions on short selling. Similar studies about the risks of arbitrage strategies can be found in Shleifer (2000).

Goetzmann, Ingersoll and Ross (1998) develop a continuous time Black Scholes like environment to model the high water mark incentive system used by many hedge funds. That is, fees are a flat amount per unit of time plus an incentive that is a percentage above a benchmark (which they take to be zero). It is assumed that the hedge fund returns the mean rate of return of the market and goes on forever with continuous redemptions unless it is closed by poor return scenario outcomes. Given these assumptions, they estimate the value of the fees paid to the manager as a call option on the investor's wealth. Kouwenberg and Ziemba (2007) investigate incentives in hedge funds and the effect of the manager's own stake in the fund. Above a 30 % own stake, risk taking behavior is greatly moderated. The call option on the other investors' money depends on this investment by the manager and is worth close to zero or as much as 18 % when the manager has little or no investment in the fund. In the empirical part of the paper, they find that the average hedge fund does not make back its fees but funds of funds do better.

GAMBLERS AS HEDGE FUND MANAGERS

I have been fortunate to work and consult with seven individuals who used investment market anomalies and imperfections and hedge funds ideas to turn a humble beginning with essentially zero wealth into hundreds of millions or billions. Each had several common characteristics: a gambling background usually obtained by playing blackjack professionally and a very focused, fully researched and computerized system for asset position selection and careful attention to the possibility of loss. These individuals focus more on not losing rather than winning. Three were relative value long/short managers consistently eaking out small edges who extensively used derivatives. One was a futures trader taking bets on a large number of liquid financial assets based on favorable trends (interest rates, bonds and currencies were the best). The fifth was a Hong Kong horse race bettor; see Benter's paper in Hausch, Lo and Ziemba (1994). The sixth, James Simons of Renaissance, was in 2005 the top hedge fund earner in the world at $ 1.4 billion and second in 2006 earning $ 1.6 billion. The seventh is a superior trader and hedge fund manager. Their gambling backgrounds led them to conservative investment behavior and excellent results both absolute and risk adjusted. They have losses but rarely do they overbet or not diversify enough to have a major blow out like the hedge fund occurrences. Good systems for diversification and determination of bet size such as that discussed in Chapters 2–5. All of them used versions of the Kelly criterion in some way. I designed such a system that was implemented by an employee of the futures trader, a Cal Tech trained physicist, to optimize bets over the ninety most liquid futures markets that he traded. It added $ 9 million per year or 18 % to profits, on average.

Dr Edward O. Thorp, a mathematician with a PhD from UCLA, became famous in 1960 by devising a simple to use card counting system for beating the card game blackjack, see

Table 9.2   The annual record of Princeton-Newport, 1969–1988 in 000's

Period Beg	End	Beg Capital	Profit (Loss)	End Capital	Added Capital +	PNP LP	S&P500 %	3-month T-Bill
1/11/69	31/12/69	1,400	57	1,457	544	4.1 %	−1.8 %	1.2 %
1/1/70	31/12/70	2,001	364	2,365	737	18.2 %	4.0 %	6.2 %
1/1/71	31/12/71	3,102	1,281	4,383	1,944	41.3 %	14.3 %	4.4 %
1/1/72	31/12/72	6,327	1,046	7,373	1,134	16.5 %	19.0 %	4.6 %
1/1/73	31/12/73	8,507	711	9,218	(2,550)	8.4 %	−14.7 %	7.5 %
1/1/74	31/12/74	6,668	751	7,419	(70)	11.3 %	−26.5 %	7.9 %
1/1/75	31/10/75	7,349	961	8,310	596	13.1 %	34.3 %	5.1 %
1/11/75	31/10/76	8,906	1,793	10,699	1,106	20.1 %	20.1 %	5.2 %
1/11/76	31/10/77	11,805	2,350	14,155	3,843	19.9 %	−6.2 %	5.5 %
1/11/77	31/10/78	17,998	2,797	20,795	(635)	15.5 %	6.4 %	7.4 %
1/11/78	31/10/79	20,160	4,122	24,282	4,349	20.4 %	15.3 %	10.9 %
1/11/79	31/10/80	28,631	7,950	36,581	9,728	27.8 %	21.4 %	12.0 %
1/11/80	31/10/81	46,309	13,227	59,536	2,343	28.6 %	22.8 %	16.0 %
1/11/81	31/10/82	61,879	18,747	80,626	18,235	30.3 %	21.8 %	12.1 %
1/11/82	31/10/83	98,861	13,842	112,703	26,342	14.0 %	10.5 %	9.1 %
1/11/83	31/10/84	139,045	20,193	159,238	(6,195)	14.5 %	11.6 %	10.4 %
1/11/84	31/10/85	153,043	21,813	174,856	(40,244)	14.3 %	11.4 %	8.0 %
1/11/85	31/10/86	134,612	41,143	175,755	(21,727)	30.6 %	24.5 %	6.3 %
1/11/86	31/12/87	154,028	52,451	206,479	17,722	34.1 %	26.7 %	7.1 %
1/1/88	31/12/88	224,201	8,918	233,119	(232,118)	4.0 %	3.2 %	7.4 %
						1382.0 %	545.0 %	345.0 %
						15.10 %	10.2 %	8.1 %

Thorp (1962). He wrote the foreword to my book with Donald Hausch, *Beat the Racetrack* published in 1984, and revised in 1987, which provided a simple to use winning system for racetrack betting based on weak market inefficiencies in the more complex place and show markets using probabilities estimated from the simpler win market.

In 1966 Thorp wrote a follow-up to *Beat the Dealer* called *Beat the Market* which outlined a system for obtaining edges in warrant markets. Thorp was close to finding the Black–Scholes formula for pricing options at least from an approximate, empirical and discrete time point of view and some of these ideas were obviously used in his hedge fund, Princeton Newport Partners (PNP) trading. The PNP hedge fund, with offices in Newport Beach, California and Princeton, New Jersey, was run from 1969 to 1988 using a variety of strategies, many of which can be classified as convergence or long-short. See Figure 6.2 for the annual record of the PNP. There is more, including Thorp's recent record, but this figure and Table 9.2 illustrate my points. Actual trades and positions used by Dr. Thorp and his

Table 9.3 Absolute and relative performance of the Chest Fund managed by J.M. Keynes, 1927–1945. *Source*: Chua and Woodward (1983)

year	Chest Fund Index	Chest Fund Return	UK Market Index	UK Market Return	T-Bill Index	T-Bill Return
1927	100.0		100.0		100.0	
1928	96.6	−3.4	107.9	7.9	104.2	4.2
1929	97.4	0.8	115.0	6.6	109.7	5.3
1930	65.8	−32.4	91.7	−20.3	112.5	2.5
1931	49.6	−24.6	68.8	−25.0	116.5	3.6
1932	71.8	44.8	64.8	−5.8	118.3	1.5
1933	97.0	35.1	78.7	21.5	119.0	0.6
1934	129.1	33.1	78.1	−0.7	119.8	0.7
1935	186.3	44.3	82.3	5.3	120.4	0.5
1936	290.6	56.0	90.7	10.2	121.1	0.6
1937	315.4	8.5	90.2	−0.5	121.9	0.6
1938	188.9	−40.1	75.7	−16.1	122.6	0.6
1939	213.2	12.9	70.2	−7.2	124.2	1.3
1940	179.9	−15.6	61.2	−12.9	125.4	1.0
1941	240.2	33.5	68.8	12.5	126.7	1.0
1942	238.0	−0.9	69.4	0.8	127.9	1.0
1943	366.2	53.9	80.2	15.6	129.2	1.0
1944	419.3	14.5	84.5	5.4	130.5	1.0
1945	480.3	14.6	85.2	0.8	131.8	1.0

Arithmetic mean:	13.06 %		−0.11 %			1.56 %
Geometric mean:	9.12 %		−0.89 %			
Standard dev:	29.28 %		12.58 %			
Beta:	1.78					
Sharpe index:	0.385	−0.129				
Treynor index:	6.46	−1.86				
Jensen index:	14.45 %					
(standard error:	4.69 %)					

colleagues are not public information, but a trade that Thorp and I jointly executed based on my ideas follows which gleans some idea of the approach he used. PNP gained 15.1 % net of fees (which were about 4 % given the 20 % of profits fee structure) versus 10.2 % for the S&P500 and 8.1 % for T-bills. PNP's initial index value of 100 in November 1, 1969 became, at the end of December 1988, 148 200 versus 64 500 for the S&P500 and 44 500 for T-bills. But what is impressive and what is a central lesson of this book, is that the risk control using various stochastic optimization procedures led to no years with losses. Of course, in comparison to Keynes, see Table 9.3 (and Figure 4.2), PNP had a much easier market to deal with. For example only in 1973, 1974 and 1976 did the S&P500 have negative returns. Such opportunities to exploit market inefficiencies apply to other markets as well.

A TYPICAL CONVERGENCE TRADE: THE NIKKEI PUT WARRANT MARKET OF 1989–90

Dr Thorp and I, with assistance from Julian Shaw (then of Gordon Capital, Toronto, now the risk control manager for Barclays trading in London), did a convergence trade based on differing put warrant prices on the Toronto and American stock exchanges. The trade was successful and Thorp won the over $ 1 million risk adjusted hedge fund contest run by Barron's in 1990. There were risks involved and careful risk management was needed. What follows is a brief description of the main points. Additional discussion and technical details appears in Shaw, Thorp and Ziemba (1995).

This edge was based on the fact that the Japanese stock and land prices were astronomical and very intertwined, see Stone and Ziemba (1993) for more on this.

The historical development leading up to the NSA put warrants

- Tsukamoto Sozan Building in Ginza 2-Chome in central Tokyo was the most expensive land in the country with one square meter priced at ¥ 37.7 million or about $ 79 000 US at the (December 1990) exchange rate of about ¥ 135 per US dollar.
- Downtown Tokyo land values were the highest in the world, about $ 800 million an acre
- Office rents in Tokyo are twice those in London yet land costs 40 times as much
- The Japanese stock market, as measured by the Nikkei stock average (NSA), was up 221 times in yen and 553 in dollars from 1949 to the end of 1989.
- Despite this huge rise, there had been twenty declines of 10 % or more in the NSA from 1949 to 1989. The market was particularly volatile with two more in 1990 and two more in 1991. Stocks, bonds and land were highly levered with debt.
- There was a tremendous feeling in the West that the Japanese stock market was overpriced as was the land market. For example the value of the Emperor's palace was reputed to be equivalent to all of California or Canada. Japanese land was about 23 % of world's non-human capital. Japanese PE ratios were 60+.
- Various studies by academics and brokerage researchers argued that the high prices of stocks and land were justified by higher long run growth rates and lower interest rates in Japan versus the US. See for example, Ziemba and Schwartz (1991) and French and Poterba (1991). However, similar models predicted a large fall in prices once interest rates rose from late 1998 to August 1990.
- Hence both must crash!

- There was a tremendous feeling in Japan that their economy and products were the best in the world.
- There was a natural trade in 1989 and early 1990
    - Westerners bet Japanese market will fall
    - Japanese bet Japanese market will not fall

Various Nikkei put warrants which were three year American options were offered to the market to fill the demand by speculators who wanted to bet that the NSA would fall.

NSA PUTS AND CALLS ON THE TORONTO AND AMERICAN STOCK EXCHANGES, 1989–92

The various NSA puts and calls were of three basic types, see Table 9.4.

Our convergence trades in late 1989 to early 1990 involved:

1. selling expensive Canadian currency Bankers Trust I's and II's and buying cheaper US currency BT's on the American Stock Exchange; and
2. selling expensive Kingdom of Denmark and Salomon I puts on the ASE and buying the same BT I's also on the ASE both in US dollars. This convergence trade was especially interesting because the price discrepancy was based mainly on the unit size and used instruments on the same exchange.

Table 9.4 NSA Puts on the Toronto and American Stock Exchanges, 1989–1992

The various puts are of three basic types. Let NSA_0 be the strike price and NSA_e the expiry price of the Nikkei stock average. Let E_0 be today's exchange rate and E_e be the exchange rate on expiry for Canadian or US dollars into yen. The symbol $(X)+$ means the greater of X or zero. Then we have

US/Cdn Dollars	Puts	Calls	Terminology
I. a $\left(\dfrac{NSA_0 - NSA_e}{E_e}\right)_+$	BT-I, SEK, BTB, London OTC	PW	Ordinary
II. b $\left(\dfrac{NSA_0 - NSA_e}{E_0}\right)_+$	BT-III, BT-IV, TFC, DXA, EXW, SXA, SXO, PXB	Sal	Product
III. c $\left(\dfrac{NSA_0}{E_0} - \dfrac{NSA_e}{E_e}\right)_+$	BT-II		Option to Exchange

	Puts
Canadian \$, Toronto	BT-I, NK; BT-II, NKA; BT-III, NKB; BT-IV, NKC; TFC, SEK
US \$, New York	BTB, DXA, SXA, SXO, EXW

In Yen	US/Cdn Person
I. a $(NSA_0 - NSA_e)_+$	I. Takes currency risk
II. b $(NSA_0 - NSA_e)_+ \dfrac{E_e}{E_0}$	II. No currency risk
III. c $\left(\dfrac{NSA_0}{E_0} - \dfrac{NSA_e}{E_e}\right)_+ E_e$	III. Currency risk in final conversion in strike price

Table 9.5 Comparison of Prices and Premium Values for Four Canadian and Three US NSA Put Warrants on 1 February 1990

Warrant	Price	% of NSA Unit	Expiry Date (yrs to ex)	Premium %	Premium % pa	Hedge Action A	Hedge Action B
BT-I	C$ 2.70	11.68 %	2/17/92(2.05)	20.1	9.8	Sell	
BT-II	C$ 1.93	10.31 %	6/15/92(2.37)	16.4	6.9	Sell	
BT-III	C$ 2.50n	14.29 %	2/16/93(3.05)	7.0	2.3		
Trilon Finl	C$ 2.75	13.7 %	2/22/93(3.05)	7.25	2.4		
K of Denmark	US$ 5.63	20 %	1/3/93(2.93)	10.1	3.4		SellL
Salomon-I	US$ 4.63	20 %	1/19/93(2.97)	10.1	3.4		Sell
BT-US	US$ 9.17	50 %	1/16/93(3.00)	8.0	2.6	Buy	Buy

Table 9.5 describes this. We performed a complex pricing of all the warrants which is useful in the optimization of the positions size, see Shaw, Thorp and Ziemba (1995). However, Table 9.5 gives insight into this in a simple way. For example, 9.8 % premium year means that if you buy the option, the NSA must fall 9.8 % each year to break even. So selling at 9.8 % and buying at 2.6 % looks like a good trade.

Some of the reasons for the different prices were:

- large price discrepancy across the Canada/US border;
- Canadians trade in Canada, Americans trade in the US;
- different credit risk;
- different currency risk;
- difficulties with borrowing for short sales;
- blind emotions vs reality;
- an inability of speculators to properly price the warrants.

I's were ordinary puts traded in yen. II's were currency protected puts (often called quantos). III's were the Nikkei in Canadian or US dollars. The latter were marketed with comments like: you can win if the Nikkei falls, the yen falls or both. The payoffs in yen and in US/Cdn are shown in Table 9.4. A simulation in Shaw, Thorp and Ziemba (1995) showed that for similar parameter values, I's were worth more than II's, which were worth more than III's. But investors preferred the currency protected aspect of the II's and overpaid (relative to hedging that risk separately in the currency futures markets) for them relative to the I's. Figures 9.1 and 9.2 show the two convergence trades.

$$\text{Relative Cost} = \frac{\text{Actual Cost - Theoretical Cost}}{\text{Theoretical Cost}} \quad \text{when } \sigma = 20\%$$

is plotted rather than implied volatility since the latter did not exist when there were deep in the money options trading for less than intrinsic as in this market. Fair value at 20 % NSA volatility and 10 % exchange rate volatility is zero on the graph. At one, the puts are trading for double their fair price. At the peak, the puts were selling for more than three times their fair price.

The BT-I's did not trade until January 1990 and in about a month the Canadian BT-I's and BT-II's collapsed to fair value and then the trade was unwound. The Toronto newspapers

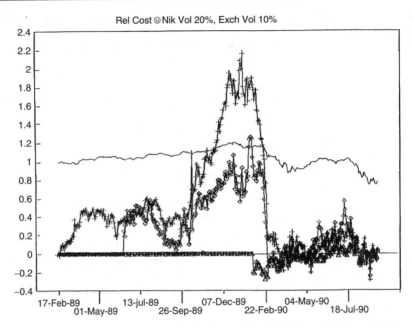

Figure 9.1 Relative costs of BT-I, BT-II and BTB NSA put warrants with NSA volatility of 20 %
and exchange rate volatility of 10 %, 17 February 1989 to 21 September 1990. Relative deviation from
model price = (actual cost − theoretical value)/(theoretical value). Key: (+) BT = I, type I, Canadian,
(◊) BT-II, type III, Canadian and (△) BTB type I, US and (−) normalized Nikkei

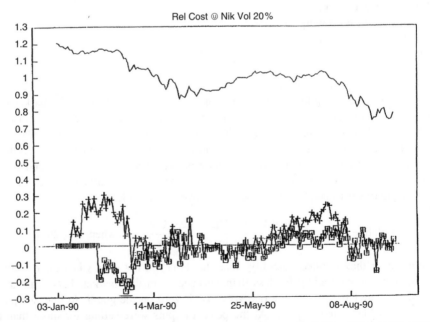

Figure 9.2 Relative costs of US type I (BTB) versus US type II (DXA, SXA, SXO) NSA put
warrants with NSA volatility of 20 %, January to September 1990. Key: ([]) BTB, type I, 0.5 NSA,
(+) avg DXA, SXA, SXO, type II, 0.2 NSA, and, (−) normalized Nikkei

inadvertently helped the trade by pointing out that the Canadian puts were overpriced relative to the US puts so eventually there was selling of the Canadians, which led to the convergence to efficiency. To hedge before January 1990 one needed to buy an over the counter put from a brokerage firm such as Salomon who made a market in these puts. The NSA decline in 1990 is also shown in Figure 9.1. Additional risks of such trades is being bought in and shorting the puts too soon and having the market price of them go higher. We had only minor problems with these risks.

Fair value at 20 % NSA volatility and 10 % exchange rate volatility is zero on the graph. At one the puts are trading for double their fair price. At the peak, the puts were selling for more than three times their fair price.

For the second trade, the price discrepancy lasted about a month. The market prices were about $ 18 and $ 9 where they theoretically should have had a 5 to 2 ratio since one put was worth 20 % and the other 50 % and trade at $ 20 and $ 8. These puts were not identical so this is risk arbitrage not arbitrage. The discrepancy here is similar to the small firm, low price effect (see Keim and Ziemba, 2000). Both puts were trading on the American stock exchange.

There was a similar inefficiency in the call market where the currency protected options traded for higher than fair prices; see Figure 9.3. There was a successful trade here but this was a low volume market. This market never took off as investors lost interest when the

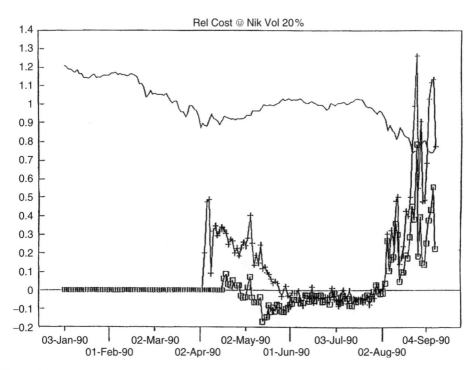

Figure 9.3 Relative costs of Paine Webber and Salomon NSA call warrants with NSA historical volatility of 20 %, April to October 1990. Relative deviation from model price = (actual cost − theoretical value)/(theoretical value). Key: (+) PXA, (+) SXZ and (−) normalized Nikkei

NSA did not rally. US traders preferred Type II (Salomon's SXZ) denominated in dollars rather than the Paine Webber (PXA) which were in yen.

The Canadian speculators who *overpaid* for the put warrants that our trade was based on made $ 500 million Canadian since the NSA's fall was so great. A great example of the mean dominating! The issuers of the puts also did well and hedged their positions with futures in Osaka and Singapore. The losers were the holders of Japanese stocks. We did a similar trade with Canadian dollar puts traded in Canada and hedged in the US. The difference in price (measured by implied volatility) between the Canadian and US puts stayed relatively constant over an entire year (a gross violation of efficient markets). The trade was also successful but again like the Nikkei calls, the volume was low.

10

The recipe for disaster: How to lose money in derivatives

Understanding how to lose helps one avoid losses

This is the second of five chapters on hedge funds. Here we discuss how to lose money in derivatives which leads to our discussion of hedge fund disasters and how to prevent them which is the subject of the next three chapters.

DERIVATIVE DISASTERS

The derivative industry deals with products in which one party gains what the other party loses. These are situations known as zero sum games. Hence there are bound to be large winners and large losers. The size of the gains and losses are magnified by the leverage and overbetting, leading invariably to large losses when a bad scenario occurs. This industry is now a staggering $370 trillion of which $262 trillion is in interest rate derivatives, according to the Bank for International Settlements in Basel; see Tett (2006).

Figlewski (1994) attempted to categorize derivative disasters and this chapter discusses and expands on that:

1. *Hedge*

   In an ordinary hedge, one loses money on one side of the transaction in an effort to reduce risk. The correct way to evaluate the performance of a hedge is to consider all aspects of the transaction. In sophisticated hedges where one delta hedges but is a net seller of options, there is volatility (gamma) risk which could lead to losses if there is a large price move up or down. Also accounting problems can lead to losses if gains and losses on all sides of a derivatives hedge are recorded in the firm's financial statements at the same time.

2. *Counterparty default.*

   Credit risk is the fastest growing area of derivatives and a common hedge fund strategy is to be short overpriced credit default derivatives. There are lots of ways to lose on these shorts if they are not hedged properly, even if they have an edge.

3. *Speculation*

   Derivatives have many purposes including transferring risk from those who do not wish it (hedgers) to those who do (speculators). Speculators who take naked unhedged positions take the purest bet and win or lose monies related to the size of the move of the underlying security. Bets on currencies, interest rates, bonds, or stock market moves are leading examples.

   Human agency problems frequently lead to larger losses for traders who are holding losing positions that if cashed out would lead to lost jobs or bonus. Some traders will increase exposure exactly when they should reduce it in the hopes that a market turnaround will allow them to cash out with a small gain before their superiors find out about the true situation and force them to liquidate. Since the job or bonus may have already been lost, the trader's interests are in conflict with objectives of the firm and huge losses may occur. Writing options, which typically gain small profits most of the time but can lead to large losses, is a common vehicle for this problem because the size of the position accelerates quickly as the underlying security moves in the wrong direction. Since trades between large institutions frequently are not collateralized mark to market large paper losses can accumulate without visible signs such as a margin call. Nick Leeson's loss betting on short puts and calls on the Nikkei is one of many such examples. The Kobe earthquake was the bad scenario that bankrupted Barings.

A proper accounting of trading success evaluates all gains and losses so that the extent of some current loss is weighed against previous gains. Derivative losses should also be compared to losses on underlying securities. For example, from January 3 to June 30, 1994, the 30-year T-bonds fell 13.6%. Hence holders of bonds lost considerable sums as well since interest rates quickly rose significantly.

4. *Forced liquidation at unfavorable prices*

Gap moves through stops are one example of forced liquidation. Portfolio insurance strategies based on selling futures during the 18 October 1987 stock market crash were unable to keep up with the rapidly declining market whose futures fell 29% that day. Forced liquidation due to margin problems is made more difficult when others have similar positions and predicaments. The August 1998 problems of Long Term Capital Management in bond and other markets were more difficult because others had followed their lead with similar positions. When trouble arose, buyers were scarce and sellers were everywhere. Another example is Metallgellschaft's crude oil futures hedging losses of over $1.3 billion. They had long term contracts to supply oil at fixed prices for several years. These commitments were hedged with long oil futures. But when spot oil prices fell rapidly, the contracts to sell oil at high prices rose in value but did not provide current cash to cover the mark to the market futures losses. A management error led to the unwinding of the hedge near the bottom of the oil market and the disaster.

Potential problems are greater in illiquid markets. Such positions are typically long term and liquidation must be done matching sales with available buyers. Hence, forced liquidation can lead to large bid-ask spreads. Askin Capital's failure in the bond market in 1994 was exacerbated because they held very sophisticated securities which were only traded by very few counterparties. Once they learned of Askin's liquidity problems and weak bargaining position, they lowered their bids even more and were then able to gain large liquidity premiums.

5. *Misunderstanding the risk exposure*

As derivative securities have become more complex, so has their full understanding. Our Nikkei put warrant trade (discussed in Chapter 9) was successful because we did a careful analysis to fairly price the securities. In many cases, losses are the result of trading in high-risk financial instruments by unsophisticated investors. Lawsuits have arisen brought by such investors attempting to recover some of their losses with claims that they were misled or not properly briefed on the risks of the positions taken. Since the general public and thus judges and juries find derivatives confusing and risky, even when they are used to reduce risk, such cases or their threat may be successful.

A great risk exposure is the extreme scenario which often investors assume has zero probability when in fact they have low but positive probability. Investors are frequently unprepared for interest rate, currency or stock price changes so large and so fast that they are considered to be impossible to occur. The move of some bond interest rate spreads from 3 % a year earlier to 17 % in August/September 1998 led even the savvy investor and very sophisticated Long Term Capital Management researchers and traders down this road. They had done extensive stress testing which failed as the extreme events such as the August 1998 Russian default had both the extreme low probability event plus changing correlations. Scenario dependent correlation matrices rather then simulations around the past correlations are suggested. This is implemented, for example, in the Innovest pension plan model which does not involve levered derivative positions (see Chapter 21). The key for staying out of trouble, especially with highly levered positions, is to fully consider the possible futures and have enough capital or access to capital to weather bad scenario storms so that any required liquidation can be done in an orderly manner or preferably prevented.

Figlewski (1994) mentions that the risk in mortgage backed securities is especially difficult to understand. Interest only (IO) securities, which provide only a share of the interest as part of the underlying mortgage pool's payment stream are a good example. When interest rates rise, IO's rise since payments are reduced and the stream of interest payments is larger. But when rates rise sharply, the IO falls in value like other fixed-income instruments because the future interest payments are more heavily discounted. This signal of changing interest rate exposure was one of the difficulties in Askin's losses in 1994. Similarly the sign change between stocks and bonds during stock market crashes as in 2000 to 2003 has caused other similar losses. Scenario dependent matrices are especially useful and needed in such situations.

6. *Forgetting that high returns involve high risk*

If investors seek high returns, then they will usually have some large losses. The Kelly criterion strategy and its variants provide a theory to achieve very high long term returns but large losses will also occur. These losses are magnified with derivative securities and especially with large derivative positions relative to the investor's available capital.

Stochastic programming models provide a good way to try to avoid problems 1–6 by carefully modeling the situation at hand and considering the possible economic futures in an organized way.

11

Hedge Fund Risk, Disasters and Their Prevention: The Failure of Long Term Capital Management

They were too smart to lose, or so they thought

Hedge fund disasters usually occur because traders overbet, the portfolio is not truly diversified and then trouble arises when a bad scenario occurs. In this and the next two chapters we discuss three sensational failures: LTCM (1998), Niederhoffer (1997) and Amaranth Advisors (2006). Stochastic programming models provide a way to deal with the risk control of such portfolios using an overall approach to position size, taking into account various possible scenarios that may be beyond the range of previous historical data. Since correlations are scenario dependent, this approach is useful to model the overall position size. In short, the model will not allow the hedge fund to maintain positions so large and so under diversified that a major disaster can occur. Also the model will force consideration of how the fund will attempt to deal with the bad scenario because once there is a derivative disaster, it is very difficult to resolve the problem. More cash is needed immediately and there are liquidity and other considerations. Chapter 21 explores more deeply such models in the context of pension fund as well as hedge fund management.

THE FAILURE OF THE TOP HEDGE FUND TEAM EVER ASSEMBLED

There have been many hedge fund failures but LTCM stands out as a particularly public one. The firm started with the talents of the core bond traders from John Merriwether's group at the Salomon Brothers who were very successful for a number of years. When Warren Buffett came on board at Salomon the culture of this group clashed with Buffett's apparently more conservative style. In truth Buffett's record is Kelly like and not all that

different from Merriwether's group
in terms of position size but Buffett's risk control is superior. A
new group was formed with an all
star cast of top academics including two future Nobel Laureates and
many top professors and students,
many linked to MIT. In addition top government officials were
involved. The team was dubbed
too smart to lose and several billion was raised even though there
was no real track record, fees
were very high (25 % of profits
plus a 3 % management expense
fee) and the entry investment was
$ 100 million minimum. The idea,

Source: Barrons. Created by Leo Cullum for Barrons.

according to Myron Scholes, was to be a big vacuum cleaner sucking up nickels all over
the world as the cartoon suggests. There were many trades, but the essence of the bond
risk arbitrage was to buy underpriced bonds in various locales and sell overpriced bonds
in other locales and then wait for the prices to revert to their theoretical efficient market
prices and then to unwind the position. These trades are similar to the Nikkei put warrant
risk arbitrage (described in Chapter 9) Thorp and I did except that the leverage they used
was much greater. I like to call these bond trades *buy Italy and sell Florence*. As shown in
Figure 11.1, the interest rate implied by the bond prices is higher in Italy than in Florence.
But the theory is that Florence, a smaller place, would have more risk. Hence, the trade
should have an advantage and be unwound when the prices reverted to their true risk priced
values. LTCM analysts made many such trades, most much more complex than this, all
across the world. They also had many other complex and innovative trades. Their belief
that markets were efficient and, when temporarily out of whack, would snap back quickly
and the continuous lognormal assumptions of option pricing hedging led them to take very
large positions which according to their theory were close to riskless.

The plan worked and the net returns for the part of the year 1994 that the fund operated
were 19.9 %. The years 1995 and 1996 had similar superb net results of 42.8 % and 40.8 %,
respectively. Indeed for the principals whose money grew fee-less, these net returns were
63 % and 57 %, respectively, with taxes deferred. There was so much demand for investment
in the fund, which in 1997 was effectively closed to new investors, that a grey market arose
with a 10 % premium. By 1997 it became harder to find profitable trades and the gains fell to
17.1 %. This was a good record for most but not satisfactory to LTCM's principals; among
other things the S&P500 returned 31 % excluding dividends. Their action was to return $ 2.7
billion of the $ 6.7 billion to the investors. The principals then put in an additional $ 100
million raised by personal bank loans. The banks were happy to lend this money basically
unsecured. Banks and others were quite keen to loan to or invest with this group and the
investors were not happy to be forced out of the fund. Still, at the start, $ 1 on February 24,
1994, was $ 2.40 net at the end of 1997. The year 1998 was difficult for the fund and then
turned into a disaster following the August 17 Russian ruble devaluation and sovereign bond
default. Bonds denominated in rubles trading for say 60 fell rapidly to 3 whereas Russian

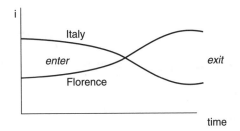

Figure 11.1   Buy Italy, sell Florence. *Source*: WT Ziemba lectures

bonds denominated in marks or dollars only fell a few percent as they were not subject to the effects of the ruble devaluation. So long 60 short 95 say became long 3 short 92 say. Also there were defaults in currency hedging contracts which added to the losses because that hedge failed.

Such losses occur from time to time in various markets and hedge funds which overbet can be very vulnerable to it. The problem for LTCM was that they had $ 1.25 trillion of positions in notional value (that's about 1 % of the December 2006 value of the world's derivatives and even more in 1998) and $ 125 billion of borrowed money. Although the trades were all over the world and hence it seemed they were diversified, they in fact were not. What happened was a scenario dependent correlation situation like that modeled in the Innovest pension application described in Chapter 21. There was an underlying variable that frequently raises its ugly head in disasters that being investor non-confidence. The graph for 1998 in Figure 11.2 illustrates the problem: all the bond rates increased for non high quality debt. For example, emerging market debt was trading for 3.3 % above US T-bonds in October 1997, then 6 % in July 1998 and then an astounding 17 % in September 1998.

LTCM was unable to weather the storm of this enormous crisis of confidence and lost about 95 % of their capital, some $ 4.6 billion including most of the principals' and employees' considerable accumulated fees. The $ 100 million loan actually put some of them into bankruptcy, although others came out better financially; see the *Barrons* cartoon. It did not help that they unwound liquid positions first rather than across all liquidity levels as the Nobles recommended, nor that many other copy-cat firms had similar positions, nor that LTCM had created enemies by being so good and so brash, nor that the lack of monitoring of margin by brokers eager for their business allowed the positions to grow to overbet levels, and finally that the $ 2.8 billion was gone and they could not draw on it when it was most needed.[1] Smart people bounce back and possibly, but not necessarily, learn from their mistakes. Various ex-LTCM members have new hedge funds and other ventures. The lessons are:

- Do not overbet, it is too dangerous.
- VAR type systems are inadequate to measure true risk but see Jorion's (2006) fine book on Var and Dunbar's (2000) for a good discussion of the VAR calculations used by LTCM. LTCM analysts did a very careful analysis but the problem was that the risk

---

[1] In Chapter 2, it was shown that using the Kelly criterion, you should never bet more than the log optimal amount and betting more (as LTCM did) is stochastically dominated as it has lower growth rates *and* higher risk. This point is **not** understood by even the top academic financial economists who insist on using positive power as well as negative power and log utility functions. The positive power ones are stochastically dominated and reflect overbetting. See, for example, Figures 2.2 and 2.3.

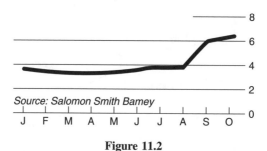

Source: Salomon Smith Barney

Figure 11.2

control method of VAR which is used in regulations does not really protect hedge funds that are so highly levered because you are not penalized enough for large losses. Indeed if you lose \$ 10 million it is penalized the same as losing \$ 100 million if the VAR number is \$ 9 million of losses. What you really need are convex penalties so that penalties are more than proportional to losses. This is discussed in Chapter 21.

You really do need to use scenario dependent correlation matrices and consider extreme scenarios. LTCM was not subject to VAR regulation but still used it.

- Be aware of and consider extreme scenarios.
- Allow for extra illiquidity and contract defaults. LTCM also suffered because of the copycat firms which put on similar positions and unwound them at the same time in August/September 1998.
- Really diversify (to quote Soros from the Quantum Funds, 'we risked 10 % of our funds in Russia and lost it, \$ 2 billion, but we are still up 21 % in 1998').
- Historical correlations work when you do not need them and fail when you need them in a crisis when they approach one. Real correlations are scenario dependent. Sorry to be repetitive, but this is crucial.

Good information on the demise of LTCM and the subsequent \$ 3.5 billion bailout by major brokerage firms organized by the FED are in a Harvard Business School case by André Perold (1998), and articles by Philippe Jorion (2000a) and Franklin Edwards (1999). Eventually the positions converged and the bailout team was able to emerge with a profit on their investment.

The currency devaluation of some two thirds was no surprise to WTZ. In 1992, we were the guests in St Petersburg of Professor Zari Rachev, an expert in stable and heavy-tail distributions and editor of the first handbook in North Holland's Series on Finance (Rachev, 2003) of which WTZ is the series editor. On arrival I gave him a \$ 100 bill and he gave me a four inch wad of 25 Ruble notes, see the photo. Our dinner out cost two inches for the four of us; and drinks were extra in hard currency.

So we are in the Soros camp; make bets in Russia (or similar risky markets) if you have an edge without risking too much of your wealth.

Where was the money lost? The score card according to Dunbar (2000) was a loss of $4.6 billion. Emerging market trades such as those similar to the *buy Italy, sell Florence* lost $430 million. Directional, macro trades lost $371 million. Equity pairs trading lost 306 million. Short long term equity options, long short term equity lost $1.314 billion. Fixed income arbitrage lost $1.628 billion.

The bad scenario of investor confidence that led to much higher interest rates for lower quality debt and much higher implied equity volatility had a serious effect on all the trades. The long-short equity options trades, largely in the CAC40 and Dax equity indices, were based on a historical volatility of about 15 % versus implieds of about 22 %. Unfortunately, in the bad scenario, the implieds reached 30 % and then 40 %. With smaller positions, the fund could have waited it out but with such huge levered positions, it could not. Equity implieds can reach 70 % or higher as Japan's Nikkei did in 1990/1991 and stay there for many months.

12

The imported crash of
October 27 and 28, 1997

You must always be prepared for unpredictable mini crashes

The Asian Financial crises, a series of banking and currency crises developed in various Asian countries beginning in mid 1997. Many East and Southeast Asian countries had currency pegs to the US dollar which made it easy for them to attract financing but they lacked adequate foreign reserves to cover the outstanding debt. Their pegs to the US dollar and low interest rates encouraged mismatches in currency (debts were in US dollars, loans in local currency) and maturities (LT debts and ST assets). Spending and expectations that led to borrowing were too high and Japan, the main driver of these economies, was facing a consumer slowdown so its imports dropped. So that effectively these countries were long yen and short dollars. A large increase in the US currency in yen terms exacerbated the crisis, which began after speculators challenged the Thai Baht and spread through the region. The countries had to devalue their currencies, interest rates rose and stock prices fell. Also, several hedge funds took significant losses, most notably, Victor Niederhoffer's fund, which had an excellent previous record with only modest drawdowns. His large long bet on cheap Thai stocks that became cheaper and cheaper quickly turned $120 million into $70 million. Further buying on dips added to losses. finally the fund created a large short position in out-of-the-money S&P futures index puts including on the November 830's trading for about $4–$6 at various times around August-September 1997.

The crisis devastated the economies of Malaysia, Singapore, Indonesia, etc. Finally it spread to Hong Kong, where the currency was pegged to the US dollar at around 7.8. The peg supported Hong Kong's trade and investment hub and was to be defended at all costs. In this case, the weapon used was higher interest rates which almost always lead to a stock market crash after a lag. See the discussion in Chapter 23 for US and Japanese cases along with other countries. The US S&P500 was not in the danger zone in October 1997 by WTZ's models nor, we presume, by those of others. Trade with Hong Kong and Asia was substantial but only a small part of total US trade. Many US investors thought that this Asian currency crisis was a small problem because it did not affect Japan very much. In fact, Japan caused a lot of it.

A WEEK ON THE WILD SIDE

The week of October 20–25, 1997 was difficult for equity markets with the Hang Seng dropping sharply. The S&P was also shaky. The November 830 puts were 60 cents on Monday, Tuesday and Wednesday but rose to 1.20 on Thursday and 2.40 on Friday. The Hang Seng dropped over 20% in a short period including a 10% drop on Friday, October 25. The S&P500 was at 976 substantially above 830 as of Friday's close. A further 5% drop in Hong Kong on Monday, October 27 led to a panic in the S&P500 futures later on Monday in the US. They fell 7% from 976 to 906 which was still considerably above 830.

On Tuesday morning there was a further fall of 3 % to 876 still keeping the 830 puts out of the money. The full fall in the S&P500 was then 10 %.

But the volatility exploded and the 830's climbed to the $ 16 area. Refco called in Niederhoffer's puts mid morning on Tuesday, resulting in the fund losing about $ 20 million. So Niederhoffer's $ 70 million fund went bankrupt and actually in the red as the large position in these puts and other instruments turned the $ 70 million into minus $ 20 million. The S&P500 bottomed out around 876, moving violently in a narrow range then settling. By the end of the week, it returned to the 976 area. So it

The cartoon from *The Economist*. Reproduced by permission of Kevin Kallaugher (Kaltoons)

really was a tempest in a teapot like the cartoon from *The Economist* depicts. The November 830 puts expired worthless. Investors who were short equity November 830 puts (SPXs) were required to put up so much margin that had to have small positions and they weathered the storm. their $ 4–$ 6, while temporarily behind at $ 16 did eventually go to zero. So did the futures puts, but futures shorters are not required to post as much margin. If they did not have adequate margin because they had too many positions, They could have easily been forced to cover at a large loss. Futures margins, at least for equity index products, do not fully capture the real risk inherent in these positions. WTZ follows closely the academic studies on risk measures and none of the papers he knows addresses this issue properly. When in doubt, or in trouble, always bet less not more. Niederhoffer is back in business having profited by this experience. (Whoops – maybe not, see the postscript!)

One of our Vancouver neighbors, we learned later, lost $ 16 million in one account and $ 4 million in another account. The difference being the time given to cash out and cover the short puts. I was in this market also and won in the equity market and lost in futures. I did learn how much margin you actually need in futures which now I use in such trading which has been very profitable with a few proprietary wrinkles to protect oneself that I need to keep confidential. A hedged strategy had a 45 % geometric mean with 74 of 79 winners with six quarters ruled too risky by an option price market sentiment danger control measure out of the 85 possible plays in the 22+ years from September 2005 to June 2007 and a seven symmetric downside Sharpe ratio as discussed in Chapter 7. Ruling out the six risky quarters, one of the naked strategies won 78 out of 79 times. In those six risky quarters, the S&P500 actually fell in four. The cumulative S&P500 loss in the six quarters was −41.7 %.

The lessons for hedge funds are much as with LTCM. Do not overbet, do diversify, watch out for extreme scenarios. Even the measure to keep one out of potentially large falls mentioned above did not work in October 1997. That was an imported fear-induced stock market crash which was not really based on the US economy or investor sentiment. My

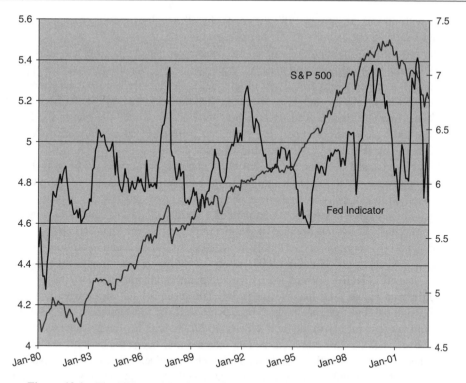

Figure 12.1 The FED model, 1980–2003. *Source*: Koivu, Pennanen and Ziemba (2005)

experience is that most crashes occur when interest rates relative to price earnings ratios are too high. Almost always when that happens there is a crash (a 10 % plus fall in equity prices from the current price level within one year), see Chapter 23 for the 1987 US, the 1990 Japan, and the US in 2000 are the leading examples as is the US in 2001, which predicted the 22 % fall in the S&P500 in 2002. Interestingly the measure moved out of the danger zone then, in mid 2001, it was even more in the danger zone than in 1999 because stock prices fell but earnings fell more. See Figure 12.1.

When long bond interest rates get too high relative to stock returns as measured by the earnings over price yield method then there almost always is a crash. Ziemba-Schwartz (1991) used a difference method and the results of that are in Ziemba (2003). Figure 12.1 here uses a ratio or log approach and is equivalent to what is now called the Fed model. I started using these measures in 1988 in my study group at Yamaichi Research, Japan. The study predicted the 1987 crash; see that on this graph. It also predicted the 1990 Japan crash. I told Yamaichi executives about this in 1989, but they would not listen. Yamaichi went bankrupt in 1995; they would have survived if they had listened to me.[1] We found for 1948 to 1988 that every time the measure was in the danger zone there was a fall of 10 %

---

[1] They could have paid WTZ a million dollars for an hour's consulting and still made more than 1000 times profit from the advice. It was more important for them to be nice to his family and him as they were than to listen to the results of a *gaijin* professor. How could he possibly understand the Japanese stock market? In fact all the economics ideas were there; see Ziemba and Schwartz (1991). WTZ did enjoy these lectures, dinners and golf but being listened to dominates.

or more with no misses. In late 1989 the model had the highest reading ever in the danger zone and predicted the January 1990 start of the crash.

In 1999 in the US, the measure entered the danger zone in April 1999 and subsequently the S&P500 fell in April 2000 and again in September 2000. Then the measure dropped out of the danger zone as prices fell. Then in late 2001, earnings fell more than prices so the measure went back into the danger zone and we had the 22 % plus fall in the S&P in 2002. In 2003, the measure then moved into the buy zone and predicted the rise in the S&P500 we had in 2003. No measure is perfect but this measure adds value and tends to keep you out of extreme trouble. This is discussed in Chapter 23.

A mini crash caused by some extraneous event can occur any time. So to protect oneself positions must *never* be too large. Koliman (1998) and Crouhy, Galai and Mark in Gibson's (2000) book on model risk discusses this. Their analysis suggests it was a violation of log-normality which I agree it was. Increased implied volatility premiums caused the huge losses of those who had to cash out because of margin calls because they had too many positions.

Some good references on hedge fund performance, risk and incentives follow for further reading. Kouwenberg and Ziemba (2007) using a continuous time model with a prospect theory S-shaped objective, where losses are more important than gains, study the effect of incentives on hedge fund manager behavior. The incentive fee encourages managers to take excessive risk but that risk tends to be much less if the fund manager has a substantial amount of their own money in the fund (at least 30 %). So look for funds where the managers *eat their own cooking.* Our empirical results indicate that hedge funds with incentive fees have higher downside risk than funds without such a compensation contract. Average net returns, both absolute and risk-adjusted, are significantly lower in the presence of incentive fees. So pick your managers well.

An incentive fee is tantamount to a call option on the value of the investor's assets. Goetzmann, Ingersoll and Ross (2003) and Kouwenberg and Ziemba (2007) show how to calculate the value of that option. The value depends directly on the manager's optimal investment style with values ranging from 17 % (with no investment) to 0 % (with 30 % + share) of the investor's capital.

In Chapter 21 we formulate some stochastic programming models and discuss pension fund, as well as hedge fund, applications. Wallace and Ziemba (2005) provides background on how to make such models and Ziemba (2003) explains enough about these models to hire someone to make one for you. Ziemba and Mulvey (1998) describe many such existing models for insurance, pension fund and other applications. The Lo (1999, 2001) and Merton (2000ab) papers set the stage for the stochastic programming models by discussing the issues.

POSTSCRIPT

The best way to achieve victory is to master all the rules for disaster, and then concentrate on avoiding them
In America, people get a second change . . . they don't get a third.

Victor Niederhoffer

After Niederhoffer's failure in 1997, his fund was closed and he lost much of his personal fortune, reputation. He had failed in 1997 because he greatly overbet and did not diversify and a bad scenario wiped him out. Was this a one time occurrence from which he learned or is it just one of a sequence of similar outcomes? Niederhoffer is a multi-talented individual who graduated with a PhD in 1969 from the Graduate School of Business, at the University of Chicago where Professors Gene Fama and Merton Miller and other great finance theorists and practitioners are on the faculty. Since his work was against the prevailing efficient markets theory and highly data dependent, he was more comfortable with the statisticians and was supervised by perhaps the world's top Bayesian statistician, Arnold Zellner. Earlier at Harvard, his senior thesis 'non randomness in stock prices: a new model of price movements' challenged random walk theory. He argued that stocks followed patterns such as Monday falls if Friday fell.

In 1967, before his PhD thesis was finished and with the title 'top US squash player', he headed to the finance department of the University of California, Berkeley business school. I was there then as well but, as a busy graduate student, never met Niederhoffer. Victor was also a whiz at chess and tennis, dating back to his Harvard undergraduate days. I was friendly with one finance legend Professor Barr Rosenberg who went on to greatness in a number of investment areas such as founding the Berkeley Program in Finance, the firm BARRA and later Rosenberg Investments. Both Barr and Victor, like me, were looking for anomalies to beat markets. Barr discovered that small caps and low price to book stocks out performed work that 25 years later in 1992 formed the basis for the famous Fama-French (1992) factors. While Barr stuck to institutional investing with low or no leverage, Victor was a high stakes futures trader using lots of leverage. Hence, if he was right, then the gains were very high but if he was wrong and his risk control was faulty, then there could be substantial losses.

While teaching at Berkeley, Victor co-founded a small investment bank, Niederhoffer, Cross and Zeckhauser (NCZ). Frank Cross was a former Merrill Lynch executive and Richard Zeckhauser, a friend from his Harvard days. Zeckhauser went to become a well known economist at the Kennedy School of Government and an avid bridge player. NCZ started with just $400 and did mail-order mergers, and sold small private companies to buyers. In 1979, Niederhoffer went into commodities and had great success, averaging 35% net for 15 years through the mid 1990s. George Soros gave him a private $100 million account in 1981 and Niederhoffer traded that until 1993. That was shut down because, as Soros said, 'he temporarily lost his edge . . . he made money while the markets were sloshing along aimlessly. Then he started losing money and had the integrity to close out the account. We came out ahead'. Earlier in 1983 Zeckhauser had quit NCZ to return to full time teaching and research partially because of Niederhoffer's high level of risk taking, saying that 'no matter what your edge, you can lose everything. You hope and believe he will learn his lesson'. Cross died and NCZ is now called Niederhoffer Henkel and is run by Lee Henkel, the former general council for the IRS.

After the 1997 blowout, it was hard for Niederhoffer to start again as there was fear of another large drawdown despite his long superior track record. So he began trading on his own account after mortgaging his house. In 2000 he started writing investment columns on websites with Laurel Kenner and in 2001 it paid off. Mustafa Zaida, a Middle East investor set up the offshore hedge fund Matador with $2 million with Niederhoffer as the trading advisor. To reign in Niederhoffer's exuberance for risk, the fund would invest only in US based S&P500 futures and options. The claim was that Niederhoffer had learned his lesson not to invest in markets he did not understand like Thailand which had set him on the road to destruction in 1997. A management fee of 2.5 + 22 was substantial. Yet with good performance, Matador grew to $350 million from non-US investors. Zaida said that 'He's definitely learned his lesson'. Recall that it was the S&P500 November largely 830 puts that turned $70 million into −$20 million in 1997 after $50 million was lost in Thai

Table 12.1 Performance of the Matador Fund, February 2002–April 2006 and Manchester Fund from March 2005–May 2007. First line is Assets where available, MM, second line is Monthly Return. *Source*: Manchester Trading, LLC (2006, 2007)

	JAN	FEB	MAR	APR	MAY	JUNE	JUL	AUG	SEP	OCT	NOV	DEC	YRTTL
Matador Fund													
2006	261.24	280.26	304.72	346									
	9.59 %	6.46 %	7.58 %	4.70 %									
2005	112.24	123.72	125.72	122.02	132.43	139.59	149.88	151.81	164.34	194.05	219.11	236.75	236.75
	1.87 %	3.76 %	1.62 %	−12.70 %	20.66 %	5.40 %	7.72 %	1.29 %	8.25 %	−5.42 %	10.05 %	6.59 %	56.28 %
2004	56.37	54.83	56.85	60.21	61.96	63.3	65.28	67.49	75.02	77.95	105.28	110.17	110.17
	1.22 %	8.35 %	0.20 %	5.17 %	4.04 %	2.15 %	3.22 %	3.38 %	2.98 %	3.90 %	3.26 %	3.67 %	50.13 %
2003	21.15	31.13	35.17	40.46	41.9	42.94	45.26	46.11	46.44	49.18	50.08	55.69	55.69
	2.47 %	7.70 %	1.65 %	1.76 %	3.54 %	2.48 %	4.75 %	1.32 %	0.52 %	5.91 %	1.21 %	1.48 %	40.55 %
2002		2.03	2.92	3.64	5.5	11.81	8.65	8.12	8.88	10.22	10.66	12.54	12.54
		1.71 %	2.71 %	−0.65 %	10.01 %	−1.16 %	−30.22 %	−6.81 %	9.29 %	15.20 %	3.55 %	7.86 %	3.12 %
Manchester Fund													
2007	20.20 %	−18.31 %	8.21 %	21.20 %	12.00 %								
2006	13.9	15.90	17.32	n/a	n/a	n/a	n/a	n/a	n/a	n/a	n/a	n/a	n/a
	10.61 %	7.44 %	8.24 %	3.28 %	−25.74 %	−7.86 %	−26.83 %	−7.88 %	19.99 %	34.29 %	0.79 %	0.04 %	−0.45 %
2005	n/a	n/a	2	1.94	2.72	4.4	4.73	5.86	6.6	7.82	8.99	11.07	1.07
	n/a	n/a	n/a	−3.10 %	11.68 %	4.09 %	7.50 %	−0.59 %	9.69 %	−4.36 %	14.98 %	5.53 %	53.23 %

equities. Niederhoffer always thinks big and bold so Matador was not enough. So in April 2005 Niederhoffer started Manchester Partners, LLC for US investors. Manchester for the Silver Cup given to the winner of the Manchester Cup Steeplechase in 1904. This trophy was one of the many art objects Niederhoffer has collected over the years and hung onto. Manchester's fees were 1 + 20, and could trade other than the S&P500 market such as fixed income and currencies. Steve 'Mr Wiz' Wisdom was Niederhoffer's risk control aide, hoping to have consistent 25 % + returns with maximum monthly losses of 15–20 %.

The bond-stock crash measure, see Chapters 23 and 25, flagged a red signal in late 2001 because earnings dropped more than stock prices. Also, my confidential investor sentiment model based on relative put/call option prices flashed red in Q4 of 2002. And indeed there was a substantial fall in the S&P500 in July 2002; Matador lost 30.22 % in that month.

Still, the February 2002 to April 2006 Matador record was a +338 % gain, 41 % net annualized, $ 350 million in assets and only 5 losses in 51 months, with a 2.81 Sharpe ratio, see Figure 12.2 and Table 12.1. This record earned Matador the number 1 ranking in 2004, 2005 and 2006 for funds managing $ 50 + million, see Table 12.2.

Manchester had only three monthly losses in the 13 months from its start in April 2005 to April 2006, a cumulative gain of 89.9 %. The approach, they said, has the following elements (from Manchester Trading, 2006):

Scientific   Rigorous statistical methodologies form the foundation of our proprietary pattern recognition process.

Empirical   *What can be tested, must be tested*. Validation through testing is the basis for all trade recommendations, impact planning and margin assessment.

Innovative   Multidisciplinary inquiry draws from such diverse fields as speech processing, information theory, and data compression to provide insight and inspiration.

Contrarian   Crowd behavior tends to create profitable opportunities. We are more often than not counter trend traders.

Focused   Undiluted application of our edge leaves the critical diversification decision in the hands of our investors.

For short term discretionary day trading:

- Systematic identification of high probability trades.
- Analysis across multiple markets & multiple time frames.

Table 12.2   Ranking of Manchester Trading. *Source*: Manchester Trading, LLC (2006)

2006	#1 performing CTA MarHedge MAPA
2005	#1 offshore managed futures fund (Tass/Lipper) for funds managing more than $ 50 million.
2004	#1 offshore managed futures (Tass/Lipper) for funds managing more than $ 50 million.
	Cumulative +338 % since inception Feb 2002: Assets under management $ 350+ million

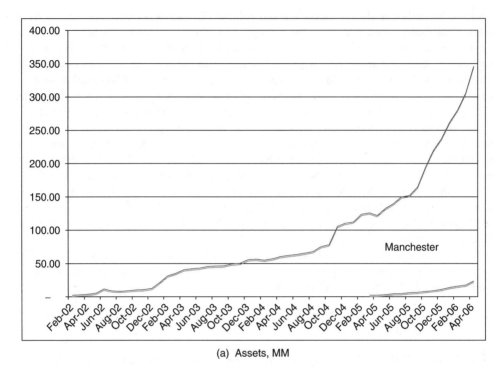

(a) Assets, MM

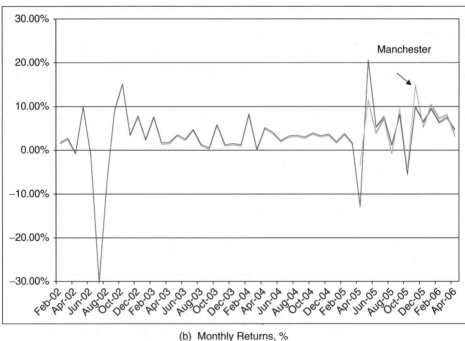

(b) Monthly Returns, %

Figure 12.2 Performance of the Matador Fund, February 2002–April 2006 and Manchester Fund from March 2005–April 2006. *Source*: Manchester Trading, LLC (2006)

- Flexible analytical methodology sensitive to changing cycles.
- Tactical execution reduces friction and slippage.

And for the option trading:

- Empirical option pricing vs. implied volatility method.
- Strategic/opportunistic seller of expensive premium.
- Forecasting techniques applied to margin pathways enhances risk modeling.
- Flexible position across multiple strikes and timeframes.
- Highly sensitive ongoing measurement of overall liquidity and margin pathway forecasting refines leverage assessment.

And what did they learn from the 1997 blowout:

- We learned our lesson and got back on our feet **fast**.
- We stick with markets and instruments we know.
- We focus on liquidity.
- We are alert to the increasing probability of extreme events, measure their potential impact and prepare for them.
- We implement safeguards and continue to refine trading and risk assessment procedures to ensure survival.

They say it cannot happen again because:

- We tailor our risk profile at all times cognizant of the impact and opportunity extreme events can bring about.
- We are constantly innovating but remain focused on what works empirically. We don't stray from our core strategy.
- Substantial co-investment by the principals of the firm is the most powerful statement we can possibly make with regard to our long term commitment to our partners.

Manchester does not like to diversify and their literature says that:

> We choose not to diversify or manage the volatility of our fund to a benchmark or index as we believe our clients and their asset allocation advisors are in a far better position to make accurate and economical diversification decisions than we are.
>
> (Manchester, 2006)

Niederhofer has historically had a long bias in his trades which are frequently unhedged with 3–6 items leverage with borrowed money.

On May 10, 2006 the Russian New Europe (RNE) fund, was trading at a 37 % premium to net asset value according the *Barron's*. RNE treated me well over the years with high returns and generous capital gains and dividends. But a 37 % premium was extraordinary. The bond-stock model and the short term investor sentiment option models I use were both way out of the danger zone and did not predict the subsequent decline. That weekend was a local peak and the S&P500 fell about 7 % in the next month with many emerging markets falling 20 % +. RNE fell more about 40 % to a no premium level. The twig that got the equity markets going on the downside was the threat of higher Japanese interest

Table 12.3 Manchester Partners net returns in various time periods versus the S&P500

Recent Returns	Latest Month	Last 3 Months	Last 6 Months	Last 12 Months	Last 18 Months	Inception 5-Apr
Partners	20.44 %	21.44 %	80.26 %	8.40 %	51.72 %	83.72 %
S&P500	1.65 %	4.38 %	12.66 %	12.36 %	17.86 %	21.82 %

rates. This caused some hedge funds with yen carry trades to unwind their positions which meant selling the S&P500 and emerging market equities. It also caused them to look closer at high-yielding emerging market currencies and bonds such as Turkey, South Africa and Iceland. Although these have high yields, thus making them attractive for Carry trades, they also have high current account deficits. Investors feared both higher interest rates and a higher yen in which they had short positions.

The Matador fund lost 25.74 % in May turning a 2006 gain of 31 % to −6 % at the end of May. The market was down 3 % but Niederhoffer was so leveraged that the loss was magnified ten times to some $100 million. This, a hedge ratio of 10, which means that Niederhoffer must have been massively long S&P500 futures and/or short S&P500 equity and/or futures puts. This is a huge long position that is not risk control safe and subject to large losses with a modest drop in the S&P500. A medium S&P500 drop, see below, would likely have led to losses around 50 % and a large 10 % + drop to losses of 75 % +. Niederhoffer said 'I had a bad May. I made some mistakes, that's regrettable ... but one sparrow does not make a spring; and nor does one bad month'. June 2006 continued badly and so did July and August; see Table 12.1 with the Matador fund 0.45 % for 2006. When the May to July debacle in the S&P500 ended it was down about 7 % but Matador lost 67 % and Manchester 45 %. Both funds are still trading and the saga continues, see Table 12.1 and the discussion below. WTZ maintains the two rules: do not overbet and do diversify in **all** scenarios. One can still make good gains in the S&P500 futures and options and other markets. But somewhat smaller than 30–40 % gains are most likely but presumably without blowouts if one has position sizes such that the fund or account will weather a 3–7 % decline in 1–4 days or a 10–15 % decline over a month.

My experience is that with proper risk control in the S&P500 market, which is not diversified, one can yield net gains in the 15 % to perhaps 25 % range. 30–40 % seems attainable only with substantial risk that likely will cause a large loss if a bad scenario occurs. Of course, other strategies could yield such higher returns as Blair Hull, Jim Simons and others have shown.

Niederhoffer was given a third and fourth chance after all! Table 12.3 shows the Manchester Partners returns to the end of January 2007, and Table 12.1 shows that up to May 2007, the fund was up 43.04 % in 2007 and 118.20 % since inception versus 7.64 % and 29.65 %, respectively for the S&P500.

The May to July 2006 blowout is seen in the 8.4 % returns in the 12 months to January 2007 in Table 12.3 then down from 89.9 % as of April 2006. But the fund gained 20.20 % in January 2007 and the April 2005 to end January 2007 net returns were back to 83.72 %, well above the S&P500. So Niederhoffer is back in business once again...perhaps till the next time. He is an investor for those grown ups who enjoyed roller coasters as kids. WTZ will stick to the Thorp model though.

13

The 2006 Amaranth Advisors natural gas hedge fund disaster

Its even optimal to bet the ranch

On September 19, 2006 the hedge fund Amaranth Advisors of Greenwich, Connecticut announced that it had lost $6 billion, about two thirds of the $9.25 billion fund, in less than two weeks, largely because it was overexposed in the natural gas market. The Greenwich, Connecticut fund was founded in 2000, employed hundreds in a large investment space with other offices in Toronto, London and Singapore. Amaranth's experience shows how a series of trades can undermine the strategy of such a hedge fund. In this chapter, we analyse how Amaranth became so overexposed, whether risk control strategies could have

prevented the liquidation and how these trends reflect the current state of the financial industry.

In previous chapters we have argued that the recipe for hedge fund disaster almost always has three parts: A trader:

1. overbets relative to one's capital; and the volatility of the trading instruments used;
2. is not diversified in all scenarios that could occur; and
3. a negative scenario occurs that is plausible ex post and likely ex ante although the negative outcome may have never occurred before in the particular markets the fund is trading.

One might expect that these two interrelated risk factors (1) and (2) would be part of the risk control assessment of hedge funds. These risks become more pronounced as the total amount traded grows – especially when traded billons. But are risks assessed in this way?

A knowledgeable risk control expert, realizing that the position is not fully diversified and that you need scenario dependent correlation matrices, would simply tell the traders that they cannot hold positions (1) and (2) since in some scenarios they will have large losses. Efficient market types have a lot to learn about real risk control. Hedges are not essentially risk free. Even a simple model would say that bets should not be made under conditions (1) and (2) because they are far too dangerous. Medium sized hedge funds are likely reasonably adequately diversified. Some type of risk control process is now standard but these systems are mostly based on the industry standard value at risk (VAR) and that is usually not enough protection in (3) as the penalty for large losses is not great enough.

On occasion, even at a large fund, a rogue trader will have such a successful trading run that careful risk control is no longer applied. Instead, people focus on the returns generated, the utility function of the trader and that of the partners of the fund, rather than the longer-term utility function of the investors in the fund. Rogue trades – those that violate (1) and (2) – can be taken as long as (3) never occurs. In the case of Amaranth's natural gas bets, their lever-

Amaranth headquarters, Greenwich, Connecticut

age was about 8:1 so $ 7 was borrowed for every $ 1 the fund had from its clients. Positions were on exchanges and over the counter and were thus very vulnerable. Those not skilled in risk control can argue that situation (3) great enough to wipe them out, simply would not occur because it is far too improbable, that is too far in the tails of the distribution of the underlying asset. They would typically assign zero to the probability of such rare events.

Even skilled risk control experts such as Jorion (2006) and Till (2006) refer to LTCM as an 8-sigma event and Amaranth as a 9-sigma event. The problem is that even modified VAR gives erroneous results and is not safe. Such wipeouts occur with events far more frequent than 8 or 9 sigma: 3-sigma is more like it. Till (2006) argues that daily volatility of Amaranth's portfolio was 2 %, making the September losses 9-sigma, but the possible losses are not stationary. We argue that this analysis is misleading; the 2 % is with typical not negative low probability disaster scenarios. Furthermore, diversification can easily fail, if, as is typical, it is based on simply averaging the past data rather than with scenario dependent correlation matrices. It is the diversification or lack thereof according to the given scenario that is crucially important, not the average past correlation across the assets in the portfolio.

Figures 13.1–13.5 illustrate the nature of the natural gas market. Figure 13.1(a) shows crude oil prices from November 1, 2005 to November 28, 2006. This shows much volatility with prices usually above $ 60 and at times exceeding the August 30 2005 post Katrina high of $ 70+. The oil prices peaked at $ 77 in July 2006 then declined to around $ 60 where they stayed for much of the fall. The price of natural gas also fell in their period. At that time, widely watched weather-forecasting centers predicted that the hurricane season would not have major storms and that the winter would be mild. Previously on August 29, September natural gas suddenly rose sharply in the last half hour of trading. Why is not known – but manipulation might have been involved. For Hunter, who was short September and long spring months, both events caused massive losses.

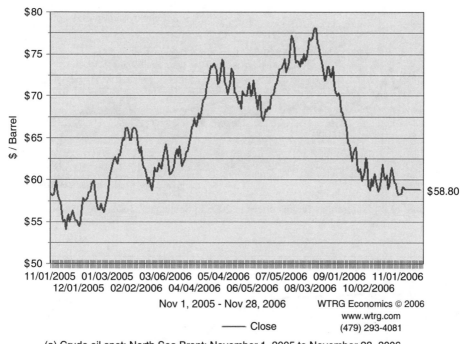

(a) Crude oil spot: North Sea Brent; November 1, 2005 to November 28, 2006

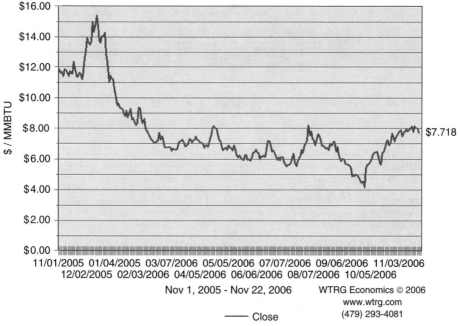

(b) NYMEX natural gas futures close, November 1, 2005 to November 22, 2006

Figure 13.1   Energy prices November 2005 to November 2006

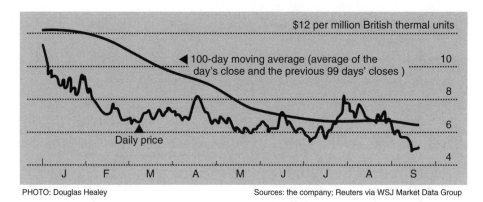

Figure 13.2   Natural gas futures prices in 2006 to September. *Source*: Wall Street Journal

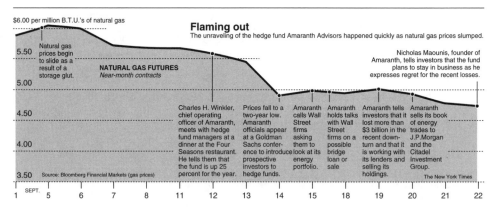

Figure 13.3   Amaranth timeline of a collapse. *Source*: New York Times, Sept 23, 2006

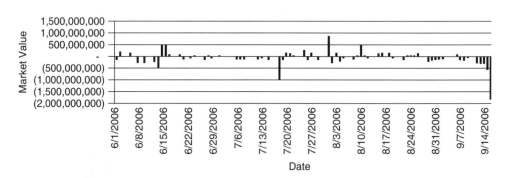

Figure 13.4   Daily change in P/L from Amaranth inferred natural gas positions, June 1 to September 15, 2006. *Source*: Till (2006)

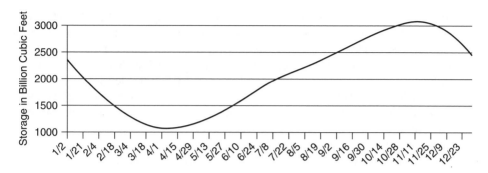

Figure 13.5 Average US natural gas inventories in BCF over the year, 1994–2005. *Source*: Till (2006)

Figure 13.2 shows natural gas futures prices in 2006. Starting from over $11/million BTU, the futures prices fell to about $5. The event that triggered the Amaranth crisis was the drop in the price of natural gas from $8 in mid July to around $5 in September. Since gas prices have climbed to $15 and fallen to $2 in recent years, such a drop is plausible in one's scenario set and should have been considered. There are fat tails in these markets. There is a large difference between the daily and long-term moving average price of natural gas, making it a very volatile commodity. Thus such a drop is not a 8–9 sigma event. In the 1990s, natural gas traded for $2–3 per million BTUs. However, by the end of 2000 it reached $10 and then by September 2001 fell back to under $2. Figure 13.1(b) shows the NYMEX natural gas futures prices from November 1, 2005 to November 22, 2006 which like Figure 13.1(a) shows much price volatility. The November 22 price of $7.718 had recovered 50% from the September lows.

Figure 13.3 shows a chronology of the collapse and Figure 13.4 presents a day-by-day recreation of Amaranth's possible losses including the disastrous last two months and final collapse (a loss of $560 million on September 14, 2006) by Till (2006). Davis, Zuckerman and Sender (2007) discuss the bailout saga and some of the winners and losers. They describe how Amaranth scrambled to unload their positions that were losing more and more day by day:

Sept 16   Agreed to pay Merrill Lynch approximately $250 million to take over some positions.

Sept 17   Agreed to pay Goldman $185 billion.

Sept 18   Gave up on Goldman deal when clearing agent J.P. Morgan would not release collateral.

Sept 20   Paid J.P. Morgan and Citadel $2.15 billion to take remaining trades after Amaranth absorbed a further $800 million in trading losses.

Valuing a fund

Actually the statement that Amaranth had $9.25 billion on September 1 is a bit of a stretch because that was the mark-to-the-market value of their portfolio, the value on which fees were charged. But, in fact, with an estimated 250 000+ natural gas contracts (about 30% of the market), an enormous position built up over the previous two years, the liquidating value of the portfolio was lower even before (3), the crisis. As a comparison, in his heyday in the

1990s, a large position for legendary hedge fund trader George Soros of the Quantum Fund was 5000 contracts. Even with one contract you can lose a lot of money: up to $20 000 in a few days. Indeed much of the previous profits were derived by pushing up of long natural gas prices in an illiquid market. WTZ once had 7 % of the ValueLine/S&P500 spread futures market while playing the January effect (see Chapter 2). Even at that level it is very difficult to get out should the market turn on you. With those January effect trades, one has a fairly well defined exit point and the futures cannot deviate too much from the cash spread but even that level is too high and risky.

So the real profits were actually much lower. Those who liquidated Amaranth's positions bought them at a substantial discount. J.P. Morgan Chase, Amaranth's natural gas clearing broker made at least $725 million after taking over most of Amaranth's positions (Davis et al, 2007). Of course, with different data forecasts such discrepancies might still occur occasionally but if they are consistently there, assumptions or risk assessments may be questioned.

The trigger for the crisis was a substantial drop in natural gas prices largely because of high levels of stored gas, coupled with an perceived drop in demand due to changing weather, altering the seasonal pattern of trade. The trading theory was based on the dubious assumption that the natural gas market would underprice winter from summer natural gas prices.

BACKGROUND

The natural gas market has two main seasons: high demand in winter and generally low demand in spring and fall. Storage facilitates provide some smoothing of the price. However, in the US, there is inadequate storage capacity for the peak winter demand. Therefore, the winter natural gas contracts trade at ever increasing premiums in summer and fall months to both encourage storage and the creation of more production and storage capacity. Basically the market tries to lock in the value of storage by buying summer and fall natural gas and selling winter natural gas forward. This section is adapted from and expands on Till (2006).

The prices of summer and fall futures contracts typically trade at a discount to the winter contracts (*contango*) thus providing a return for storing natural gas. An owner of a storage facility can buy summer natural gas and simultaneously sell winter natural gas via the futures markets. This difference is the operator's return for storage.

When the summer futures contract matures, the storage operator can take delivery of the natural gas, and inject it into storage. Later when the winter futures contract matures, the operator can make delivery of the natural gas by drawing it out of storage. Figure 13.5 shows the average build-up of inventories over the year. As long as the operator's financing and physical outlay costs are under the spread locked in through the futures market, this will be profitable. This is a simplified version of how storage operators can choose to monetize their physical assets. Sophisticated storage operators actually value their storage facilities as an option on calendar-spreads. Storage is worth more if the calendar spreads in natural gas are volatile. As a calendar spread trades in steep contango, storage operators can buy the near-month contracts and sell the further-out month contracts, knowing that they can ultimately realize the value of this spread through storage. But a preferable scenario would be for the spread to then tighten, which means that they can trade out of the spread as a profit. Later if the spread trades in wide contango again, they can reinitiate a purchase of the near-month versus far-month natural gas spread. As long as the spread is volatile, the operator/trader can continually lock in profits, and if they cannot trade out of the spread at a profit, they can then take physical delivery and realize the value of their storage facility that way. Till (2006) believes that both storage operators and natural gas producers were the ultimate counterparties to Amaranth's spread trading.

In the winter, natural gas demand is inelastic. If cold weather comes early then there is fear that there will not be enough storage so prices are bid up. The fear of inadequate supplies lasts for the entire heating season. Winter 2005 was an example. At the end of the winter, storage could be completely depleted. For example during February to March 2003, prices had moved up intraday $ 5.00 /MMBtu, but settled only $ 2.50 higher, which is why Amaranth hoped for a long winter. As a weak hedge they short the summer (Apr-Oct). Demand for injection gas is spread throughout the summer and peak usage for electricity demand occurs in July/Aug. Being more elastic, this part of the curve does not rise as fast as the winter in a upward moving market. This was their hedge.

The National Weather Service issued an *el nino* forecast for the 2006–7 winter so gas storage was at an all-time record and the spreads were out very wide. This plus the fact that the market basically knew about Amaranth's positions, led to their downfall, which was a result of their faulty risk control.

THE TRADE AND THE ROGUE TRADER

Let's take a closer look at the trade that destabilized Amaranth. Brian Hunter, a 32 year old Canadian from Calgary, had fairly simple trades but of enormous size. He had a series of successful returns. As a youth in Alberta he could not afford ski tickets but at 24, with training as an instant expert on derivatives from courses at the University of Alberta (including ones from two colleagues), he headed to a trading career. He was bold and innovative with nerves of steel while holding enormous positions. Typically he was net long with long positions in natural gas in the winter months (November to March) and short positions in the summer months (April to October).

Amaranth Advisors was a multi-strategy fund, which is quite fashionable these days since they only have one layer of fees rather than the two layers in a fund of funds. On their website it states: 'Amaranth's investment professionals deploy capital in a broad spectrum of alternative investment and trading strategies in a highly disciplined, risk-controlled manner.' They provide a false sense of security from the assumed diversification across strategies. The problem is that diversification strategies can be correlated rather than hedged or independent, especially in extreme scenario cases. As a result, too much can be invested in any one strategy negating diversification. In the case of Amaranth, some 58 % of assets were tied up in Hunter's gas trades but risk adjusted, these trades made up 70–90 % of Amaranth's capital allocation.

Hunter made huge profits for Amaranth by placing bullish bets on natural gas prices in 2005, the year Hurricane Katrina shocked natural gas refining and production. Hoping to repeat the gains, Amaranth wagered with a 8:1 leverage that the difference between the March and April futures price of natural gas for 2007 and 2008 would widen. Instead it narrowed. The spread between April and March 2007 contracts went from $ 2.49 at the end of August 2006 to $ 0.58 by the end of September 2006. Historically, the spread in future prices for the March and April contracts have not been easily predictable. The spread is dependent on meteorological and political events whose uncertainty makes the placing of such large bets a precarious matter (Wikipedia, 2006).

Jack Doueck of Stillwater Capital pointed out that while a good hedge fund investor has to pick good funds to invest in, the key to success in this business is not to choose the best performing managers, but actually to avoid the frauds and blowups. Frauds can take on various forms including a misappropriation of funds, as in the case of Cambridge, run by John Natale out of Red Bank, NJ, or a mis-reporting of returns as in the case of Lipper, or Beacon Hill, or the Manhattan Fund. Blowups usually occur when a single person at the hedge fund has the power to become desperate and *bet the ranch* with leverage. With both frauds and blowups, contrary to public opinion (and myth), size does *not* seem matter: examples are Beacon Hill ($ 2 billion), Lipper ($ 5 billion), and Amaranth ($ 9 billion).

Amaranth's investors will be seeking answers to questions including: to what extent did leverage and concentration play a role in recent out-sized losses? We think the latter; (1) and (2) are the main causes here of the setup before the bad scenario caused the massive losses.

IS LEARNING POSSIBLE?

Do traders and researchers really learn from their trading errors? Some do but many do not. Or more precisely, do they care? What lessons are taken from the experience? Hunter previously worked for Deutsche Bank. In December 2003 his natural gas trading group was up $ 76 million for the year. Then it lost $ 51.2 million in a single week leading to Hunter's departure from the Deutsche Bank. Then Hunter blamed 'an unprecedented and unforeseeable run-up in gas prices'. At least he thought about extreme scenarios. Later in a lawsuit, he argued that while Deutsche Bank had losses, his group did not.

Later in July 2006, after having billion dollar swings in his portfolio (January to April +$ 2B), −$ 1B in May when prices for autumn delivery fell, +$ 1B in June – he said that 'the cycles that play out in the oil market can take several years, whereas in natural gas, cycles are several months'. The markets are unpredictable but most successful traders would lower their bets in such markets. Our experience is that when you start losing, you are better off taking money off the table not doubling up in the hope of recouping the losses. It is better to lose some resources and be able to survive then to risk being fully wiped out. However, instead they increased the bets.

Amaranth was a favorite of hedge funds of funds, investment pools that buy into various portfolios to try to minimize risk. Funds of funds operated by well known and successful investment firms Morgan Stanley, Credit Suisse, Bank of New York, Deutsche Bank and Man Investments all had stakes in Amaranth as of June 30, 2006. From September 2000 to November 30, 2005, the compound annual return to investors, net of all costs was a decent, but not impressive, 14.72 %. This is net of their 1.5 % management fee and 20 % of the net new profits. Amaranth had liquidated a significant part of its positions in relatively easy to sell securities like convertible bonds, leveraged loans and blank check companies or special purpose acquisition companies. Liquid investments were sold at a small discount while others, like portfolios of mortgage-backed securities, commanded a steeper discount.

As is common among hedge funds, Amaranth severely restricts the ability of investors to cash in their holdings. For example, investors could withdraw money only on the anniversary of their investments and then, only with 90 days' notice. If they try to withdraw at any point outside that time frame there is a 2.5 % penalty. If investors redeem more than 7.5 % of the fund's assets, Amaranth can refuse further withdrawals.

My experience is that if you lose 50 % of a $ 2 million fund, you will have a hard time relocating to a new fund or raising new money, but if you lose 50 % of $ 2 billion the job/fund prospects are much better. So Hunter moved on to Amaranth whose founder and chief executive, Nick Maounis, said on August 11, 2006, that more than a dozen members of his risk management team served as a check on his star gas trader: 'what Brian is really, really good at is taking controlled and measured risk'. Nick will forever eat these words.

Amaranth said they had careful risk control but they did not really use it. Some 50 % of assets in one volatile market is not really very diversified at any time and is especially vulnerable in a crash and doubly so if one's bets make up a large percentage of the market. Such a large position is especially dangerous when the other traders in the market know a fund is overextended in this way and many hedge funds such as Citadel and J.P. Morgan were on the other side of the market. Then, when the crisis occurred, spreads widened, adding to the losses. Hunter's response was to bet more and more (in effect doubling up) until these trades lost so much they had to be liquidated. That is exactly what one should not do based on risk control considerations, but, as discussed below, it makes some sense with traders' utility functions.

Successful traders make a large number of hopefully independent favorable bets which, although they may involve a lot of capital, are not a large percentage of the capital nor are they in on illiquid market should one need to liquidate. Warren Buffett's Berkshire Hathaway closed end hedge fund frequently makes $ 1 billion risky bets but these have a substantial edge (positive expected value) and about 1 % or less of Berkshire Hathaway's more than 140 billion capital. A typical Buffett trade was a loan of some $ 945 million to the Williams pipeline company of Oklahoma at some 34 % interest in 2002 during the stock market crash, when the oil price was low and the pipeline company was in deep financial trouble. Banks refused to bail them out. But Buffett knew he had good collateral with the land, pipeline and buildings. Williams recovered largely due to this investment and better markets and paid off the loan early and Berkshire Hathaway made a large profit.

The problem is that rogue traders are grown in particular organizations and are allowed by the industry. While they are winning, they are called great traders, then they become rogue traders when they blow up their funds. The Hunter case is similar to those of Nick Leeson and Victor Niedorhoffer but different than Long Term Capital Management (LTCM). In the first three cases, there was a major emphasis on trade in one basic commodity. The trouble was the risk control, namely our (1) and (2) and combined with the bad scenario (3). As discussed below the firm's and rogue trader's utility function likely caused this problem by making it optimal for these utility functions to over bet. LTCM is much more subtle. The confidence scenario that hit them was the result of faulty risk control based on VAR and historical data. They needed scenario dependent correlation matrices like those discussed in Chapter 21.

POSSIBLE UTILITY FUNCTIONS OF HEDGE FUND TRADERS

One way to rank investors is by the symmetric downside Sharpe ratio (DSSR) as discussed in Chapter 6. By that measure, investors with few and small losses and good sized gains have large DSSRs. Berkshire Hathaway has a DSSR of about 0.90. The Harvard and Ford Foundations endowments are about 1.0. The highest we have seen is Thorp's Princeton Newport's 1969–88 DSSR of 13.8. Those with high DSSRs have smooth wealth curves. For example, Figure 6.3 which is from a futures account run from January 1, 2002 to

December 29, 2006 for a personal account of the second author run very carefully with strict risk control and trades with advantages.

This is not a utility function but the results of the choices made using a utility function. Those who want high DSSRs are investors trying to have smooth returns with good returns with low volatility and very few losses. Thorp only had three monthly losses in 20 years; the Harvard and Ford endowments and Berkshire Hathaway have 2–3–4 per year.

Consider a rogue trader's utility function.[1] The outcome probabilities are:

1. x % of the time the fund blows up and loses 40 %+ of its value at some time; the trader is fired and gets another trading job keeping most past bonuses.
2. y % of the time the fund has modest returns of 15 % or less; then the trader receives a salary but little or no bonus.
3. z % of the time the fund has large returns of 25 % to 100 %; then the trader gathers more assets to trade and large bonuses.

At all times the rogue trader is in (1) and (2), that is, the total positions are overbet and not diversified and move markets. There is no plan to exit the strategy since it is assumed that trades can be made continuously. Then in a multiperiod or continuous time model it may well be that for the fund managers and traders specific utility functions that it is optimal to take bets that provide enormous gains in some scenarios and huge losses in other scenarios. Kouwenberg and Ziemba (2006) show that in a theoretical continuous time model with incentives, risk taking behavior is greatly moderated if the hedge fund manager's stake in the fund is 30 % or more.

In the case of Amaranth and similar rogue trading situations, there are additional complications such as the fund manager's utility function and his wealth stake inside this fund and outside it. Then there is the rogue trader's utility function and his wealth inside and outside the fund. According to Aumann (2005) in his Nobel lecture: a person's behavior is rational if it is in his best interests given his information. Aumann further endorses the late Yale Nobel James Tobin's belief that economics is all about incentives. In the case of Hunter, his share of $ 1B plus gains (real or booked) was in the $ 100 million range. What's interesting, and this is similar to LTCM, is that these traders continue and increase bets when so much is already in the bank. Recall in LTCM, that they had a $ 100 million unsecured loan to invest in their fund. Finally, in such analyses, one must consider the utility functions and constraints of the other investors' money. In the case of Amaranth, Deutsche Bank who had first hand knowledge of Hunter's previous trading blowups, was an investor along with other well known firms.

WINNERS AND LOSERS

Who are the winners and losers here? Hunter is a winner and will get relocated soon. He has hundreds of millions, having made about $ 75 million in 2005 (out of his team's $ 1.26 billion profit), and will likely make more later. Of course, his reputation is tarnished but $ 100+ million in fees over the years helps. Like many others, Hunter had to leave 30 % of this in the fund so some of the $ 75 million was lost. There might be some lawsuits but he likely will not be hurt much. At 32, he is set for life financially, despite the losses.

---

[1] An academic treatment of a rogue trader is in Ziemba and Ziemba (2007). Here we sketch some ideas.

He is likely to begin again. An executive recruiter has offered to help introduce Hunter to investors. He sees opportunities for Hunter to make a fresh start with high-net-worth investors, possibly in Russia and the Middle East.[2] Betting on fallen hedge-fund stars is not all that uncommon. John Meriwether, who led Long-Term Capital Management until its 1998 implosion, now runs another hedge fund. Nicholas Maounis, Amaranth's founder and CEO, is exploring starting a new hedge fund. Instead of being ahead 27 % for 2005 his fund had to be liquidated. He lost much of his previous fees by leaving much of it in the fund. Since 2005 produced $ 70 million in management fees and $ 200 million in incentive fees, his cut was substantial but like LTCM, he should have diversified more.

Other winners are those on the other side of the trade if they followed proper risk control and could weather the storm created by Amaranth's plays and those like Citadel Investment Group, Merrill Lynch and J.P. Morgan Chase who took over Amaranth's portfolio and the Fortress Investment group, which helped liquidate assets. J.P. Morgan was named 'Energy Derivatives House of the Year, 2006' by *Risk* magazine.

The losers are mainly the investors in Amaranth including various pension funds which sought higher returns to make up for 2000–2003 equity investment mistakes. As of January 30, 2007, they have received about $ 1.6 billion which is less than 20 % of their investment value in August 2006. They will receive a bit more but their losses will exceed 75 %. Those who invested in mid 2005 have received about 27 % of their original investment or about 18 % of the peak August value. Other losers are hedge funds which were swept up by the Amaranth debacle including those that lost even though they bet on the right (short) direction because Hunter moved the market long on the way up like Mother Rock LP and those who lost along with Amaranth on the way down. They were long October and short September futures. According to Till (2006), they likely were forced out of their short position August 2, 2006 when the spread briefly but sharply rallied. Another loser was Man Alternative Investments Ltd., a fund of hedge funds listed on the London Stock Exchange in 2001 by the Man Group PLC, which shut down after recent losses tied to Amaranth's collapse and persistently poor liquidity in the shares. It is a small fund with little active trading interest, a concentrated shareholder base, and positions that were both difficult to build up and unwind. It had about $ 31.5 million invested in a portfolio selected by Man Group's Chicago-based Glenwood Capital Investments LLC unit, is part of Man Group PLC, which has $ 58 billion in assets under management. The fund lost about one-fifth of its gains this year from the collapse of Amaranth though it was up 6.5 % through October.

Archeus Capital, a hedge fund that in October 2005 had assets of $ 3 billion, on October 31, 2006, announced it would close returning $ 700 million to their investors. The fund, founded and run by two former Salomon Brothers bond traders, Gary K. Kilberg and Peter G. Hirsch, was like Amaranth, a multistrategy fund. However, it had a more conservative approach that focused on exploiting arbitrage opportunities in convertible bonds. Archeus began experiencing redemptions last year after its main investment strategy fell out of favor. The fund's founders blamed its administrator for failing to maintain accurate records. Their subsequent inability to properly reconcile the fund's records, led to a series of investor

---

[2] Indeed in late March 2007, it was widely reported that Hunter was soliciting money for a series of commodity funds with the name Solengo Capital. It is believed that cash rich investors in the Middle East and Europe are likely to invest. To assuage fears of another meltdown, investors will be able to pick specific managers and commodities. The new fund will impose margin and other restrictions on managers and will eliminate all lock-in restrictions if these controls are violated. The prices of the natural gas contracts Mr Hunter is known to favor had been increasing in anticipation of his return to the market.

withdrawals from which they were not able to recover. Also, Archeus's 2006 performance did little to inspire its clients. Through the first week of October 2006, Archeus's main fund was down 1.9 % for the year. However, the fund had returned 18.5 % since July 2005. Still, during a period when hedge fund returns have come under increased scrutiny and have, on average, lagged the returns of the major stock market indexes, such a return was insufficient to keep investors on board.

The $ 7.7 billion San Diego County Employees' Retirement Association has retained the class-action firm Bernstein Litowitz Berger and Grossmann to investigate the Amaranth implosion. Its $ 175 million investment in Amaranth, which was valued at $ 234 million in June 2006, is now estimated to be worth only $ 70 million, thus a $ 100+ million loss. They should have done better due diligence in advance. Those who bet the ranch on every trade eventually lose it. Investors should have known that was what they were investing in with Amaranth.

Following Amaranth's collapse, while investors were seeking someone to blame, some argued that these bets showed the need for greater or a different sort of regulation of hedge funds, or at least their over the counter trades. Others including Gretchen Morgenson of the New York Times, pointed to the persistence of what many of have called the *Enron Loophole*, created in 1993, when the Commodity Futures Trading Commission (CFTC) exempted bilateral energy futures transactions from its regulatory authority. This exemption was extended in 2000 in the commodity futures modernization act to include electronic facilities. Many have argued that Enron used such trades to increase the value of long-term contracts. In the run-up of gas prices in 2005/2006, some analysts and politicians pointed to the role of speculators in changing the demand structure, leading a congressional subcommittee to release a report urging that such trades all be the concern of US regulators. Amaranth's collapse brings a different aspect to this debate, as it shows the limits to such self-regulation by market actors. While it is unclear what policy actions might be taken in this matter, this concern is likely to continue and may change the environment in which such trades are made in the future. However, there are limits to the role that can be played by such regulation.

Other small losers are funds of funds of Morgan Stanley and Goldman Sachs who lost 2.5 % to 5 % from their Amaranth holdings. However as they helped unwind the trades they may well have recouped their losses as the energy markets subsequently increased.

There is little impact from this on the world economy. The hedge fund industry now has a bit more pressure to regulate position sizes but most regulators steer away from risk control. When you mention risk control, you are usually encouraged to change the subject. What regulators are interested in is operational risk. The exchanges have limits but rogue traders are able to get around these rules. In any event, if VAR were to be used it would most likely not work unless one is blessed with no bad scenarios. As long as risk control is so poorly understood, misapplied and disregarded and pension funds and others are desperate for high returns, such disasters will occur from time to time; and this is fully expected. It is simply part of the hedge fund zero sum gain. For every Jim Simons or Blair Hull eaking out steady profits using a lot of careful research, excellent execution, position sizing and strict risk control; there is a rogue trader trying to make it by over-betting with very little research and a firm which improperly applies risk control. Improper regulation may well hurt more than help.

This chapter is dedicated to our late friend and colleague University of Chicago Professor Merton Miller; he would have enjoyed it and hopefully would agree with our analysis.

Part III
Towards Scenarios: Country Studies

14
Letter from Cairo

Is Egypt's recent growth sustainable? The impact of the currency devaluation on Egypt's quest to attract investment

This chapter, like the ones that follow, provides a case study of a country or regional economic climate, highlighting the macroeconomic conditions, and prospects for growth and investment. Such case studies provide the basis for building scenarios to guide investment strategies and highlight key vulnerabilities where present. This chapter looks at Egypt's attempts to attract and absorb foreign direct investment as an example of economic performance. It also analyzes how Egypt's exchange rate shift has affected economic performance. Some of the broader regional issues are also discussed in Chapter 17 on Cyprus and the Mediterranean region.

Towards the end of 2003, a rising concern with foreign direct investment (FDI) or rather its lack became a common explanation for Egypt's relatively low economic growth rate. Bemoaning the lack of foreign investment, a series of conferences have been held where investors, analysts, researchers and government officials have tried to solve the difficult question of what motivates investors and what scares them into removing their assets and, most importantly, how best to capitalize on this resource. At recent conferences aimed at international investors, the rhetoric has been a mix of almost unbelievable promises on the part of the government to streamline economic policies and desperation on the part of some long-term investors who fear that the Egyptian economic climate is deteriorating. Investors cite policies as the floatation of the Egyptian pound and its subsequent rapid depreciation over the course of 2003 and the slow pace of reforms as adding uncertainty to their business decisions. It is possible to sketch a brief picture: the downturn in the global economy limits the amount of money available to emerging markets. Most of the limited supply of FDI for developing countries is destined for Asia and Eastern Europe, leaving little investment for a bureaucracy-laden country in a politically unstable region of the world.

As it is the aggregate of individual investment assessments of Egypt's possibilities, FDI provides a lens to view economic opportunities and challenges. Thus, low levels of FDI seems to be a symptom rather than a cause of Egypt's development struggle – a confluence of local, regional and global economic adjustment costs. As such, Egypt's experiences provide a useful case to analyse the allocation of international investment to developing countries and their ability to utilize it. First a look at the fundamentals.

Cairo is an incredibly vital city of 22 million people (about half of Egypt's population). Arriving in the midst of Ramadan (November 2003), when people swarm the streets to eat and shop by night, with traffic jams to match, it seemed that everyone was participating in the global economy from the craftsmen to the food vendors to those selling clothes for the coming celebration. All this vitality, despite spiraling prices (as much as 40 % in the 2003) as a result of the devaluation of the local currency, demonstrates the resilience of the Egyptian economy and domestic demand.

Looking at its fundamentals, Egypt would seem to be a good candidate for FDI. It possesses the largest population in the Middle East, a plentiful labour force, a stable government, large and growing tourism industry, participant in many bilateral or regional trade agreements, commitment to increasing economic liberalization and growth of the private sector, which also increased ability to absorb investment. Following its *Infitah* (opening) liberalization in the 1980s, Egypt derived some benefits from its IMF structural adjustment program in the early 1990s, during which it increased its foreign exchange reserves, privatized key corporations and decreased its debt stock. However, as in other such programs, there were high costs to following the IMF prescriptions.

SOME CHALLENGES: CURRENCY DEPRECIATION

Egypt provides a good example of the struggles of development, with a large and growing population, but one which continues to have high un- and under-employment, and obstacles to opening businesses (as documented in the annual World Bank Doing Business surveys). There continue to be problems in accessing credit, especially for individuals and small enterprises, though this is changing, with some of the first mortgage programs and increasing support to SMEs. While rich in resources (oil, natural gas), only 5 % of Egypt's landmass is arable. A series of reclamation projects and expansion of oases are extending that area, yet costs are high and potential environmental impact uncertain.

Yet economic fundamentals, either good or bad, are not enough to determine investment strategies. The quality of confidence and the perception of international and local investors about doing business, is crucial to investment, as emerging markets compete for resources. There are a lot of trends which could make investors wary including, the increasing budget deficit, the downgrading the Egyptian pound and its bonds by Standard and Poors and uncertainty about the exchange rate and progress of economic reform. The government has sent mixed messages. Following the Prime Minister's January 2003 announcement that the Egyptian pound (LE) would be floated, initial uncertainty and significant divergence between the official and unofficial rates, the government continually intervened in the foreign exchange market. More than a year following the *floatation*, there was still a 15 % differential between the market price and the black market rate. Following the floatation the government (and in particular) the central bank lacked a monetary policy but instead reacted to crises, further diminishing certainty and stability. Exchange rate uncertainty made it difficult for companies to make effective plans.

THE CHALLENGE IN ATTRACTING INVESTMENT

Net FDI to Egypt has averaged about $ 600 million per year from 2000–2003. FDI for fiscal year 2002–2003 totaled $ 700.6 million, an increase of about $ 200 million dollars over each of the previous two years (Central Bank of Egypt Monthly Statistical Bulletin, January 2004). According to the World Bank, the level of FDI has declined by almost half over the past three years (statement at December 2003 Egypt Invest conference). However, such numbers and their significance remain contested. At the January 2004 Economist Conference, the Prime Minister Nazif argued that the real effective value of FDI was much greater than the amount quoted abroad since they include only inland and new projects and exclude investment, petroleum, export oriented free zones and investment in capital markets, which are main growth areas. Instead he asserted that the real amount of FDI inflows reach approximately $ 2.3 billion.

Egypt, like other developing countries, has received increasing investment as it liberalized, although not at the same high rates as its counterparts in Asia and Eastern Europe, being in a different class of emerging market. In the 1990s, short and long-term FDI flows increased, as investors sought new investments and greater returns on their investment. China was by far the greatest developing country recipient of FDI, attracting $ 47 billion dollars in the first 11 months of 2003. (Reuters, 2003). Egypt's FDI woes are fairly typical in the Middle East and North African (MENA) region. In 2002, Morocco's FDI totaled $ 533 million (World Investment Directory). Even in the 1990s, though Egypt had exchange rate stability by virtue of its peg to the US dollar, it received fairly low capital flows, partly because there was little to buy, as only limited privatization had taken place. The capital controls meant that Egypt was sheltered from some of the short-term capital flows that emerging markets received in the mid-1990s to detrimental effect. However slow growth meant that it was slow to attract some of the companion investment flows. However, the stability and size of the market encouraged some investment, with many companies setting up regional offices.

Global, regional and national economic and political factors explain the difficulty of attracting FDI. After a peak in 2000, investment flows decreased dramatically in 2001 (UNCTAD world investment report 2001). Since a general reluctance to invest in emerging markets limits supply, most investors seek a guaranteed return on their investment and are unwilling to enter new and less proven markets. Most of the companies investing in Egypt today are long term investors including Shell and Vodafone. A series of regional and national political factors undermine confidence. Unlike emerging markets in Latin America, Asia or Eastern Europe, Egypt suffers from regional instability. Yet Egypt is an important ally of the United States, being its second largest aid recipient.[1] Egypt's political regime

---

[1] In 2006, Egypt became the third largest recipient of US aid, as funds to Iraq increased.

is stable, in fact, an overarching goal is political stability, being unwilling to undertake potentially destabilizing reforms. The collapse of President Mubarak in November 2003 while giving a speech, revived concerns about political succession. Since he has been unwilling to name a vice president, some fear that a power vacuum might ensue upon his death.

Regional conflict and uncertainty has an impact on Egypt's economy. Having endured economic losses during the 1990–91 Gulf war, particularly the cessation of remittances and loss of tourism and Suez canal earnings, negative economic effects were expected from the 2003 US invasion of Iraq. Conflict can increase or divert demand. In fact, there can be some positive economic spillovers of recent action in Iraq, largely because of increased Suez Canal earnings, and a concurrent rise in the price of oil.

For many years, the Egyptian pound (LE) was pegged at 3.5 to the dollar. As the dollar appreciated and the currencies of Egypt's competitors depreciated (either as a result of policy or speculative attacks), the pound became overvalued. During this period of stability and increasing overvaluation, Egyptian companies became accustomed to cheap imports of raw materials and intermediate goods, including essential food products. But this overvaluation was not sustainable in the long term. From 2001 onwards, a shortage of hard currency emerged, increasing the spread between the bank and black market exchange rates. At this point, the government launched a gradual devaluation which culminated in the floatation of the pound in January 2003. The timing of the floatation was at least somewhat triggered by the predicted US intervention in Iraq, which was expected to increase demand for hard currency. Following the devaluation, a lack of foreign currency forced further real depreciation. Lack of a functioning money market made it difficult for banks to access foreign exchange, making them in turn reluctant to sell it to customers. Exporters and others sought currency on the black market that they could not get from banks.

Policy uncertainty and the inability to predict the exchange rate discouraged some investment. The actual exchange rate is less important, than the ability to predict and repatriate revenues. To protect their assets, some import-export companies priced their product in dollars. Fearing that the pound would devalue further, others were locked into specific LE rates with contractors, weakening their profit margins. To secure the hard currency necessary for international transactions, they were forced to the black market. This vicious cycle of devaluation was exacerbated in the short-term by the government requirement that all companies engaged in foreign trade surrender 75 % of hard currency received within 30 days. As there is often a lag between payment for imports and receiving the goods, this policy leading to fears that people would not be able to access currency when needed, thus leading to greater recourse to the black market, which furthered the differential between official and unofficial rates. However, in the longer term, these requirements increased the supply of foreign currency in the banking system. The interbank market, introduced as part of the banking law of 2004, increased trade in dollars between banks, increasing access to dollars, leading to lower black market sales.

The impact of investment is mixed. While new jobs were created and GDP has continued to grow slowly, FDI has not had the spillover effect some expected – perhaps because amounts were relatively low and not primarily in high labour-intensive industries. Furthermore, the rate of return on such investment varied. Official unemployment rates, which are likely understated, remain at around 11 %. Much job growth continues to be in the public sector.

Egypt could learn from the experiences of its neighbours. To an extent, Morocco and Tunisia have used their ties with Europe to restructure their economies to take advantage of their increased access to the European market. The current draft Agadir agreement between Egypt, Morocco, Tunisia and Jordan would pool rules of origin for export to the EU and is a step in the right direction, as could increase cooperation between North African countries. The reforms of several GCC countries to transform themselves into financial centres and attract investment provide a model. Countries like the UAE and Bahrain have attracted foreign investors by making it easier to open and conduct business. As the regional head of a large multinational company told me:

> in contrast to Egypt, Dubai in the United Arab Emirates is very business oriented. They are focused on doing whatever is necessary to keep business happy . . . they cut through the bureaucracy. Egypt will need to make such changes to keep its existing investment. Furthermore, these countries have converted their energy assets into capital markets. . .

Having focused on many of the challenges faced by Egypt, there are positive signs. In March 2004, Standard and Poors ranked Egypt highest for return on share value among emerging markets with the Cairo and Alexandria stock exchanges main index rising 120 % in 2004 and 110 % in 2005. However, some of this rise reflects the volatility of the market and the adjustment implicit in devaluation. Egypt's existing and future trade agreements (both bilateral and regional) place it in a prime location to produce goods for local and foreign markets. Through the soon to be implemented EU association agreement, Egypt with has agreed to liberalize its market, strengthening reformers within the ruling party in internal struggles.

Recognizing the need to restore confidence in its monetary and fiscal policies, the Egyptian government has responded by making strong statements and taking some needed policy action, even if progress is slow. To this end, they are instituting policies necessary to support the – now managed – exchange rate and build confidence. These changes include a new banking law increasing the independence of the central bank. In December 2003, a new central bank governor and board was appointed, a move. Previously, political disputes and empty spots on the board stopped policy action. This new central bank was seen to be more skilled and more willing to seek outside expert advice in crafting monetary policy. At the beginning of 2004, Egypt was soon to launch an inter-bank market and in the longer term, an inflation-targeting monetary policy. At the same time, the legislative agenda involves fiscal reforms including among others, further streamlining of customs and tax collection.

On balance, there are good opportunities for foreign and domestic investors in Egypt. The government has made progress in economic reforms, both in the legislation and implementation, though further progress is needed. By focusing on attracting and retaining FDI, the government will be forced to maintain its commitment to reform and transparency. by 2004, Egypt had somewhat recovered and even mitigated its losses. Revenues from the Suez Canal reached their highest levels. At the same time, tourism revenues increased recording the highest figures since the mid 1990s, a recovery following a drop off after the terrorist attacks in the mid 1990s. Egypt also received increase visits from the region. Egypt is no more risky than other emerging economies provided that the challenges described above are taken into consideration. It is a land blessed with many resources and opportunities. After all, the land which created the last surviving wonder of the Ancient world, the Great Pyramid, has been able to recover from shocks and recreate itself many times over the millennia.

POSTSCRIPT: RIDING THE PETRODOLLAR BOOM: IS RECENT GROWTH SUSTAINABLE?

Almost three years later, at the beginning of 2007, Egypt's economic environment continued to improve significantly, from the moderately pessimistic outlook described above. Growth rates in the spring and summer of 2006 reached 7 %, heights not achieved for almost 20 years. Many of the promised reforms above have come to pass, including a new banking law and the harmonization of tariffs and some speeding of customs procedures. The new 'business-oriented' cabinet sworn in 2004, was able to enact several reforms, including the creation of a new ministry of investment, headed by Mahmoud Mohieddin, which brought together groups dealing with investment across the government. Egypt has continued to benefit from the external climate including the demand for commodities, Egypt is the recipient of increasing 'petrodollar' flows from neighbouring gulf countries, which have also flowed to other less-resource rich Arab countries like Lebanon and Jordan.[2] Of course many challenges remain, as it is difficult to make substantial changes so quickly, but recent economic figures including higher growth rates and exports and lower unemployment point to positive changes.

The divergence with the GCC has increased. The attractiveness of these areas has intensified as the price of oil climbed as investors have flocked to manage the new oil wealth. Increased spending both on consumer goods and infrastructure as well as the growth of the non-oil private sector has also had a positive effect on growth, even if many of these countries have not been very successful in diversifying away from oil and gas.

Several developments have assisted in this growth, including a new trade agreement, encouraging the development of Qualified Industrial Zones (QIZ), in which goods would gain duty-free access if they included some Israeli components. The agreement, several years in negotiation, was spurred on by the approaching expiration of the multi-fiber agreement which limited chinese textile exports. Signing the QIZ agreement was seen to be a largely short-term response to in effect buy time for the Egyptian textile market to adjust.

Along with the increase in growth rates, Egypt received almost 40 greenfield (new) FDI projects per year from 2003–2005, similar to that of its North African neighbours, higher than any other Middle Eastern countries aside from the UAE, but fewer than most Latin American and Asian countries (UNCTAD 2006). According to the Ministry of Investment calculations, which now include previously excluded oil and gas projects, FDI rose to $ 3.9 billion in 2004/05 and $ 6.1 billion in 2005/06, or just under 6 % of GDP. Projections for 2006/07 are as high as $ 8 billion, which would bring it close to the FDI received by South Africa, the largest recipient of FDI in Africa. On a sector basis, Egypt's FDI has become more diversified. with oil and gas related projects accounting for only 30 % of FDI, a decrease from the over 60 % received in 2004/5 (Oxford Business Group, 2006). So the steady increase in FDI goes along with internal reform that is facilitating higher growth and taking advantage of positive external environment.

However risks remain. Some analysts, most notably Morgan Stanley's Serhan Cevik worry about the liquidity that has helped fuel growth in Egypt as it has done in much of the Middle East and North Africa. He argues that the expansionary fiscal and monetary policies (and petrodollar inflows) will continue to drive inflation and may be a limiting factor on growth. Furthermore, the possibility of lower commodity prices (while benefiting Egypt, which has become a net importer of oil), may destabilize growth. Yet some of the reforms place Egypt is a stronger position.

---

[2] For more information on the size of these flows entering the financial market, see Setser and Ziemba (2006).

15
Threats, challenges and opportunities of China

Chinese influence is growing dramatically across the globe

Drawing on our June 2004 trip, this chapter and the one that follows discuss opportunities and risks of investing in China and its interdependence with the global economy. This chapter assesses overall economic prospects, including the risk of a growth slowdown, giving particular attention to the exchange rate regime. The following chapter focuses on the Chinese financial markets and their correlation to world markets.

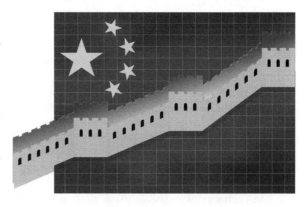

Our June 2004 departure for China coincided with continued media frenzy surrounding the possibility that China's high growth would falter, with differing opinions about the likelihood and severity of such a change in growth patterns on China and the global economy. Some said that the Chinese economy was heading for a massive crash, which would send the whole world into a spiral because of decreased demand for commodities. Others argued that Chinese government policies would orchestrate a *soft landing* by moderating demand.

Others were even more optimistic, thinking that growth would continue to propel global commodity prices and drive growth in Asia. Another area of concern was planning for any fallout from the possible revaluation of the Chinese renmimbi. Much of China's role in driving Asian and global growth and economic competition and opportunity for investors is strangely similar to that played by Japan in the mid and late 1980s; see Ziemba and Schwartz (1991, 1992). Although there are many differences including the role of and receptiveness to foreign investment and the level and speed of development, there are lessons to be learned from the comparison.

We looked on this trip as a chance to see how much truth there was in these debates. And while a three week trip, with a very rudimentary understanding of Chinese language, could only give us a glimpse of this dynamic, rich, fast-changing country, it gave us a basis to assess the likelihood of different economic outcomes. On the basis of meetings with a variety of representatives from academia and business communities as well as a few policymakers, we were led to the three scenarios that are discussed later in this chapter.

What we learned is that many of the clichés being shared about China are true, especially the contradictory ones. We take a look at some of them in turn.

Cliché 1   There is massive and sustained growth in China. Riding the train around the country, we could see the scope of construction and reconstruction that has propelled

China's demand for concrete and steel. This investment, while largely focused on business sectors, extended to preserving and restoring China's heritage, including some related to groups which the government had previously sought to suppress. The business and financial centers showed signs of continuing rapid construction. In Shanghai we marveled at the construction and the ever-taller towers of Pudong, the new financial district on the east bank of the river Huangpu. What made it even more impressive was the realization that fifteen years ago there was little development there. However this massive growth varies dramatically, with some regions receiving little growth, contributing to increased inequality within China and a related domestic political challenge.

Cliché 2   The massive population of China is well known and the coincidence of internal migration and population growth with rising incomes have brought many changes in demand. We saw evidence of this in many areas from waiting to cross the river in Shanghai or cross the street in Beijing. China's large population means that it needs its massive rate of growth to maintain and increase its standard of living. Even the small cities in China, with one to three million people are large by Western standards.

Cliché 3   There is a growing middle class. Aside from providing fodder for articles about plastic surgery and other conspicuous consumption, it is clear that the middle classes are growing. It is hard to identify how large it is, how it compares to our US or European notions of a middle class and the size of its wealth and disposable income. In each city we visited, there were gigantic modern malls, many of which carried international brands. Obviously there must be people purchasing these products, even if some shops might originally have been introduced to prove that China was modern and world-class. Statistics show that the middle class is growing. However, given the size of the population this does not mean that the entire country is acceding to middle-class status. Yet, by necessity, China has been successful at moving millions of people above the poverty line, accounting for much of the global decrease in poverty rates. (WB paper)

China is a land of contrasts: while there has been much urban development, 66 % of the population is employed in rural areas and 43 % of those remain engaged in agricultural production. Unlike many developing countries, China has been able to moderate the flood of internal migration, by limiting who can change one's residence permits. But there is important interdependence between the urban core and its satellite rural regions. Pressure to move to urban areas is defused but in an increasingly privatized economy other incentives are used to keep people from flooding to urban areas. We heard of one project undertaken by the city of Shanghai to foster technological innovation in a rural region in the west, with the assumption that it would minimize migration.

China accounts for 21 % of world population but at June 2004 exchange rates, only 4 % of world GDP (13 % at purchasing power parity rates). At the same time, employment patterns have shifted. More and more employment is moving out of the public sector. This trend is exacerbated by privatization of state owned enterprises. Since 1990, employment in state and collective enterprises has fallen from 21 % to 12 %.

All of the construction and reconstruction demonstrate China's great hunger for raw materials. The demand for energy is very high and likely to rise.

In 2003, China used

- 40 % of the world's cement production;
- 31 % of world coal;
- 7.4 % of global oil output.

China generated half of the global growth of GDP and is the third largest exporter after US and Germany. There are increasing signs of consumerism:

- 12.4 million privately owned cars in 2003; an increase of 24.8 % over 2002. Volkswagen sold more cars in China than Germany.
- Increasing private ownership of houses apartments, 82 % of urban housing is privately owned.

COSTS OF DEVELOPMENT

In many developing countries, rapid growth and large populations have led to massive use of energy, little green space and often wall-to-wall buildings. And parts of China certainly match this picture, but new development seems to be taking account of externalities. More and more Chinese wish to live in areas with better air. Arriving in Shanghai, we were struck both by its monumental size and by the amount of green space. However, the means for getting better air is often to live farther from the urban manufacturing areas, necessitating private transportation which increases release of greenhouse gases. As China develops, the externalities of pollution grow more costly, e.g. in water supply, air quality and traffic. And they appear to be aware of this, as the *China Daily*, the government newspaper, told us proudly on Earth Day.

Shanghai is once again China's face to the world and economic centre. Shanghai was the centre of European power in the mid-19th century. It is a very modern city and seems like a new sort of China dream, that of modernizing in a Chinese manner. Pudong across the river from the bund (the locus of European power in Shanghai in the 19th century and home of the banks and customs house) epitomizes this *Chinese modernization*. It has become a showcase, intended to outmodernize the Europeans, to show that the Chinese directed liberalization can be

Nanjing Road, Shanghai with view to Pudong across the river.

better than the Western one. Many Chinese from other parts of the country visit the city to see how modern it is. Parts of Shanghai's old city made us think of Disneyland's Mainstreet USA, but of course it is Chinatown for Chinese tourists. Tourism, both domestic and foreign is becoming very important. In particular we were surprised by how many Chinese tourists there were everywhere. In fact, not surprisingly, the only place we went that was not full of Chinese tourists was the mosque in X'ian.

The Shanghai Stock Exchange is representative of these developments and the importance of symbols of modernity. It opened just a couple years ago in an ultra modern facility with a massive trading screen and seats and computers for more than 1000 traders. However it sits essentially empty. When we visited in the middle of one trading day there were only about 15 people on the **largest trading floor in Asia**; some were reading newspapers, see the photo. The trading screen was active but most trading is done on-line. The stock exchange might be seen as a symbol of Chinese achievement, yet the emptiness of the trading floor also reflects the efficiency. The Chinese have been able to introduce the sort of technology which eliminates the need to use open outcry trading on the exchange. We discuss the Chinese stock exchanges, trading results, returns, risk, and relationships with other markets in more depth in the next chapter.

Outside the Shanghai Stock Exchange

There is much change in modern China. Though the mode of government is communist, it is very capitalistic in its mode of every

Inside the Shanghai Stock Exchange during trading hours

day economics. Still the economy is centralized. So to a large extent the government, which still owns all the land, can control where development happens. Its cities and municipalities are playing an increasingly important role even establishing links with other cities across the country.

Now that we have set the scene, we would like to assess the risks of investing in China and its impact on the global economy. In so doing, we assess the likelihood and possible nature of a slowdown, emphasizing how one might hedge against these risks. In fact, we argue that this focus on a slowdown and particularly on a crash is beside the point. Instead it is critical to more fully understand China's longer-term challenges. In the rest of this chapter, we present a number of different scenarios of possible short and longer horizon outcomes and considering what impact these scenarios might have on China, the Asia-Pacific region and the world. While we have economic policies as our primary focus, we briefly consider the geo-political implications of such policies.

Table 15.1 The changing nature of trade, as a percentage of exports and imports. *Source*: General Administration of Customs, China in UBM Economic & Market Trends Q2/04

	Exports		Imports	
By Product	1994	2003	1994	2003
Food, beverages, tobacco	9.1	4.2	2.8	1.5
Raw materials, fuels, chemicals	11.8	8.1	20.4	27.3
Basic manufactured goods	19.2	15.7	24.3	15.5
Machinery & transport equip	18.1	42.9	44.6	46.7
Misc manufactures	41.3	28.8	5.9	8.0
Others				
By Region				
North America	29.5	29.1	13.7	9.3
Europe	25.0	24.2	19.0	16.1
Asia	40.8	39.8	59.5	66.0
Oceania	1.4	1.8	2.5	2.1
Latin America	2.0	2.8	2.5	3.7
Africa	1.4	2.4	0.8	2.0

Before developing scenarios, we now turn our attention to some key factors that presage change and thus potential risk factors for investment in China:

What is most dramatic about China's export growth is the shift from simple labor-intensive manufacturing to more complex products, see Table 15.1. As a result, China has been able to attract factories away from competitors in developed or developing countries and so increasingly produce higher-level goods.

Trade surplus. While a source of political tension today, the trade imbalance between China's imports and exports to the US and Europe is not a new story. For much of its history, China has had less interest in importing products than industrial countries have had in its exports. Or rather Western countries have been unable to provide cheap enough or interesting enough goods that the Chinese wanted. Even in the 19th century, the Americans and British worried about the amount of foreign exchange being shipped to China in exchange for cheap Chinese goods, This precursor to today's rising Chinese foreign reserves led the British to begin exporting opium from India to China (not one of the best moments in British commercial history) in an attempt to balance the trade relationship. Yet, the story of the trade deficit is more complicated; while China has a deficit with many partners, it is a net importer of raw materials and commodities and runs a trade deficit with many commodity exporters or other Asian countries which may provide imputs for manufacturing.

Chinese labor is producing cheap goods, but also inexpensive quality goods. Many countries are hooked on Chinese products which are of good quality at very low prices. It is very difficult for the US or anyone else to make things as cheap with as good quality as the Chinese. The quality is improving dramatically and products are increasing in complexity, in part because of the sort of joint ventures in which foreign companies take part. Unlike many developing countries, China has been able to negotiate technology and knowledge transfer as well as the actual work. There is increasing amounts of R&D taking place in China.

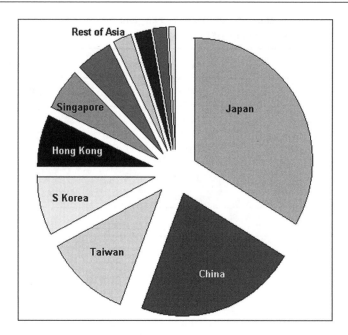

Figure 15.1   Foreign exchange reserves. *Source*: The Economist, July 10, 2003

As shown in Figure 15.1, China has the second largest holdings of foreign reserves after Japan. These holdings have been increasing rapidly since the end of 2001. In fact in the year ending March 31, 2004, foreign reserves rose by 39.2 % (see postscript). This has several implications. First, as US external debt through outstanding securities increases, China is one of its largest and fastest growing creditors. Should China try to divest themselves of their dollar investment, it would have a substantial impact on the US dollar debt. Also, it makes a substantial revaluation of the RMB less likely since a revaluation would decrease the value of their US dollar assets. These assets would make it possible to uphold the currency peg if challenged but are not likely to be used as the costs of doing so are high.

OVERSEAS INVESTMENT

There are substantial barriers to overseas investment by Chinese citizens. So the Chinese must invest in the domestic market although cracks in this strict policy are appearing.[1] The restrictions have pushed price earnings ratios to high levels, especially in comparison to the more open Hong Kong equity markets. These restrictions go along with the those on foreign investment in China, where foreigners are restricted to certain sectors. The first stage of a qualified international investor program is in place, which might make it easier to purchase Chinese equities. Much investment is funneled through Hong Kong because of its banking hub and favorable regulations.

---

[1] The government wants mainland Chinese to invest in Hong Kong. But the people are hestitant because they fear a currency loss in doing this because their RMB must be converted into Hong Kong dollars which are fixed to the US currency which is declining. They fear that when converted back to RMB they will not have enough to justify the risk.

The auto sector is seen as one of the greatest opportunities. China is a country with a burgeoning middle class who have an increasing demand for private transportation and more can afford it. In addition to the domestic market, as production improves, there may be increasing demand for Chinese produced vehicles. For car manufacturers, a country where there are only eight cars for every 1000 people (compared to 940 cars per 1000 in the US) it seems too good to be true. While most other world markets are becoming saturated, China presents a large population with growing disposable income and high demand for personal vehicles. As a result multinationals have been fighting to set up factories in China since the early 1990s, creating cars for all market segments. These cars vary from very expensive models to more affordable ones – like the omnipresent mini-vans (cost around US$ 15 000). But at the same time, reports indicated that sales were down, partly driven by increasing difficulties in gaining loans to finance purchases (China Daily). Even though car saturation is still low, there are traffic jams everywhere.

Another great media debate concerns foreign direct investment and the prospect of over-investment in certain sectors and government attempts to restrict credit in these areas. It is likely that there was overinvestment and that loans in some sectors were too easy to obtain. However some overinvestment was the likely result of restricting investment in other sectors. However, the fact is that loans were granted based not on the fundamentals of the project but on connections. Recent studies such as that of HSBC have shown that the government policies to discourage investment have been effective and make it less likely for loans to be granted because of connections and not on the merit of the investment. There has been so much investment in China that some has probably been less efficient. The investment has also led to substantial inflation, a risk which we address in our scenarios.

We discuss three basic scenarios for China's growth patterns:

1. A sharp crash, followed by a medium term decrease in growth.
   This scenario would require a major decrease in growth of reaching perhaps 3 % GDP growth. If a hard crash happened, one would expect an impact on world commodity demand, with commodity prices falling from their recent rise. However, not all of the rise reflects increased demand, some of the rise reflects the depreciation of the US dollar, the currency in which most commodities are priced. Some commodities remain considerably cheaper in real terms. Also, terrorism premia are built in to protect against commodity production shocks. A crash in China would be most destabilizing domestically since it would impact domestic demand, harming local companies and foreign joint ventures. However, it is unclear what kind of hard landing could result because of the still centrally directed economy. The rate of non-performing loans is a potential problem, but most of those loans are held by still unprivatized banks which are unlikely to be allowed to default. In many cases, these non-performing loans may already have been absorbed by the banks. The combination of the exchange controls, the fixed exchange rate and large supply of foreign reserves make it unlikely or almost impossible for China's currency to collapse (see more about the currency issues below). And in such a lower growth scenario, depreciation would be even less likely, as a revaluation/appreciation would harm recovery in such a low growth outcome. The majority of direct investment in China is illiquid, being investment in companies, largely joint ventures. Such investment is by its nature long term and investors are unlikely to pull out lightly, though they may be unlikely to reinvest or increase their investments. The stock exchange effects would be negative and are estimated in the next chapter. Thus it would seem that China is

somewhat insulated from such a hard landing. So this scenario has low probability, at most 10%.

2. A slowdown, with GDP growth between 3–6%.

For many developed countries, a slowdown is usually defined as the lack of GDP growth, but as China which has average GDP growth of about 9% for the last decade, even a 3 or 4 or 5% GDP growth might be disastrous. Because of the size of its population, economists say that China needs around 7% GDP growth or unemployment will rise and rural urban inequality will not be sustainable. Such a decrease in growth, if sustained, might postpone new projects, could jeopardize existing ones and be destabilizing for China and its trading partners. Since investment and trade with China are driving many countries in Asia, a slowdown in China might also threaten other Asian economies. A slowdown in China might even negatively impact the United States if it decreases labor costs in China, further decreasing the costs of production. With such a slowing Chinese output, demand for inputs would suffer, albeit less than in scenario (1). Some argue that growth may slow slightly in this scenario but that might still lead to a stock market crash. But, like the US, it does not look like either market will enter the danger zone unless there is a larger rise in interest rates than projected and a larger drop in earnings. This scenario has probability of about 20%.

3. Similar or slightly lower growth but well within the rate of replacement: 7–9% GDP growth.

The third scenario is probably the most likely (estimated to be about 70%) and the most sustainable in the long run. While it might reflect a decrease in growth, GDP growth of 7% might be more sustainable in the longer term. Since much of the very high growth was driven by FDI which has been as high as 50% of GDP.[2] More directed investment is better for China in the long-run since there are only so many infrastructural projects which can be built at once. The probability of this scenario stems from the relative success of Chinese government policies in discouraging overinvestment. They rightly fear that this investment is likely to spur inflation which would hamper domestic demand. Instead of a hard shift, slightly lower growth is possible. For several years, China has maintained growth of 9%. It is difficult to sustain growth at such levels, but we believe that China's resources and labor along with government policies make sustained growth at or around replacement levels likely. In fact, if this scenario comes to pass, government officials are likely to claim that it was a part of the overall plan to cool down several overheated sectors.

Aside from any of the reasons we have just cited, it is clear to us that China must avoid a hard landing since its costs would be too hard economically and politically. While wishing will not make it so, the determination of the Chinese communist élites to retain power has led to much flexibility of economic programing, and this is likely to continue with the government keeping substantial control on reform and investment to ensure that they do not lose political control. Too sharp a landing, and a resulting decrease in the standard of living would likely threaten the government politically.

Perhaps the largest source of risk is the Chinese currency and its regime. The Chinese Yuan or Renmimbi (the peoples' currency, RMB) has been pegged to the US dollar at approximately 8.28 Y to one dollar since 1994.[3] This peg and capital controls enabled it to

---

[2] This may include some double counting of FDI routed through Hong Kong on its way to the mainland. Current estimates in July 2007 are $50–60 billion US per year.

[3] We discuss the recent changes in the RMB exchange rate level and regime in the post script.

survive the Asian currency crises of 1997 and 1998. There has been no currency risk in doing business in China because they have maintained this peg; they have the reserves to support the rate, and the control over convertibility. Unlike other Asian tigers, China was reluctant to liberalize capital flows. While this restriction limited the amount of foreign capital which could be invested in the country, it also allowed more control of this same investment, discouraging so-called hot money. This restriction follows Robert Mundell's *impossible trinity*, the argument that countries could only maintain two of the three following: free capital movement, fixed exchange rates, and effective monetary policy, that is control of interest rates. China was able to maintain monetary policy and its exchange rates since it rejected free movement of capital.

Most international economists and central bankers believed that the current (June 2004) fixed exchange rate regime was not sustainable in the long term and did not reflect China's growth patterns. Chinese officials have also announced that the RMB would become more freely convertible, and we have seen the RMB appreciate from 8.2 to 7.6 as of July 2007. Discussions with students and others showed us that they also see the level and regime of their currency to be one of the biggest challenges that China faces.

The RMB exchange rate has become a international issue, with China facing international pressure to revalue (increase the level of) the RMB. This pressure has mainly come from the United States, though the Europeans are also concerned about the exchange rate. As the US dollar depreciates, the yuan depreciates along with it, making Chinese goods even cheaper for European consumers and making it just as difficult for US products to compete. Thus, some Americans argue, the exchange rate presents an unfair advantage since it artificially depresses the prices. Yet, while Chinese have a stable low currency for exports, the depreciation of the US dollar means that commodities, which make up a large proportion of Chinese imports, have become more expensive. At the same time, Americans win and lose from the current Chinese exchange rate. China is a great source of cheap products enabling them to buy more with their money. Also many American companies have operations in China and are reaping the profits.

We must also separate a potential revaluation from free floatation and freely exchangeable currency. Because of international interest in China, it is likely that upon first becoming freely exchangeable, the RMB would appreciate dramatically, above its *natural* level, as investors seek to guarantee their investment. Since market prices of currencies reflect confidence and other intangible trust or distrust in a currency as well as its economic fundamentals, the currency may shift from being undervalued to overvalued. Thus, a revalued yuan would not solve all the problems of the imbalance of trade. There are several choices for the Chinese government:

1. A new peg to the dollar, probably revalued slightly but maintaining the exchange rate regime and capital controls.

   Such a shift in the peg might be welcomed by many American specialists, who see the currency as one of many ways that China threatens US interests. Many economists argue that it would be in China's interest to revalue the currency as it would help to rebalance the economy and remove the implicit subsidy on the export sector. This policy would increase the cost of Chinese exports, perhaps making them less competitive. Revaluing the peg might be very risky for the Chinese since it would introduce uncertainty. If they revalue once, an investor might expect them to do so again. In addition, even if current restrictions are maintained, such a move might encourage investors to buy real estate and whatever RMB they can attract in the hopes that the currency will appreciate. Thus a new valued peg is an unlikely first step since it is likely to challenge China's interests: stability, sustainability, and flexibility.

2. Maintain peg but increase capital mobility.

   The combination of lifting some capital controls and keeping the peg contradicts Mundell's well-proved trinity. More capital freedom would make maintaining the peg and monetary transmission even more difficult. Not only would the Chinese government lose some of its channels to discourage hot money, but, if done on its own, it would result in uncertainty. Freeing capital would limit the central bank's control of the money supply and might result in outflow of RMB. However, some form of convertibility will be necessary without opening completely, as money is already flowing in even though financial flows for investments are tightly controlled. In a Bloomberg article, DeRosa (2004) addresses this loophole, by focusing on China's growing money supply and the central bank's loss of control. Pushed up by exports and the foreign currency surrender requirements, the money supply has grown. This growth shows how the government is losing control of this supply and inflation is likely to result. In fact inflation is up on the year.

3. Float the currency.

   If China floated its currency, it would join most of the major currencies. However, there are risks in such floatation since it might encourage speculation, it would eliminate much control over the currency. In addition, instead of real free floatation, the government might use it as a cover for a managed peg, or at least a partial one. All of these might increase the uncertainty surrounding the regime and by extension the Chinese economy.

4. A peg to a basket of currencies (the dollar, yen and euro) reflecting China's most important trading partners and key reserve and vehicle currencies.

   This is one of the most likely policies to be adopted in the medium term and is under serious consideration by Chinese officials. A basket would provide stability and more flexibility but would allow (even require) that China maintain its control of capital flows. Pegged to a basket, China's currency would respond to the market forces indirectly. Most of the disadvantages of this option are similar to option one, that is, lack of credibility and difficulty of picking the right level. However, we offer a few caveats. Firstly, a basket is difficult to put together, and may require some adjustment to find the right balance, particularly if the US dollar continues to be volatile. Just as the right basket would protect the Chinese economy from this volatility and that of commodity prices, the wrong one would accentuate it. In addition this delicate balancing might limit trust in the Chinese ability to manage their exchange rate. If the currency becomes more openly traded before this basket is clear (or before the central bank is trusted), speculation may occur. Should this option be accompanied by freer capital flows, the risk of instability and speculation would be that much greater.

5. Maintain the existing peg but move towards a more flexible exchange rate in the longer/medium term.

   This option is some form of cheat since it combines several of the previous ones. Since there are so many uncertainties involved in changing an exchange rate regime and the issue of domestic and foreign investor confidence is so variable, a longer term multi-faceted approach is necessary. Several policies which must be in place to support a free exchange rate. Primary among these are policies relating to the banking system. China will need to proceed in privatizing more of its banks, eliminate the large number of non-performing loans, improve the interbank market, etc. Also it would need to free domestic trading of foreign currency. It is possible that option (4) a basket would be one of the interim steps. However transparency or at least credibility is one of the most important prerequisites to this long-term policy change.

Floatation and steps toward currency convertibility are long-term goals for the Chinese, since its currency regime does not allow for the growth. If the Chinese maintain the peg they are likely to continue to suffer growing domestic inflation. One of the biggest risks, however, is of doing nothing or appearing to do nothing. The Chinese government and central bank must make its commitment to the chosen policy clear and be as transparent as possible in its actions. Although RMB is not available on the international markets it is increasingly available as a regional currency. (It has been used in trade with China's neighbors in South East Asia such as Vietnam.) As a result, demand for RMB will go up ahead of a proposed revaluation or rebalancing.

Revaluing gracefully is something that few countries have been able to achieve. We hope that China will be able to learn from the experiences of others so that it could be the first. In general, when countries exit a currency peg, they are forced to do so to devalue, often because they lack adequate foreign reserves (e.g. Egypt, Turkey, Argentina, and several Asian countries). China is unlikely to be forced from its perch. Yet if the RMB is freer, devaluation is unlikely in the short term since there has been so much pent-up demand for the currency and the Chinese economy for which it could be seen as a surrogate. Chinese officials are rightly concerned about the potential negative fallout of revaluation. If investors are uncertain of the final objectives, they may be cautious or they may force the currency to an inappropriate level. A non-credible peg will open China up to speculation.

In addition to currency risk, other risks persist. China still is a developing country with much inequality. There is a major gap in development between rural and urban residents. While urban residents tend to be increasing their standard of living, this makes the gap with their rural counterparts more pronounced. Should this inequality continue to grow, it might be destabilizing for the government and investors. One of the sources of stability in China has been the government's ability to gradually increase the standard of living of the majority of the population. This improvement in the quality of life has limited political challenges to authority.

There seems to be little risk of policies which would threaten the reform process and freeing market. The peaceful transition of power from Jiang Zemin to the new leaders seems unchallenged. The upcoming party congress will provide more clues of the next transition. The government has been successful in gradually raising standards of living to maintain their political control.

Yet, China is different from other developing countries, even those that share a socialist, command economy-past. China has had two advantages over Russia. Firstly, it had a stronger and more recent entrepreneurial past and many overseas Chinese who sought to develop it. Secondly, because of the swift but gradual reform process there was time to create institutions where they were necessary rather than focus on completely creating a free-market economy from day 1. Additionally, China has had the benefit of tremendous FDI flows. Throughout the 1990s, China was second only to the US in the amount of FDI and China-bound flows tended to exceed those for all other developing countries combined. Its low labor costs combined with its large potential domestic economy have made it an irresistible location for multinational companies to enter. For while production in China for export has boomed, Chinese imports or Chinese consumption of foreign products has not increased to the extent hoped for as China's domestic supply chain deepens, this may increase.

To paraphrase the chairman of a automobile company: While there are risks in investing in China just like in any developing country, the biggest risk is not being there. We would argue that the biggest risk for an investor is not paying attention to China, whether one has investments there currently or not. China's share of world population, of international trade and power on the international stage means that one cannot ignore developments there, either the positive or the negative. Yet one should not accept either the doomsday statements or the projections of boomtown, rather, like anywhere else, it is important to know the investment environment and the companies in which one is investing and to monitor the situations as they change. The key is not to get sucked into the *China dream* but to enjoy the ride.

POSTSCRIPT

More than a year after broadening the currency peg, the RMB has still had very little movement against the US dollar. Although it is now pegged to a basket of currencies used by China's main trading partners, the RMB still seems largely to be pegged to the US dollar in effect. Since exiting the peg, appreciation has been slow, and includes no real appreciation. As a result, the exchange rate continues to be a divisive political issue in its relationship with the US. The effects of US Treasury Secretary Henry Paulson's widely anticipated ongoing strategic economic dialogue with China on the exchange rate regime are still unclear, but gradual changes from China are likely to stave off congressional efforts. The Treasury Department again declined to label China a currency manipulator and a long threatened legislative alternatives have not been introduced. However, China's exchange rate and thus the real costs of its products remain a issue of concern for the US and the EU. China increased exports to Europe at a higher rate than to the US China continued to increase holdings of foreign reserves, reaching over $1 trillion late in the fall of 2006. Several papers have discussed the implications of china's growing reserves and imagined ways in which they might be spent.

China's growth rates have continued to climb, with 2006 GDP growth exceeding 10.5 % in comparison to 9.9 % in 2005 with even higher growth in the first half of 2007. However concerns about China's impact on global demand continue. Now the discussion has evolved from concern about China's hard or soft landing to a debate over whether China's demand can allow the rest of the world to decouple sufficiently from the US economy in case of a slowdown in US demand, that is, if China can continue to be a motor for Asian growth as well as African and Latin American economies which have grown to depend on Chinese purchases. Much focus has been on China's demand for commodities, and its continuing to lock-up supplies of oil in African and the Middle East, and in the market force China might play as it begins to build up its strategic oil reserves. We discuss further developments in the Chinese financial markets in Chapter 16.

Since writing about China's economy has become a growth industry, it was hard to devise a short list of references and we learned things from a variety of sources in preparing our lectures for China. However, for tracking developments in China, we recommend sources like *The Economist, Bloomberg,* and *The China Economic Quarterly.* See also Cao et al (2007), Chow (2007), and Haitao and Ruoen (2007). Additional items cited are in the bibliography.

16
Chinese investment markets: Hedge fund scenario analysis

Is China the new Japan: will they hang onto the foreign exchange or waste it like Japan by investing in things they already owned-their land and their stocks. The key is to invest outside China and in new ventures in China.

China's growth and challenges have remained high on the economic news but we have so far been correct in our prediction that Chinese government policies would avert a *hard landing*. Estimates for China's GDP growth in 2004 range from 7 % (perhaps wishful thinking) and 9 % (the IMF's recent report drawing on numbers released by the government). In this chapter we discuss stock market returns, IPOs, resource sustainability and how one might get involved in the China game. In addition, we consider several risk factors which will impact China's ability to maintain growth in the long-term.

In Chapter 15, we discussed China's rapid economic growth, its absorption of high levels of investment and its interdependent role in the world economy, which will only increase. We argued that a slowdown of growth from 9 % GDP growth was likely but that a crash was unlikely given the restrictions on withdrawing foreign  investment, continuing interest in China (what some have called the need to get to China's party before it is too late) and, most crucially, continuing central direction of critical aspects of the economy. Recent economic data from China seems to support our suggestion that China would not suffer a crash but would instead have a slowdown of growth. The government policies designed to slow down overheated sectors have had some desired effect, although it is far too soon to predict the long-term effect of these policies or of investment decisions see postscript for current government attempts to slow and rebalance its reaccelerating economy. And some would point out that the very success of government policies reveals that China is far from a market economy, since it was a regulated cool-down of overheated sectors. However this has reversed in 2007.

We also discussed various currency scenarios, suggesting that in the long term, as it becomes a more developed and open economy, China may need to increase currency flexibility. While its exchange rate currently provides stability and very competitive pricing, it may be unstable in the long-term, requiring high interest rates and strict currency controls. Yet, international actors such as the IMF should be wary of urging a rapid change in currency regime since credibility of the currency is critical and any currency revaluation or floatation requires supporting policies. Especially as any revaluation would cause market actors to indirectly purchase RMB (or directly if capital controls are lifted) on the anticipation that its value will continue to rise.

In the past decade, China has become increasingly dependent on foreign investment and foreign purchase of Chinese goods which have enabled a rapid growth in domestic standard of living to the extent that Chinese companies are now seeking foreign acquisitions – both to lock up resources and to spend the results of their trade. In particular, it has been increasing trade with resource-rich African and Central Asian countries. China is playing a more powerful role in investment trade and politics in Asia, filling the vacuum left by the United States. In fact Chinese exports to Japan were greater than those of the US and in smaller East and Southeast Asian countries, China is increasingly the superpower to be appeased. However, some attempts to purchase foreign companies have been blocked by some of the recipient countries, such as CNOOC's attempt to buy UNOCAL.

To better understand the equity market dynamics, we will make some general comments about the Chinese economy.

CHINA'S ECONOMY

With high (albeit slowing) growth and increasing numbers of middle class in urban areas, a vast country and population and many workers who can produce at very low prices, there are many investment opportunities. Yet, this picture obscures certain challenges which can curb growth. While the middle class is growing, so are its costs. In the past, education, health care and other social services were provided by the state, but now individuals must pay for these services themselves. These costs are particularly onerous in rural agricultural areas away from the booming coastal areas where standards of living are ever higher. Recent studies have shown that these wage increases are not equally allocated and there are limitations to the ability to gradually increase labor rates. Instead it is becoming harder to fill all the positions in some coastal free trade zones, especially as some rural areas are also increasing revenues.

Income growth is by no means evenly distributed. This makes the dream of the capturing the domestic market that much harder to achieve. China is likely to remain inward focused (e.g. supplying many of its goods domestically) since it is so large, and it will be difficult for foreign firms to realize the sort of profits of which they have been dreaming. Because of its size and power, China has always been able to have more leverage with foreign firms than other emerging markets, requiring joint ventures rather than merely assembling parts. Now Chinese firms are increasingly recruiting the staff of foreign companies to improve their businesses (WSJ, 2004). Since income growth has been solid at about 9 % but there is still a huge differential between urban per capita disposable income (2639 RMB) and rural household per capita cash income (834 RMB) (China Economic Quarterly, 2004).

China's policies and growth do not take place in a vacuum. Because of China's currency peg (and high FDI to GDP ratio), Chinese interest rates are very dependent on global trends. As of June 2004, we are now in the midst of an environment of global interest rate increases. Many countries such as England and Australia have been increasing rates for some time, while others such as the US are just beginning this tightening phase. Since the Chinese currency is pegged to the US dollar, both the interest rate cycle and currency competitiveness of China will be related to US policy decisions. In addition, China's vast holdings of US treasuries will increase the impact of such interest rates choices. As a result, watching changes in the Fed funds rate would provide an indication of policy moves in China and enable predictions of China's continuing ability to attract investment. In addition to responses to global trends in interest rates, there are local factors also at stake. The Chinese government ordered banks to restrict loans to overheated sectors to stop rapid growth.

THE EFFECT OF CHINESE DEMAND FOR RESOURCES

A major factor relating to China's success relates to its supply of resources, both human and energy. Earlier we discussed the important role China played in recent global commodity price increases. In fact it was only in 2003/2004 that global commodity prices have returned to their higher levels of the mid-1990s. However since Chapter 15 was written, a related aspect of China's energy dependency has emerged: insufficient energy to sustain their production machine. Even though China imports and produces increasing amounts of energy, its demand for energy was too great in the summer of 2004. As a result, the government was forced to institute a series of brownouts or forced reductions in usage forcing companies to cut down on their factory hours of operations and sending workers on forced vacations for the months of July and August. These lost hours of work were to be made up in the early fall. This decline in production and deferred work made some companies unable to meet their orders for goods, especially for the crucial back-to-school market in the US. The energy shortage even carried over to luxury hotels that were asked to turn down air conditioners (to keep temperatures at 26C or above) and to ask staff to refrain from using the elevators and escalators when possible.

While successful in the short term, none of these measures are sustainable in the long term, since they only reflect short-term solutions; instead, substantial conservation policies and or new sources of energy are needed. And China is planning for both. However, it also reflects the degree to which China is still centrally regulated that these brownouts could be used, since unlike the increasingly common air-conditioner overuse blackout threat in industrialized countries. It did highlight vulnerabilities of the just-in-time global supply chain.

Aside from the intricacies of supply chain management, China's demand for energy and its subsequent price rises also increased domestic inflation. During 2004, grain and oil prices drove inflation up. China is the second largest energy consumer after the US, with oil making up 8 % of its imports and 7.6 % of world oil consumption.

Energy is refueling international territorial disputes. China and Japan are fighting over the oil supply route from Siberia. One of the key gas pipelines in construction is from the Tarim Basin to Shanghai – through the separatist Uighur area of Xinjiang. China is negotiating to buy Singapore's stake in oil in Ecuador. This is an important sector is highlighted by the fact that Buffett in 2003 held 13 % of the publicly available equity in PetroChina (China's national petroleum company). As pensions have been increasingly privatized, the retirement funding is helping to drive the expanding capital market.

CHINESE STOCK MARKETS

We now take a closer look at stock market trends to see how the results of the Shanghai and Shenzhen exchanges compare to New York markets. While it is beyond the scope of this chapter, data comparison of Chinese markets with European markets, as well as other emerging markets in general and those in the region in particular would reveal what commonalities and anomalies characterize the Chinese situation.

In analysing the stock market trends, we are struck by similarities with Japan in the 1980s. Like Japan in the late 1980s, China is booming and accumulating huge US dollar reserves because of the trade surplus. It is a population of savers. Yet, the motivations of Chinese savers differ from the Japanese. This also reflects the changing nature of the resource and production chain. It is now even easier to outsource aspects of production. Like Japanese, China needs to import vast amounts of energy and commodities. The study of anomalies and other aspects of the Chinese markets is just beginning and lessons can be applied from Japan. Bill's studies at the Yamaichi Research Institute and the University of Tsukuba were stock market crashes, anomalies (seasonal and fundamental) and return predictability using factor models. He found that there were strong anomalies and they were very similar to those of the US; see Ziemba and Schwartz (1991). We share some preliminary findings of the Chinese markets drawing on some existing studies.

First, a little Chinese stock history: China's stock market began in January 1984 with the issue of shares by Feilo Acoustics of Shanghai though these shares did not begin trading in the OTC market until August 1986. Regular trading in the Chinese stock markets did not commence until December 1990 in Shanghai (SHSE) and July 1991 in Shenzhen (SZSE). In the beginning there are only A-share stocks, which are limited to domestic investors and institutions and selected foreign institutional investors and traded in RMB (US$ 1 = 8.3 RMB). In contrast, H shares are of companies incorporated in Mainland China but listed on the Hong Kong Stock Exchange and other foreign stock exchanges. The Chinese and Hong Kong markets are the largest in Asia except for Japan (Wang, 2003). Only shares of Mainland Chinese companies are traded in China. As of April 2001, there were 1,123 listed companies on Mainland stock exchanges (597 and 526 on the SHSE and the SZSE, respectively) [1300 in early 2004], with a total capitalization of US$ 617 billion (5,101 billion RMB). In contrast the H-shares traded in HK had a cap of US$ 569 billion (HK$ 44 442 at the fixed rate of 7.80) in April 2001.

B-shares trading on the SHSE and SZSE are denominated in US or other foreign currencies or Hong Kong dollars and were designated for overseas investors. Because they were open to foreign investors, the B-shares fell dramatically following the 1997 Asia crisis. While the B-shares were decimated, the Chinese-held A-shares remained steady. In March 2001, investment in B shares was opened up to domestic investors with access to foreign currency.

Most listed Chinese firms have been created from formerly state-owned or state-controlled enterprises (SOEs). This makes them very different from the typical IPO. In the US or UK, firms tend to begin as a privately held company and then opens up to market ownership. In China, the primary reason for creating the stock markets was to allow state-owned enterprises (SOEs) to raise capital from Chinese households and from foreign entities. Other domestic institutions buy some of the other shares. Typically the state retains shares in these companies and uses the IPO process as a means to replace state responsibility for investment and employment in the enterprise. So share ownership is divided into state (central or local government), legal-entity (other domestic institutions including listed companies, SOEs and banks) and tradable shares. State and legal-entity shares are not traded publicly creating a class of shares similar to crossholding shares in Japan and Germany. Tradable shares are the only class that can be traded on the domestic stock exchanges and these are in turn divided into A- and B-shares with A-shares selling in RMB and B-shares in foreign currency.

In 2002 China opened the A-share RMB market to *Qualified Foreign Institutional Investors* and since that time 11 financial institutions have been approved. However they are subject to a lock-up period of at least a year during which period they cannot sell and stock is limited, thus isolating the A-Share market.

THE SHARE ALPHABET: DEFINITIONS OF SHARES AVAILABLE IN MAINLAND CHINESE COMPANIES

A-shares: shares of mainland companies traded in the mainland exchanges. The prices of A-shares are quoted in RMB, and currently only mainlanders and selected foreign institutional investors are allowed to trade A shares.

B-shares: shares of mainland companies traded in the mainland exchanges B-shares are quoted in foreign currencies and in the past, only foreigners were allowed to trade them. Since March 2001, mainlanders have been able to trade B-shares as well. However, they must trade with legal foreign currency accounts. Since these shares are open to foreign investors and foreign currency, these shares are more vulnerable to capital flight. More recently, B-shares were opened to domestic Chinese as a way of providing a place for them to store their foreign currency within China.

H-shares: mainland companies and are listed on the Hong Kong Stock Exchange and other foreign stock exchanges.

A vs H shares: this is the difference between the A share index and the H share index which is about +33% in July 2007.

Figure 16.1 shows the capitalization as a function of GDP for various countries in 2003. Observe that Hong Kong is the highest and China is the lowest. So while the mainland Chinese stock markets have been growing dramatically, they still lag behind on a per capita basis. Figure 16.2 shows A and H share differentials during December 2002 to February 2004.

H-shares rose strongly in early 2004 while A-shares went up only slightly. Large players can have a big role in IPOs, such as BP which has participated in the IPOs for Petrochina and Sinopec and then quickly sold the shares (H) for a profit of more than US$1 billion (CEQ). The A-share index is dominated by a number of key state-owned companies notably Sinopec, Baosteel, Yangtze Power, and Shanghai Auto – with earnings growth of 50% or

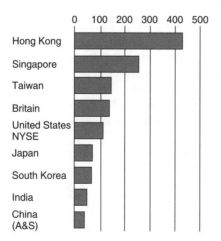

Figure 16.1   Stock market capitalization as a percent of GDP, 2003. *Source*: The Economist, March 18, 2004

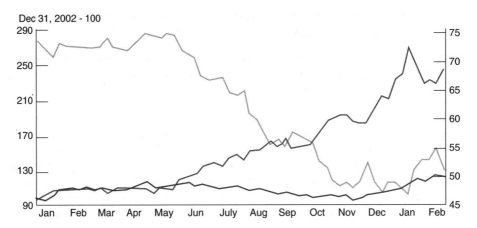

Figure 16.2 A and H shares (left scale) and the discount rate (the right scale), December 2002 to February 2004. *Source*: CEQ (2004)

more in 2003. The Shanghai 50, a new index of the 50 largest stocks on the Shanghai exchange is also beginning to have a major impact on the A-share market. At the beginning of 2003 these stocks accounted for less than one-third of Shanghai's market capitalization; by year-end they were over 45 %. This index is dominated by SOEs apparently favored by investors.

ESTIMATING THE RETURNS ON THE CHINESE STOCK MARKETS: IPOS, OWNERSHIP AND RETURNS

As the Chinese stock exchanges are young and most shares were IPOs of mature state owned firms (many listed Chinese IPOs were companies near bankruptcy in desperate need of cash injections), one would expect different return patterns than in developed markets. Due to the need to attract investors, some firms are likely to state their assets in a misleading way. The public offerings are a way to increase the amount of capital within the system, allowing more promising firms to subsidize weaker ones.

The unique ownership structure of Chinese listed companies influences the impact of privatization and ownership on performance. Using 1995–96 data Xu and Wang (1997) found that firm value increased with increases in the level and concentration of legal-entity ownership but state ownership had no impact on value. Tian (2000) investigating 1994–98 found that state ownership lowered firm value but the relationship was convex. Sun and Tong (2003) confirm that state ownership has a negative impact, and legal entity ownership had a positive impact.

Looking at this in a different way, Wang (2003) investigates the pre- and post-IPO valuation changes using 747 Chinese firms that went public during 1994–99 (369 on the SHSE and 378 on the SZSE). Figure 16.3(a) shows the returns by year and (b) by industry.

Only utilities come close to maintaining the past ROA. There has been a growing discrepancy between the before and after ROA. Wang (2003) observes that post IPO price performance in Chinese markets is significantly lower than the pre-IPO level. The median ROA drops from 9.3 % three years before the IPO to 6.4 % in the three years after the IPO. Firms in real estate and agricultural sectors experienced the largest declines and utility firms the least.

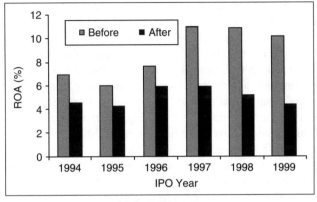

(a) overall, by year

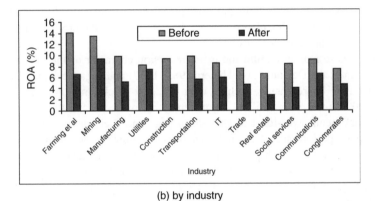

(b) by industry

Figure 16.3   Median Return On Assets (ROA) three years before and after IPO. The performance is measured by ROA, in percent. The median ROA is the median of average ROA of a firm three years before and after the IPO. Firms are classified using the CSRC's – digit classification system. *Source*: Wang (2003)

The only significant impact of ownership that Wang (2003) found was that legal-entity ownership and the concentration of non-state ownership is the best determinant of performance changes. He found a convex relationship between legal-entity ownership and non-state concentration and stock performance, that is, low and high levels of legal- entity ownership or non-state concentration increase along with post issue performance, whereas intermediate levels of legal-entity ownership or non-state concentration decrease with performance.

For several years, the Shenzhen stock exchange had been closed to IPOs. However in 2003, there was a major new listing of the TCL Corp., an unlisted holding company. They first delisted their telephone equipment subsidiary with a share swap then sold additional shares raising 2.5 billion RMB in new capital. The price had been set at 16 times 2002 earnings consistent with current IPOs (interestingly, at the time of its delisting, TCL Communications was trading at 61 times earnings.) This suggests that IPOs are priced at a common level independent of fundamentals (CEQ, 2004 Q1).

Also in 2003, there were a number of large share issues in H-shares. The first insurance company, the People's Insurance Co of China, raised US$ 700m and the shares increased 50 % in one day. Next was China Life which offered US$ 3.5 billion, had bids of US$ 80 billion and rose 27 % on the first day and later was trading at nearly a 70 % increase above the issue price. CEQ reports that these IPOs are *priced to do some favors*. One seventh of the China Life offering was allotted to Li Ka-shing and other Hong Kong investors despite the general retail and institutional interest. This suggests that the underpricing is intended to give select investors quick profits. These offerings continued into 2004 but by March the market was weakening, the HIS lost 18 % from March to May. The China Enterprises Index for H-shares fell 23 %. An offering of the China Shipping Container delayed its offering as it would have been difficult to get 9 times earnings (Dow Jones news, Yahoo, May 13).

The Chinese market also has different valuation characteristics than the American one. Using past returns and volume to predict medium term results, Wang and Chin (2004) found that low-volume stocks outperform high-volume stocks, volume discounts are more pronounced for past winners than for past losers, low-volume stocks trend and high- volume winners mean revert. Their findings are not entirely consistent with the US literature and are likely to result from such Chinese market characteristics as the prohibition of short sales and the dominance of individual investors.

Does the Chinese market exhibit the mean reversion character of the US market? Wang (2004) investigates the DeBondt and Thaler (1985, 1987) and Jagadeesh and Titman (1993) theses for Chinese shares using A-share data on most stocks trading from July 1994 to December 2000 on the Shanghai and Shenzhen stock exchanges. In the US, there is long-term (five year) mean reversion and short-term (e.g. one year) momentum. He found that stocks with poor performance over the past 6 to 24 months continued to underperform. However, when combined with past winners, the short-term momentum strategy of buying winners and selling losers was not profitable. Small stocks outperform large stocks and value stocks outperform growth stocks. Market factors such as beta, size and book-to-market do predict price movements as in the US.

As with any investment or loan, it is important to consider how the capital is being used. As the Chinese stock market went through bull market periods, the nature and purpose of being listed changed and the goal became that of obtaining money from private investors to increase liquidity, which in turn gave more benefits to managers and directors of the companies. These funds were rarely used for continued investment and/or long-term profitability of the company that would benefit shareholders and increase value. Many domestically listed companies massaged their books to make their earnings more appealing thus increasing their abilities to attract investment.

These motivations pose a dilemma for investors. Because the original intent of the Chinese stock market was to save and improve the near bankrupted state owned enterprises by attracting capital and making them more competitive, it is hard to find enough qualified companies in which to invest in China's domestic A-share or B-share markets. In Hong Kong, H-shares present higher quality companies, but these are at a premium. However, the very best Chinese companies, especially private companies, are yet to be listed domestically or abroad.[1] While China is in a high growth period, and will continue to grow rapidly in the next a few decades, the question remains how to best benefit from the growth?

---

[1] But more of them were in 2005/6 investing in Chinese companies: domestically listed A-share companies in which the government still owns 30 % is presently illegal for most foreign investors. Investing in Chinese companies listed in Hong Kong and abroad, one is limited to investing in few companies and in restricted industries.

HOW CAN ONE PARTICIPATE IN THIS *CHINA BOOM* PERIOD?

Chinese and New York Stock Exchanges

Having discussed the effects of IPOs on stock returns, we will now look more broadly at the Chinese stock exchanges by comparing the Shanghai and New York stock exchange and the Hang Seng. In so doing, we draw on Chow and Lawler (2003) who studied the relationship between the rates of return and volatilities of the Shanghai and New York markets. They found that the overall rates of returns and volatility in the two markets were basically uncorrelated. They use a absolute deviation volatility measure as well as variance to measure volatility. The almost zero and insignificant correlation between the rates of return to Shanghai and New York stocks indicates that the two markets are not integrated.

- As to be expected from an emerging market which is rapidly changing and accepting massive investment, rates of return and volatility of the Shanghai market were higher than New York. It would be expected that equity markets in a more mature developed economy would be less volatile.
- Volatility of the two markets are negatively correlated and to Granger cause volatility in the other market negatively.
- This lack of correlation is explained by the differences of macroeconomic fundamentals in the United States and China. These differences are also indicated by a negative correlation between the rates of change in their GDP. In addition, their capital markets are not integrated.

We would be surprised to discover that the Shanghai stock exchange would be directly correlated with NY because it is a very different sort of market. First, China is an emerging market rather than a stable world economic leader. Second, the countries and markets responded to the Asian financial crisis in different ways. Third, the stocks listed on Chinese exchanges represent a still relatively small, though ever increasing amount of the Chinese economy, much of which remains under at least some government oversight. Certain industries are over – represented In fact, it would be useful to compare Chinese returns with other markets, both within the region, other emerging markets and also the European ones.

Differences between the US and Chinese stock exchanges reflect their divergent economic histories and fundamentals underlying the economies. For most of the period studied (1992–2002) the US had sustained economic growth, partly driven by a revolution in information technology. In contrast, China began this period with the aftermath of the Tiananmen incident, followed by Deng Xiaoping's revolutionary policy in 1992 of deepening market reform that led to China's amazing expansion and inflation in the 1990s. This growth was followed by tight monetary policy to control inflation. The Chinese markets were negatively affected by the Asian financial crisis of 1997–99, which scared foreign investors and in the short term, decreased the amount of FDI available to emerging markets. However, after 1999, investment resumed. In addition, the two stock markets are driven by different fundamentals. The Shanghai stocks had a higher mean rate of return than New York stocks. This higher mean rate of return for the entire period is partly but not solely the result of a higher inflation rate in China. Even after the rate of inflation became zero or slightly negative in China, the rate of return in Shanghai remained higher than that of New York, but the difference in the rate of return between the two markets narrowed in the second sub-period, since the 1997 Chinese takeover of Hong Kong. The second measure of volatility itself reflected greater uncertainty in Shanghai. As an emerging market the Shanghai market had a higher volatility and the volatility itself had a higher variance, but the difference from the New York market was reduced in the second sub-period as the Shanghai market matured.

The Shanghai and New York stock markets were not correlated during January 1992 to February 2002. This observation is one indicator that the Chinese capital market was not integrated with the world market. However, the degree of integration may increase in the future as China has become a member of WTO.

Table 16.1 gives the price/earnings ratios of the various Chinese, the Hong Kong and the S&P500 indices from June 1996 to August 2004. Observe that the average PE ratios of the A-shares are about double those of the B-shares and substantially above the rather high S&P500 values during this period. From Figure 16.5(a) we see that these indices were higher than the S&P500 throughout except for the brief period from October 2001 to June 2002.

Table 16.2 shows the correlation matrix of these stock markets. Figure 16.5 shows this visually. Observe how close the Shanghai and Shenzhen A-shares are. Shanghai and Shenzhen B-share exchanges followed similar paths in the beginning but diverged. Recently the Shanghai exchange was opened to domestic investors with foreign currency.

Table 16.1 Statistics on the price earnings ratios for various exchanges, monthly, June 1996 to August 20, 2004. *Source*: Bloomberg

	S&P500	Hang Seng	Shanghai A	Shanghai B	Shenzhen A	Shenzhen B
Average	29.03	15.85	41.89	21.77	41.81	14.97
Median	28.32	15.37	40.81	16.92	41.49	13.85
St Dev	8.29	4.02	8.50	12.92	8.04	6.79
Low	18.31	8.62	25.69	5.11	20	.46 4.71
High	62.26	28.05	60.84	59.86	59.07	38.85

Table 16.2 Correlation Matrix for PERs for various exchanges, monthly, June 1996 to August 20, 2004. *Source*: Bloomberg

	S&P500	Hang Seng	Shanghai A	Shanghai B	Shenzhen A	Shenzhen B
S&P500		0.06	0.15	0.36	0.12	0.27
HSI			−0.14	0.09	−0.08	0.20
Shanghai A				0.25	0.89	0.33
Shanghai B					0.27	0.94
Shenzhen A						0.33
Shenzhen B						

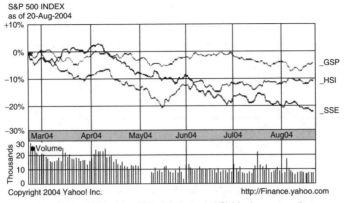

(a) 6-months, SSE dropping, SPX relatively steady, HSI rising in recent months

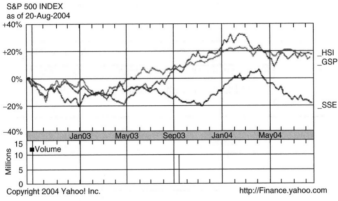

(b) 2-years originally sort of tracking each other

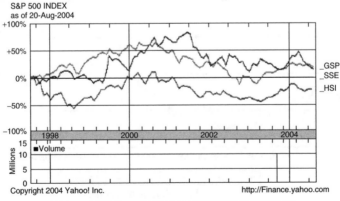

(c) from end of 1997, over the longer period, HSI is the worst performer

Figure 16.4 Hang Seng, Shanghai and the S&P500 indices for different time periods from 3 months to 7 years. Recalibrated to base at each start date. *Source*: Yahoo-Finance

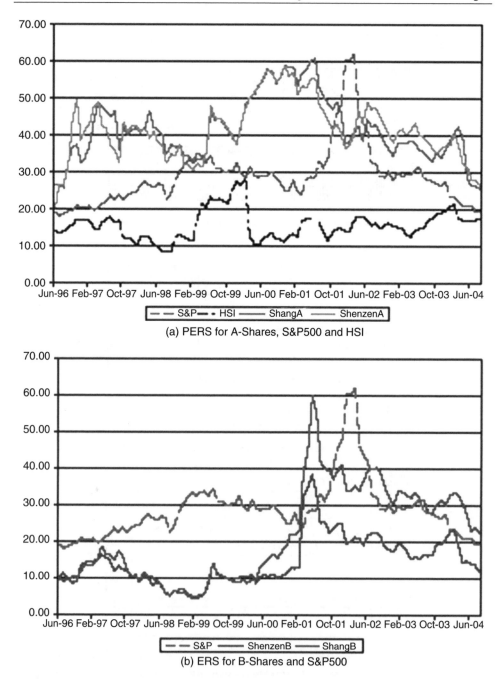

(a) PERS for A-Shares, S&P500 and HSI

(b) ERS for B-Shares and S&P500

Figure 16.5 The price earnings ratios for various exchanges, monthly, June 1996 to August 20, 2004. *Source*: Bloomberg

THE FUTURE: INVESTING IN CHINA REQUIRES A LEAP OF FAITH

The cycles will be much wider and more frequent in China because of the lack of information. Having said that, if you're investing, you should put a fairly large part of your total assets in China because within as short a period as 30 years, China is likely to have the largest gross national product any nation has ever had.

John Templeton, April 1, 2004 in Smart Money

Opportunities for private Chinese and foreign investors are expanding, making it more critical to assess what makes for a good investment. The critical issues to consider are past good investments and determining what looks good for the future, including broader global trends that affect and are affected by policies in China.

Other limits to investment include ownership regulations, e.g., what items can be bought by foreigners especially related to stock issues and types and nature of joint ventures. The government still owns all the land so property is leased. With a shortage of apartments and a continuing move to the cities, there is constant upward pressure on housing prices. Higher interest rates and a slowdown pose the greatest danger to investment.

There are several options for those who would like to directly or indirectly invest in China; any of these options would require in-depth research to maximize the investment. Indirect investment includes investing in China-related stocks, companies that do business with China and/or will profit from China's long term economic growth. There are many companies that would fit that description. Natural resource companies, or producers of raw materials or other intermediate inputs for Chinese goods, including energy, agriculture, minerals and parts. Other alternatives include investing in China-related funds, which include mutual funds, closed-end funds, hedge funds and/or offshore funds, focusing on China. There are new funds opening everyday. There are still a lot of opportunities in China, but savvy investors will have to do their research to mitigate against the asymmetry of information and make sure that each investment is sound.

Of course, risks remain: country risk factors in China and abroad (political instability, rising interest rates), which could negatively impact the value of the companies. In addition, investors must prepare for currency risk between the country of investment and their home countries since depreciation of the currency may decrease returns. Fluctuation in resource prices is another source of uncertainty. Therefore, it is necessary to invest in countries that are politically stable, economically open, and that have a currency appreciation prospect (or at least are likely to remain stable), or else to hedge against the potential risk factors involved.

It is difficult to assess the information regarding the Chinese markets. John Templeton about sums it up, we don't really know exactly the returns expected, or in what sectors they are most likely to come but we are convinced that being invested in the long haul is important. This was essentially the same feeling expressed by Jim Rogers in his recent book Adventure Capitalist (2003) in which he mentions buying B-shares when they fell out of favor following the 1997 Asian crash and he expects to just hold on for the long term. However, his advice is not to invest indiscriminately but to do as much research as possible on investments – a policy he follows all over the world. He is convinced in China's importance enough to expect his young daughter will learn Mandarin! But what we do predict is that China will become an even more important player in the world economy and political arena.

POSTSCRIPT: CHINESE EQUITY MARKETS

In the 30 months since this article was written, China's financial markets have only become more dynamic. There have been a growing number of initial public offerings, which have been oversubscribed. The largest of these was the ICBC IPO, which has since become one of the largest global banks. At the same time the number of and quality of companies listed has increased in number and in quality. This has resulted in better performing indices. In 2006 and 2007, in particular, better companies have been listed on the stock exchanges. This has coincided with increased demand from Chinese investors. But the number of tradeable shares is low.

These high earners propelled the Shanghai and Shenzhen stock markets up by 140 % from February 2006 to the end of January 2007 and further through June 2007. See Figure 16.6. The public is very active in buying mutual funds and is redeploying savings account money into what has so far been higher yielding equities. Since capital gains are not taxed added fuel to the rally. The introduction of the qualified foreign investor program as discussed above has eased the way for some foreign investors, and added to the liquidity of the exchange.

> Across China, similar tales of riches are captivating the country and enticing millions. Investors opened an estimated 50 000 retail brokerage accounts a day in December. A new mutual fund from a Beijing-based money manager partly owned by Germany's Deutsche Bank AG raised the equivalent of $ 5.1 billion in its December launch, a new record.

Measured by the price earnings ratios, the valuations are not cheap and are well above those in most other countries. The end of December 2006 PE ratios on the Shanghai stock exchange were 37.57 for the Chinese traded A-shares and 28.15 for the hard currency B-shares traded by foreigners. The Shenzhen stock exchange had a similar PE ratio for the A-shares (37.46) but the B shares were lower at 23.2.

The B-share market is still small and illiquid with an average daily volume in 2006 of about US$ 65 million. Its purpose to provide foreign investors with access to Chinese equities was usurped by the Hong Kong H-shares which have a market capitalization of over US$ 800 billion versus US$ 19 billion for the B-shares. Rumors suggest that the B-shares

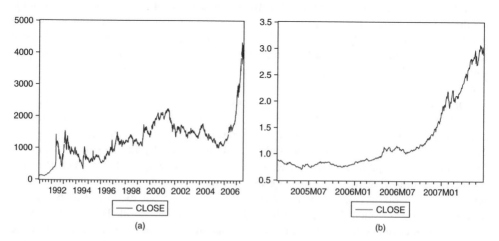

Figure 16.6 Chinese stock markets: (a) Shanghai stock index January 1, 1990 to June 29, 2007; (b) 50 Exchange traded funds January 1, 2005 to June 29, 2007. *Source*: Ruoen (2007)

might be merged with the A-shares. As of December 2006, there were 109 listed B-shares of which 85 also have yuan-denominated A-shares. Since the A-shares trade at a discount of about 30 %, they could be bought back. But Chinese companies historically prefer to invest in growth opportunities rather than in buybacks. Moreover, they would have to raise cash on the A-share market in competition with other companies trying to expand. The conversion from B's to A's would require compensation, another undesirable.

However, continuing growth, does make some of these equities vulnerable. In 2007 there were increasing fears that the stock markets might be overvalued – and markets likely to be volatile. As any conversion of B's to As could be complex, it may not occur.

Figure 16.7 (a & b) shows the long bond (5-year) Treasury bond rates on the Shanghai stock exchange from 2002 to June 2007. These rates were about 2.9 % in January 2007 so the bond-stock model discussed in Chapters 23 and 25 is not in the danger zone in China despite these high PE ratios. The measure is about $2.9 - (100/37.57) = 0.24$, which is below the danger level. Since Chinese interest rates have historically been below those in the US, the danger zone was well below the about 3 % bond/stock danger level for the US. By June 2007, see Figure 16.7 a, b, the long bond increased to about 4.33 % but despite the great rise in the Shanghai stock index, the PE ratios have actually fallen because earnings are rising faster than prices. The bond–stock model is thus about $4.33 - 3.33 = 1.00$ still below the danger zone but more risky.

China is now more comparable to Japan in the early 1980s rather than the US.[2] In Japan from 1948 to 1988, the stock market rose 220 times in yen and 550 times in dollars, yet had 20 declines of 10 % or more. Historically, the Shanghai market has had many large declines with daily changes as high as the -16.39% on 23 May 1995. The 50 best and largest listed companies had a dramatic rise of over 40 % in late December 2006 to end

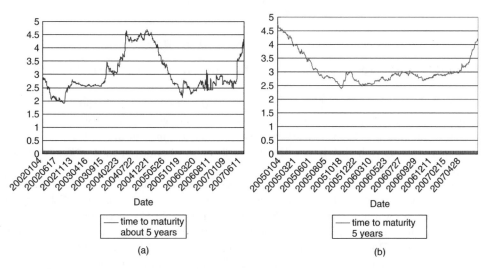

Figure 16.7 Long bond (5 years) yield to maturity on Treasury bonds on the Shanghai stock exchange: (a) January 1, 2002 to June 29, 2007; and (b) January 1, 2005 to June 29, 2007. *Source*: Ruoen (2007)

---

[2] In Japan's early development period, foreign exchange reserves were controlled by the MITI. These were doled out to support development of the economy. Soon firms were able to hold onto their foreign earnings and reinvest them according to their own plans. We know that some of these were spent on trophy purchases.

Table 16.3 Large declines in the Shanghai stock exchange. *Source*: Burton (2007)

1995-05-23	−16.39	1997-05-22	−8.83
1993-12-20	−13.08	1992-05-26	−8.46
1994-08-29	−12.67	1994-07-28	−8.43
1993-03-22	−11.75	1998-08-17	−8.36
1992-10-27	−11.18	1992-05-27	−8.31
1994-10-05	−10.71	1993-05-04	−8.21
1994-10-13	−10.64	1994-09-29	−8.00
1993-03-01	−10.46	1992-10-22	−7.84
1992-08-11	−10.44	1994-10-26	−7.82
1993-05-24	−10.30	1996-04-30	−7.78
1992-12-09	−10.28	1999-07-01	−7.61
1996-12-16	−9.91	1992-12-10	−7.57
1992-08-12	−9.52	1993-02-24	−7.49
1996-12-17	−9.44	1996-11-21	−7.31
1992-10-26	−9.43	1994-09-07	−7.30
1992-09-08	−8.92	⋯	⋯
1997-02-18	−8.91	2007-01-25	−3.96

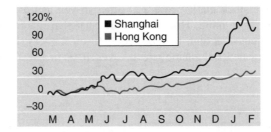

Figure 16.8 The Shanghai A price index vs the Hong Kong H index, May 2006 to February 9, 2007

January 2007 with a −3.9 % fall on 25 January 2007. See Figure 16.6 and Table 6.3. So with growth rates of more than 10 % and a wide and growing trade surplus and a world awash in liquidity, the Chinese markets may well mirror Japan in the 1980s with a large but bumpy ride up to higher levels. Eventually there will be movement towards the Hong Kong H share level, see Figure 16.8.

Indeed, over the course of 2007, there have been many declines in the A-Share market.[3] Moreover, the fear of a Chinese crash is rising in the US and Asia. The February 27 decline plus the warning from Alan Greenspan of a possible US recession and weak US data contributed to a nearly 4 % fall in the US and global markets that day and a six week correction period. However, aside from the February crash, there has been little contagion to other markets, which may be more vulnerable to a slowdown in Chinese economic growth than an equity crash. See the discussion in Chapter 23.

Most of the declines in the Shanghai and Shenzhen indices were triggered by actual or rumored government policy changes, including crackdowns on speculative activity, changes

---

[3] These include February 27 (−8.84 %), April 19 (−4.52 %), May 30, (−6.65 %), June 4 (−8.26 %), June 28 (−4.03 %) and July 5 (−5.23 %).

in monetary policy instruments and use of administrative tools like reducing the stamp tax. Still, the index was up over 110 % in the past 12 months and over 60 % for the first half of 2007. One measure to watch is that of new brokerage accounts being opened, as when this growth slows there likely will be trouble. For now such inflows contribute to price rises. After record account openings, the number of new accounts slowed in early July, subsequently rebounding. Mainland equity markets were relatively isolated from global risk aversion.

These declines have triggered concerns about a broader correction in China's equity markets. The official script is that the market will rise after government policies become clearer, the price-earnings ratios return to a reasonable level and the results of listed companies in the first half of the year are announced. Any correction might be limited by the large proportion of non-tradeable shares and of tradeable shares held by public actors, who might be more likely to hold even if prices slide. However, those in last, retail investors, are likely to suffer. Restrictions on other domestic investments (real estate) and negative real returns on bank deposits in the face of skyrocketing equity returns are likely to keep driving investors to the exchange. Though likely policy initiatives (encouraging more IPOs, a decrease of the tax on bank deposits and opening to investment abroad) may increase inflows, it sure looks like Japan in the mid to late 1980s; see Stone and Ziemba (1993) and Ziemba and Schwartz (1991, 1992).

In 1988–89 at the peak, Japan had PE ratios in the range of 60, until the interest rates rose in mid 1989 into August 1990 to crash the market; see Figures 9.1, 9.3, 23.2 and 23.3 and Ziemba and Schwartz (1991).

According to calculations by Professor Ren Ruoen of Beihang University, Beijing, there is price parity at an exchange rate of about 5 yuan per dollar. So the slight drift upward in the yuan of 6 % that we have seen from July 2005 to December 2006 might bring the yuan to this level in about 10 years. The drift is expected to be about 3–5 % per year but more likely being about 5 %.

The *nationalization* of global financial flows evidenced by the increase of Asian reserves due to the US trade and current account deficit, as well as the willingness of Asian countries to buy US assets, has created a huge liquidity problem which so far has resulted in concentration of assets in low yielding treasuries. A number of countries manage their exchange rates and therefore must hold on to growing reserves as they attempt to neutralize the flows; this concentration helps to explain the conundrum of the insatiable demand for bonds, even at very low yields and the lack of demand for equities, even at low valuations.

So far, China's reserves, growing by nearly $ 200 billion a year, have been managed by the State Administration for Foreign Exchange, a department of the Central Bank, and invested almost entirely in government bonds and other low-yielding presumably risk-free assets. Recently China has created a new unit, to be named the China Investment Company to manage a portion of China's $ 1.3 trillion of foreign exchange reserves. The new corporation has a different mandate, to diversify into various assets including non-Chinese equities, property and direct investments. The fund is likely to have at least $ 200 billion in assets when it launches, though diversification may take some time. This policy change in China, while still concentrating assets in the hands of the government, will likely generate a major change in global markets, including the relative valuations of bonds and equities. A first major move is their $ 3 Billion investment in the private equity firm Blackstone (at a 4.5 % discount to the IPO value). Besides a potentially good investment this may give them entry to future private equity deals in the U.S., China and elsewhere. Others have suggested that it and other deals may include training to be given to Chinese fund managers. Such clauses were included in some of Singapore's (GIC and Temasek) purchases. The Blackstone holding will be transferred to the new investment company when it is created (likely September 2007). To finance further investments, rather than just investing US dollars they hold as they do to purchase US Treasury and Agency bonds, the central government will issue bonds in RMB with a coupon rate to be determined which will then be released by the central bank as part of money market operations. In return the central bank will then transfer the equivalent in fx to the investment company to make the equity purchase. It is unclear (but likely) if this procedure will be followed for future transactions.

POSTSCRIPT ON ECONOMIC GROWTH AND DEVELOPMENT

The Chinese economy's continued progress toward market liberalization has spurred high projections for economic growth to 2050 with Fogel (2005, 2007), Maddison (1998, 2005), Ruoen (1998) and others pointing to the ability of the economy to continue to experience rapid growth. Long-term projections are based on assumptions of greater labour productivity, increased education levels, investments in capital equipment and, importantly, inter-industry shifts out of agriculture into higher value added sectors which at the same time may increase the productivity in agriculture. Such growth also reflects increased moves up the value added chain within sectors as well and a deepening of the domestic supply chain. In terms of worker productivity, from 2000 to 2005 China has shifted from being 26 % less productive than ASEAN countries to being 5 % more productive. The gap is projected to increase as Chinese productivity has been growing at about 6.6 % a year, almost double that of ASEAN.[4] According to the ILO, China's productivity growth has coincided with the growth in secondary school and university attendance and relatively high level of research and development spending (1.23 % of GDP) (The Economist, 2007).

By 2020 China's per capita income is predicted to reach the level of Korea in the early 1990s and at that point, due to the population size, the Chinese economy would be 30 times that of Korea (in the early 1990s) (Ruoen, 1997). Fogel (2007) projects that, despite potential political and economic constraints, by 2040, the Chinese economy will reach $ 123 trillion or nearly three times the output of the whole world in 2000 with a per capita income of $ 85,000, more than twice that forecast for the EU15 and much higher than India but below the US. If this is the case, clearly a series of adjustments to higher Chinese wage rates will occur, in particular, to what extent wage costs will be passed on to importers of Chinese goods.

China's economy grew 11.1 % in 2006 with a total output of US$ 2.705 trillion according to the National Bureau of Statistics. Recent projections from the World Bank and even Chinese authorities expect growth at or over 10 % in 2007. Thus China is close to overtaking Germany, whose output was US$ 3 trillion but with a much lower growth rate of 2.5 %. To bring this about smoothly will require a lot of organization including building industrial cities and suburbs and the relocation of hundreds of millions of people. Whether or not these projections are accurate it is clear that the impact of China and the rest of Asia's growth will be substantial in the next 30+ years.

---

[4] Productivity in the ASEAN group varies from that of Singapore which is higher than Japan to Cambodia's which is half that of India.

17
Springtime in Buenos Aires: prospects for investment, how deep is the recovery?

Back to Commodity-Driven Growth? Renewed exchange rate competitiveness combined with more centralized control.

As I wrote this chapter in November 2005, Argentina was again much in the news, as it was hosting the leaders of the western Hemisphere for the fourth Summit of the Americas. Hoping to solidify hemispheric links, fight poverty and promote trade, leaders of government presented contending visions for the Americas and in particular the US role within it. Met with protest from many, especially in the host country of Argentina, which has been and is still a testing ground for both the liberalizing and populist trends common to much of Latin America, the summit ended inconclusively with Venezuela and the Mercosur countries refusing to agree to preliminary talks surrounding much-discussed free trade area of the Americas (FTAA), calling into question the development paths for

many Latin American countries and the prospect of regional and sub-regional trade, political and economic zones. The summit discussions illustrate questions which arose during my recent visit to Argentina and Uruguay on the eve of the Southern Hemisphere's spring (September 2005). How much room is there for these overlapping zones? What do recent events say about the prospects for sustained and equitable growth and investment in Latin America? While this chapter will not engage in a regional survey, and instead focuses on the effects of Argentina's 2001–2 crisis and recent recovery, its experience is similar to many emerging markets in Latin America and beyond.

As 2006 begins, Argentina is likely to be in the news for another reason, the fourth anniversary of the financial crisis of 2002. Thus it is a key time to make a checkup, to ask how Argentina has recovered from the crisis that transfixed much of the financial world in the end of 2001. In late December 2001–January 2002, Argentina defaulted on its international debt, experienced protests leading to riots, limits on withdrawing assets from bank accounts, had five presidents within the span of three weeks and abandoned the decade long peso-dollar peg which had given stability following the high inflation and monetary uncertainty of the 1980s.

Comparing Argentina's currency crisis to the almost contemporary physical introduction of the euro, reveals the political and economic importance of currency and monetary choices. As the streets of Buenos Aires filled with those protesting the aftermath of the exit from the decade long dollar-peso peg, which had provided the basis for the growth, stability, high foreign investment of the early to mid-1990s, while reducing flexibility, eleven European countries were trying to convince their citizens and the global financial community that the future was in tying their currency and monetary policy together. While it is difficult to these two currency decisions, as the European monetary union was based on decades of economic and political integration while the argentine peg to the US dollar was a unilateral policy to bring stability to economic and financial systems.

For Argentina in the 1990s, the peg to the US dollar provided credibility and refocused the central bank on its primary goal of ensuring monetary stability and preserving the value of money. Convertibility was very effective at bringing economic stability by banishing the hyperinflation of the late 80s and 1990. But as the US dollar appreciated against the currencies of Argentina's trading partners, this stability was bought at a high price, encouraging deflation in the domestic economy. Following the devaluations of the Asian financial crisis, and the 40 % devaluation of the Brazilian real in 1999, Argentina's currency peg became increasingly costly to bear. At that time, fears of devaluation made commitment to the currency board that much more essential to maintain the inflows of foreign currency. Throughout the 90s, largely as a result of the currency board and successive structural adjustment programs, Argentina was shown off as a prime example for the IMF and other international actors.

Yet by the late 1990s, Argentina was in the midst of one of the most devastating recessions in its history, which was exacerbated by decreasing demand for primary products and the global slowdown. The dollar peg made Argentina's currency increasingly uncompetitive and

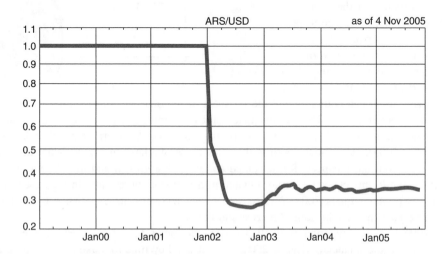

Figure 17.1 Argentine peso versus US dollar

the series of dollar-denominated contracts, led to deflation, increasing unemployment at the time when social spending cuts limited the safety net available.

The memory of hyperinflation strengthened the public resolve to maintain convertibility, fearing a collapse in stability if the peg was changed. The perceived cost of change was too high. It was not until the spring and summer of 2001 that the debt situation and the exchange rate policy became untenable. Hoping for further loans from international actors to avoid default and devaluation it was too late and as currency fled the country, it was impossible to make the interest payments on the foreign debt in late 2001. At the same time, restrictions on withdrawing funds at the old one-dollar to one peso exchange rate began, leading to the protests mentioned above as people feared that they would not be able to access their assets. But there was no longer an alternative to exiting the currency board. Figure 17.1 above shows the dollar peso exchange rate for the last decade, focusing on the last five years of the devaluation and more recent *managed* float which has kept the peso around 2.8 pesos to one American dollar.

DEVALUATION OF THE ARGENTINE PESO

So four years after that tumultuous December and January, how is Argentina faring? What is the level of recovery and what does it mean for foreign investors? In many ways, the prognosis seems much better and the recovery somewhat swifter than some predicted three years ago. Argentina had a successful debt swap with the vast majority of their private creditors in the spring of 2005, with all but 11 % accepting 30c on the dollar for their investment. Argentina has had very high growth rates from 2003–5, averaging about 9 % GDP growth. This recovery was accomplished without further foreign funds and the debt level has progressively decreased. It is a mark of the extreme crisis prior to the devaluation that GDP levels and output levels (in pesos) are only recently returned and to the levels they reached in the late 1990s. Poverty and inequality levels which rose dramatically in the aftermath of the crisis are returning to their slightly less elevated levels of the late 1990s. Argentina's recovery can be explained by two main factors: a favorable external environment especially in key agricultural exports and the ability to react to the competitive exchange rate with human and physical capital resources. Yet, three main challenges remain to be overcome to make long-term growth possible: (re) integrating the 50 % of the population below the poverty line, maintaining and increasing human capital to support future growth and regaining trust of the international financial community, which was lost in the default and accompanying dissolution of the dollar-denominated contract system. Some of these are well on their way to being achieved.

Just as the negative external climate exacerbated the recession of the late 1990s, growing external demand, especially for commodities, has facilitated the economic recovery. Argentine producers were able to take advantage of the new competitive exchange rate for exports. At the same time global demand for several agricultural products that Argentina produces, especially soybeans, increased dramatically, led by Chinese demand. Agricultural production and exports make up an increasing amount of GDP and a major supply of foreign currency. The production of soybeans is very profitable, especially in the north. As exports increased, imports decreased, especially from non-Mercosur countries. The export prices are very competitive, even with high export tax rates, leading more land to be cleared for soybean production. This move towards mono-cropping worries some, given that the environmental effects are unclear, and it may limit the arable land for other crops destined for domestic consumption and the meat for domestic and export. Meat exports have also increased. But it is unclear at present how much the production can be expanded for export, especially as the costs to domestic consumers are already rising.

The resilience of the domestic economy supported this growth, as domestic producers who had previously been unable to compete against imports have been able to expand sales. For example the publishing industry has grown since devaluation as imported books from Mexico and Spain became three times more expensive, prompting more domestic production in this literate and literary country.

Social costs and effects of the crisis remain high, especially the still high levels of unemployment and poverty and increased levels of inequality. These social effects are the result of the

'enough of garbage contracts' in the heart of the microcentro, the downtown business and financial district refers to the dollar denominated utilities contracts.

two-phase crisis – the recession and the sudden devaluation, in which assets and wages were devalued but liabilities remained constant, at the same time, uncertainty led to some inflation. Argentina has not reached the levels of inequality of several of its neighbors, especially Brazil, one of the most unequal countries in the world. The recession led to deflation, shrinking in growth, loss of jobs, decrease in real wages, government revenues, etc. All of which was exacerbated by the financial and economic collapse of 2002. Yet, from the fourth quarter of 2002, growth was already beginning even without any access to private credit. This early growth was driven by competitive exports. By midway through 2003, high levels of growth were enabled by increased supply of capital.

This inequality is largely the result of economic changes, e.g. the move to large production farms, which are increasingly mechanized. The manufacturing industries are recovering from the recession of the 90s, labor intensive manufacturing is increasingly expensive, and it is hard to compete with East Asia. Many firms could not afford to make capital investments in the 1990s even though such imports were cheap. But recent research shows that firms that were able to adapt and survive during the recession are now very flexible and have been able to adapt well. But there is a limit to how fast these can grow and how many new jobs can be created in the process, given that these companies succeeded by becoming increasingly productive and limiting their hiring.

Through the decade from 1992–2002, the poverty rate increased from around 20 % to as much as 60 % immediately following the crisis. This increase in poverty was shared between the recession and devaluation. During the recession many people lost their jobs, and those who kept their jobs had considerable losses in real wages. Many turned to the informal economy and did so increasingly through the devaluation crisis. However these traditional coping strategies were insufficient. The increase in poverty led the government to respond with a temporary targeted transfer to poor households. This program, Jefes y Jefas, guaranteed a minimum income to households with children. It included a work requirement of 20 hours per week and has been largely credited with cushioning the effects of the crisis. While some concerns have been raised about its ability to target those who most needed the money, it is seen to be an effective program implemented in a very short period of time, when it was desperately needed. And while some fear that the increased subsidies are creating a culture of entitlement among the poorer members of society, they are a necessary means to an end to promote political and social stability and the survival of the lower classes.

Does Argentina have the capacity to absorb new wealth and distribute it? The current growth is concentrated in some areas and in a few hands and the money is not necessarily staying in the country, as the financial system has yet to regain its credibility. Capital controls have been quite effective in keeping money in the country and hot money speculation from entering. While foreign companies can repatriate their assets, there are many restrictions and penalties on short-term inflows. It has the most to gain from long-term foreign direct investment and that the hot money of the 1990s brings costs as well as benefits.

CHALLENGES FOR THE FINANCIAL SECTOR

As in many developing countries, the lack of depth of the tax base limits growth and results in inefficiencies. There is little corporate tax, little income tax, though collection rates have increased and the most major are export and value-added taxes. With the new exchange rate, prices remain competitive even with taxes of as high as 22 % on soybeans.

The breakdown of the system of contracts provides a major source of instability in the financial sector derives from debt default, exit from convertibility and pessification brought with it the collapse of the dollar-denominated contract system. The limitations on withdrawing assets, the forcible conversion of dollars to pesos at differential rates and the breaking of contracts especially in the utilities sector have had a long term impact on the credibility and stability of the financial sector from which it is only now beginning to recover. Since the currency board guaranteed constant convertibility of pesos to dollars, it implied that pesos were dollars for the purposes of most transactions. Under the stability of Convertibility, the majority of contracts were denominated in dollars. This perception of stability was a key part of the national and sometimes local government contracts with the private providers of essential services, many of whom were foreign conglomerates. Throughout the recession of the late 1990s, when wage rates fell the dollar based prices remained constant and in many cases increased as they were based on US inflation rather than Argentine deflation. Following the devaluation, these contracts were forcibly de-dollarized, a response which led some utility providers to refuse to provide service at the lower peso prices. Many of these providers have now exited the market, some selling to domestic companies, others are still waiting the results of pending court cases. This instability is making international investors wary. While I have focused on the utility contracts this situation is representative of many other contract systems, the breakdown of which had negative effects on many aspects of the financial system.

The debt swap of spring 2005 was a necessary step towards resolution of the external debt imbalance which was needed to attract both domestic and foreign investment. Understandably the causes of the financial crisis and the debt default continues to be a national fascination, one product of which is one of the more surreal museums I have visited, one devoted to external debt. Housed in the basement of a building used by the economics department of the University of Buenos Aires, the debt museum takes as its mission to explain how Argentina's indebtedness to foreign debtors ebbed and flowed through the 1980s and 90s. This museum, a joint venture between the University of Buenos Aires and the local government, depicts the economic changes of the last quarter century in Argentina to explain how it became so indebted, from the debt crisis of the 80s, to the increasing multilateral loans which supported the dollar-peso currency peg. One of its most powerful sections is a **black hole** out of which one can pull examples of all the public goods such as health, education and infrastructure on which spending was cut to maintain debt payments. The museum fulfils a role to encourage debate on the economic condition; when I visited, it was the site of a heated symposium on the lingering costs of the debt.

The costs of the debt remain a key part of the domestic political debate, frequently mentioned in the October 2005 parliamentary elections. In both Argentina and Uruguay, Argentina's smaller neighbor, which also suffered a currency crisis in 2002, there have been numerous calls for money to be spent not on continuing to pay off the debt but on increased social services, especially the education and health sectors and supporting traditional farming industries.

To what extent is Argentina's recovery a success story and what leverage does it have with international actors especially the IMF as it nears an upcoming deadline for renegotiating its multilateral debt? Following the debt swap, which most investors, Argentina seems to be in much stronger position vis-á vis international investors and multilateral creditors. By choosing to delay a settlement on its IMF loans until most of the private loans were settled, Kirchner and his finance minister Lavagna have more political leverage. Also, in the last two years, Argentina has paid all of the required interest payments and has

Protest: no to the payment of the foreign debt in the Plaza de Mayo, directly in front of the Casa Rosada, home of the President of the Republic of Argentina.

been paying down some of its debt. President Kirchner, buoyed by the strong showing of his supporters in the mid-term parliamentary elections, has the political space to take some unpopular decisions. It is still unclear if those decisions will be unpopular to the IMF or to his supporters, or both. Visiting Argentina during the presidential election, many people mentioned the difference between Kirchner's populist rhetoric and his actions that please the international financial markets. More recent actions have tilted to the populist side. And while he has been unwilling to fall in line with all requests from the financial community, he is unlikely to take the anti-IMF stance many of his compatriots desire. They are likely to negotiate a settlement in the coming months. Yet Argentina may not able to determine the prices, earlier in 2005, they had to withdraw a bond issue because investors demanded higher interest for their investment.

People are investing in Argentina again, North American and European investment is up in specific sectors. The cheap exchange rate is driving a burgeoning tourism industry as the number of American and European tourists rediscover the charms of the *Paris of the south*. Also property values are rising especially in the sought-after areas of Buenos Aires such as Recoleta, Palermo and Puerto Madero. In some of these areas, the prices are as high as in the late 1990s. Investors from Brazil are increasingly evident, whether it is in the tourist sites of the Buenos Aires or the fancy restaurants of Puerto Madero. Investment in Argentina is attractive for Brazilians and many have bought out the contracts of European and American companies who fled. But two additional sources come to mind.

Along with some traditional sources, some new investors are stepping up. China, is more and more interested in securing mineral and agricultural products to fuel its growth, and is increasingly investing in many South American countries. In Venezuela President Chavez is increasingly using its oil wealth to subsidize the energy costs of his own country and other Latin American countries fighting against what he sees as the yoke of American capitalism. In recent months he has been making agreements with members of the southern cone and has announced Petrosur, an oil-based regional agreement, for increasing Latin American cooperation. Venezuela is also

The new bridge designed by Santiago Calatrava in Puerto Madero, one of the fastest growing areas of Buenos Aires, one of several in which rich Argentines and foreigners are investing, notable as the home of expensive hotels and high-tech companies.

buying bonds from Argentina at very favorable rates, without insisting on the high interest rates demanded by the international markets.

There are many ways in which progress is happening and more is likely but there are some challenges and limiting factors to widespread growth and investment – and in that way is quite indicative of many Latin American countries and to Argentina's particular history. In 1900, Argentina had similar per capita GDP to many European countries – and has since spent a century asking what happened. The period of highest growth in 1890s and early 1900s was driven, like today's, by the sale of primary agriculture products to a global market clamoring for resources. For Argentina, one of the breadbaskets of the world, agricultural exports were a major driver of growth and source of wealth, the results of which trade can still be seen whilst wandering around Buenos Aires today, a city full of early 20th century europeanesque buildings. But agricultural prices and those of all primary products are subject to the whims of global demand. Today that demand comes from China, and while that demand is unlikely to disappear, sustained growth is only likely to continue if trade can be diversified and add value.

THE CHALLENGE OF PROMOTING LONG-TERM VALUE-ADDED PRODUCTION

Current challenges call into question the ability to expand and the opportunity for sustained long-term production, The shift to one crop for export is decreasing the amount of land available for domestic food production and thus increasing the costs.

Education and human capital development are limiting factors to growth. Argentina has been better able to respond to changes and opportunities brought by its new, more competitive exchange rate and favorable external market because of its traditionally high levels of education, in comparison to some of its neighbors. Argentina has attracted high-tech investment, particularly centered on the city of Cordoba. Future growth will rely on increasing human capital growth and flexibility. Some question how long Argentina can rely on past educational strengths and how long can it absorb new technical growth without trained professionals. There's a lack of engineers and specialized tradespeople, especially in the younger cohorts, a trend that much of the developed world is also facing. Especially as educational funding decreased dramatically in the 1990s and through the crisis period. While there is general agreement that spending should be increased people disagree on how much and where it should be targeted.

Some sectors have natural limitations to growth either in their capital requirements or in their production methods, making scaling up production for the external market difficult. An example is the wine industry which has an increasing international market. International demand coincided with the financial crisis which made wine more expensive for the domestic market. Yet they were unable to take advantage of the competitive pricing because of three factors (a) the inability to make capital investment in the 1990s to facilitate later expansion, (b) the bad harvest in 2002, and (c) difficulty in breaking into international markets. Additionally the wine industry is uses labour-intensive procedures such as extensive handpicking of grapes which raises the quality and also the price. Thus, capacity to expand was limited by labor and resource distribution issues. Many companies are still reacting to the challenges of doing business that emerged in the 1990s and are heightened by the costs of doing business under increasing global integration.

Over all, Argentina is recovering well from a decade of financial highs and lows, but there are many challenges to be addressed, particularly relating to the strength of institutions, trust from domestic and international actors and the government need to steer a fine line between the populist anti-IMF rhetoric and the desire to attract capital to finance Argentina's growth. Most disconcertingly, the distributional imbalances between the provinces and the rich and poor, pose a challenge to the recovery and to long-term growth. The country can only grow if it has a sustainable basis of human and economic capital as well as a basis of social services. With a proper assessment of the country and currency risks and the opportunity in certain key sectors, Argentina is again a place for targeted investment.

POSTSCRIPT: THE NEW KIRCHNER ERA

As mentioned above, Kirchner gained legislative and regional gubernatorial support in the elections of the fall of 2005, solidifying his powerbase. This allowed him to move in two directions, paying off Argentina's debt to the IMF early (something also done by Brazil) to avoid both increasing interest payments and the advice and restructuring and also placing the economy under more central control. Such efforts included imposing price controls, limiting meat exports and other related policies. Coasting on high popularity, the Kirchner era seems likely to continue for sometime, with Nestor's wife Christina to be the party's nominee in upcoming elections.

Investment has continued to rise. Although volatile, Argentine equity markets rose in 2006, an average rise of 35 % over the year, considerably higher than that of 2005. Argentine GDP growth leveled off slightly to around 8 % after having averaged 9 % growth for the past four years, a noted recovery. Rising inflation rates, averaging over 10 % for most of 2005 and 2006 provide concern for some investors as do increasing central controls over the economic sector. Argentina's dependence on commodity exports makes it vulnerable to changes in global demand.

18
Cyprus: On the outer edge of Europe, in the middle of the Mediterranean

EU convergence and Mediterranean trade hub?

Half-way through a six month-stint working in Egypt, I decided it was time to investigate some of the developments on the Mediterranean from a different perspective, one of the newly acceded EU member states. I chose Cyprus, an island by geography closer to Syria than to any European country, but one of the strongest new EU members. Cyprus's location has historically made it a key base for control of either end of the Mediterranean, determining strategy in conflicts ranging from the Crusades to the

Suez crisis. Its geography makes it a crossroads of Mediterranean history, explaining the confluence of the multitude of Greek and Roman sites, crusader castles and more recent remains that marked the touristic portion of my visit there. Cyprus remains a crossroads today and the trip prompted reflection upon today's Mediterranean region, and different models of economic cooperation and political, economic and social interests in the Mediterranean region.

But before we get to Cyprus and how it has been integrated into euroland, a bit of an aside on international currency fluctuations (particularly the drop in the dollar/euro exchange rate) which illustrate one aspect of how the US and EU project economic power globally. In the latter half of 2004, the big economic news story was the fall of the dollar against most international currencies, but especially the euro. In November 2004, the US dollar reached an 11-year low against the euro or combined basket of European currencies. It is perhaps slightly misleading to focus on the decade-long history as the dollar is being compared to two very different measures, pre and post- European united currency. It was not until January 2002, the introduction of the coin and paper currency, that there could be a real demand for the euro as a store of value and unit of trade. So for our purposes, a three-year horizon is sufficient to show the fluctuation in the exchange rate.

Long-term predictions about the dollar/euro exchange rate abound, and contend with the statements of politicians which range from recent US official support for a strong dollar to protests that Europe's share of dollar adjustment is too high, not to mention ongoing criticism of China's exchange rate policy (see Chapter 15). The large American balance of payments deficit and the substantial holdings of US currency in Asia remain sources of instability in

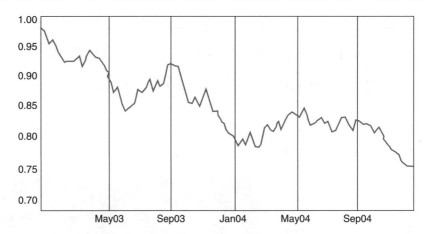

Figure 18.1   Euro/Dollar Exchange Rate, two years ending December 17, 2004. *Source*: Yahoo Finance

the dollar. It is likely that the dollar will continue to fall in response to these imbalances. Yet, the exchange rate is not so easy to predict, I do not believe that the market is that self-adjusting. Since a continued decline in the value of the dollar would devalue the assets held by many Asian countries, most would be unlikely to engage in major dollar selling.

US AND EU POLICIES TOWARDS USE OF THEIR CURRENCIES

A related issue are the distinct American and European policies towards international use of their currencies. While European and US policies are similar in that they encourage international use of their currencies (though the US has supported this more than the EMU members) they diverge in their policies toward unilateral dollarization, that is official use of the dollar or the euro by a third country as is done in several states in Latin America and the former Yugoslavia. (R Ziemba 2003) The US has had a policy best described as 'benign neglect', that is, it will not encourage the adoption of the dollar by giving incentives such as the sharing seignorage or being a lender of last resort, yet it will not actively oppose dollarization as it increases demand for the dollar. The US benefits from the dollar's hegemonic role as it allows it to borrow in its own currency. The dollar's widespread use as vehicle currency can increase demand. Yet the dollar holdings held outside of the US are less responsive to the traditional monetary policy transmission mechanisms, especially the interest rate. There are several reasons why Asian countries such as China are likely to continue to hold a significant portion of reserves in dollars. One of the most compelling reasons is that selling dollars would devalue both their assets (predominately dollar reserves) and revalue their dollar-pegged currencies, thus bringing two sources of instability.

However, the European approach is somewhat different. The ECB and different EU governments have been much more circumspect about internationalization of the euro. Since the EMU is a regional multilateral currency arrangement, there exists a process of economic and political convergence for eligible members which EU member states do not want to threaten with the prospect of unilateral euroization. Believing the euro seal of approval should be earned rather than appropriated, existing members fear either changing the Maastricht criteria or allowing countries to unilaterally adopt the euro without having proved their understanding of the culture of currency stability through two years of training in the ERM II. However, the European countries welcomed the currency pegs of the aspiring member states as it provided training in preparation to entry into the euro zone when conditions were met.

CYPRUS: A MODEL EU STUDENT

Cyprus has been firmly in the euro zone, from the tourists you see on the beach, to the EU funded infrastructural projects of Nicosia's inner core to its trade with other EU member states (43 % of Cyprus' exports and 54 % of its imports are with EU member states.) As such it provides a snapshot of how the new EU member states are being integrated and of some of the dilemmas they face as they seek to accede to the euro zone. Concurrent enlargement programs extended the EU's borders and created a greater internal skeleton in the shape of the new EU constitution.

In many ways, Cyprus has been a model student. Unlike some other new member states, Cyprus has had years of currency stability. Cyprus has maintained a peg to either the euro or a basket of European currencies for more than 10 years. Cyprus first pegged its currency to the ECU in 1992, coinciding with its first application to become a member of the European Community. Maintaining the peg was an important policy move for the successive governments as it signaled that it was committed to both currency stability and the EU. With its stable currency, educated workforce, and competitive interest rates for offshoring Cyprus became a center for financial services, attracting foreign investment. Cyprus was able to maintain the exchange rate because it had the needed supporting policies in place, including relatively low levels of debt and adequate reserves and substantial controls on currency outflows from citizens and high interest rates. As part of EU accession, Cyprus has eliminated currency controls.

Cyprus has a high-valued, stable currency, and recently liberalized its capital account. Although its history proves its ability to maintain a currency peg, its public finances are stopping it from applying to join the euro. In response to external shocks including the global economic slowdown and the decline in international tourism, the government of Cyprus undertook a number of expansionary policies to cushion the blow to the economy and to maintain political and economic stability. As a result of these policies, Cyprus had significantly high rates of public debt and higher deficits. In 2003, the deficit was 6.3 % with the public debt more than 70 % of GDP. However recent deficit projections of less than 3 % in 2005 would fulfill the Maastricht criteria. But this dramatic reduction will not be easy, especially as it is likely to require a cut in public sector employment.

Cypriot public finance struggles are similar to those of other European countries, especially its fellow new members. As of fall 2004, 10 out of 25 members of the EU have deficits that broach the Maastricht 3 % deficit limit, including six new EU members. All of these countries are required to follow the Maastricht criteria and are not able to join the euro until they are met. This illustrates instabilities in the Stability and Growth Pact which underlies the euro. There have been a variety of suggestions to soften the pact, mainly led by the larger member states. This might include increased emphasis on where the extra money is being spent rather than just on how much a state overruns the budget. However, given the coordination needs and the uncertainty which results from increasing deficits, dramatic changes are unlikely. Many smaller states are already unhappy that larger states such as France and Germany were not penalized for their deficits. The budgets of new member states entering the EMU will be analysed carefully since it was discovered that Greece and possibly Italy misstated their spending in order to qualify to join the euro. Other figures have pointed out insecurities in the system. In April 2004, George Soros warned that the ERM could be dangerous for many central and Eastern European countries since it would leave them open to currency speculation. He suggested that they not enter the ERM until their economic fundamentals are strong and that they remain in such a vulnerable peg for as short a period as possible.

Yet all of this stability might come at a cost to sustainability. The high level of the Cypriot pound makes Cyprus seems expensive to an outside observer, with a higher-valued currency than the British pound. This high value makes it seems to share some characteristics with countries which maintain an over-valued currency. Cyprus has avoided high levels of private debt in international currency, having relatively high saving rates partly due to capital controls and a steady source of foreign currency. Yet, studies assert the appropriateness of the exchange rate, and the cost of living is currently 65 % of the EU average. While the high value must keep inflation low, one wonders about the effects, especially for an island nation which must import food, energy and intermediate products, while making Cypriot exports more expensive. However, these labour costs have encouraged Cypriot companies to focus on higher value-added products, especially in the service sector and to offshore more of the production. Cyprus continues to have high productivity levels, leading to its positive terms of trade.

Cyprus has higher costs of production than many of its Middle Eastern and Eastern European neighbours. Cypriot companies have opened factories for manufacture of shoes and furniture in neighboring Middle Eastern countries, especially Syria. Yet there is no shortage of employment, with a low 4 % unemployment rate. Cyprus must import labour at an increasing rate, with foreign temporary workers making up 11 % of the total working population. They provide the services that allow Cyprus' economy to thrive, and the household workers in particular help fill the gap created. One woman explained the high numbers of (women) workers thus: since the scars of civil strife and invasion remain, all young people were encouraged to get an education and to get a good job so that if they ever had to flee again they would always have their degrees and experience to support them. And that sentiment in itself explains a lot of the recent Cypriot experience and determination to succeed?

The lack of resolution to the *Cyprus situation* provides ongoing political uncertainty. After the failure of the last April's referendum, in which the Turks said yes and the Greeks said no, prospects for future unification remain unsure. The referendum was based on a UN negotiated plan which proposed a two-community federation with a limited federal government. Unfortunately, the economic aspects of the UN plan were among the least detailed and many Greek Cypriots worried about paying the costs of unification. Yet the lack of settlement produces several paradoxes, while Cyprus acceded to the EU as a unit, the government does not have control over the northern third of the country. So technically, northern Cyprus could export to the EU, but there are no approved ports for shipping and there are concerns about the liabilities since the Republic of Cyprus is the only recognized government. The recent compromise selection of a start date for Turkey's accession to the EU shows that these negotiations will continue to overshadow relations in the region, especially between Cyprus, Turkey, Greece and the EU. It also made it easier for Cypriots and foreign visitors to cross the border. However it remains a key political risk and delays the island from achieving its potential.

PROMOTING TRADE AND INVESTMENT ACROSS THE MEDITERRANEAN: IN WHOSE INTEREST?

I returned to the Mediterranean's southern shore, as a new attempt to encourage growth, development and reform was being announced in Egypt, that is an agreement on Qualified Investment Zones (QIZ) signed by Israel, Egypt and the US. This agreement provides an opportunity to compare American and European approaches to the Middle East and North Africa. Both use a series of economic incentives (market access) in response to political and economic change but the EU policy is much more widespread, encompassing almost all of the Middle Eastern countries. EU policy to most of its southern neighbors comes under the framework of the Barcelona process, the euro Mediterranean partnership. The EU has signed and is in the process of implementing cooperation agreements that encompass aid, economic, political and social cooperation with most of its Mediterranean neighbors, as well as sponsoring some intra-regional cooperation. The US and the EU share many of the same objectives in the Middle East, political stability, economic growth, increased standard of living and quality of life, etc, but somewhat different approaches to meet these goals. The EU is much farther along as it has signed trade agreements with most of the southern Mediterranean and has tried to do so on a broader regional basis when possible. Secondly, EU assistance has tried to foster some intra-regional trade. For example, Egypt, Morocco, Tunisia and Jordan, all of whom have association agreements with the EU, last year signed the Agadir agreement to share rules of origin which will facilitate the number of goods allowed duty free entry into the EU, expanding the scope and maximizing the benefits separate agreements with the EU.

The US relationship with the southern shores of the Mediterranean is focused on relations with individual countries within the framework of encouraging Arab state relations with Israel. In December 2004, eight years after negotiations started, the United States and Israel recently concluded and signed a modified free trade agreement with Egypt. The goal of this newest economic agreement is largely political, that of increasing cooperation between Israel and her Arab neighbors. The agreement follows a similar one with Jordan, which later led to a full-fledged free trade agreement. Goods produced in these zones can be sold duty free in the US as long as they contain 11.7 % Israeli products. This new agreement will promote Egyptian-Israeli economic cooperation, and is seen as the best means to preserve and enhance Egypt's access to the US textile and clothing market. When existing quotas are lifted in January 2005, it is expected that large Asian producers will swamp the market, closing the door to other suppliers. But duty free access is not enough on its own to lure more clothing manufacturers. These requirements include a more streamlined tax and customs regime, more credible and transparent monetary policy and easier pathways through bureaucratic wranglings. And all of these policies are part of a work in progress. As always, things are happening in the Mediterranean and there are prospects for growth.

POSTSCRIPT

Since it joined the EU formally in May 2005, Cyprus has progressed towards joining the euro, officially joining ERM II at that point. It has decreased its fiscal deficit to below the 3 % benchmark, stabilizing its debt to GDP ratio (which remains above 70 %). Cyprus is widely expected to apply to join the EMU in 2007, following Slovenia who became the first new member state to join in January 2007. In February 2007, Cyprus announced its intention to enter the EMU, though a timeline for accession is not yet known. Cyprus's aging population is expected to place a great burden on its finances, and to encourage an economic slowdown in the coming decade as the dependency ratio grows at a faster rate than the EU average. The lack of resolution to the island's division is holding back development as well as providing an obstacle to Turkey's accession talks which we do not have room to discuss here.

A number of EU cooperation agreements have been further implemented and the EU and its member states have added more direct multilateral and bilateral negotiations to achieve their goals including stemming the flows of illegal immigration by directing development aid (a topic which is discussed in Chapter 19.)

The war in Iraq has shaped and limited the American ability to foster economic cooperation in the Middle East and North Africa, partly as the economic carrots are more limited. A variety of broader Middle East initiatives have fallen relatively flat. However, the US has continued to push forward with a number of individual free trade agreements (FTAs) with southern Mediterranean countries, countries to form a basis for a broader US-Middle East Free Trade Agreement (see Lawrence, 2006 for more details on such plans and how they might interact with existing agreements). While many of these agreements are primarily motivated by politics, given the fact that no middle eastern countries are major US trading partners. To date, the US has FTAs with Jordan, Morocco and Bahrain and recently signed an agreement with Oman. However, to date, US trade with all of these countries is quite small, owing to the size of the partner economies and the fact that their major trading partners remain in Europe and Asia, though in certain sectors, especially the financial sector, there is potential for growth. The QIZ agreement between Egypt, Israel and the US has had promoted some Egyptian sectors, diverting assembly of some goods from Israeli factories which had used Palestinian low-cost labour – which has been increasingly difficult to use given travel restrictions. However, the scope of the agreement is limited. These agreements are some of many being pursued both by the US and middle eastern countries, many of which are seeking to add trade agreements with their Asian trading partners. and it is not clear how easily such new agreements can be rationalized with EU agreements.

19

Is Iceland's growth spurt threatened by financial vulnerabilities?

Is it a well planned country or a small city state?

The next two chapters assess economic risks in countries in or closely tied to the eurozone. This chapter discusses Iceland, a member of the European Free Trade Area (EFTA) and the smallest country to have an independent free-floating currency. Because of its economic openness and its high yielding bonds, it has been seen as a kind of 'canary' in the coalmine of the global economy, warning of risks to high-yielding emerging market economies, especially those with high current account deficits such as Turkey or South Africa. We assess the macroeconomic trends and risks to the currency and asset prices in the open economy. This article was inspired by a trip Bill took to Iceland in July 2006 to attend the 21st Euro Conference on 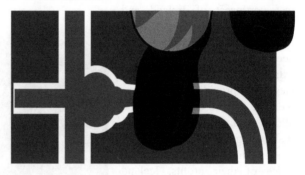 Operational Research in Iceland. Bjarni Kristjansson, the president of the software firm Maximal, was one of the main organizers and Bill gave a keynote speech on the Kelly criterion. As Iceland's financial vulnerabilities were much in the news early in 2006, the trip provided a key chance to investigate its prospects for investment and vulnerabilities.

This chapter sets out to investigate the case of Iceland, a small, open economy, dependent on foreign financing, whose financial stability and prospects for long term growth were called into question earlier in 2006. Concerned by the high current account deficit and foreign currency debt on bank balance sheets, several rating agencies, including Fitch, downgraded Iceland's debt in February 2006. This downgrading was followed by concerned reports from some European analysts including those at Danske Bank. The uncertainties raised by these reports triggered a 20 % depreciation in the value of the Icelandic Krona (against the euro) and a similarly sized temporary drop in the stock index. This chapter asks whether the equity sell-off and currency crash of earlier this year was just a blip or a marker of deeper instability. In either scenario, Iceland is vulnerable to swings in investor confidence, the impact of which is exacerbated by its dependence on external financing.

Although Iceland's economy and population is very small in global terms, it illustrates a number of key trends in the global economy, including the degree to which countries can maintain policy independence, and whether economic growth that is highly dependent on external financing can be sustainable and independent. However Icelanders abroad and foreign acquisitions by Icelandic companies are the source of some of this external financing. Some compare Iceland to a medium sized city acting as a country that has been able to stay independent by enacting effective policies it is dependent on global trade and financial flows.

But just as Iceland has recently been buffeted by global investors, it has also been strengthened by access to wider markets and credit.

Iceland presents a remarkable economic growth story which includes a 250 % increase in the stock market index from December 2001 to July 2006. A small, open economy like Iceland is challenged to retain independent policies (including social programs). Yet this small country just northwest of Ireland and Scotland, with a population of less than 300 000 people, has been able to maintain a set of extremely favorable social policies while providing an environment friendly to business, which allows Icelandic companies to make extensive investments overseas, from which they derive much of their profits. Iceland has low corporate tax rates and derives much of its revenue from value added taxes.

This chapter highlights the issues facing Iceland and discusses scenarios for the future of the economy and financial markets, including the significance of the vulnerabilities exposed earlier this year. Before detailing these vulnerabilities, it is helpful to discuss some attributes of Iceland's economy, especially the carefully planned process of opening to the global economy.

A key driver of growth was Iceland's rapid shift to outward economic orientation, This came about as part of a 20-year process in which the economy evolved from a very closed economy, protected by those seeking to maintain the status quo to one in which many of Iceland's successful and growing companies and banks have invested abroad, making most of their revenues offshore where they have more access to credit at lower interest rates and can benefit from larger markets. Two main external factors encouraged this transition, European Integration and global trade and capital liberalization, both beginning to speed up in the early 1970s. In this period, Iceland was challenged by very high inflation. Although Iceland did not want to join the precursor to the EU, they wanted to gain access to the market, so became a member of the European Free trade area from the beginning, which required trade liberalization and the adoption of certain regulations. Other key policies in this shift include privatization of government banks, removing price and currency controls, simplifying the tax system (including a shift to VAT and decreasing corporate taxes) and freeing foreign exchange. These policy changes, though requiring significant time and political contestation, enabled the creation of the current market drivers.

Iceland's small size required an outward orientation, as there are limits to growth and access to credit in such a small economy. Iceland's size posed a few obstacles to reforms, as it is vulnerable to global fluctuations. There is some pride in Iceland in being the smallest country with an independent floating currency. However, its size makes it vulnerable to capital flows may be quite volatile, as a relatively large amount may stem from an individual project. While Iceland's economy has grown greatly and diversified in the past few years, traditional sources of income, particularly fish and related products, remain very important. Although the profit margin remains relatively small, fish represents the highest amount of export revenues. However investment in aluminum projects will be playing an increasing role in the coming years.

To understand the context and import of the February 2006 crisis, we need to delve into the determinants of the recent boom, which has been characterized by high levels of Icelandic investment abroad. This investment has been concentrated in the UK, Scandinavia and Eastern Europe, particularly in the retail sector. Since late 2005 and early 2006, investors have been attracted to Iceland's high yielding bonds, and some have been heavily invested in carry trades, that is, borrowing in a low interest rate currency (i.e. the Japanese Yen) and investing where large gains might be made (a high yielding currency, like the Icelandic Krona). Generally this is a profitable trade unless the high yield investments suffer a large currency depreciation.

Basic country facts; see also
Nordel and Kristinsson(1996)

Size: 39,768 square miles; about the size of Kentucky (also filled with horses – for riding).
Highest point: 6923 ft
Population: 293 557
(31/12/04), almost half of which is in the capital, Reykjavik, population 113 848.
Life expectancy: Females 83, Males 79.
High quality of life.
Education: Free through college, education rate about average for Europe.
Settlement: Settled by Norwegian and Celtic (Scots and Irish) immigrants during the late 9th and 10th centuries. Gained independence from Denmark in 1944.
Climate: Cool, temperate, variable, warm, Gulf Stream and Arctic currents; short tourist season making hotels expensive but not very profitable.
Location: 1884 km northwest of London.
4208 km northeast of New York.

Basic Economic Facts

Currency: ISK, Icelandic Krona
Per capita GDP: 34,700 euros in 2004
Labor force: 160,000 (2004 est.)
Labor force – by occupation:
Agriculture 5.1%, fishing and fish processing 11.8%, manufacturing 12.9%, construction 10.7%, services 59%. (1999).
Public debt: 24% of GDP (2006 est.), a decrease by half in the last five years.
Sales tax: 24% (10% on food); a primary source of government revenue.
Income tax: companies – 18% for (among the lowest of OECD countries), individuals – wage income – 38.54% above about ISK 809 616 (USD 7,845 in 2001), and extra 7% above ISK 3 980 000 (USD 38,566), financial income – 10%
Economy: Iceland's small economy is heavily dependent on fishing and related industries, which account for more than 60% of export earnings through the Icelandic group of companies. Smallest economy (number 177 in size in the world). to have its own currency and a flexible exchange rate.
Pension system: fully funded with assets over 1.2 times GDP, but largely in risky equity.
Health: Free health care cradle to grave.
Unemployment: 2.1%

To some this strength seems to come out of nowhere. Iceland remains a relatively young economy, with the country gaining its independence in 1944 from Denmark. It is only since the late 1990s that high levels of liberalization and privatization have taken place along with restructuring of the financial sector. Iceland's transition from a small, relatively paternalistic economy was accomplished with considerable political battles, as the establishment was threatened by the emergence of a new sources of investment income. Proceeds from the sale of fishing quotas and the pension funds, provided this liquidity which was then invested, allowing the diversification of the economy. These policies have allowed Iceland to rapidly diversify the economy. At the same time, Iceland combines aspects of socialistic and individualistic economic policies. The limited size of the economy and politically charged nature of some of the privatization and regulation debates meant that many companies sought investments overseas, where they could enjoy economies of scale in a way not possible in Iceland alone. This access to the international markets provides one source of strength, just as it presents some weaknesses. The banks have high levels of external debt, so high that the central bank might find it difficult to act as a lender of last resort, should any of the banks fail.

AMID THE STRENGTHS, THERE ARE ISSUES OF CONCERN

With high short-term interest rates already costing 13 % and approaching 14 % (on debt of over $ 3 billion); a huge and growing current account deficit (over $ 2 billion), a potential housing bubble and huge private debts, there is considerable reason for concern. On the positive side, Iceland has low and decreasing levels of government debt, a fiscal surplus, foreign exchange and gold reserves of $ 1 billion, and a fully funded pension plan.

Starting in February 2006, a number of international bond rating agencies such as Fitch and Barclays downgraded Icelandic country debt. In June, S&P revised the outlook to negative, fearing a hard landing. These negative assessments were based on the large and growing current account deficit, and concerns about the increasing foreign debt accrued from 2003–06, particularly the liabilities on the bank balance sheets; see Figure 19.1. These downgrades had a temporary devastating effect as investors fled the short-term investments made to take advantage of Iceland's high interest rates. The following section analyses in turn a series of vulnerabilities in the Icelandic economy and attempts to assess the likelihood of a negative outcome.

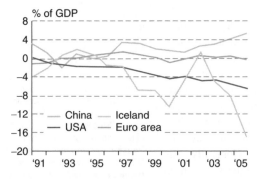

Figure 19.1   Current account balance as % of GDP, 1991–2005. *Source*: CBI (2006, p. 8)

THE CURRENT ACCOUNT DEFICIT

As of mid 2006, the current account deficit represented 16.5 % of GDP, well above that of the US (6 %). In the US consumption drives spending which accounts for the level of debt. In Iceland much of the deficit reflects overseas investments of Icelandic companies. Given the small size of the economy, a large project, such as investment in aluminum production, could swamp the accounts for a given year. However, unlike the Americans, Iceland does not have the luxury of borrowing in its domestic currency; most of its debt is dollar or euro denominated. While high current account deficits pose some reason for concern, the source of the deficit determines the level of vulnerability. Worries about Iceland's current account imbalance coincided with new concern about those of other countries particularly in emerging economies such as Turkey and South Africa.

Unlike many industrialized countries, Iceland is not facing a pension crisis. Its pension system underwent significant reforms beginning in the mid-1990s. The demand of its pension fund for investment opportunities in Iceland and overseas, was one of the factors driving the liberalization, and re-regulation of its financial system. The investments of the pension fund (largely equities) mirror the demographic profile of Iceland's population (relatively young) compared to most European countries. The pension fund is currently 120 % funded so assets exceed liabilites by 20 %.

The Central Bank of Iceland (CBI) used a macroeconomic simulation model to predict how the current account deficit (as a percentage of GDP) might be affected by a series of shocks, as shown in Figure 19.2, currency depreciation, declining asset prices, increasing foreign interest rates and all three of these shocks. Depending on which scenario materializes, results may form an improvement or a further 3 % decline depending on the future scenario.

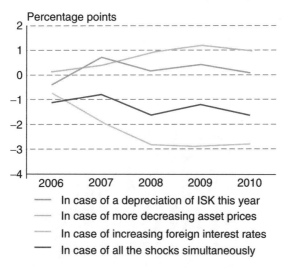

Figure 19.2 Simulations of current account balance as % of GDP under different scenarios. *Source*: CBI (2006, p. 41)

DEBT

Both households and Icelandic companies have a lot of debt compared to most countries although Australia and New Zealand are similarly indebted; see Table 19.1.

However, most companies hedge against their currency risk by earning money in the foreign currencies of the debt; see Figure 19.3. Some would argue that the growing current account deficit is offset by this significant increase in foreign currency denominated-assets. However maturity mismatches remain. Investment, liabilities and debt have all significantly increased in the period from 2004–6; see Table 19.1.

Figure 19.4(a) shows the net wealth of households compared to their after tax income. Household net wealth has had a large relative rise since 2002, much of which is related to housing values and would mostly be lost with a 15 % fall in real estate prices. Figure 19.4(b) shows the steady increase in household debt, which is offset by increasing asset values.

Table 19.1 International investment position of selected OECD countries as % of GDP. *Source*: CBI (2006, p. 44)

	Assets	Debt	Net IIP
UK	356	369	−13
Canada	80	95	−15
Australia	79	141	−62
New Zealand	62	154	−92
Switzerland	551	404	147
Ireland	1163	1188	−25
Luxembourg	256	253	3
Iceland	247	333	−86

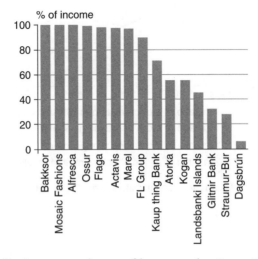

Figure 19.3 Foreign currency income of key companies. *Source*: CBI (2006, p. 46)

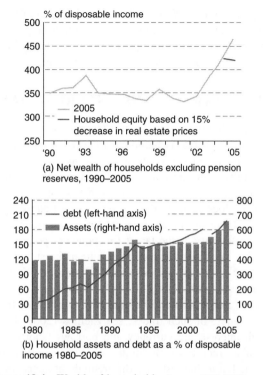

Figure 19.4   Wealth of households. *Source*: CBI (2006, p. 19)

INFLATION

Like many other OECD countries including Canada, the UK and New Zealand, Iceland uses inflation targeting to guide its monetary policy; see Bernanke (2005) and the CBI (2006). Inflation has been significantly overshooting its 2.5 % target for much of 2006. Inflation in Iceland is high and rising, being about 8.4 % in July 2006 and it is projected to reach 9 % in late 2006 and peak about 11 % in Q2 2007 and then to decelerate in late 2007 and fall to 4.5 % in late 2008 and then to 2.5 %; see Figure 19.5. Driven by domestic demand,

Figure 19.5   Inflation. *Source*: Kaupthing Bank (2006)

depreciation, and wage growth, the inflation rate has not been very responsive to the increase in the policy interest rate. The CBI would prefer a much more rapid disinflation, (a quicker reaching of the target) and hence may raise short rates significantly higher, possibly as high as 18 % unless significant signs of contraction become evident.

THE CURRENCY AND INTEREST RATES

The Icelandic Krona is free floating, being the smallest economy to have a floating exchange rate. It's real effective exchange rate is based on a basket of currencies weighted annually according to their share in traded goods and services, as in Figure 19.6. The Krona then trades freely in inverse relation to the index of these currencies. So the currency regime is a mixture between a peg and a float; the currency floats freely against major currencies, although the central bank does manage the currency on a trade-weighted basis. Focusing on price stability, the CBI uses an inflation target for to set monetary policy, thus having abandoned exchange rate stability as the target for monetary policy. Fischer (2001) among others argues that floating rates provide much safer financial stability than fixed exchange rates. This makes it easier to see the impact of global currency shocks and is in line with its foreign currency denominated liabilities, lowering currency risk and transactions costs.

Part of the 20 % decline in the Krona in February 2006 was from forex traders and hedge funds unwinding carry trades. In such trades, see Ziemba (2003) for examples, one goes long in assets of a high interest rate currency and borrows (shorts) a low yield currency. This is usually a profitable trade but if the high yield currency quickly depreciates, all the gains and more are lost. Large interest rate differentials attracted investors to enter such trades with investments in Krona and other currency assets.

Figure 19.7 shows the ISK index from 1999 to June 2006. A look at its path shows the impact of the 2006 currency crisis and concern about the current account. One explanation for the limited slide in the stock market and reversal, is that even as foreign investors sold Icelandic securities, residents did not flee and actually increased their holdings.

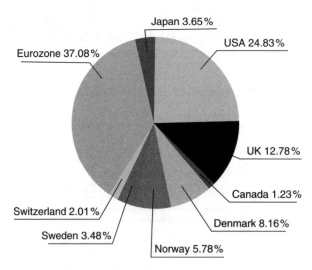

Figure 19.6 Official currency basket, 2002. *Source*: Invest in Iceland Agency (2006, p 5)

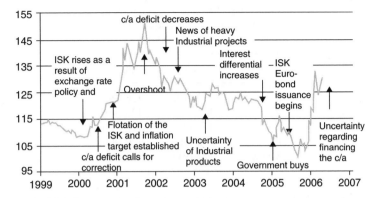

Figure 19.7 The ISK index, 1999–2006. *Source*: Glitnir (2006a)

In July 2006, the index was about 129 or 93 ISK/euro. During the currency crisis in early 2006, the index rose from 110 or 79/euro to a peak of 135 or 99/euro. Glitnir's forecast, shown in Table 19.3, is for a gradual rise in late 2006, returning the index to 120 or 87/euro area in 2007. Our conclusion is that the currency is supported by the high interest rates and there is no serious currency crisis and not comparable to Asia in 1997 (see Ziemba, 2003). In contrast to the countries that suffered currency and financial crises in the 1990s, Iceland has fewer currency and maturity mismatches, with a stronger financial system and has only a current account and not a fiscal deficit.

Table 19.2 International investment position. *Source*: Central Bank of Iceland (2006, p. 42)

NP at the end of period in b.kr	2000	2001	2002	2003	2004	2005
Total Assets	303.1	415.9	409.4	708.2	1,153.5	2,398.4
Direct investment abroad	56.2	86.8	101.3	122.5	245.0	597.0
Portfolio assets	173.6	197.3	159.7	262.3	374.2	627.6
Other investment, assets	39.1	95.2	11.2	265.2	468.7	1,106.5
Reserves	34.2	36.6	37.2	58.1	65.6	67.3
Total liabilities	766.3	1,012.2	989.1	1,266.1	1,819.2	3,227.3
Direct investment in Iceland	42.1	70.7	64.3	84.6	121.9	242.0
Portfolio liabilities	347.7	471.3	490.2	776.1	1,302.3	2,297.9
Other investment liabilities	376.2	470.2	434.6	405.4	395.1	687.5
International investment position	−462.9	−596.3	−579.7	−557.9	−665.7	−828.9
Equity capital net	178.1	188.8	150.5	234.6	392.9	723.7
Net external debt position	−641.0	−785.1	−730.2	−792.5	−1,058.6	−1552.6
Monetary authorities	18.6	21.7	20.8	58.1	65.5	67.2
General government	−167.2	−239.8	−227.2	−220.9	−212.4	−168.8
Deposit money banks	−329.4	−373.7	−361.8	−471.1	−778.2	−1,268.5
Other sectors	−163.0	−193.2	−167.0	−158.6	−133.5	−182.6
Exchange rate ISK/USD	84.47	102.95	80.58	70.99	61.04	62.98

1. Summary from Central Bank of Iceland Statistics webpage
2. Preliminary data

Table 19.3 SK index (ISK/euro) in
Q1, Q2 2006 and forecasts to Q4 of
2007. *Source*: Glitnir (2006)

	2006	2007
2Q	110 (79)	130 (94)
2Q	128 (93)	125 (90)
3Q	135 (98)	120 (87)
4Q	133 (96)	120 (87)
Average	127 (91)	124 (89)

Through the 70s and 80s, Iceland suffered from high inflation, averaging 60 %. A key part of the economic reforms involved indexing salaries to inflation. In 2001, they adopted an inflation targeting monetary policy. Interest rates in Iceland have echoed the US increases since early 2004 starting from a higher base of 5.25 %. A sequence of rises to July 2006 increased the rate to an eye-popping 13 %. With more rises likely, perhaps as high as 14.5 % in September (Glitnir's forecast) or possibly 18 % according to CBI statements. Although inflation is high, these high interest rates may begin to have a negative impact on growth and financial assets. See Figure 19.8. The CBI is well managed and will likely drop rates in 2007 but it is easy to overshoot. WTZ points to the example of Japan where the BOJ raised rates in 1988–89. They continued to do so even after the stock market began to fall in January 1990 and proceeded to raise rates until August 1990, a full eight months more. See Figure 23.3. This was a major cause of many bankruptcies and the 15-year slump in Japan's economic and financial markets. However in an environment of global tightening, especially with the Fed unlikely to stop tightening until September 2006 at the earliest, the CBI may be unable to get out of step for fear of a decreasing interest rate differential, even if that results in an overshoot. Given high and rising inflation in Iceland, the CBI will have domestic reasons to continue to raise interest rates.

Many analysts have spoken about a possible housing bubble. A government policy of subsidizing interest rates at 5 % for personal housing is one contributing factor to encourage this overheating. However, commercial and industry held property does not benefit from this subsidy. However, the policy of many companies of selling property and leasing it back to access further credit many have contributed to this boom. It is hard not to foresee

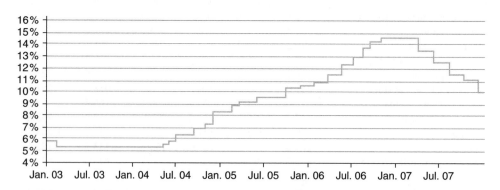

Figure 19.8 Short interest rates 2003–2007. *Source*: Glitnir (2006a)

trouble in the housing sector especially with steady increases in nominal prices since 2002 and yearly gains in the 30–40 % range in 2004 and 2005 and a 20 % rise the first half of 2006. Since there is an increased supply of land, much construction, a softening market with prices higher than construction costs, coupled with the higher interest rates, less credit available for housing loans, declining consumer confidence, the prediction of Glitnir (2006) that nominal prices might decline 5–10 % in 2007 might even be optimistic. A key question is whether they will fall softly or there will be a hard landing.

FINANCIAL (IN)STABILITY?

In their report, which responds to many of the vulnerability analyses of Iceland, Mishkin and Herbertsson (2006) drawing from the economic literature, argue that there are three routes to financial instability, none of which are present in the Iceland today. These drivers of instability are:

1. financial liberalization with weak prudential regulation and supervision;
2. severe fiscal imbalances; and
3. imprudent monetary policy

They conclude that Iceland's economy has adjusted to financial liberalization and there is prudent regulation and effective supervision. Government debt has decreased to low levels and the pension system is fully funded. Monetary policy has kept core inflation (excluding housing) on target, although inflation is increasingly resistant to the current policy rate, likely leading to further hikes. While there is a large current account deficit, they argue that the economy is much stronger and more stable than the emerging market economies which lack the degree of regulation and depth of the financial system. Thus they conclude that the current account by itself does not pose a financial instability. Iceland does face small country risk with much external debt. However, Mishkin and Herbertsson conclude that the risk of a financial meltdown with a massive withdrawal of Icelandic assets is small, They base this on the theory of multiple equilibria which suggests that self-fulfilling prophecies are unlikely to occur when fundamentals are strong as in Iceland in 2006. Let us look in detail at one possibly vulnerable area, the stock market.

PREDICTING GDP, RECESSIONS AND THE STOCK MARKET

Ecklund (2007) uses an econometric factor model analysis to predict the future state of the business cycle in Iceland and in particular the GDP and possible recessions. Since GDP is only computed quarterly, the model aggregates the macro-economic data into quarterly values. It is assumed that there is a single common unobservable element that drives the cyclical evolution of many macroeconomic variables (coincident, lagging or leading) which in turn drive the economy measured as an index. Using monthly data on 104 macroeconomic and financial variables from a number of different sectors and markets during the period January 1999 to September 2005 gives the results in Figures 19.9(a) and 19.9(b).

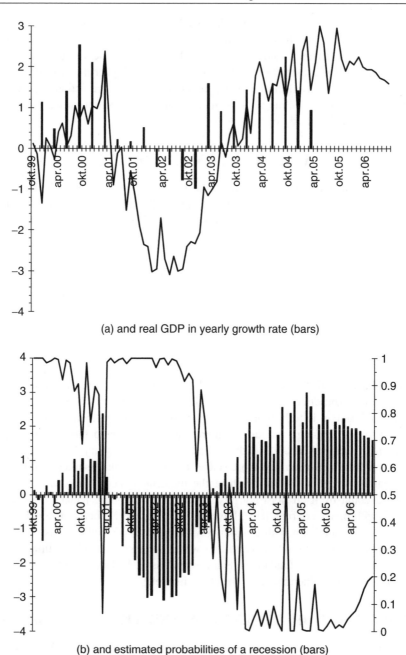

(a) and real GDP in yearly growth rate (bars)

(b) and estimated probabilities of a recession (bars)

Figure 19.9 Estimated state of the economy. *Source*: Ecklund (2007)

These forecasts are consistent with the expansion from 2003 into 2006 that we have seen and show that the probability of a recession remains low but is currently about 20 % and climbing.

WILL THE STOCK MARKET CRASH AND WOULD IT INFLUENCE OTHER MARKETS?

There are several ways to analyse risk in the stock markets. WTZ uses two basic models to predict stock market crashes including the bond-stock return difference, discussed in Chapters 23 and 25. It is very good at predicting crashes over about a one year period, based on long term (10 to 30 year) interest rates compared to the current past earnings yield; and a short term behavioral finance sentiment measure based on relative put and call option prices (high relative call prices presage crashes). Since puts and calls on the index in Iceland are not publicly traded but rather are over the counter between banks and their customers, it is hard to get the data for the latter measure. But the data is available for the bond-stock measure.

To put the experience of Iceland in context, we first look at the bond-stock measure for the US, the UK, Japan, France, and Germany (as of July 12, 2006). The danger zone requires a long bond rate well past 2.5 % and close to 3 %. We see from Table 19.4 that despite the weak global stock markets of May to July 2006, none of these countries are in the danger zone. It would take a large increase in long bond rates (which seems unlikely) and/or a large decrease in the earnings yield to reach the danger zone which would imply a large chance of a fall of 10 % plus within one year. See Chapters 23 and 25.

There are 15 stocks in the index with weights from 26.5 % to 1.0 % of the market capitalization; as in Table 19.5. The three large banks – Kaupthiing (most aggressive thus likely most vulnerable in any crisis), Landsbanki Islands and Gitnir (most conservative) dominate the index adding to 51.8 %. Many of the other companies have significant foreign investments.

Figure 19.10 shows the dramatic rise of these key stock-trading values particularly since 2004. It also shows how quickly these drops can occur. However, the notable sharp sell-offs, have to a large extent been blips and there is a question whether these investments can continue to produce similar returns, and if not, whether that will prompt investors to seek other markets.

Index funds such as Gitnir's (No. 6) track the market and essentially duplicate it as shown in Figure 19.10. Such index funds have slightly overweighted the large banks, thus leading to higher returns. These values are net of real inflation (2–4 %) and show a high rate of return since 1995. There were losses during 2000 and 2001 but very large gains in 2002–5.

The stock market increased in 2006 then declined during the 20 % currency depreciation that started in February. The real issue is whether these high prices are sustainable, and how much they depend on continuing high returns from the foreign assets of the banks and companies. The PE ratio of the index in April 2006 was 16.3 (with a 44 % real increase in

Table 19.4 Long-bond (10 yr) versus earning yield differentials for major countries, July 12, 2006

	S&P500	FTSE200	Nikkei225	CAC40	DAX30
Index	1259	5861	15249	4942	5638
A) PE ratio	16.86	16.61	36.26	13.82	13.33
B) Stock Return (1/A)	5.93 %	6.02 %	2.76 %	7.24 %	7.50 %
C) Bond Return (10 yr)	5.10 %	4.67 %	1.94 %	4.10 %	4.09 %
Crash Signal (C-B)	−0.83	−1.35	−0.82	−3.14	−3.41

Table 19.5   Stock market index. *Source*: Glitnir (2006b)

Weights				Real rates of return	
Company	Fund	Index		Fund	Index
1 Kaupthing Banki hf.	27.2 %	26.5 %	2005	56.5 %	54.5 %
2 Landsbanki Islands hf.	13.1 %	13.0 %	2004	49.1 %	47.2 %
3 Glitnir Banki hf.	12.5 %	12.3 %	2003	42.7 %	40.7 %
4 Straumur Buróarás Fjárfes	8.9 %	8.9 %	2002	20.7 %	19.2 %
5 Actavis Banki hf.	10.1 %	9.9 %	2001	−16.4 %	−16.6 %
6 FL Banki hf.	6.3 %	6.2 %	2000	−16.7 %	−17.2 %
7 Bakkavör Group hf.	4.0 %	4.1 %	1999	36.7 %	36.4 %
8 Avion Group hf.	3.7 %	3.7 %	1998	6.3 %	3.4 %
9 Mosaic Fashions hf.	2.7 %	2.6 %	1997	9.0 %	10.2 %
10 Ossur hf.	2.2 %	2.2 %	1996	44.1 %	57.3 %
11 Tryggingami tö in hf.	2.1 %	2.0 %	1995	33.4 %	31.1 %
12 Dagsbrún hf.	1.5 %	1.5 %			
13 Alfresca hf.	1.2 %	1.2 %			
14 Fjárfestingafélagi Atorka	1.0 %	1.0 %			
15 Grandi hf.	1.0 %	1.0 %			

Figure 19.10 The 15 stocks in the Iceland equity index and their growth in real terms from 1997–2006. *Source*: Glitnir (2006b)

stock prices since April 2005 when the PE ratio was 17.3). At the same time, the current account deficit increased from 9.3 % of GDP to 16.5 %. According to the CBI, there is a future PE ratio of 11.1 when financial companies are included and 14.2 without.

Figure 19.11 shows the long term nominal bond yields and Figure 19.12 shows the term structure of interest rates as of June 16, 2006, a short rate of 13 % and a long rate (5 year) of 9.4 %. Using the future PE ratio of all 15 stocks (financial and non-financial) gives the bond-stock measure at +0.39 % and out of the danger zone; see Table 19.6.

Table 19.6 provides two bond stock measure calculations. The measure is 0–5 % so while it is below ideal conditions is not in the danger zone but could well be.

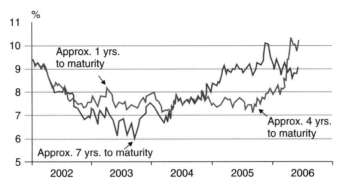

Figure 19.11   Long term nominal Treasury bond yields, June 16, 2006

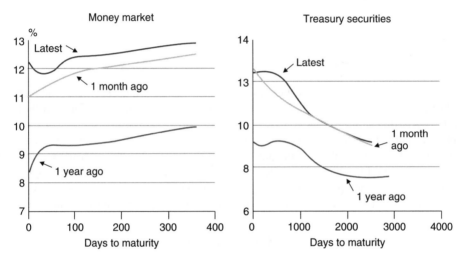

Figure 19.12   Term structure of nominal interest rates, June 16, 2006

Table 19.6   Bond-stock measure calculations in Iceland

Index	16 nonfin	15 in index
A) PE ratio		11.1
B) Stock Returen (1/A)	6.13 %	9.01 %
C) Bond Returen (5 yr)	11.00 %	9.4 %
Crash Signal (C-B)	4.87 %	0.39 %

Doing the calculation with the past earnings PE multiple on the non financials and a blended short/long interest rate of 11 % puts the measure at 4.87 % (which is in the danger zone). So the conclusion is cloudy. A crash may be avoided but the market looks very risky.

Table 19.7 indicates that the banks own 41.5 %, and the pension funds 29.1 % so they who have been the major benefactors of the 2002–06 (Feb rise) and would be the major losers (unless they sell or hedge) in a crash.

Table 19.7   Main owners of securities in February 2006. *Source*: CBI (2006, p. 32)

M.kr	Equities	%	HFF bonds	%
Households	285,690	11.7 %	3,042	0.8 %
Housing Financing Fund		0.0 %	18,275	4.9 %
Commercial banks and saving banks	242,051	9.9 %	153,492	41.5 %
Investment banks	70,921	2.9 %	10,927	3.0 %
Securities companies	18,646	0.8 %	1,093	0.3 %
Investment funds	39,362	1.6 %	32,663	8.8 %
Pension funds	217,292	8.9 %	107,541	29.1 %
Insurance companies	58,094	2.4 %	5,951 ·	1.6 %
Businesses	864,701	35.4 %	2,890	0.8 %
Non-residents	523,776	21.4 %		
Others	7,663	0.3 %	1,545	0.4 %
Custody accounts	113,701	4.7 %	32,327	8.7 %
Total	2,441,897	100.0 %	369,746	100.0 %

PROSPECTS FOR THE FUTURE

The second half of 2006 and 2007 will be a crucial period in Iceland. The rising inflation and overheated economy are likely to lead naturally to higher interest rates. These in turn will lead to other stresses on the economy. It will be essential that the investments of Icelandic companies and banks continue to perform well; should some of these deals fail, the impact on investor confidence could be damaging to the currency, stock and bond markets. However the, strength of the financial system, the hedging and operating environment, has significant strengths. The evidence points to a weak housing market, high interest rates, a risky stock market and an economy that, despite the troubles, will limp through for better times in 2008.

POSTSCRIPT

Since July 2006 we have the following developments. First, inflation is dropping from a yearly rate of 7.3 % in November 2006, to 7.0 in December and a projected 6.7 % in January 2007 according to the Kaupthing Bank. Second, economic growth is slowing to 0.8 % in Q3 2006 for a yearly rate of about 3 % in 2006. The rate of increase of the property index is dropping dramatically but there are no losses yet though they loom on the horizon. The property index was up 4.8 % in 2006. Third, the trade deficit remains high and is increasing because imports continue to increase while exports are flat. Fourth, consumer confidence remains very high. Fifth, short term interest rates which were 13 % in July 2006 are now 14.25 % with an unexpected 25 basic point rise on December 21, 2006. Long rates remain in the 9 % area. Some, like the Kaupthing Bank, think this is the last interest rate hike but that rates will remain high. But others, like the Danske bank, think the short rates might go to 16 % and that a severe growth slump and likely a recession are very likely.

So the country is risky for investment. Sensing this the S&P rating agency lowered the foreign currency sovereign credit ratings of long term debt from AA− to A+ and for short term debt from A-1+ to A-1. Finally the stock market continues to rise and is just now slightly above the February 2006 peak when it fell about 20 % during the financial crisis at that time as described above. The 15 stock index was up 15.8 % in 2006 and dividends

19.0 % with a 3.8 % increase in December 2006. In January 2007 the index has risen an additional 8.3 % to the 22nd, Glitner forecasts a 21 % rise in 2007. With the long term (5 year bond) interest rate still at 9 % and the price earnings ratio such that the earnings to price yield is in the 10 % area the bond stock measure is still not in the danger zone. But the least slip in earnings would put it in the danger zone. The drop in housing price increases which look like they will turn to decreases soon and the possible recession and at least a major slowdown suggest that these earnings will drop. That coupled with the very high short term interest rates which seem to be either staying high or going even higher suggest that the stock market is very risky.

20

Would a bridge connect Sicily's economy to Europe's heart?

Distance and institutions pose challenges to Sicily's growth and attempt to catch up to the rest of Italy.

In mid-September 2006, southern Italians held a series of strikes in Rome and in Sicily over the decision of Prime Minister Romano Prodi's government to postpone or cancel the construction of a bridge to con-nect Sicily to Italy's mainland. Discussed for many years, this link would be the world's largest suspension bridge. A part of former Prime Minister Berlusconi's election platform, the project would take five years. It was delayed by its large cost and possible environmental damage including concern that a shifting seabed might make it unsafe. Proponents point to the likely benefits of decreasing trans-portation costs, leaving the island less vulnerable to ferry strikes, and speeding up the transportation time. Not only would trains no longer need to be loaded onto ferries for the crossing, but it might provide an opportunity to use faster trains throughout a region of southern Italy which lacks Eurostar connections and remains time consuming to reach. Thus it is possible that easier connections with Sicily might also promote development for the neighboring regions of southern Italy, which have recently sustained some of the lowest growth and income levels in Italy. This may be a lot to expect from one, albeit large, infrastructure project. Those opposing the bridge point to the cost, environmental impact and question whether money could be better spent on other infrastructure projects in southern Italy. Others, particularly in cities like Messina just across from the Italian mainland, fear that they would lose business as people would no longer stop there to access the ferry.

This chapter is not intended to assess the merits of such a bridge or the challenges it might pose, but the issues highlighted in the controversy illustrate broader tensions in less developed regions within the European Union. The arguments for and against the bridge correspond to competing proposals for economic and social progress and the obstacles faced by such regions in attracting investment and encouraging inclusive growth. Especially as the EU continues to integrate newer members, the challenge of encouraging growth in less developed regions within EU member states persists. This will become more important now that Bulgaria and Romania are progressing along the path to EU accession and the EU continues to negotiate with Turkey and to deepen its cooperation agreements with African and Middle Eastern neighbors. Although many such regions have received significant investment from national governments and European structural funds, in many cases they remain poorer than other regions, with weaker institutions and infrastructure, having difficulty attracting and retaining human and other forms of capital. In many cases, such regions have had more difficulty evolving into the type of industrial and post-industrialized society which characterizes much of Europe. In this chapter, I take a closer look at the investment climate in Sicily and risks to its development. Sicily provides an interesting case study to look at how such regions are integrated within the EU amid increasing globalization.

SICILY'S ECONOMIC CHALLENGES

A little background on Sicily can put its challenges and prospects into perspective. Although having lower growth and productivity than most other Italian regions, it also had lower costs. Although Sicily is the largest region in Italy by size, it has the third lowest GDP, being ahead only of neighboring regions of Calabria and Campania. Sicily has sustained a per capita GDP of approximately 71 % of the EU average. In comparison, Italy's GDP is slightly above the average of all 25 EU member states. Unemployment is high, at 20.1 %, double the Italian average in 2003, as is emigration. All of which is partly explained by continuing high levels of participation in the informal economy.

Sicily's economy and that of much of southern Italy is diversifying. The share of GDP contributed by manufacturing and agriculture is decreasing and the slack is being picked up in services sector, much of which serves the local community. Sicily has a different economic structure than much of Italy. Sicily tends not to be competitive in the areas where Italy is normally strong including food, clothing and furniture production and has lower levels of exports than Italy as a whole. Sicily's exports tend to be primary and secondary natural resources including refined petroleum. Manufactured exports are largely the result of the investments from the public sector. Agriculture and construction are significant drivers of the economy with manufacturing's share decreasing. However, the agricultural industry faces sharp competition from other Mediterranean countries. Sicily is sparsely populated with challenging terrain, making large scale agriculture difficult. Much of the arable terrain is being utilized mostly by relatively small sized family farms. However, Sicily does have a significant manufacturing sector especially around Catania. As the manufacturing sector shrank, services grew, making up the largest share of GDP.

Through the 1990s, Sicily had low levels of exports, averaging 6 % of production, contrasting with an Italian average of 20 %. However, this may partly be explained by transportation issues as Sicily is farther from most European countries, the destination of more than 50 % of Italy's exports. The composition of its exports also varies, with petrochemicals making up a significant proportion of Sicily's export revenues.

Sicily has not been able to attract high amounts of foreign and national direct investment, with most of the investment coming from governmental sources, both national and European. Yet there has been investment in the real estate sector, factories, construction and reconstruction of residential and commercial property. While more infrastructure investment might be beneficial, Sicily's ports and other maritime installations are substantial. All of this might seem to be a laundry list of challenges that would be difficult to overcome.

So what does looking at Sicily show us about how less developed regions have fared within the EU? Regions have differed in the ability to promote growth and provide a dynamic investment climate. The countries and regions that have been most able to take advantage of European structural and cohesion funds have tended to be smaller countries that already had plans for infrastructure and skills development but lacked financial resources to implement them (eg. Ireland).

European and global integration, and decrease in transportation costs, have put pressure on manufacturing sector even in areas with stronger levels of growth such as in northern Italy. Lower-priced consumer goods in Italy face increased competition from lower cost labour. Italy's shoe, clothing and bag manufacturers have been particularly hard hit by competition from East and Southeast Asian imports, causing some producers to demand increasing tariffs on many of these products entering the EU. However, such tariffs are at best a short-term solution, unlikely to have a longer-term effect on producers as trade may be diverted to other countries in East Asia. However some small Italian firms have been able to continue to grow by moving up the production chain, producing higher quality products and in some cases sourcing parts of the production overseas or in less expensive areas of Italy. However, it is harder to create such a resurgence without existing linkages or levels of production.

Much of Sicily's land, especially away from the coast, continues to be used for agricultural production. Some have blamed the strong euro for making the products less competitive. The strength of the euro in recent years, particularly as it appreciated against the US dollar when the currencies of many exporters to Europe remained stable, put increasing challenges on manufacturing exports. This leads some politicians to call for Italy to leave the eurozone. In addition to the argument that the euro is over-

valued for Italy's economy, others including opposition politicians bemoan the budget deficit requirements of being a member of the eurozone which limits (imperfectly) the depth of fiscal adjustment possible. However this argument about whether the real exchange rate of the euro is overvalued seems to be an excuse that obscures some of the other challenges listed above which include labour productivity changes and the value added to products. Some might see these recurring threats to exit the euro as a risk to investing in Italy. However an exit is not very likely given the high costs of exiting the monetary union and the benefits that accrue from being part of the eurozone, even if vulnerabilities exist.

In the increasingly integrated European economy, are less developed regions left out or is integration a way to bring back in? Are underdeveloped regions condemned to stay underdeveloped? Weaker official institutions and infrastructure compound differentiation between emerging regions.

The challenges Sicily and other areas of the Mezzogiorno face in evolving to higher value added products question whether such areas can create industrial hubs, technology or other clusters. There have been some significant investments in new industries including a computing center in Calabria. But some question whether such development is sustainable, that is if there is enough local demand and supply of skilled labour. Such policies are a shift from the industrial investment in the 50s and 60s, much of which focused on setting up industrial areas and promoting the production of goods.

Unlike some other areas of Italy and Europe, Sicily continues to have some similarities with emerging markets. Although it is much richer, with a higher standard of living and human development indicators than emerging markets in Latin America and the Middle East, its economic structure has some similarities. Sicily has high commodity exports, often of primary and secondary agricultural and mineral products. However unlike many emerging markets, it is not a very open economy, with little exports. For the most part, it has not benefited from the recent commodity boom because its currency and labour costs make it difficult for products to be competitive. However, it receives from transfer payments and the remittances from its emigrants to Italy or through the EU.

SICILY'S TIES TO THE MEDITERRANEAN REGION

Sicily's economy and economic challenges are tied to its Mediterranean neighbors in Europe and North Africa. Like Spain, Italy is a main entry point for migrants from the African continent. Being so close to the coast of Africa, Sicily and Lampedusa, a small nearby island to its south, receives its share of migrants. From January–July 2006, 12 000 illegal immigrants were discovered by Italian police while trying to reach Sicily. In addition to existing cooperation agreements with all of its southern neighbors which include migration issues, EU members are increasingly negotiating directly with North African countries to manage these flows of workers. Recently both France and Spain signed migration agreements with Senegal which are an attempt to manage such flows. Libya became the first North African country to be integrated into the EU's deportation policy. More such agreements might follow.

So how much do transportation links matter? A look at one
of Sicily's Italian neighbors might
show a model for economic development. Although it has a significant tourist industry, it has not
received the type of investment that
some of its neighbors like Cyprus
or even other regions in Italy have.
Transportation costs made it difficult to attract just-in-time production or other flexible schedules,
given the greater distance and number of competitors. A 2000 study of
the differences between Sicily and

Abruzzo, the most northerly and richest region of Italy's Mezzogiorno shows how economic structures influenced their growth patterns. Proximity matters; Abruzzo received consider-ably higher investment inflows than regions to the south. The shorter distance between Abruzzo and North and Central Italy, encouraged companies to locate operations there, which then facilitated diversification of its economic base and development of skilled work-ers. Even within Abruzzo, the most northern areas received highest levels of investment. This result would make an argument for strengthening and speeding up the transportation between Sicily, and the rest of Italy, i.e. by investing in the roads, ferries and possibly a bridge to increase access. However, transportation is insufficient. Areas like Abruzzo could

capitalize on geography to become part of the Italian supply chain, allowing its companies to become subcontractors from firms in northern Italy who facing labor unrest. Such investment led to spillovers and locally driven growth, but it required certain skills to be available. In contrast, in Sicily, government and public sector invested significant capital in large factories, which encouraged few spin-offs and local sub contracting and less development of skilled workers. Instead it was the public sector that absorbed most workers and instead of local production, products continued to be imported from the north.

Other risks to investment include weaker institutions and governance although these are improving. Italy continues to have high level of work in the informal economy, and in Sicily this is higher than other areas. In the past, organized crime thrived in the less-developed areas, creating alternative structures in power vacuums. Even when public investments were made, there were fears of corruption, that public funds were being siphoned off or not spent effectively. The same might hold true with private investment. Fearing investment might not bring returns, investors were wary of contributing to the region. In turn, this situation became self-fulfilling as less developed areas remained so. Furthermore, as a greater proportion of public spending focused on consumption rather than capital investment, efforts including spending on social services, were beneficial in the short term but had limited effect on building the investment climate in the longer term. However there were notable exceptions, particularly in the building of roads and other infrastructure in the main pathways of the island and construction projects. Recent local government reforms and a commitment to law and order have played a considerable role in improving these institutions and will continue to have positive spillovers on the economic climate.

So, the bridge itself, if completed, would only be part of a longer term solution and perhaps not the most economical. However, connecting Sicily more directly to the heart of Italy and Europe would benefit both the island and its neighbors. Even in the North, Italy's industrial base, manufacturing stagnated in the 1990s only to revive in recent years. many of Italy's export competitors in Asia and Mexico have lower income costs, making it difficult for Italy to compete on price with products that use cheaper technology and for which consumers have high price elasticity.

Given the risks in region like Sicily and the distance from other economic centers, it is likely that investors will either continue to focus on value added industries of northern and central Europe or on the manufacturing sectors in Asia which are also increasingly moving up the value added chain. Investments in human capital and infrastructure and an increased employment in construction and reconstruction will hopefully increase local and regional demand without which Sicily would continue to suffer lower growth. But support from national and regional government to provide infrastructure investment and support for governance reforms might create positive spillovers that can foster development and improve the investment climate.

Part IV
Scenario Analysis: The Stochastic Programming Approach to Managing Risk

21
Hedge and pension fund risk, disasters and their prevention

Scenario dependent correlation matrices are crucial to model risk in all scenarios

Hedge fund and pension fund disasters occur at different speeds. With a hedge fund, it is usually immediate in one or two days or over a month or so. That is because their positions are usually highly levered. The action is quick and furious when things go wrong. A pension fund on the other hand rarely makes decisions on an hourly, daily, or weekly basis. Rather, their decisions are how to allocate their funds into broad investment classes over longer periods of time. Review decision periods are typically yearly or possibly quarterly after meetings with their fund managers.

There have been many hedge fund disasters such as Long Term Capital Management (1998), Niederhoffer (1997), and Amaranth (2006), see Chapters 11–13. They almost invariably have three ingredients: the fund is over bet, that is, too highly levered; the positions are not really diversified for all scenarios; and then a bad scenario occurs. Once the trouble starts, it is hard to get out without excess cash. So it is better to have the cash in advance, that is, to be less levered in the first place.

Pension funds have had their share of disasters as well. And the loss can be substantial. In 2003, the University of Toronto announced that their pension fund lost $450 million in the past year. The British universities pension system was in a shortfall of more than 18 %, some $6 billion in 2006. These losses

were largely attributable to being overweighted in equities just before the 2000/2 crash. Worldwide pensions had a shortfall of $2.5 trillion in January 2003, according to Watson Wyatt. Most of these losses could have been avoided with better scenarios that reflected current distributions of asset returns; see Chapter 23. With equity rises the shortfall in July 2007 is less.

Defined benefit pension funds that owe a fixed stream of money, are the source of the trouble. Many governments such as those in France, Italy, Israel and many US states have such problems. On the other hand, defined contribution plans, like that of my university, where you put the money in, get contributions from the university, manage the assets and have what you have, create no consequences for the pension plan. Losses and gains are the property of the retirees not the plan sponsor. So these have no macro problem though, for individuals, their retirement prospects can be bleak if the funds have not been well managed.

The key issue for pension funds is their strategic asset allocation to stocks, bonds, cash, real estate and other assets. Stochastic programming models provide a good way to assess the risk control of both pension and hedge fund portfolios using an overall approach to position size which takes into account various possible scenarios that may be beyond the range of previous historical data. Since correlations are scenario dependent, this approach is useful to model the overall position size. The model will not allow the hedge fund to maintain positions so large and so under diversified that a major disaster can occur. Also the model will force consideration of how the fund will deal with the bad scenarios because once there is a derivative disaster, it is very difficult to resolve the problem. More cash is needed immediately and there are liquidity and other considerations. For pension funds, the problem is a shortfall to its retirees and the political fallout from that.

Let's first discuss fixed mix versus strategic asset allocation.

FIXED MIX AND STRATEGIC ASSET ALLOCATION

Fixed mix strategies, in which the asset allocation weights are fixed and the assets are rebalanced at each decision point to the initial weights, are very common and yield good results. An attractive feature is an effective form of volatility pumping since they rebalance by selling assets high and buying them low. Luenberger (1998) presents a general discussion of the gains possible from volatility pumping. Fixed mix strategies compare well with buy and hold strategies: see, for example, Figure 21.1 which shows the 1982 to 1994 performance of a number of asset categories including mixtures of EAFE (Europe, Australia and the Far East) index, S&P500, bonds, the Russell 2000 small cap index and cash.

Theoretical properties of fixed mix strategies are discussed by Dempster et al (2003) and Merton (1990) who show their advantages. In stationary markets where the return distributions are the same each year, the long run growth of wealth is exponential with probability. The stationary assumption is fine for long run behavior but for short time horizons, even up to 10 to 30 years, using scenarios to represent the future will generally give better results.

Hensel, Ezra and Ilkiw (1991) showed the value of strategic asset allocation. They evaluated the results of seven representative Frank Russell US clients who were having their assets managed by approved professional managers who are supposed to beat their benchmarks with lower risk. The study was over sixteen quarters from January 1985 to December 1988. A fixed mix benchmark was: US equity (50 %), non-US equity (5 %), US fixed (30 %), real estate (5 %), cash (10 %). Table 21.1 shows the results concerning the mean quarterly returns and the variation explained. Most of the volatility (94.35 % of the total) is explained by the naive policy allocation. This is similar to the 93.6 % (Brinson, Hood & Beebower, 1986). T-bill returns (1.62 %) and the fixed mix strategy (2.13 %) explain most of the mean returns. The managers returned 3.86 % versus 3.75 % for T-bills plus fixed mix so they added value. This added value was from their superior strategic asset allocation into stocks,

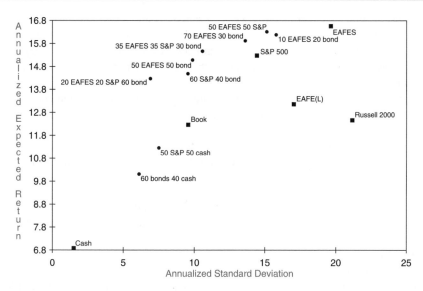

Figure 21.1   Historical performance of some asset categories, January 1, 1982 to December 31, 1994.
Source: Ziemba and Mulvey (1998)

Table 21.1   Average return and return variation explained (quarterly by the seven clients), percent. *Source*: Hensel et al (1991)

Decision Level	Average Contribution, %	Additional variation explained by this level (volatility), %
Minimum Risk (T-bills)	1.62	2.66
Naive Allocation (fixed mix)	2.13	94.35
Specific Policy Allocation	0.49	0.50
Market Timing	(0.10)	0.14
Security Selection	(0.23)	0.40
Interaction and Activity	(0.005)	1.95
Total	3.86	100.00
T-bills and fixed mix	3.75	

bonds and cash. The managers were unable to market time or to pick securities better than the fixed mix strategy.

Further evidence that strategic asset allocation accounts for most of the time series variation in portfolio returns while market timing and asset selection are far less important has been given by Blake, Lehmann and Timmerman (1999). They used a nine-year (1986–94) monthly data set on 306 UK pension funds with eight asset classes. They find also a slow mean reversion in the funds' portfolio weights toward a common, time varying strategic asset allocation. The UK pension industry is concentrated in very few management companies. Indeed four companies control 80 % of the market. This differs from the US where in 1992 the largest company had a 3.7 % share (Lakonishok, Shleifer & Vishny, 1992). During the 1980s, these plans were about 50 % overfunded. Fees are related to performance usually relative to a benchmark or peer group. They concluded that:

1. UK pension fund managers have a weak incentive to add value and face constraints on how they try to do it. Though strategic asset allocation may be set by the trustees these are flexible and have wide tolerance for short-run deviations and can be renegotiated.
2. Fund managers know that relative rather than absolute performance determines their long-term survival in the industry.
3. Fund managers earn fees related to the value of assets under management not to their relative performance against a benchmark or their peers with no specific penalty for underperforming nor reward for outperforming.
4. The concentration in the industry leads to portfolios being dominated by a small number of similar *house positions* for asset allocation to reduce the risk of relative underperformance.

The asset classes from WM Company data were UK equities, international equities, UK bonds, international bonds, cash, UK property and international property. UK portfolios are heavily equity weighted. For example, the 1994 weights for these eight asset classes over the 306 pension funds were 53.6, 22.5, 5.3, 2.8, 3.6, 4.2, 7.6 and 0.4 %, respectively. In contrast, US pension funds had 44.8, 8.3, 34.2, 2.0, 0.0, 7.5, 3.2 and 0.0 %, respectively.

Most of the 306 funds had very similar returns year by year. The semi-interquartile range was 11.47 to 12.59 % and the 5th and 95th percentiles were less than 3 % apart.

The returns on different asset classes were not very high except for international property. The eight classes averaged value weighted 12.97, 11.23, 10.76, 10.03, 8.12, 9.01, 9.52 and 8.13 (for the international property) and overall 11.73 % per year. Bonds and cash kept up with equities quite well in this period. They found, similar to the previous studies, that for UK equities, a very high percentage (91.13) of the variance in differential returns across funds because of strategic asset allocation. For the other asset classes, this is lower: 60.31 % (international equities), 39.82 % (UK bonds), 16.10 % (international bonds), 40.06 % (UK index bonds), 15.18 % (cash), 76.31 % (UK property) and 50.91 % (international property). For these other asset classes, variations in net cash flow differentials and covariance relationships explain the rest of the variation.

STOCHASTIC PROGRAMMING MODELS APPLIED TO HEDGE AND PENSION FUND PROBLEMS

Let's now discuss how stochastic programming models may be applied to hedge fund pension fund problems as well as the asset-liability commitments for other institutions such as insurance companies, banks, pension funds and savings and loans and individuals. These problems evolve over time as follows:

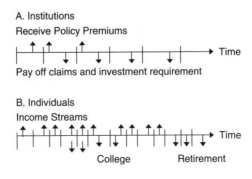

The stochastic programming approach considers the following aspects:

- Multiple discrete time periods; possible use of end effects – steady state after decision horizon adds one more decision period to the model; the tradeoff is an end effects period or a larger model with one less period.
- Consistency with economic and financial theory for interest rates, bond prices, etc.
- Discrete scenarios for random elements – returns, liabilities, currencies; these are the possible evolutions of the future; since they are discrete, they do not need to be lognormal and/or any other parametric form.
- Scenario dependent correlation matrices so that correlations change for extreme scenarios.
- Utilize various forecasting models that handle fat tails and other parts of the return distributions.
- Include institutional, legal and policy constraints.
- Model derivatives, illiquid assets and transactions costs.
- Expressions of risk in terms understandable to decision makers based on targets to be achieved and convex penalties for their non-attainment.
- This yields simple easy to understand risk averse utility functions that maximize long run expected profits net of expected discounted penalty costs for shortfalls; that pay more and more penalty for shortfalls as they increase.
- These utility functions are highly preferable to VaR which does not consider the size of the loss at all but just whether a loss has occurred.
- Model various goals as constraints or penalty costs in the objective.
- Maintain adequate reserves and cash levels and meet regularity requirements.
- We can now solve very realistic multiperiod problems on modern workstations and PCs using large scale linear programming and stochastic programming algorithms.
- The model makes you *diversify* – the key for keeping out of trouble.

Figure 21.2 from Cariño and Turner (1998) shows that the stochastic programming approach generally is superior to fixed mix. fixed mix A (a 64/36 stock/bond mix) and B (46/54) are dominated by the optimal stochastic programming dynamic frontier trading off expected wealth and expected shortfall cost.

More evidence regarding the performance of stochastic dynamic versus fixed mix models

However, Fleten, Høyland and Wallace (2002) compared two alternative versions of a portfolio model for the Norwegian life insurance company Gjensidige NOR, namely multistage stochastic linear programming and the fixed mix constant rebalancing study. They found that the multiperiod stochastic programming model dominated the fixed mix approach but the degree of dominance is much smaller out-of-sample than in-sample, see Figure 21.3. This is because out-of-sample the random input data is structurally different from in-sample, so the stochastic programming model loses its advantage in optimally adapting to the information available in the scenario tree. Also the performance of the fixed mix approach improves because the asset mix is updated at each stage.

We now focus on a model WTZ designed for the Siemen's Austrian pension fund which was implemented in 2000 and built together with Alois Geyer of the University of Vienna. The model is described in Geyer et al (2002) and Geyer and Ziemba (2007) and summarized below.

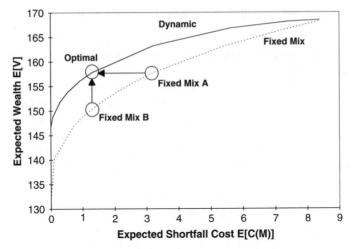

Expected Wealth and Shortfall Costs of Strategies

Strategy	Initial Equity/Bond Allocation (%)	Expected Wealth at Year 5	Expected Penalized Shortfall
Optimal	59/41	158 (9.6% pa)	1.3
Fixed Mix A	64/36	158 (9.6% pa)	3.2
Fixed Mix B	46/54	150 (8.5% pa)	1.3

Figure 21.2   The optimal stochastic strategy dominates fixed mix

INNOALM, THE INNOVEST AUSTRIAN PENSION FUND FINANCIAL PLANNING MODEL

Siemens AG Österreich, part of the global Siemens Corporation, is the largest privately owned industrial company in Austria. Its businesses with revenues of € 2.4 B in 1999, include information and communication networks, information and communication products, business services, energy and traveling technology, and medical equipment. Their pension fund, established in 1998, is the largest corporate pension plan in Austria and is a defined contribution plan. Over 15 000 employees and 5000 pensioners are members of the pension plan with € 510 million in assets under management as of December 1999.

Innovest Finanzdienstleistungs AG founded in 1998 is the investment manager for Siemens AG Österreich, the Siemens Pension Plan and other institutional investors in Austria. With € 2.2 billion in assets under management, Innovest focuses on asset management for institutional money and pension funds. This pension plan was rated the best in Austria of seventeen analyzed in the 1999/2000 period. The motivation to build InnoALM, which is described in Geyer et al (2002), is part of their desire to have superior performance and good decision aids to help achieve this.

Various uncertain aspects, possible future economic scenarios, stock, bond and other investments, transactions costs, liquidity, currency aspects, liability commitments over time, Austrian pension fund law and company policy suggested that a good way to approach

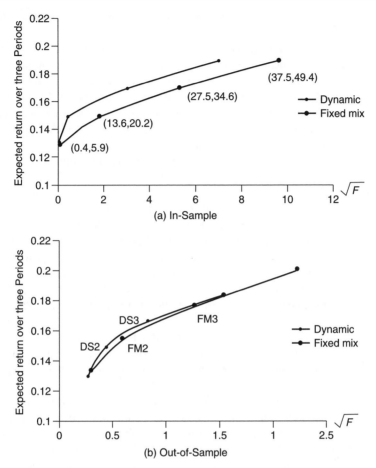

Figure 21.3 Comparison of advantage of stochastic programming over fixed mix model in and out of sample. *Source*: Fleten et al (2002)

this was via a multiperiod stochastic linear programming model. These models evolve from Kusy and Ziemba (1986), Cariño and Ziemba et al. (1994, 1998), Ziemba and Mulvey (1998) and Ziemba (2003). This model has innovative features such as state dependent correlation matrices, fat tailed asset return distributions, simple computational schemes and user-friendly output.

InnoALM was produced in six months during 2000 with Geyer and Ziemba serving as consultants with Innovest employees Herold and Kontriner giving advice. InnoALM demonstrates that a small team of researchers with a limited budget can quickly produce a valuable modeling system that can easily be operated by non-stochastic programming specialists on a single PC. The IBM OSL stochastic programming software provides a good solver. The solver was interfaced with user friendly input and output capabilities. Calculation times on the PC are such that different modeling situations can be easily developed and the implications of policy, scenario, and other changes seen quickly. The graphical output provides pension fund management with essential information to aid in the making of informed investment decisions and understand the probable outcomes and risk involved with these actions. The model can be used to explore possible European, Austrian and Innovest policy alternatives.

The liability side of the Siemens Pension Plan consists of employees, for whom Siemens is contributing DCP payments, and retired employees who receive pension payments. Contributions are based on a fixed fraction of salaries, which varies across employees. Active employees are assumed to be in steady state; so employees are replaced by a new employee with the same qualification and sex so there is a constant number of similar employees. Newly employed staff start with less salary than retired staff, which implies that total contributions grow less rapidly than individual salaries.

The set of retired employees is modeled using Austrian mortality and marital tables. Widows receive 60 % of the pension payments. Retired employees receive pension payments after reaching age 65 for men and 60 for women. Payments to retired employees are based upon the individually accumulated contribution and the fund performance during active employment. The annual pension payments are based on a discount rate of 6 % and the remaining life expectancy at the time of retirement. These annuities grow by 1.5 % annually to compensate for inflation. Hence, the wealth of the pension fund must grow by 7.5 % per year to match liability commitments. Another output of the computations is the expected annual net cash flow of plan contributions minus payments. Since the number of pensioners is rising faster than plan contributions, these cash flows are negative so the plan is declining in size.

The model determines the optimal purchases and sales for each of N assets in each of T planning periods. Typical asset classes used at Innovest are US, Pacific, European, and emerging market equities and US, UK, Japanese and European bonds. The objective is to maximize the concave risk averse utility function expected terminal wealth less convex penalty costs subject to various linear constraints. The effect of such constraints is evaluated in the examples that follow, including Austria's maximum limits of 40 % in equities and 45 % in foreign securities, and a minimum 40 % in Eurobonds. The convex risk measure is approximated by a piecewise linear function so the model is a multiperiod stochastic linear program. Typical targets that the model tries to achieve and if not is penalized for, are wealth (the fund's assets) to grow by 7.5 % per year and for portfolio performance returns to exceed benchmarks. Excess wealth is placed into surplus reserves and a portion of that is paid out in succeeding years.

The elements of InnoALM are described in Figure 21.4. The interface to read in data and problem elements uses Excel. Statistical calculations use the program Gauss and this data is fed into the IBM0SL solver which generates the optimal solution which generates the optimal solution to the stochastic program. The output used Gauss to generate various tables and graphs and retains key variables in memory to allow for future modeling calculations. Details of the model formulation are in Geyer et al (2002) and Geyer and Ziemba (2007).

Some typical applications

To illustrate the model's use we present results for a problem with four asset classes (Stocks Europe, Stocks US, Bonds Europe, and Bonds US) with five periods (six stages). The periods are twice 1 year, twice 2 years and 4 years (10 years in total). We assume discrete compounding which implies that the mean return for asset i (μ_i) used in simulations is $\mu_i = exp(\overline{y})_i - 1$ where $\overline{y}_i$ is the mean based on log-returns. We generate 10 000 scenarios using a 100-5-5-2-2 node structure. Initial wealth equals 100 units and the wealth target is

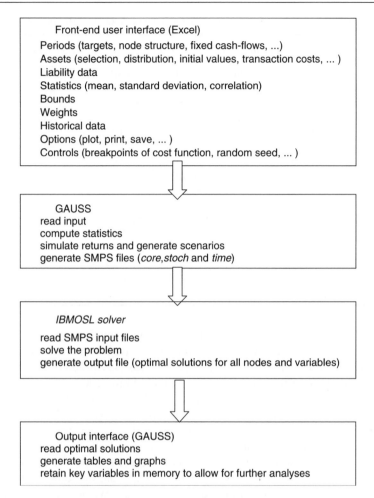

Front-end user interface (Excel)

Periods (targets, node structure, fixed cash-flows, ...)
Assets (selection, distribution, initial values, transaction costs, ...)
Liability data
Statistics (mean, standard deviation, correlation)
Bounds
Weights
Historical data
Options (plot, print, save, ...)
Controls (breakpoints of cost function, random seed, ...)

GAUSS
read input
compute statistics
simulate returns and generate scenarios
generate SMPS files (*core,stoch* and *time*)

IBMOSL solver

read SMPS input files
solve the problem
generate output file (optimal solutions for all nodes and variables)

Output interface (GAUSS)
read optimal solutions
generate tables and graphs
retain key variables in memory to allow for further analyses

Figure 21.4   Elements of InnoALM. *Source*: Geyer et al (2002)

assumed to grow at an annual rate of 7.5 %. No benchmark target and no cash in – and outflows are considered in this sample application to make its results more general. We use risk aversion $R_A = 4$ and the discount factor equals 5 %. which corresponds roughly with a simple static mean-variance model to a standard 60-40 stock-bond pension fund mix; see Kallberg and Ziemba (1983).

Assumptions about the statistical properties of returns measured in nominal Euros are based on a sample of monthly data from January 1970 for stocks and 1986 for bonds to September 2000. Summary statistics for monthly and annual log returns are in Table 21.2. The US and European equity means for the longer period 1970–2000 are much lower than for 1986–2000 and slightly less volatile. The monthly stock returns are non-normal and negatively skewed. Monthly stock returns are fat tailed whereas monthly bond returns are close to normal (the critical value of the Jarque-Bera test for a = .01 is 9.2).

However, for long term planning models such as InnoALM with its one year review period, properties of monthly returns are less relevant. The bottom panel of Table 21.2 contains statistics for annual returns. While average returns and volatilities remain about

Table 21.2   Statistical Properties of Asset Returns. Source: Geyer et al (2002)

	Stocks Eur		Stocks US		Bonds Eur	Bonds US
monthly returns	1/70 −9/00	1/86 −9/00	1/70 −9/0	1/86 −9/00	1/86 −9/00	1/86 −9/00
mean (% p.a.)	10.6	13.3	10.7	14.8	6.5	7.2
std.dev (% p.a.)	16.1	17.4	19.0	20.2	3.7	11.3
skewness	−0.90	−1.43	−0.72	−1.04	−0.50	0.52
kurtosis	7.05	8.43	5.79	7.09	3.25	3.30
Jarque-Bera test	302.6	277.3	151.9	155.6	7.7	8.5
annual returns						
mean (%)	11.1	13.3	11.0	15.2	6.5	6.9
std.dev (%)	17.2	16.2	20.1	18.4	4.8	12.1
skewness	−0.53	−0.10	−0.23	−0.28	−0.20	−0.42
kurtosis	3.23	2.28	2.56	2.45	2.25	2.26
Jarque-Bera test	17.4	3.9	6.2	4.2	5.0	8.7

the same (we lose one year of data, when we compute annual returns), the distributional properties change dramatically. While we still find negative skewness, there is no evidence for fat tails in annual returns except for European stocks (1970–2000) and US bonds.

The mean returns from this sample are comparable to the 1900–2000 one hundred and one year mean returns estimated by Dimson et al. (2002) (see also Dimson et al, 2006 for updates). Their estimate of the nominal mean equity return for the US is 12.0 % and that for Germany and UK is 13.6 % (the simple average of the two country's means). The mean of bond returns is 5.1 % for US and 5.4 % for Germany and UK.

Assumptions about means, standard deviations and correlations for the applications of InnoALM appear in Table 21.4 and are based on the sample statistics presented in Table 21.3. Projecting future rates of returns from past data is difficult. We use the equity means from the period 1970–2000 since 1986–2000 had exceptionally good performance of stocks that is not assumed to prevail in the long run.

Table 21.3   Regression Equations Relating Asset Correlations and US Stock Return Volatility (monthly returns; Jan 1989–Sep 2000; 141 observations). *Source*: Geyer et al (2002)

correlation between	constant	slope w.r.t. US stock volatility	t-statistic of slope	R
Stocks Europe – Stocks US	0.62	2.7	6.5	0.23
Stocks Europe – Bonds Europe	1.05	−14.4	−16.9	0.67
Stocks Europe – Bonds US	0.86	−7.0	−9.7	0.40
Stocks US – Bonds Europe	1.11	−16.5	−25.2	0.82
Stocks US – Bonds US	1.07	−5.7	−11.2	0.48
Bonds Europe – Bonds US	1.10	−15.4	−12.8	0.54

Table 21.4 Means, Standard Deviations and Correlations Assumptions. Source: Geyer et al (2002)

		Stocks Europe	Stocks US	Bonds Europe	Bonds US
normal periods	Stocks US	.755			
(70 % of the time)	Bonds Europe	.334	.286		
	Bonds US	.514	.780	.333	
	Standard deviation	14.6	17.3	3.3	10.9
high volatility	Stocks US	.786			
(20 % of	Bonds Europe	.171	.100		
the time)	Bonds US	.435	.715	.159	
	Standard deviation	19.2	21.1	4.1	12.4
extreme	Stocks US	.832			
periods	Bonds Europe	−.075	−.182		
(10 % of the	Bonds US	.315	.618	−.104	
time)	Standard deviation	21.7	27.1	4.4	12.9
average period	Stocks US	.769			
	Bonds Europe	.261	.202		
	Bonds US	.478	.751	.255	
	Standard deviation	16.4	19.3	3.6	11.4
all periods	Mean	10.6	10.7	6.5	7.2

The correlation matrices in Table 21.4 for the three different regimes are based on the regression approach of Solnik et al (1996). Moving average estimates of correlations among all assets are functions of standard deviations of US equity returns. The estimated regression equations are then used to predict the correlations in the three regimes shown in Table 21.4. Results for the estimated regression equations appear in Table 21.3. Three regimes are considered and it is assumed that 10 % of the time, equity markets are extremely volatile, 20 % of the time markets are characterized by high volatility and 70 % of the time, markets are normal. The 35 % quantile of US equity return volatility defines *normal* periods. *Highly volatile* periods are based on the 80 % volatility quantile and *extreme* periods on the 95 % quartile. The associated correlations reflect the return relationships that typically prevailed during those market conditions. The correlations in Table 21.4 show a distinct pattern across the three regimes. Correlations among stocks increase as stock return volatility rises, whereas the correlations between stocks and bonds tend to decrease. European bonds may serve as a hedge for equities during extremely volatile periods since bonds and stocks returns, which are usually positively correlated, are then negatively correlated. See Figure 21.5 for this phenomenon during 2000–2 in the US when stocks fell and bonds rose. See Figure 21.6 for such correlations (rolling) from 1930–2000. The latter is a major reason why using scenario dependent correlation matrices is a major advance over sensitivity tests using one correlation matrix.

Optimal portfolios were calculated for seven cases – with and without mixing of correlations and with normal, t- and historical distributions. Cases NM, HM and TM use mixing

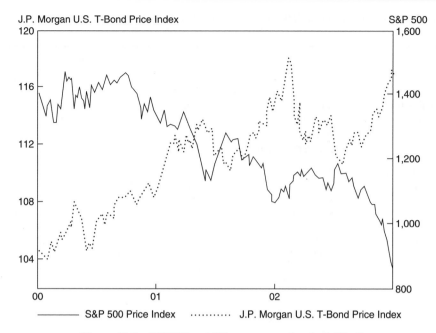

Figure 21.5   S&P500 and US government bonds, 2000–2

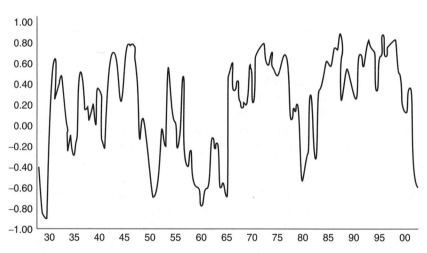

Figure 21.6   The correlation between US equity and government bonds with rolling windows, 1930–2000. *Source*: Schroeder investment management (2002)

correlations. Case NM assumes normal distributions for all assets. Case HM uses the histori-cal distributions of each asset. Case TM assumes t-distributions with five degrees of freedom for stock returns, whereas bond returns are assumed to have normal distributions. The cases NA, HA and TA use the same distribution assumptions with no mixing of correlations matrices. Instead the correlations and standard deviations used in these cases correspond to an 'average' period where 10 %, 20 % and 70 % weights are used to compute averages of correlations and standard deviations used in the three different regimes. Comparisons of the average (A) cases and mixing (M) cases are mainly intended to investigate the effect of mixing correlations. TMC maintains all assumptions of case TM but uses Austria's constraints on asset weights that Eurobonds must be at least 40 % and equity at most 40 %, and these constraints are binding.

Some test results

Table 21.5 shows the optimal initial asset weights at stage 1 for the various cases. Table 21.6 shows results for the final stage (expected weights, expected terminal wealth, expected reserves and shortfall probabilities). These tables show that the mixing correlation cases initially assign a much lower weight to European bonds than the average period cases. Single-period, mean-variance optimization and the average period cases (NA, HA and TA) suggest an approximate 45-55 mix between equities and bonds. The mixing correlation cases (NM,HM and TM) imply a 65-35 mix. Investing in US Bonds is not optimal at stage 1 in any of the cases which seems due to the relatively high volatility of US bonds.

Table 21.6 shows that the distinction between the A and M cases becomes less pronounced over time. However, European equities still have a consistently higher weight in the mixing cases than in no-mixing cases. This higher weight is mainly at the expense of Eurobonds. In general the proportion of equities at the final stage is much higher than in the first stage. This may be explained by the fact that the expected portfolio wealth at later stages is far above the target wealth level (206.1 at stage 6) and the higher risk associated with stocks is less important. The constraints in case TMC lead to lower expected portfolio wealth throughout the time horizon and to a higher shortfall probability than any other case. Calculations show

Table 21.5 Optimal Initial Asset Weights at Stage 1 by Case (percentage). *Source*: Geyer et al (2002)

	Stocks Europe	Stocks US	Bonds Europe	Bonds US
Single-period, mean-variance optimal weights (average periods)	34.8	9.6	55.6	0.0
Case NA: no mixing (average periods) normal distributions	27.2	10.5	62.3	0.0
Case HA: no mixing (average periods) historical distributions	40.0	4.1	55.9	0.0
Case TA: no mixing (average periods) *t*-distributions for stocks	44.2	1.1	54.7	0.0
Case NM: mixing correlations normal distributions	47.0	27.6	25.4	0.0
Case HM: mixing correlations historical distributions	37.9	25.2	36.8	0.0
Case TM: mixing correlations *t*-distributions for stocks	53.4	11.1	35.5	0.0
Case TMC: mixing correlations historical distributions; constraints on asset weights	35.1	4.9	60.0	0.0

Table 21.6 Expected Portfolio Weights at the Final Stage by Case (percentage), Expected Terminal Wealth, Expected Reserves, and the Probability for Wealth Target Shortfalls (percentage) at the Final Stage. *Source*: Geyer et al (2002)

	Stocks Europe	Stocks US	Bonds Europe	Bonds US	Expected Terminal Wealth	Expected Reserves at Stage 6	Probability of Target Shortfall
NA	34.3	49.6	11.7	4.4	328.9	202.8	11.2
HA	33.5	48.1	13.6	4.8	328.9	205.2	13.7
TA	35.5	50.2	11.4	2.9	327.9	202.2	10.9
NM	38.0	49.7	8.3	4.0	349.8	240.1	9.3
HM	39.3	46.9	10.1	3.7	349.1	235.2	10.0
TM	38.1	51.5	7.4	2.9	342.8	226.6	8.3
TMC	20.4	20.8	46.3	12.4	253.1	86.9	16.1

that initial wealth would have to be 35 % higher to compensate for the loss in terminal expected wealth due to those constraints. In all cases the optimal weight of equities is much higher than the historical 4.1 % in Austria.

The expected terminal wealth levels and the shortfall probabilities at the final stage shown in Table 21.6 make the difference between mixing and no-mixing cases even clearer. Mixing correlations yields higher levels of terminal wealth and lower shortfall probabilities.

If the level of portfolio wealth exceeds the target, the surplus $\widetilde{D}_j$ is allocated to a reserve account. The reserves in t are computed from $\sum_{j=1}^{t} \widetilde{D}_j$ and as shown in Table 21.6 for the final stage. These values are in monetary units given an initial wealth level of 100. They can be compared to the wealth target 206.1 at stage 6. Expected reserves exceed the target level at the final stage by up to 16 %. Depending on the scenario the reserves can be as high as 1800. Their standard deviation (across scenarios) ranges from 5 at the first stage to 200 at the final stage. The constraints in case TMC lead to a much lower level of reserves compared to the other cases which implies, in fact, less security against future increases of pension payments.

Summarizing we find that optimal allocations, expected wealth and shortfall probabilities are mainly affected by considering mixing correlations while the type of distribution chosen has a smaller impact. This distinction is mainly due to the higher proportion allocated to equities if different market conditions are taken into account by mixing correlations.

The results of any asset allocation strategy crucially depend upon the mean returns. This effect is now investigated by parametrizing the forecasted future means of equity returns. Assume that an econometric model forecasts that the future mean return for US equities is some value. between 5 to 15 %. The mean of European equities is adjusted accordingly so that the ratio of equity means and the mean bond returns as in Table 21.4 are maintained. We retain all other assumptions of case NM (normal distribution and mixing correlations). Figure 6.6 summarizes the effects of these mean changes in terms of the optimal initial weights. As expected, see Chapter 4, the results are very sensitive to the choice of the mean return. If the mean return for US stocks is assumed to equal the long run mean of 12 % as estimated by Dimson et al. (2002, 2006), the model yields an optimal weight for equities of 100 %. However, a mean return for US stocks of 9 % implies less than 30 % optimal weight for equities.

Model Tests

Since state dependent correlations have a significant impact on allocation decisions it is worthwhile to further investigate their nature and implications from the perspective of testing the model. Positive effects on the pension fund performance induced by the stochastic, multiperiod planning approach will only be realized if the portfolio is dynamically rebalanced as implied by the optimal scenario tree. The performance of the model is tested considering this aspect. As a starting point it is instructive to break down the rebalancing decisions at later stages into groups of achieved wealth levels. This reveals the 'decision rule' implied by the model depending on the current state. Consider case TM. Quintiles of wealth are formed at stage 2 and the average optimal weights assigned to each quintile are computed. The same is done using quintiles of wealth at stage 5.

Figure 21.7 shows the distribution of weights for each of the five average levels of wealth at the two stages. While the average allocation at stage 5 is essentially independent of the wealth level achieved (the target wealth at stage 5 is 154.3), the distribution at stage 2 depends on the wealth level in a specific way. If average attained wealth is 103.4, which is slightly below the target, a very cautious strategy is chosen. Bonds have the highest weight in this case (almost 50 %). In this situation the model implies that the risk of even stronger underachievement of the target is to be minimized. The model relies on the low but more certain expected returns of bonds to move back to the target level. If attained wealth is far below the target (97.1) the model implies more than 70 % equities and a high share (10.9 %) of relatively risky US bonds. With such strong under-achievement there is no room for a cautious strategy to attain the target level again. If average attained wealth equals 107.9, which is close to the target wealth of 107.5, the highest proportion is invested into US assets with 49.6 % invested in equities and 22.8 % in bonds. The US assets are more risky than the corresponding European assets which is acceptable because portfolio wealth is very close to the target and risk does not play a big role. For wealth levels above the target most of the portfolio is switched to European assets which are safer than US assets. This 'decision' may be interpreted as an attempt to preserve the high levels of attained wealth.

The decision rules implied by the optimal solution can be used to perform a test of the model using the following rebalancing strategy. Consider the ten year period from January 1992 to January 2002. In the first month of this period we assume that wealth is allocated according to the optimal solution for stage 1 given in Table 21.5. In each of the subsequent

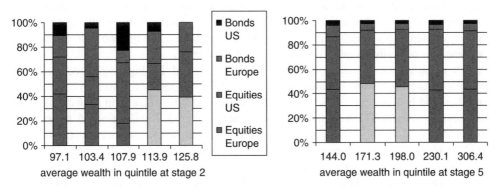

Figure 21.7 Optimal weights conditional on quintiles of portfolio wealth at stage 2 and 5. *Source*: Geyer et al (2002)

Table 21.7 Results of asset allocation strategies using the *Decision rule* implied by the optimal scenario tree. Source: Geyer et al (2002)

	complete sample 01/92-01/02		out-of-sample 10/100-01/02	
	mean	std.dev.	mean	std.dev.
NA	11.6	16.1	−17.1	18.6
NM	13.1	15.5	−9.6	16.9
HA	12.6	16.5	−15.7	21.1
HM	11.8	16.5	−15.8	19.3
TA	10.0	16.0	−14.6	18.9
TM	14.9	15.9	−10.8	17.6
TMC	12.4	8.5	0.6	9.9

months the portfolio is rebalanced as follows: identify the current volatility regime (extreme, highly volatile, or normal) based on the observed US stock return volatility. Then search the scenario tree to find a node that corresponds to the current volatility regime and has the same or a similar level of wealth. The optimal weights from that node determine the rebalancing decision. For the no-mixing cases NA, TA and HA the information about the current volatility regime cannot be used to identify optimal weights. In those cases use the weights from a node with a level of wealth as close as possible to the current level of wealth. Table 21.7 presents summary statistics for the complete sample and the out-of-sample period October 2000 to January 2002. The mixing correlation solutions assuming normal and t-distributions (cases NM and TM) provide a higher average return with lower standard deviation than the corresponding non-mixing cases (NA and TA). The advantage may be substantial as indicated by the 14.9 % average return of TM compared to 10.0 % for TA. The t-statistic for this difference is 1.7 and is significant at the 5 % level (one-sided test). Using the historical distribution and mixing correlations (HM) yields a lower average return than no-mixing (HA). In the constrained case TMC the average return for the complete sample is in the same range as for the unconstrained cases. This is mainly due to relatively high weights assigned to US bonds which performed very well during the test period, whereas stocks performed poorly. The standard deviation of returns is much lower because the constraints imply a lower degree of rebalancing.

To emphasize the difference between the cases TM and TA Figure 21.8 compares the cumulated monthly returns obtained from the rebalancing strategy for the two cases as well as a buy and hold strategy which assumes that the portfolio weights on January 1992 are fixed at the optimal TM weights throughout the test period. Rebalancing on the basis of the optimal TM scenario tree provides a substantial gain when compared to the buy and hold strategy or the performance using TA results, where rebalancing does not account for different correlation and volatility regimes.

Such in- and out-of-sample comparisons depend on the asset returns and test period. To isolate the potential benefits from considering state dependent correlations the following controlled simulation experiment was performed. Consider 1000 ten-year periods where

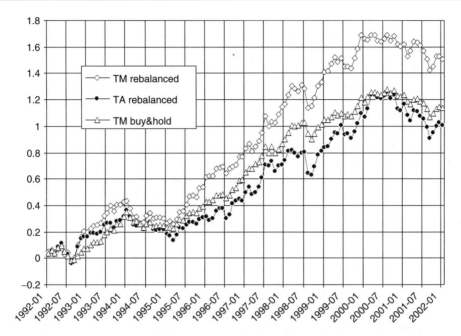

Figure 21.8 Cumulative monthly returns for different strategies. *Source*: Geyer et al (2002)

simulated annual returns of the four assets are assumed to have the statistical properties summarized in Table 21.4. One of the ten years is assumed to be a 'extreme' year, two years
correspond to 'highly volatile' markets and seven years are 'normal' years. We compare
the average annual return of two strategies: (a) a buy and hold strategy using the optimal
TM weights from Table 21.5 throughout the ten-year period, and (b) a rebalancing strategy
that uses the implied decision rules of the optimal scenario tree as explained in the in- and
out-of-sample tests above. For simplicity it was assumed that the current volatility regime is
known in each period. The average annual returns over 1000 repetitions of the two strategies
are 9.8 % (rebalancing) and 9.2 % (buy and hold). The t-statistic for the mean difference is
5.4 and indicates a highly significant advantage of the rebalancing strategy which exploits
the information about state dependent correlations. For comparison the same experiment was
repeated using the optimal weights from the constrained case TMC. We obtain the same average mean of 8.1 % for both strategies was obtained. This indicates that the constraints imply
insufficient rebalancing capacity. Therefore knowledge about the volatility regime cannot be
sufficiently exploited to achieve superior performance relative to buy and hold. This result
also shows that the relatively good performance of the TMC rebalancing strategy in the
sample period 1992–2002 is positively biased by the favorable conditions during that time.

Conclusions and final remarks

The model InnoALM provides an easy to use tool to help Austrian pension funds' investment
allocation committees evaluate the effect of various policy choices in light of changing
economic conditions and various goals, constraints, and liability commitments. The model
includes features that reflect real investment practices. These include multiple scenarios,

non-normal distributions and different volatility and correlation regimes. The model provides a systematic way to estimate the likely results of particular policy changes and asset return realizations in advance. This provides more confidence and justification to policy changes that may be controversial such as a higher weight in equity and less in bonds than has traditionally been the case in Austria.

The model is an advance on previous models and includes new features such as state dependent correlation matrices. Crucial to the success of the results are the scenario inputs and especially the mean return assumptions. The model has a number of ways to estimate such scenarios. Given good inputs, the policy recommendations can improve current invest-ment practice and provide greater confidence to the asset allocation process. The following quote by Konrad Kontriner (Member of the Board) and Wolfgang Herold (Senior Risk Strategist) of Innovest emphasizes the practical importance of InnoALM:

> The InnoALM model has been in use by Innovest, an Austrian Siemens subsidiary, since its first draft versions in 2000. Meanwhile it has become the only consistently implemented and fully integrated proprietary tool for assessing pension allocation issues within Siemens AG worldwide. Apart from this, consulting projects for various European corporations and pensions funds outside of Siemens have been performed on the basis of the concepts of InnoALM. The key elements that make InnoALM superior to other consulting models are the flexibility to adopt individual constraints and target functions in combination with the broad and deep array of results, which allows to investigate individual, path dependent behavior of assets and liabilities as well as scenario based and Monte-Carlo like risk assessment of both sides. In light of recent changes in Austrian pension regulation the latter even gained additional importance, as the rather rigid asset based limits were relaxed for institutions that could prove sufficient risk management expertise for both assets and liabilities of the plan. Thus, the implementation of a scenario based asset allocation model will lead to more flexible allocation restraints that will allow for more risk tolerance and will ultimately result in better long term investment performance. Furthermore, some results of the model have been used by the Austrian regulatory authorities to assess the potential risk stemming from less constrainec pension plans.

22

Setting the scenario

Rare events are not so rare these days

The key to successful investment performance over time is to get the mean right, to properly diversify and not to overbet. Getting the mean right is the strategy element – how do you devise a winning strategy? One measure of how good a strategy is its mean return. The other element is money management which now goes by the more fashionable term risk control. As argued in Chapter 21, scenario dependent correlation matrices are crucial for this risk control since correlations are scenario dependent. So some way of estimating these correlations based on given scenarios is crucial for successful risk control.

This chapter discusses ideas about scenarios. Chapters 24–26 go more deeply into procedures for scenario generation and aggregation, more technical aspects and some applications. This is a complex subject.

The stochastic programming community and other research areas such as fixed income have made considerable progress on the construction of such scenarios. We also must aggregate them in some situations and to focus on some areas of them in other situations. In the stochastic programming literature and community, scenario generation and aggregation has been and continues to be one of the most active research areas. Considerable progress has been made but still there is much to be done.

EXTREME SCENARIOS

Here is a short quiz: An index of the damages from earthquakes in California in the years from 1970 to 1993, according to Embrechts, Resnick and Samovodmitsky (1998), is shown in Figure 22.1.

In this data some years have zero damage, some have five, etc. The highest is 129. The question is how much earthquake damage occurred in California in the next year? Can you

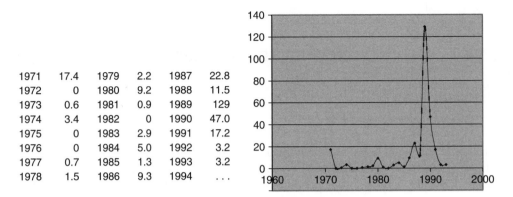

1971	17.4	1979	2.2	1987	22.8
1972	0	1980	9.2	1988	11.5
1973	0.6	1981	0.9	1989	129
1974	3.4	1982	0	1990	47.0
1975	0	1983	2.9	1991	17.2
1976	0	1984	5.0	1992	3.2
1977	0.7	1985	1.3	1993	3.2
1978	1.5	1986	9.3	1994	...

Figure 22.1   Earthquake loss indices per year

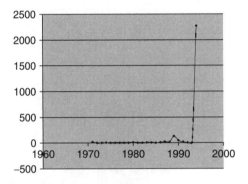

Figure 22.2   Earthquake loss ratios per year to 1994

forecast the 1994 value? When I present this in lectures, most of the answers are ten or less. The 1989 peak of 129 and the 47 in 1990 are not considered in most observers' calculations since they look like outliers with the main probability mass in the years 1972 to 1986 where the maximum damage was less than ten.

The answer for 1994 is actually 2272.7. The big 129 peak that was so high in Figure 22.1 became very small when the next year's data is included. Hence, as shown in Figure 22.2, extreme events can occur that are beyond the range of all previous events. There may have been earthquakes in California 400 years ago that were bigger than Northridge's (greater Los Angeles) in 1994 but there were few people and buildings there then so there was not much to destroy. Figure 22.2 shows the years 1989 and 1990 as similar to the 1972 to 1986 years and all the years 1971 to 1993 appear to have values which are essentially zero.

Insurance companies are in the business of predicting and insuring these rare catastrophic events. This is difficult to do even for such organizations with considerable resources. The year 1998 was a difficult one for LTCM and others as thirty-two insurance companies in the US went bankrupt. Post 9/11 they have had more trouble and subsequent years have also been difficult. The result is more restrictive and more expensive policies. Still the insurance industry has not been very profitable.

The number of such extreme scenario events is increasing. Table 22.1 is a list of events that occurred in 1998 that were beyond the range of the previous data. Figure 22.3 shows

Table 22.1   Seventeen rare events in 1998

May 18	Indonesia's rupiah collapses from 25 000, to 17 000 to the US dollar.
Aug 17	Russia defaults on ruble denominated debt; ruble collapses by two thirds.
Aug 31	The Dow plunges 512.61 points or 6.37 % (on −1 day, strongest trading day of the month).
July–Sept	US banks suffer worst derivatives losses ever $445 million.
Sept 24	Hedge fund Long-Term Capital Management is bailed out with $3.6 billion.
Sept 27	Japan Leasing files for bankruptcy with $17.9 billion in liabilities; biggest financial failure since World War Two.
Oct 5	30-year US treasury yields hits record 4.74 % low.
Oct 7	The US dollar plunges 7.8 % against the yen, largest one-day loss in 12 years.
Oct 8	China's yuan soars to an all-time high of 8.2777 to the US dollar.
Oct 9	Japan's Nikkei index sinks to 11 542, lowest since 1984.
Oct 13	London's FTSE-100 index soars a record 214.2 points.
Nov 2	The US savings rate sinks to 0.2 %
Nov 5	Some leading Western banks cut yen deposit rates to negative values.
Nov 11	Shares of theglobe.com skyrocket more than tenfold in first day of trading.
Nov 30	US mortgage rates fall to 6.64 %, the lowest since 1967.
Dec 3	11 European countries cut interest rates simultaneously.
Dec 10	World oil prices slide below $10 a barrel, the lowest since 1986.

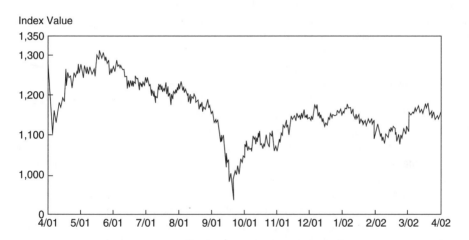

Figure 22.3   The S&P around September 11, 2001

the S&P500 around the September 11, 2001 bad scenario. There was a 14 % fall in one week! However from the perspective of the markets, these adverse effects have short term effects on prices.

These seemingly rare, *beyond-previous-experience* events are not so rare. Highly levered speculative investing has occurred for hundreds of years but recently there are more and more complex derivative instruments which is one of the causes of the growth of these rare events. The New York risk management consultants Capital Markets Risk list *'first-time'* market events – events that conventional (not stochastic programming) risk control models cannot foresee because the events have occurrences way beyond the range of previous history. Normally, there are four or five such events each year. Seventy-seven occurred in 1998!

David Lewis, a Princeton philosophy professor argues that there are a plurality of worlds. Bill Miller, the famed manager of the Legg Mason Value Trust, who beat the S&P500 every year from 1990 to 2005, fifteen straight years – a great record and a very good example of *getting the mean right* and not being over levered and being diversified enough to do well, views Lewis' ideas as

> One of the things capital markets do is consider possible worlds. The level and direction of prices reflect the markets' assessment of the probabilities of possible worlds becoming actual. . . . There are advocates for many of these views. Investors consider the risks and rewards and allocate their money accordingly.

Scenarios are a means to describe and approximate possible future economic environments. In our modeling applications, scenarios are represented as discrete probabilities of specific events. Together all the scenarios represent the possible evolution of the future world. There is a set of T period scenarios of the form $S^T = (S_1, S_2, \ldots, S_T)$, where $s_t \in S_t$ are the possible outcomes of all random problem elements where s_t occurs in period t, with probability $p_t(s_t)$.

A typical scenario tree is shown here, where S_1 has three possible outcomes, S_2 has three and S_3 has two. There are eighteen separate economic futures usually with different chances/probabilities of occurrence. Each can occur and together they approximate the possible future evolution of the economic environment relevant to the problem at hand. I argue that for asset-liability modeling, the most important parts of the distribution are the means and the left tail. The mean drives the returns and the left tail, the losses. We cannot include all possible scenarios but rather focus on a discrete set that best approximates the possible important

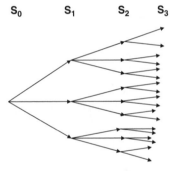

S_0 $\quad$ S_1 $\quad$ S_2 $\quad$ S_3

events that could happen. Since we have S^T total scenarios, we can include those we want. Once a scenario is included, the problem must react to the consequences of that scenario. This is a very important and flexible feature of stochastic programming modeling not usually available in other approaches.[1] We frequently aggregate scenarios to pick the best N out of the S^T so that the modeling effort is manageable. The true distribution P is approximated by a finite number of points $(w^1, \ldots, w^S)$ with positive probability p^s for each scenario s. The sum of all scenario probabilities is one. I argue that getting all the scenarios and their probabilities right is impossible and does not matter much anyway. What is important is to cover the board of possible occurrences. Then you will make sound decisions with risks under control.

The generation of good scenarios that well represent the future evolution of the key parameters is crucial to the success of the modeling effort. Scenario generation, sampling and aggregation is a complex subject and I will discuss it by describing key elements and then provide various developed and implemented models.

---

[1] The inclusion of such extreme scenarios means that the model must react to the possibility of that scenario occurring. This is one of the ways a stochastic programming overall model would have helped mitigate the 1998 losses and collapse of LTCM, the 1997 bankruptcy of Niederhoffer's hedge fund and Amaranth's collapse in 2006. The model would not have let them hold such large positions. See the discussion in Chapters 11–13.

Scenarios should consider among other things:

1. mean reversion of asset prices;
2. volatility clumping in which a period of high volatility is followed by another period of high volatility;
3. volatility increases when prices fall and decreases when they rise;
4. trending of currency, interest rates and bond prices;
5. ways to estimate mean returns;
6. ways to estimate fat tails;
7. arbitrage opportunities must be eliminated or their effects minimized.

An example of the first item, see Figure 22.4, is the S&P500 from 1991 to 2003. The straight line shows the mean reversion. My bond-stock relative return crash model as well as those of others predicted this decline, see Chapter 23, Ziemba (2003) and Shiller (2000).

Scenarios come from diverse sources and are used in many applications. They can come from a known discrete probability distribution or as the approximation of a continuous or other probability distribution which is estimated from past data, economic forecasting models or comparison with similar past events. The latter is especially useful for situations that have *never* occurred. If there is a potential crisis in Brazil whose effects must be estimated and no data or models are available but similar crises have occurred in Russia where the effects are well estimated then the Russian data can be used. This data is useful as a proxy for scenario estimation, especially for disastrous scenarios.

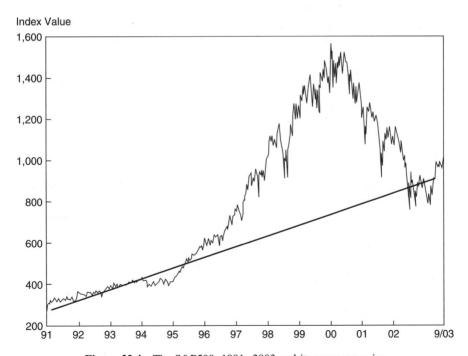

Figure 22.4   The S&P500, 1991–2003 and its mean reversion

Economic variables and actuarial predictions drive the liability side, whereas economic variables and sentiment drive financial markets and security prices. Hence, estimating scenarios for liabilities may be easier than for assets as there often are mortality tables, actuarial risks, legal requirements such as pension or social security rules, well-established policies, etc; see Embrechts (2000). Such scenarios may come from simulation models embedded into the optimization models that attempt to model the complex interaction between the economy, financial markets and liability values. Examples include Kingsland (1982) and Winklevoss (1982) and Boender (1997).

Abaffy et al (2000) and Dupačová et al (2000) survey scenario estimation and aggregation methods, that represent a larger number of scenarios by a smaller number. We can use the following classification:

1. There can be full knowledge of the exact probability distribution. This usually comes from a theoretical model. However, it is possible to use historical data or an expert's experience.
2. There can be a known parametric family based on a theoretical model whose parameters are estimated from available and possibly forecasted data. For example, there is a huge literature of scenario generations for interest rate, fixed income, and bond portfolio management using Vasicek (1997), Heath-Jarrow-Morton (1992) and Black, Derman and Toy (1990) and other interest rate models. For example, the prices of Treasury bonds can be computed on a lattace grid (basically parallel horizontal and vertical lines; then you compute on the places where the lines cross) subject to the initial yield curve. Then the prices of other relevant interest rate dependent securities can be estimated.

   Stochastic differential equation modeling can be used to generate scenarios for asset returns and liability commitments using a cascade of models that feed one into another. See, for example, Jamshidian and Zhu (1977), Chan et al (1992) and the Towers Perrin scenario generation system discussed in Mulvey (1996) and Mulvey and Thorlacius (1998).

   Methods used to evaluate Value at Risk can also be used to create scenarios since they estimate probability distributions; examples include Jorion (2000), Jamshidian and Zhu (1997) who estimate market and currency risk, and Jobst and Zenios (2001) and Duffie and Singleton (2003), who estimate market and credit risk.
3. Scenarios can be formed by sample moment information that aggregates large numbers of scenarios into a smaller easier set or generate scenarios from assumed probability distributions.
4. The simplest idea is to use past data that is in comparable circumstances and assign them equal probabilities. This can be done by just using the raw data or through procedures such as vector autoregressive modeling or bootstrapping which samples from the past data.
5. When there is no reliable data, one can use expert's forecasts (examples include Markowitz and Perold, 1981) or governmental regulations. Abaffy et al (2000) point out that to test the surplus adequacy of an insurer, New York State Regulation 126 suggests seven interest rate scenarios to simulate the performance of the surplus. Liability commitments are frequently easier to estimate than assets since there may be demographic data, regulations, etc.

The following schema is typical:

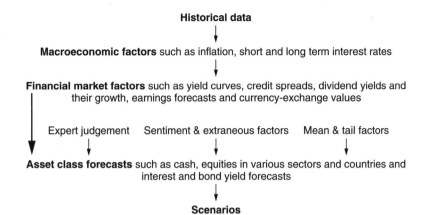

Historical data

↓

Macroeconomic factors such as inflation, short and long term interest rates

↓

Financial market factors such as yield curves, credit spreads, dividend yields and
their growth, earnings forecasts and currency-exchange values

Expert judgement   Sentiment & extraneous factors   Mean & tail factors

Asset class forecasts such as cash, equities in various sectors and countries and
interest and bond yield forecasts

↓

Scenarios

Whatever method is used to generate the scenarios relying on the merging of decision maker subjective estimates, expert judgment and empirical estimation, it is crucial to validate the estimated distributions and to make sure that the decision maker has not defined the range too narrowly. One should reflect on the distribution by asking what would make the value be outside the range and then assess the probability of this occurring. This will help expand the range and make the probability assessment more realistic.

Chapter 24 discusses scenario generation and aggregation in more depth along with other technical details and some examples.

23

Hedge fund scenario analysis

The long bond vs equity yield model is useful to predict stock market crashes

This chapter focusses on hedge funds in the context of the mid April 2004 stock market to illustrate scenario generation and aggregation. There is more on the technical aspects of the latter topic, as well as more on valuation measures, in Chapters 24 and 25. I focus on the US and S&P500 index  as it is the most important in the world and greatly influences other markets. See Siegel (2003) for the definitive treatment of benchmarks and indices and their use in portfolio management worldwide. I manage, for others in private accounts, and BVI based offshore pooled hedge funds, and with my own and family money, what amount to hedge funds in the equity and racetrack markets so it's useful for me to collect my thoughts as well. The past two plus years since the end of 2001 have been good for me and my futures account was up about 100% per year annualized to April 2004. Returns have continued to come in steadily but at a slower pace; Figure 6.3 updates the account to May 4, 2007.

I continue to argue that getting the mean right; and watching risk control and, especially, not overbetting are the keys to success. I have done three types of trades (I am small by fund standards, so that's enough for my resources in this futures account):

1. hedged currency trades where the key is to get the mean right and devise strategies and positions to capture this;
2. security market anomaly trades like the turn-of-the-year effect; and
3. exploiting systematic biases in the S&P500 futures put and call markets.

Readers of this book will have their own favorite trades so let me turn to the US stock market. I use several valuation measures for the S&P500. Of greatest importance is to stay out of crashes if you are long and especially if levered long. I have used the bond-stock yield difference model since my days at Yamaichi Research in Tokyo in 1988. I first wrote about it in Ziemba-Schwartz (1991) and there is a good discussion in Ziemba (2003). The idea is simple. Bonds and stocks compete for the money. When interest rates are high bonds look better. When interest rates are low, stocks provide more return and are preferred. A steep yield curve like that in Figure 23.1, is very good for stocks and dangerous for bonds. You want to buy bonds before interest rate

---

*Dedicated to my 1988-89 Yamaichi Research Institute colleagues who lost their jobs when Yamaichi Securities went bankrupt in 1995. Had the YRI management, then the sixth largest brokerage firm in the world, listened to the research they paid for in my crash study group, they would have taken actions to avoid this bankruptcy. The model presented here is simple but it works to predict great crashes.

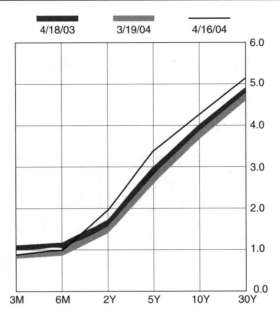

Figure 23.1   US Treasury yield curve, April 10, 2003, March 19 and Apirl 16 2004. *Source*: Bloomberg

declines and avoid them before interest rate rises. Bonds are very complex because inflation is crucial as well and there is so much discounting and various types of expectations.

THE EFFECT OF INTEREST RATES

Let's go first to the interest rates. On April 16, 2004, the odds favored a rather sharp increase in short term rates and sooner rather than later.

The crash measure comes in various versions but simply subtracting the 30-year T-bond rate from the reciprocal of the S&P500 price earnings ratio (using trailing earnings) is a good way to measure market risk. Table 23.1 shows the measure around the 1987 crash. The measure went into the danger zone (above a 95 % confidence band) in April 1987 with the S&P at 289.32. Then the S&P500 went higher before the eventual crash in October 1987. The danger points are in bold in the column on the right. The measure called the 1990 crash in Japan. It was no surprise. The indicator was further in the danger zone at the end of 1989 than it ever was in the previous 40-years including the 1987 crash. Whenever this measure was in the danger zone in Japan from 1948–88, there was a crash of at least 10 % in one year with *NO* misses: 12/12. There were eight other crashes. So this measure is more like a sufficient rather than a necessary condition for a crash. I can refer the reader to Ziemba and Schwartz (1991), Berge and Ziemba (2006) and Koivu, Pennanen and Ziemba (2005) for more on Japan. When the measure goes into the danger zone, the market ignores it and usually continues to rally. But eventually, within one year, there is a crash of at least 10 % from the initial value of the index when the measure went into the danger zone. Timing the fall is difficult. Just ask George Soros. His funds lost $ 5 billion shorting the Nasdaq in early 2000 when it was in the danger zone but still rising. Had his funds waited to start shorting in April 2000 they might have made $ 50 billion. Soros also shorted the Nikkei in 1988 more than a full year before the decline that started in January 1990.

Table 23.1   S&P500 index, PE ratios, government bond yields and the yield premium over stocks, January 1984 to August 1988. *Source*: Ziemba and Schwartz (1991)

		S&P Index	PER	(a) 30 Yr G bd	(b) 1/pe, %	(a)-(b)
1986	Jan	208.19	14.63	9.32	6.84	2.48
	Feb	219.37	15.67	8.28	6.38	1.90
	Mar	232.33	16.50	7.59	6.06	1.53
	Apr	237.98	16.27	7.58	6.15	1.43
	May	238.46	17.03	7.76	5.87	1.89
	Jun	245.30	17.32	7.27	5.77	1.50
	Jul	240.18	16.31	7.42	6.13	1.29
	Aug	245.00	17.47	7.26	5.72	1.54
	Sep	238.27	15.98	7.64	6.26	1.38
	Oct	237.36	16.85	7.61	5.93	1.68
	Nov	245.09	16.99	7.40	5.89	1.51
	Dec	248.60	16.72	7.33	5.98	1.35
1987	Jan	264.51	15.42	7.47	6.49	0.98
	Feb	280.93	15.98	7.46	6.26	1.20
	Mar	292.47	16.41	7.65	6.09	1.56
	Apr	289.32	16.22	9.56	6.17	3.39
	May	289.12	16.32	8.63	6.13	2.50
	Jun	301.38	17.10	8.40	5.85	2.55
	Jul	310.09	17.92	8.89	5.58	3.31
	Aug	329.36	18.55	9.17	5.39	3.78
	Sep	318.66	18.10	9.66	5.52	4.14
	Oct	280.16	14.16	9.03	7.06	1.97
	Nov	245.01	13.78	8.90	7.26	1.64
	Dec	240.96	13.55	9.10	7.38	1.72
1988	Jan	250.48	12.81	8.40	7.81	0.59
	Feb	258.10	13.02	8.33	7.68	0.65
	Mar	265.74	13.42	8.74	7.45	1.29
	Apr	262.61	13.24	9.10	7.55	1.55
	May	256.20	12.92	9.24	7.74	1.50
	Jun	270.68	13.65	8.85	7.33	1.52
	Jul	269.44	13.59	9.18	7.36	1.82
	Aug	263.73	13.30	9.30	7.52	1.78

In 1988 the bond-stock measure was not in the danger zone because the interest rates were so low; see Figure 23.2. It was only later in 1989 that it moved into the danger zone as interest rates rose and the stock market rose as well. In late 1989 the measure was the furthest into the danger zone in 41 years in Japan as shown in Figure 23.2. Then the big crash started on the first trading day of 1990. Eventually the market fell to one quarter of its end of December 1989 value. See Figures 9.1–9.3. Figure 23.2 shows that the Bank of Japan made an error of disastrous proportions; it raised interest rates in 1988 and 1989 getting the January 1990 crash going. But then they raised these rates for eight more months

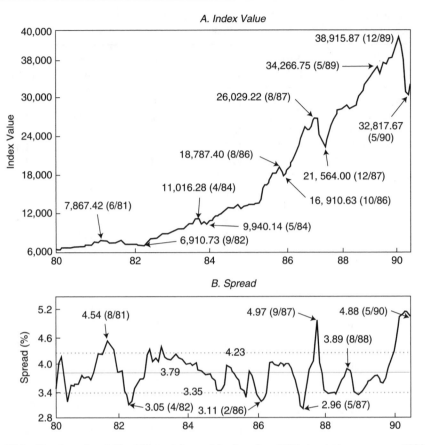

Figure 23.2 Bond-stock yield differential model for the Nikkei stock average, 1980–89.
Source: Ziemba and Schwartz (1991)

from January to August 1990. This absolute crushing of the bubble economy had a lot to do with the weak economy and stock market for the next ten plus years since many people and institutions were forced into bankruptcy by these high interest rates.

THE 2000–2002 CRASH IN THE S&P500

Table 23.2 shows that the measure entered the danger zone in April 1999 when the spread was 3.03 %; see the column on the right, with the S&P500 at 1335.18. The bond-stock return crash danger model went deeper into the danger zone as the year progressed. The spread was at 3.69 % in December 1999 and the S&P500 rose from 1229.23 at the end of December 1998 to 1469.25 at the end of December 1999. The stage was set for a crash that did occur; see Figure 12.1. Meanwhile, the P/E ratio was flat, increasing only from 32.34 to 33.29, and long-bond yields rose from 5.47 to 6.69 %. The S&P500 fell to 1085 on September 17, 2000, prior to 9/11. Again, the S&P500 went higher and hit 1527.46 on March 24 2000 and then again reached 1520 on September 1, 2000. But when it fell it went to 1085 in September 2000 and eventually to 768.63 on October 10, 2003. On April 21, 2004 the index closed at 1122.60.

Table 23.2 Bond and stock yield differential model for the S&P500, 1995–1999. *Source*: Ziemba (2003)

year	month	S&P500 Index	a PER	b 30-yr gov't bond	c = 1/a return on stocks	b-c crash signal
1995	Jan	470.42	17.10	8.02	5.85	2.17
	Feb	487.39	17.75	7.81	5.63	2.18
	Mar	500.71	16.42	7.68	6.09	1.59
	Apr	514.71	16.73	7.48	5.98	1.50
	May	533.40	16.39	7.29	6.10	1.19
	Jun	544.75	16.68	6.66	6.00	0.66
	Jul	562.06	17.23	6.90	5.80	1.10
	Aug	561.88	16.20	7.00	6.17	0.83
	Sep	584.41	16.88	6.74	5.92	0.82
	Oct	581.50	16.92	6.55	5.91	0.64
	Nov	605.37	17.29	6.36	5.78	0.58
	Dec	615.93	17.47	6.25	5.72	0.53
1996	Jan	636.02	18.09	6.18	5.53	0.65
	Feb	640.43	18.86	6.46	5.30	1.16
	Mar	645.50	19.09	6.82	5.24	1.58
	Apr	654.17	19.15	7.07	5.22	1.85
	May	669.12	19.62	7.21	5.10	2.11
	Jun	670.63	19.52	7.30	5.12	2.18
	Jul	639.96	18.80	7.23	5.32	1.91
	Aug	651.99	19.08	7.17	5.24	1.93
	Sep	687.31	19.65	7.26	5.09	2.17
	Oct	705.27	20.08	6.95	4.98	1.97
	Nov	757.02	20.92	6.79	4.79	2.01
	Dec	740.74	20.86	6.73	4.79	1.94
1997	Jan	786.16	21.46	6.95	4.66	2.29
	Feb	790.82	20.51	6.85	4.88	1.97
	Mar	757.12	20.45	7.11	4.89	2.22
	Apr	801.34	20.69	7.23	4.83	2.40
	May	848.28	21.25	7.08	4.71	2.37
	Jun	885.14	22.09	6.93	4.53	2.40
1997	Jul	954.29	23.67	6.78	4.22	2.56
	Aug	899.47	22.53	6.71	4.44	2.27
	Sep	947.28	23.29	6.70	4.29	2.41
	Oct	914.62	22.67	6.46	4.41	2.05
	Nov	955.40	23.45	6.27	4.26	2.01
	Dec	970.43	23.88	6.15	4.19	1.96
1998	Jan	980.28	24.05	6.01	4.16	1.85
	Feb	1049.34	25.09	6.00	3.99	2.01
	Mar	1101.75	27.71	6.11	3.61	2.50
	Apr	1111.75	27.56	6.03	3.63	2.40
	May	1090.82	27.62	6.10	3.62	2.48
	Jun	1133.84	28.65	5.89	3.49	2.40
	Jul	1120.67	28.46	5.83	3.51	2.32
	Aug	97.28	27.42	5.74	3.65	2.09
	Sep	1017.01	26.10	5.47	3.83	1.64
	Oct	1098.67	27.41	5.42	3.65	1.77
	Nov	1163.63	31.15	5.54	3.21	2.33
	Dec	1229.23	32.34	5.47	3.09	2.38
1999	Jan	1279.64	32.64	5.49	3.06	2.43
	Feb	1238.33	32.91	5.66	3.04	2.62
	Mar	1286.37	34.11	5.87	2.93	2.94
	Apr	1335.18	35.82	5.82	2.79	3.03
	May	1301.84	34.60	6.08	2.89	3.19
	Jun	1372.71	35.77	6.36	2.80	3.56
	Jul	1328.72	35.58	6.34	2.81	3.53
	Aug	1320.41	36.00	6.35	2.78	3.57
	Sep	1282.70	30.92	6.50	3.23	3.27
	Oct	1362.92	31.61	6.66	3.16	3.50
	Nov	1388.91	32.24	6.48	3.10	3.38
	Dec	1469.25	33.29	6.69	3.00	3.69

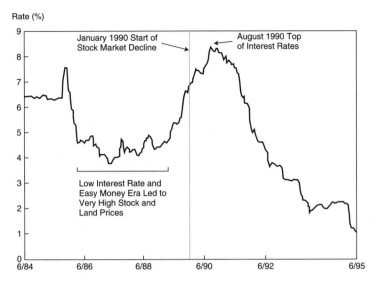

Figure 23.3 Short-term interest rates in Japan, June 1984–June 1995. *Source*: Ziemba (2003)

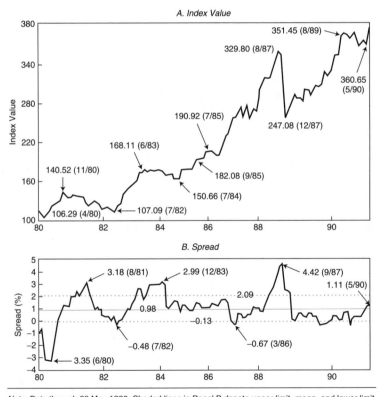

Note: Data through 29 May 1990. Shaded lines in Panel B denote upper limit, mean, and lower limit.
Source: Based on data from Ziemba and Schwartz (1991).

Figure 23.4 Bond-stock yield differential model for the S&P500, 1980–90. *Source*: Ziemba (2003)

Measure (%)

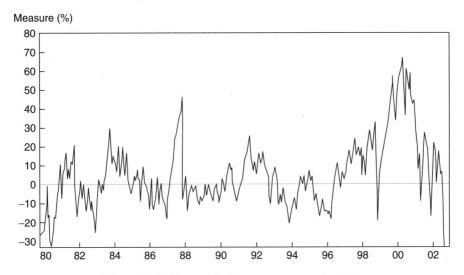

Figure 23.5   Race to the bottom. *Source*: Davis (2003)

Figure 23.5 shows the late 2002 values for the crash indicator using the Fed model. That model uses 10-year bond yields and computes the ratio of the bond and stock yields in terms of a percentage over- or under-valued. This measure is close to our difference crash model. This graph from Ned Davis' research indicates that, since 1980, very under-valued markets have historically had high returns. When the measure is above 15 % then mean S&P returns average a loss of 6.7 %. From 5 to 15 % had mean gains of 4.9 % and below −5 % had mean gains of 31.7 %. In late 2002/early 2003, the market was at one of its steepest discount to *fair value*. See Figure 12.1 for our calculations which mirror those of Davis. The length and depth of the 2000–2003 decline is seen in the jagged parts of Figure 12.1. One sees the initial danger zone for the measure in April 1999 but then the market returned to the danger zone in 2001 and 2002 because stock prices fell but earnings fell even more. This was a period where consensus future earnings forecasts were invariably far too optimistic. The S&P500 index fell from 1460.25 at the end of December 1999 to 885.76 on October 31, 2002 down 37 %. The S&P500 fell 22 % in 2002. This was a phenomenal call since many institutions assumed, wrongly, that the trouble was over. The short term measure based on behavioral finance ideas about option prices that I use predicted the circa July 2002 fall in the S&P500 when the bulk of the 2002 decline occurred.

What is the bond-stock earnings yield model saying now in April 2004 and what are the prospects for the S&P500 for the rest of 2004 and 2005? As of April 16, 2004 the price-earnings ratio of the S&P500 was estimated to be 23.28. Hence, the earnings yield was 4.30 %; see www.spglobal.com/earnings.html. This is based on reported earnings of 48.74. Dividends of 18.95 provided a yield of 1.67 %. The book value, for fiscal year 2002, was 324.14 providing a 3.50 market to book value ratio.

On April 16, 2004, the 30-year T-bond was yielding 5.19 % and the much more liquid 10-year bond was yielding 4.37 %. My original studies used 30-year bond rates but Berge and Ziemba (2006) and Koivu, Pennanen and Ziemba (2005) use 10-year rates since they more accurately reflect long term interest rates as they are more liquid. The conclusion though is that with either bond rate, the S&P500 was *NOT* in the danger zone in April

Table 23.3   The Fed funds futures contracts, April 2004. *Source*: Bloomberg

Month	April 13	April 14	April 21	
April	1.01 %	1.01 %	1.01 %	
May	1.02 %	1.02 %	1.02 %	
June	1.03 %	1.03 %	1.03 %	
July	1.11 %	(1.04 %)	1.10 %	
August	1.22 %	(1.08 %)	1.24 %	
September	1.33 %	(1.13 %)	1.335 %	
October	1.42 %	(1.18 %)	1.46 %	
November	1.57 %	(1.27 %)	1.59 %	
December	1.70 %	(1.35 %)	1.70–1.75 %	no trades
January '05			1.80–1.95 %	no trades
February '05			1.90–2.20 %	no trades

2004, nor any time later through June 29, 2007. The short term measure was not in the danger zone either. That does not mean that there cannot be a 10 % plus decline but the cause for this would seem to have to come from elsewhere. Terrorism is one possibility not to be discounted. A sharp increase in interest rates coupled with higher price-earnings ratios is another and then these measures would go into the danger zone later.

The best predictor of short term interest rate movements that I know is the Fed funds futures contract. Its prices yield useful scenarios for this variable, see Table 23.3. The recent CPI and core CPI, retail sales, and non-farm March payroll increases led to a sharp increase in the Fed funds futures prices on Wednesday, April 14, 2004.

The market prices suggest about 50-50 odds on the initial 25bp tightening move occurring on June 30 above the current (April, 2004) Fed funds target of 1.00 %. The first 25bp tightening move is now more than fully discounted at the August 10 meeting (versus 45 % before the March employment report), and a second 25bp move is about two-thirds discounted at the ensuing meeting on September 21. A cumulative tightening of 75 bp is discounted following the December 14 FOMC meeting.

So the 1 % dream world of low interest rates for more than 40 years will soon change. There is no crash coming based on earnings and interest rate concerns until the bond stock measure moves into the danger zone, and even for some time after,. The other big event in addition to the short term interest rate rise is the 2004 election, which I now discuss.

THE EFFECT OF THE 2004 PRESIDENTIAL ELECTION

The effect of the election is complex. First, who will win? Second, what is the likely impact of each possible outcome? There are various polls but the best odds/probabilities are likely from the betting exchanges. The largest of them is Betfair in London. You can access their website without an account to find out the odds, just look under special bets and go to the US presidential election. US residents cannot have such accounts but those in Canada, the UK and other countries can. On April 21, 2004 the odds that Kerry would get the Democratic nomination were 1-33 or 97 % based on bid-ask prices of 1.02 and 1.04. Using the British odds system, this means bet 33, collect 34 and win one. So it's not 100 % certain that he will get the nomination but it's quite likely. These prices stabilized. Earlier, Dean was 1.8 (British odds), 4-5 (US odds) and I shorted him at that. Later he jumped to 6-1, then 16-1.

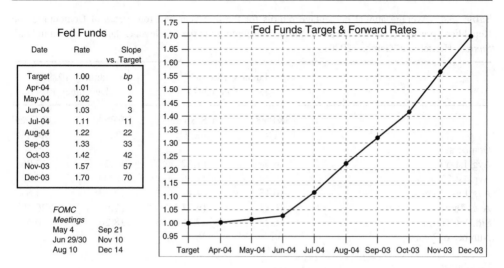

Fed Funds

Date	Rate	Slope vs. Target
Target	1.00	bp
Apr-04	1.01	0
May-04	1.02	2
Jun-04	1.03	3
Jul-04	1.11	11
Aug-04	1.22	22
Sep-03	1.33	33
Oct-03	1.42	42
Nov-03	1.57	57
Dec-03	1.70	70

FOMC
Meetings
May 4   Sep 21
Jun 29/30   Nov 10
Aug 10   Dec 14

Figure 23.6 US forward rate analysis, April 14, 2004

He is now 75-95. Hillary Clinton is 95-130. I somehow shorted her at 5-1, remember stink bids often get filled at great prices and hedged long at 11 − 1. Edwards is 160 – 390. These are the leading longshots.

A great stink bid was the 5000 trade on the Nikkei stock index in 1990 when the index was over 20 000. If you are the only bid and someone goes market, you fill your stink bid.

Let's assume that Kerry wins or if one of the others pulls an upset then the candidate will have similar policies vis-à-vis the stock market prospects. For the election, the April 21, 2004 odds are

Republicans   1.73-1.77

Democrats   2.30-2.38.

There is no market for any candidates besides Bush for the Republican nomination. So the candidates are in the ratio of about 1.75 to 2.34. So Bush's chances are about 57 % and Kerry's 43 %.

The effect of presidential election results on stock prices is studied by several authors. My work appears in Hensel and Ziemba (1995, 2000). The main conclusions are that, on average, returns are higher with Democrats than with Republicans, that returns in the last two years of electoral terms are much higher than in the first two years and that small cap stocks are much higher with Democrats than with Republicans, especially outside of the small cap dream month of January. Tables 23.4 and 23.5 detail this across years for the first, first two and last two years of the administration; and by month, respectively.

Ned Davis, in an interview in *Barron's* provides further insights. Table 23.6 shows the 1900 to 2000 results if the incumbent wins or loses versus all election years. From the Hensel-Ziemba results above, we assume that the last year, the election year of the cycle, has high returns. This is borne out in Davis' results; see Table 23.6. Interestingly, Davis' results separate the year into January to May and June to December. For both cases, incumbent wins or loses, the January to May returns are much lower than the June to December returns. The latter average 14.70 %. So if Bush were to win, the return in the latter part of the year

Table 23.4　Average annual percentage returns for the first year and four years of Democratic and Republican presidencies. Statistically significant differences at the 5 % level (2-tail) are shown in bold. *Source*: Hensel and Ziemba (2000)

	January 1937 to December 1997		January 1929 to December 1997	
	S&P500 TR	US Small Stk TR	S&P500 TR	US Small Stk TR
Democrat				
Avg 1st Yr	6.58	11.32	10.24	19.06
Avg 1st 2Yrs	6.14	11.85	8.09	15.90
Avg Last 2Yrs	16.13	24.11	17.40	24.65
Avg. Term	10.81	16.71	12.62	20.15
Std.Dev. Term	16.35	27.76	18.26	30.69
Number of Years	36	36	37	37
Republican				
Avg 1st Yr	1.87	−6.22	0.54	−14.45
Avg 1st 2Yrs	6.98	1.39	3.77	−6.29
Avg Last 2Yrs	15.03	16.95	9.06	10.18
Avg. Term	11.00	9.17	6.42	1.94
Std.Dev. Term	15.12	19.89	21.17	27.81
Number of Years	28	28	32	32
Diff 1st Yr	4.72	17.54	9.71	33.51
Diff 1st 2Yrs	−0.84	10.46	4.32	22.19
Diff Last 2Yrs	1.10	7.16	8.33	14.47
Diff Term	−0.19	7.55	6.20	18.21
1st year t-values (Ho:Diff=0)	0.67	1.39	1.15	**2.58**
First 2-years t-values (Ho:Diff=0)	−0.14	1.13	0.69	**2.39**
Last 2-years t-values (Ho:Diff=0)	0.20	0.69	1.20	1.41
Term t-values (Ho:Diff=0)	−0.05	1.04	1.29	**2.57**

would average 14.70 % with probability 57 % and with Kerry 4.24 % with probability 43 %. So the forecast is for a 10.20 % gain versus 10.68 % for the 26 previous elections since 1900.

There were 81 % winners: 94 % when the incumbent is re-elected but only 60 % when the incumbent loses. Davis adds that his research shows that after the first Fed interest rate rise the market typically rises for the next year. The first hike is usually a response to higher earnings which offset the short term interest rate rise. Only after a series of interest rate rises is the result a negative. Since the Fed funds rate already predicts a greater than 1 % rise by February 2004, and Fed governors are talking about a 3–3.5 % neutral Fed funds rate, there likely will be many increases.

So what do we conclude? Bonds look the most risky. Stocks probably can eke out gains in 2004 especially if Bush wins. But 2005 looks much more difficult as interest rates will

Table 23.5 Average percentage monthly small- and large-cap stock returns during Democratic and Republican presidencies, January 1929–December 1997. *Source*: Hensel and Ziemba (2000)

	Democratic Administrations			Republican Administrations		
	S&P500 Total Return	US Small Cap Total Total Return	Small Cap minus Large Cap	S&P500 Total Return	US Small Cap Total Return	Small Cap minus Large Cap
January	1.72	6.45	4.72	1.65	5.93	4.28
February	−0.38	0.74	1.11	1.59	2.78	1.19
March	−0.58	−0.91	−0.34	0.96	1.21	0.25
April	2.25	2.58	0.33	−0.24	−1.82	−1.57
May	1.07	1.40	0.33	−0.50	−1.52	−1.02
June	1.57	1.71	0.14	0.78	−0.40	−1.18
July	1.95	2.81	0.86	1.69	1.11	−0.58
August	1.17	1.65	0.47	1.73	1.25	−0.47
September	0.40	0.78	0.38	−2.87	−3.31	−0.45
October	0.42	−0.24	−0.67	−0.40	−2.66	−2.26
November	1.44	1.61	0.17	0.44	−0.53	−0.97
December	1.56	1.58	0.02	1.59	−0.09	−1.68

Table 23.6 Historical reaction of the market to elections. *Source*: Ned Davis Research, *Barron's*, April 19, 2004

	Incumbent Wins		Incumbent Loses		All Election Years		Non-Election Years	
Month	Avg Gain	Time Mkt Is Up, %	Avg Gain	Time Mkt Is Up	Avg Gain	Time Mkt Is Up, %	Avg Gain	Time Mkt Is Up, %
January	0.23	53	−0.48	40	−0.04	50	1.42	68
February	−0.46	50	−1.59	40	−0.83	48	0.13	51
March	2.80	88	1.31	60	2.06	74	0.24	56
April	−0.87	44	−2.26	40	−1.41	42	1.95	59
May	−0.73	56	−1.87	40	−1.17	50	0.29	53
June	1.04	62	0.61	50	0.87	58	0.22	49
July	1.99	56	2.65	50	2.24	54	1.00	64
August	2.59	81	3.86	50	3.08	69	0.38	62
September	0.61	44	−1.05	40	−0.03	42	−1.60	40
October	2.95	88	−1.52	40	1.23	69	−0.13	52
November	3.75	69	−0.40	60	2.15	65	0.53	60
December	0.99	62	0.55	50	0.82	58	1.76	78
January-May	1.78	60	−4.53	40	−0.75	52	4.12	65
June-December	14.70	94	4.24	60	10.68	81	2.15	63

then be higher and it's the first year of a presidential term. Davis points out that with $34.5 trillion of debt, the US cannot afford much higher interest rates. He is buying bonds when the rates in the 10-year get to 4.75 to 5.00 %. These rates are 4.40 % in 2004.

POSTSCRIPT

In 2004, the S&P500 gained 2.00 % in January and 6.86 % in the remaining 11 months for a total gain of 8.99 %. In 2005 the S&P500 lost −2.53 % in January and gained 5.67 % in the next 11 months for a total gain of only 3.00 %. And in 2006 it was up 2.54 % in January, 10.80 % in the next 11 months and 13.30 % for the year. Hensel and Ziemba (1995), updated in Ghosh, Bhalla and Ziemba (2007), have studied the January barometer. The results indicate that if January is positive then the probability of a gain in the next 11 months is high (85 %) and so is the absolute amount. But if January is negative, then the rest of the year is noise, going up or down about half the time and if the S&P500 rises, on average the gain is small. In these three years the results bear out the script.

We end this postscript with some large declines in the Dow Jones Industrial Average and the recoveries that followed some declines that we could not predict. First Table 23.7 displays the ten worst DJIA declines, according to Dustin Woodard, see Maranjian (2007) writing for *The Motley Fool*. While some of these declines have been long and large, the historical record is that the various US stock markets including the DJIA have always recovered as shown in Figures 23.7 and 23.8.

The evidence is strong that stocks outperform bonds, T-bills, and most other financial assets in the long run; see Siegel (2002); Dimson, Marsh, and Staunton (2002, 2006), Table 23.9, and Figures 23.7 and 23.8. Stocks generally outperform in times of inflation and bonds outperform in times of deflation (see, for example, Smith 1924). Why do stocks generally outperform bonds? As has been said, a major reason is that businesses retain earnings, which go on to create more earnings and dividends too.[1] In times of growth, firms borrow at fixed cost with the expectation of earning positive economic profit, so in the long term, equities, as a reflection of this positive income creation, should grow at the rate of productivity.

Occasionally, stocks underperform alternative asset classes for long periods. Figure 23.8 shows this phenomenon for the DJIA from 1885 to 2001 in 2001 dollars, and Figure 21.5 shows the 2000–02 period for the S&P500 and US Government bonds. When bonds outperform stocks, as in this latter period, they are usually negatively correlated with stocks as

Table 23.7 The 10 Largest Declines in the DJIA, 1900–2007.
Source: The Motley Fool

Began	Ended	DJIA fell...	Change, %
6/17/1901	11/9/1903	57 to 31	−46
1/19/1906	11/15/1907	75 to 39	−49
11/21/1916	12/19/1917	110 to 66	−40
11/3/1919	8/24/1921	120 to 64	−47
9/3/1929	11/13/1929	381 to 199	−48
4/17/1930	7/8/1932	294 to 41	−86
3/10/1937	3/31/1938	194 to 99	−49
9/12/1939	4/28/1942	156 to 93	−40
1/11/1973	12/6/1974	1,052 to 578	−45
1/15/2000	10/9/2002	11,793 to 7,286	−38

---

[1] From the review of Smith by J.M. Keynes in 1925, quoted in Buffett (2001).

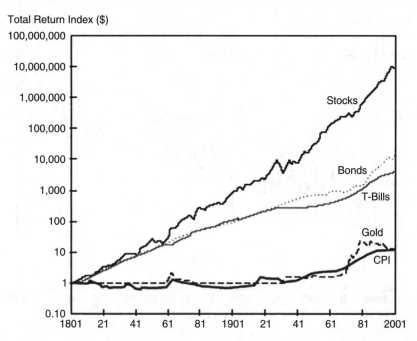

Figure 23.7 Total nominal return indexes, 1801–2001. Note: CPI = Consumer Price Index. *Source*: Siegel (2002)

well; see Figure 21.6, which has rolling correlations. Between 1982 and 1999, the return of equities over bonds was more than 10 % a year in European Union countries. The question is whether we are moving back to a period during which the two asset classes move against each other or whether the phenomenon will prove to be temporary. Moreover, the historical evidence, since 1802 for the United States and since 1700 for the United Kingdom, indicates that the longer the period, the more likely this dominance. Siegel showed that in all 20-year periods from 1926 to 2001, US equities outperformed bonds, and for 30-year horizons, based on the past data, it is optimal (with a mean-variance model) to be more than 100 % in stocks and have a short position in bonds; see Tables 23.8 and 23.9. Siegel used various risk tolerance measures, such as ultraconservative and risk taking. These measures are easy to devise using the Kallberg and Ziemba (1983) results; just assign Arrow-Pratt risk-aversion values, as was done in the second column of Table 23.8. Values over 100 % mean more than 100 % stocks or a levered long position, which would be a short position in bonds or cash.

WTZ used two crash risk measures that are very effective for anticipating large 10 %+ declines in the S&P500 and other stock indices. These measures can help investors assess risks and minimize the effects of such crashes. Here we briefly re-review these two measures and explore three declines in the US and world markets that were not predicted by these measures. From this background, we try to draw out lessons for predicting and responding to such shocks in a variety of markets.

The two measures are:

bond-stock which compares bond versus stock yields, and

Index Value

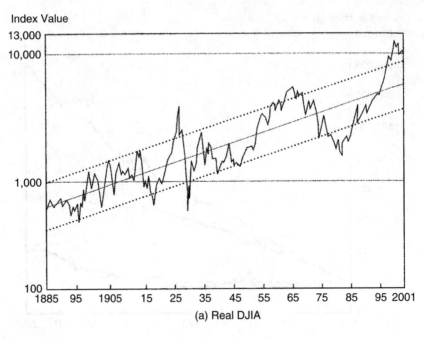

(a) Real DJIA

Index Value

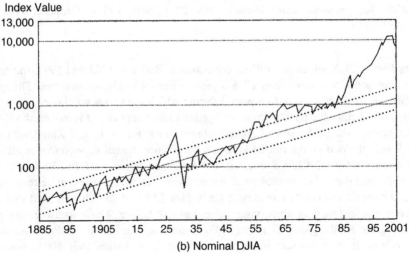

(b) Nominal DJIA

Figure 23.8   The real and nominal DJIA. *Source*: Siegel (2002)

T-option a measure of market confidence sentiment related to puts versus calls prices

The three declines not explained by the two measures are:

1. September 11, 2001,
2. May to June 2006, and
3. February 27 to April 2007

Table 23.8 Portfolio allocation: percentage of portfolio recommended in stocks based on all historical data (R_A = risk aversion index). *Source*: Siegel (2002)

Risk Tolerance	R_A	Holding Period			
		1 year	5 years	10 years	30 years
Ultraconservative (minimum risk)	10	8.1%	23.3%	39.5%	71.4%
Conservative	6	25.0%	40.6%	60.1%	89.7%
Moderate	4	50.0%	63.1%	87.2%	114.9%
Risk Taking	2	75.0%	79.8%	108.3%	136.5%

Table 23.9 Equities have generated superior returns in the long run, December 1925–December 1998. *Source*: Ibbotson (1999) in Swensen (2000)

Asset Class	Multiple	
Inflation	9	times
Treasury bills	15	times
Treasury bonds	44	times
Corporate bonds	61	times
Large-capitalization stocks	2,351	times
Small-capitalization stocks	5,117	times

Some background on crash measures

Historically, the bond-stock crash measure has been successful in predicting 10%+ market corrections, including the declines in October 1987 (us and Japan), the 1990 Japan, the 2000 US and the 2002 US. In Japan from 1948-1988, there were twenty 10%+ declines even though the market went up 221 times in yen (and 550 times in US dollars). The bond-stock measure had a 12/12 record in predicting crashes in that period, that is, whenever the measure was in the danger zone, there was a fall of 10%+ within one year from the time the measure went into the danger zone. This is a very good forecasting record, but eight declines in Japan during these 40 years were not predicted by this measure. Berge, Consigli and Ziemba (2007) present an analysis of this measure in five equity markets (US, Japan, UK, Germany and Canada) from 1970–2005. Similarly, the short term confidential T-measure WTZIMI uses in trading has good short term predictability (3–6 months). Since 1985 the T-measure has had $T < 0$, that is, in the danger zone, for the S&P500, six times. These are summarized in Table 23.10.

T is negative when the market is over confident as measured by relative put and call option prices. Then it is very dangerous since there are no sellers and only buyers but some sellers will usually appear to drive the market down. Of these six $T < 0$ occurrences, we have the October 1987 crash and the 3Q2002 crash when the S&P500 fell 22% in this quarter. The S&P bias trade is not done when $T < 0$; see Table 23.10. Otherwise the S&P bias trade of WTZIMI is very successful when $T > 0$. From 1985, there were no losses for $T > 100$, as it has been since 3Q2003.

In the six quarters when $T < 0$, there were four losses and two times the measure did not predict correctly. Still the sum of the six returns yielded a combined arithmetic loss of -41.7%. Hence, these two measures are useful but they do not predict all 10 %+ crashes nor do they predict some small declines. For these two declines under 10 % and the September 11, 2001 14 % decline, other reasons must be found, which we will consider below.

Declines and crashes not predicted by the measures[2]

Although the bond-stock and proprietary T measures have a good record, there are some key episodes which they did not predict. Studying these declines and their triggers helps US to assess shocks. The September 11, 2001 attacks and the stock market decline of 14 % in the S&P500 that followed after a one week market closure was largely a random, that is unforeseen event. But the size of the decline was exacerbated due to the then weak stock market and US economy which had a recession starting in spring 2001; see Figure 23.9 a, b. The stock market was weak because although prices had fallen, earnings had fallen more. The bond-stock model which had been in the danger zone in April 1999, predicting the April 2000 decline, then returned to the danger zone in the fall of 2001 predicting the 22 % fall in the S&P500 in 2002, see Figure 23.9. The T-measure for 3Q2002 at -142.8 predicted the 12 % fall in the S&P500 that quarter; see Table 23.10.

The S&P500 fell 37 % from 1460.25 at the end of December 1999 to 885.76 on 31 October 2002.

In May to June 2006 the S&P500 fell 7 % and markets in some emerging economies fell 20 % or more. Worries that valuations of some emerging market stocks were too high enlarged their losses. For example, the closed end emerging market fund RNE (Russian New Europe) was at a very high 37 %+ premium on May 10 to net asset value – an amount way above historical values. The trigger for the decline was a rumor that the Bank of Japan

Table 23.10 Results of the six times out of 85 quarters the T-measure was negative for the S&P500

Quarter	3Q 1986	4Q 1986	4Q 1987	4Q1990	3Q2002	3Q2003
T Strategy	−3.20	−.95	−3.50	−1.9	−142.8	−50.4
Return	2.278 %	26.42 %	−123.49 %	−0.123 %	−34.94 %	−4.415 %
	Profit	Large profit	Bond/stock measure in danger zone	Small Loss	T-measure worked well extreme danger zone	small loss
S&P Return in Quarter	−8.20 %	+3.70 %	−24.50 %	+4.80 %	−12.00 %	−4.5 %

---

[2] There have been additional small corrections including several 6–9 % declines from July to September 2004 and March to June 2005. In an April 9, 2007 Barron's article, Michael Santoli notes that there has been one such pullback each year since 2004. In each case, a recovery quickly followed each decline and each retreat has been shallower than the preceding one and a faster recovery of the loss. Buying on the declines has been rewarded as bidders try to beat the crowd and speed up the recovery. Buying on these dips has worked so far, as has selling put options during the greatly expanded volatility which returned to low levels after the decline. There is evidence that the current decline is following this pattern. As of April 6 2007, the futures market returned to pre-decline levels with the VIX at 13.23, so this 2007 decline was essentially over and the S&P500 rose to new highs above 1500 in early May 2007.

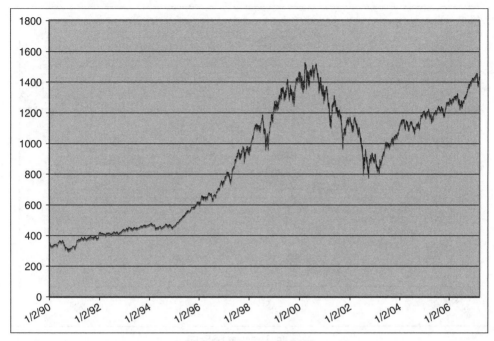

(a) Seventeen year S&P500

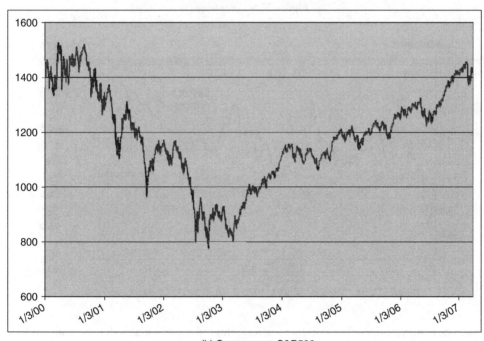

(b) Seven years S&P500

Figure 23.9   S&P500, Daily over time. *Source*: Yahoo Finance

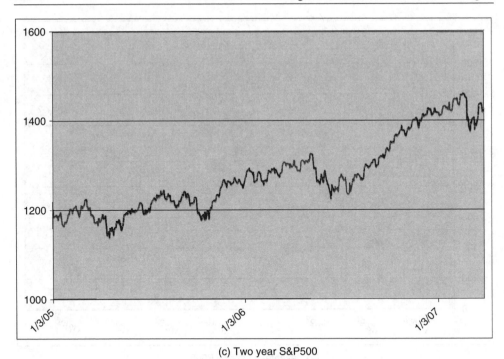

(c) Two year S&P500

Figure 23.9   (*continued*)

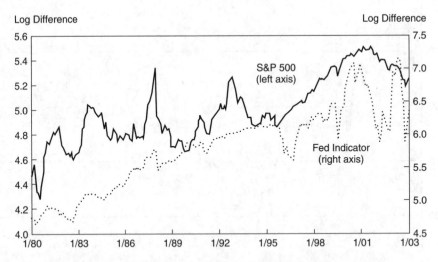

Figure 23.10   The Fed Model, 1980 to May 2003. *Source*: Ziemba (2003)

would raise interest rates. These higher interest rates did not materialize but the fear that they would spark a rally in the yen led some yen carry trade players to unwind their short yen, long higher yielding non-Japanese asset positions, especially emerging market currencies. In turn this led to sales of various stocks and indices including the S&P500 and the decline was largest (elements of mean reversion) in those areas that had gained the most, namely

CBOE SPX MARKET VOLATILITY INDE
as of 30-Mar-2007

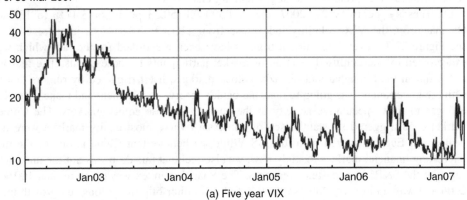

(a) Five year VIX

CBOE SPX MARKET VOLATILITY INDE
as of 19-Mar-2007

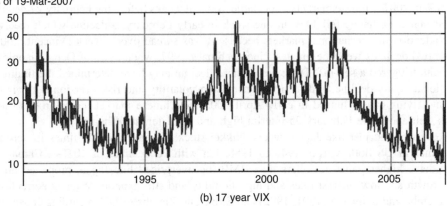

(b) 17 year VIX

Figure 23.11 VIX. *Source*: Yahoo Finance

the emerging markets. The VIX volatility index, see Figure 27.7 rose from around 10 % before the crisis to the 22 % level before dropping back to 10 % after the sell-off.

The third decline is February 27 through April 2007 with February 27 and March 13 lows of 1399.04 and 1377.95, respectively. This decline gradually faded away although the VIX never got back to 10 % even with the S&P500 over 1500 in early July 2007. For months, there has been talk of the current period being the longest time without a 2 % decline in one day or a large monthly decline. The stock market had low volatility since the 2006 decline; see Figure 27.7 which plots the VIX for the last five years and the last 17 years.

An example of these sentiments was made by Bob Stovall, a 50-year Wall Street veteran, in a talk on November 15, 2006 to investment students at Stetson University. Stovall argued that given the current real economic growth in 2006, it would be very difficult for stocks in the S&P500 to continue to increase in price (Moffatt, 2006). Without economic growth, companies would have trouble meeting earnings expectations. He said that the average bull market in US history lasts approximately 56 months. At that time, the US was approaching the 50th month of the bull market. He concluded that a shift toward steady cash flow stocks with dividends was preferable to large capital gains stocks.

On Tuesday, February 27, 2007, the S&P500 fell 50.33 points or 3.47 % to 1399.04. On that drop, the VIX volatility index rose from 11.15 to 18.31 %, a jump of 64.22 %; see Figure 27.7. Several concurrent triggers have been mentioned for the fall, which were exacerbated by the confused reaction of market participants to these events. The first was a 9 % fall in the Shanghai and Shenzhen stock markets, itself triggered by rumors that the Chinese government was going to raise the bank's reserve requirement and make regulatory changes to slow speculative activity in the soaring Chinese equity markets. The Chinese market drop triggered substantial sell-offs in Asia (where most equity markets were near peaks) and Europe as well as in the US While *we* believe that China is one of the most interesting financial markets to study now, we also feel that this drop was **not** the underlying cause of the S&P500 persistent weakness. The Shanghai index was up more than 100 % in 2006 and way up in early 2007 so the 9 % fall is a minor blip in the long run growth trend, and likely motivated by profit-taking and a concern about over-valuation. Furthermore, it is not an indication of slowing of the Chinese economy which is expected to grow around 9–10 % in 2007. Chinese markets are volatile. Several weeks before the February 27 decline, the Shanghai exchange fell 11 % in one week in early February, a decline which received little attention in international markets because it was spread over a week (Vincent, 2007). These two declines were the greatest since February 1997, when news of Deng Xiaoping's ill health triggered a sell-off. Thus, the Chinese decline may have determined the timing of the global equity decline, and return of increasing volatility and risk aversion but it is not the underlying cause. Indeed in early April 2007 the Chinese market indices rose to new highs well above the February 25 interim high and fell later, see Chapter 16.

We expect that just like Japan, whose Nikkei stock average rose 221 times in yen and 550 times in US dollars from 1948 to 1988, but with 20 declines of 10 %+, China will likely have higher gains in dollars than RMB, be overpriced like Japan, propelled up by fast growth and low interest rates and high liquidity and still experience many corrections. See Ziemba and Schwartz (1991, 1992) and Stone and Ziemba (1993) regarding Japan. But the *market* did *not* understand this. Rather many market actors tend to react as a herd to such events, seeking to minimize their losses, but the more recent response appears to be buy on dips. See our primer on Chinese investment markets below for more description of Chinese markets.

Other news also contributed to the fall in the S&P500 and worldwide markets Tuesday included a statement by former Fed Chair Alan Greenspan that a recession in the US was a possibility although it was not probable as well as some weak economic numbers.

Greenspan later said the probability of a recession was 25 %. At the time, bond prices were actually estimating a higher probability. We assume, that even though it might be wise for a former Fed chair to let the current Fed chair do the talking, audiences like the one in Hong Kong, require that Greenspan say something interesting to earn his $ 150 000 speaking fee.

The decline was exacerbated by a large unwinding of yen carry trades who sold stock and created a short covering rally in the yen that moved the USD/JPY exchange rate from 127 to 116; see Figure 23.12 on the yen dollar rate from March 30, 2006 to March 30, 2007. However, it appears that those who foresaw the end of the yen carry trade spoke too soon. Although the Bank of Japan recently doubled interest rates (in February 2007), the benchmark rate of 0.5 % remains far below other interest rates – encouraging Japanese retail

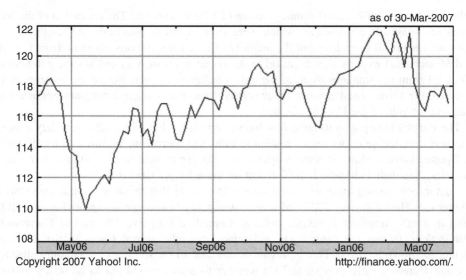

Copyright 2007 Yahoo! Inc.   http://finance.yahoo.com/.

Figure 23.12   Daily yen, one year from March 30, 2006 to March 30, 2007

and institutional investors to continue to seek higher returns abroad, and foreign investors to use the weak yen as a financing currency – even if Morgan Stanley recently argued that yen-denominated loans to retail investors remain very small (Morgan Stanley 2007)

Accentuating the tension were political as well as economic risks. Many commentators such as Lawrence Summers (former Treasury Secretary and Harvard President and current DE Shaw hedge fund consultant) have argued that the market was not pricing in the worldwide risks in most assets including the S&P500. However, both of WTZ's large crash 10%+ measures were not in the danger zone. The decline in February 27 to early April, and possibly beyond, had not reached a 10% fall and the VIX which reached 19% was bouncing around the 13–16% range most of the time.

We turn to the Eurasia group's list of top seven political risks for 2007 for an assessment of some of the geopolitical risks and their possible effect on the global economy. The risks as reported by Ian Bremmer (2007) are as follows:

1. Iran
2. Nigeria
3. Iraq
4. Turkey
5. Russia
6. China
7. Afghanistan/Pakistan

The majority of these risks are challenges of political transition and succession that could impact energy supply (Russia, Nigeria, Iran), regional power plays in the Middle East (Iran, Iraq, Turkey), the war on terror (Afghanistan/Pakistan, Iraq) or involve challengers to US dominance in the global politics and economy (Chinese succession, Russia).

The top risk, how to respond to Iran's nuclear ambitions and the potential impact of a military escalation on asset prices, has regained increasing urgency in recent weeks, following the March 23, 2007 Iranian capture of British hostages. The escalation of the Iran crisis has again lifted oil prices, which were slow to fall considerably. Although the US does not import oil from Iran and the majority of its energy imports originate from Canada and Mexico, Iran exports significant oil to American allies in Asia and has the potential to block oil from the southern shore of the gulf. Furthermore, even though the hostages were released, the crisis raised a series of questions about Iran's nuclear program, influence in Iraq and the role of the US-UK alliance.

The Eurasia Group also isolated four longer term risks that will challenge policy makers and investors for years to come: pandemic influenza, terrorism, resource nationalization, and protectionism. Many of these longer-term risks are present in their list of 2007 issues to watch. See their February 2, 2007 report on these longer term risks.

Rumors are moving these nervous markets. The rumor that failed Amaranth trader Brian Hunter (see Herbst-Baylis, 2007 and others) was going to manage a commodities volatility fund in a new series of funds for Solengo Capital of Calgary, Alberta and Greenwich, Connecticut, moved the natural gas and related calendar spread trades in the direction Hunter is known to favor. That is, higher winter and lower summers. Amaranth collapsed because Hunter greatly overbet and his weather forecasts turned out to be wrong and he foolishly doubled his position. The March 28, 2007 rumor of an Iran attack on a US warship moved the dollar and oil prices. This rumor caused oil to spike to $5 to $68 and then fall quickly to $64. US and global markets are very reactive to any negative news about the US economy and the fears that it might spark a global slowdown. Other fears include the fallout of subprime housing loan defaults and its effect on consumer credit and the drop in consumer confidence which fell from 111.2 in February to 107.2 in March and declining housing sales, starts and prices. WTZ will stick to his two crash measures and Buffett's measure of the ratio of stock value to GDP for the big crashes but nervousness can easily drop prices in the short-term and investors need to be hedged against such reversals and have plenty of cash available to weather such storms. Also the S&P500 earnings are projected to rise only 3.8 % following 4Q2006, the first below 10 % rise since 2003; and only 6.7 % in 2007 versus 16 % in 2006. The April/May 2007 S&P500 rise to new DJIA and S&P500 highs was partially based on reported earnings exceeding these forecasts.

The ugly head of the sub-prime loan problem in the US, that is loans to unqualified buyers that are in or near default, caused turbulence in June 2007 when two Bear Stearns hedge funds lost billions. As usual it was overbetting, not being diversified and being hit with a bad scenario (in this case rising interest rates). See Lo (2007) re the rising interest rates and Kelly, Ng and Reilly (2007) re the Bear Stearns crisis and its bailout. By July 6 this tempest in a teapot was basically over with the S&P500 in record territory at 1530.44. But the higher VIX volatility in the 15 % area remained. Then on July 26, 27 the S&P fell over 50 points and the VIX exploded to over 24%. While well below the 44% in 2000 this sharp decline added much fear to the equity markets and more to the woes of those trying to borrow money in the bond market to finance private equity deals.

24
Some approaches for scenario generation and reduction

There are many ways to generate scenarios

Scenario generation is a complex subject in stochastic programming as well as one deeply studied by those making fixed income, interest rate, bond and other models.[1] In this chapter I present some scenario generation ideas using the vector auto-regressive approach and through stochastic differential equations. In Chapter 25 I discuss other scenario generation approaches such as moment matching and using a Wasserstein distance measure.

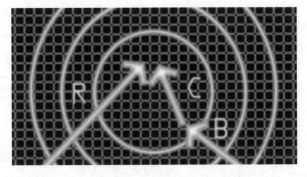

Figure 24.1 shows a typical multiperiod scenario tree.

1. There can be full knowledge of the exact probability distribution, P. Such a situation usually comes from a theoretical model that explains perfectly the past and future data. If the probability distribution is discrete then you have all possible scenarios and their exact probabilities. You have covered the board perfectly. The only issue is do you need to aggregate to a smaller number of scenarios and if so you can use a scenario reduction approach like one of those discussed below. If the theoretical model has a continuous distribution or part of it is not discrete then you will need to sample to obtain the scenarios needed and their probabilities which will likely not be exact. So basically this situation is like case (2).

2. There is a known parametric family based on a theoretical model whose parameters are estimated from available and possibly forecasted data. For example, for interest rates one could use

   (a) a generalized Hull and White (1990–96) process

$$dr(t) = [\theta(t) - \alpha r(t)]dt + \sigma(t)dw(t),$$

   or

   (b) a Ho and Lee (1986) process

$$dr(t) = \theta(t)dt + \sigma dw(t),$$

   or

---

[1] There are good surveys such as Abaffy et al (2000), Birge and Louveaux (1997), Dupačová et al (2001), Jamshidian and Zhu (1997), Kouwenberg and Zenios (2007), Siegel (2003), Wallace and Ziemba (2005) and Ziemba (2003). In these papers are references to many of the technical papers whose references are not cited here. There are also technical articles by Birge and Wets (1986), Casey and Sen (2003), Dupačová, Groewe-Kuska and Roemisch (2000), Edirisinghe and Ziemba (1996), Frauendorfer (1996), Hochreiter and Pflug (2002), Pennanen and Koivu (2002), Pflug (2001), Roemisch and Heitsch (2003), and Wright (1994).

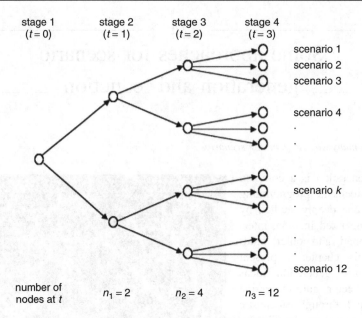

Figure 24.1 A typical three period scenario tree with four stages

(c) a Black-Derman-Toy (1990) process

$$dlog(r(t)) = \left[\theta(t) + \frac{\sigma'(t)}{\sigma(t)} log(r(t)) \right] dt + \sigma(t) dw(t)$$

where w is a Weiner process, $r(t)$ is the instantaneous interest rate, $\sigma(t)$ the instantaneous volatility, $\theta(t)$ the drift component and $\alpha(t)$ the mean reversion rate.

VECTOR AUTOREGRESSIVE MODELS

A useful approach is via vector auto regressive or VAR models. This was used in the Russell-Yasuda Kasai model, see Cariño, Ziemba (1998) and Cariño, Myers and Ziemba (1998) and the discussion in Ziemba (2007).

VAR models were introduced by Sims (1980) as a forecasting method using past data. A typical model is

$$y_t = \mu + A_1 y_{t-1} + \ldots + A_p Y_{t-p} + \varepsilon_t$$

where μ_t, y_k, and ε_t are n vectors, the A_i are nxn, and the ε_t are $N(0, \Sigma)$, $t = 1, \ldots, T$, with variance-covariance matrix Σ. Such models are estimated by generalized least squares using Zellner's (1962) seemingly unrelated regression approaches since the individual equations are tied together by the variance-covariance matrix Σ of the n errors in equations.

A scenario tree may be constructed assuming a root with initial value y_0 at time 0. Then sample n_0 times one-period forecasts y_{T+1}, where each forecast is a scenario at time 1 with probability $1/n_0$. This is then repeated to generate the entire scenario tree over the horizon

$t = 1, \ldots, T$. Berkelaar et al (2002) using annual Dutch data for 1956 to 1997 estimated the VAR model

$$cash(t) = 0.013 + 0.769cash(t - 1) + \varepsilon_1(t),$$

$$bond(t) = -0.002 + 1.366cash(t - 1) + \varepsilon_2(t),$$

$$stock(t) = 0.095 + \varepsilon_3(t),$$

$$infl(t) = 0.020 + 0.645infl(t - 1) + \varepsilon_4(t),$$

with covariance matrix of the errors

$$10^{-5} \begin{Bmatrix} 28.466 & -12.702 & -150.027 & 13.972 \\ -12.702 & 393.538 & 134.710 & 32.563 \\ -150.027 & 134.710 & 2430.607 & -166.369 \\ 13.972 & 32.563 & -166.369 & 92.465 \end{Bmatrix}$$

where $cash(t)$ is the short term interest rate, $infl(t)$ is the inflation rate, and $bond(t)$ and $stock(t)$ are the returns on a diversified bond and stock portfolio, respectively.

Towers Perrin is a global management consulting firm which uses the stochastic differential equation economic projection model CAP:Link for generating scenarios for asset returns using economic models for pension fund and insurance company management applications. The model has been used in 17 countries in North America, Europe and Asia using data from the US, Japan and Germany as a driver of economic activity in other countries. It is assumed that the three drivers affect economic activity in the smaller countries but not vice versa.[2] These elements are used to generate discrete scenarios for various asset and liability asset classes such as cash, government bonds, various types of equities, fixed income assets and foreign assets. The model is documented in Mulvey (1996) and Mulvey and Thorlacius (1998) who also present a sample application. The model has the following elements:

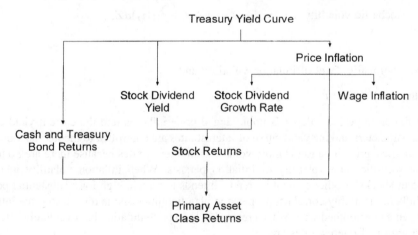

___
[2] This is generally a good assumption. The 10 % crash in the S&P500 of October 27 and 28, 1997 imported from Hong Kong was a dramatic exception which took many highly levered traders such as Victor Niederhoffer by surprise; see Chapter 12 for a discussion of this.

The submodels use the following forms:
Interest rates use the equations

$$\text{Short rate: } dr_t = f_1(r_u - r_t)dt + f_2(r_u, r_t, l_u, l_t, p_u, p_t)dt + f_3(r_t)dZ_1$$

$$\text{Long rate: } dl_t = f_4(l_u - l_t)dt + f_5(r_u, r_t, l_u, l_t, p_u, p_t)dt + f_6(r_t)dZ_2$$

where

r_u is the normative level of short interest rates,

r_t is the level of interest rates at time t,

l_u is the normative level of long interest rates,

l_t is the level of interest rates at time t,

p_u is the normative level of inflation,

p_t is the level of inflation at time t,

$f_1, \ldots, f_6$ are vector functions that depend upon various economic factors up to period t, and

dZ_1 and dZ_2 are correlated Wiener disturbances.

Similar interpretations are for the dZ_i and f_{ij} listed below. This is a variant of the two factor Brennan-Schwartz model (1982). These two vector diffusion equations provide input for the remaining spot interest rates and the yield curve. At any point t, the mid-rate is a function of the short and long rates; other points on the spot rate curve are computed using a double exponential equation for the spot rate of interest.
Inflation uses the equations

$$\text{Price inflation: } dp_t = f_7 dr_t + f_8(r_u, r_t, l_u, l_t, p_u, p_t)dt + f_9(v_t)dZ_3$$

$$\text{Stochastic volatility: } dv_t = f_{10}(v_u - v_t)dt + f_{11}(v_t)dZ_4$$

where

v_u is the normative level of inflation volatility and

v_t is the level at time t.

Price inflation in period t depends upon lagged price inflation and the current yield curve. Internal parameters and the yield curve of interest rates are controlled to theoretical values. In most countries, price inflation is more volatile than interest rates because there are no traded inflation securities and volatility of inflation persists. When inflation volatility increases because of shocks or other economic trends, it tends to remain high for a substantial period. Wage inflation is highly correlated to pension plan liabilities and is related to price inflation in a lagged and smoothed way. Wages react slowly to price inflation but eventually catch up.
Long term real interest rates are

$$dk_t = f_{12}(k_u, k_t, l_u, l_t, p_u, p_t)dl + f_{13}(k_u, k_t, l_u, l_t, p_u, p_t)dt + f_{14}dZ_5$$

where

k_u is the normative level of real yields and

k_t is the actual level at time t.

Real interest rates are the excess of nominal interest rates over inflation. Index linked bonds, that relate nominal interest rate changes, inflation and future inflation expectations are traded in various countries, see Campbell and Viceira (2001).

To derive the real yield curve, one computes a short-term real yield based on the short term nominal interest rate and current inflation and interpolates along the nominal interest rate curve.

Currency strength is measured (see Mahieu and Schotman, 1994, and Kritzman, 1992) by:

$$ds_t = f_{15}(r_u, r_t, p_u, p_t, pp_t)dt + f_{16}dZ_6$$

where

s_i/s_j is the exchange rate between currency i in units of j and

pp_t is the average cost of goods in foreign countries relative to domestic cost.

Currencies theoretically depend heavily on purchasing power parity (ppp) since exchange rates ought to reflect price inflation. However, currencies tend to trend and may depend on trading arguments and economic factors such as trade deficits. In the model, ppp is used with mean reversion over 2–12 years. For its risk analysis, CAP:Link considers the strength of the relationship within individual scenarios and the strength of the relationship across multiple simulations.

Stock returns use ideas from Poterba and Summers (1988) that divide stock returns into dividends and capital gains and relate the linkages to interest rates and inflation. Dividend growth provides additional current income plus the end of period dividend rate using the equation:

$$dg_t = f_{17}(p_u, p_t, g_u, g_t)dt + f_{18}(g_t)dZ_7$$

where

g_u is the normative level of dividend growth and g_t is the level at time t.

Dividend growth rates are highly dependent upon inflation. The dividend equation is

$$dy_t = f_{19}dr_t + f_{20}dl_t + f_{21}ds/s_t + f_{22}(y_u, y_t, r_u, r_t, k_u, k_t)dt + f_{23}(g_t)dZ_8$$

where

y_u is the normative level of dividend yield and

y_t is the level at time t.

Dividend yield which mean reverts depends upon interest rate and currency changes and there are long term relationships between the level of real yields.

These equations are used to generate discrete scenarios for various asset and liability classes such as cash, government bonds, various types of equities, fixed income assets and foreign assets. The calibration to accurately estimate parameter values uses an iterative process. The system provides scenarios for cash, government bonds and large cap equities plus other assets including real estate, venture capital; small cap stocks; emerging market investments; catastrophe related securities and derivatives. A VAR method is combined with equilibrium conditions, see Boender (1997) and Boender et al (1998), to generate the actual scenarios. As in other applications, more scenarios are needed when risk aversion is higher since the solutions depend to a greater degree on rare events; see Mulvey and Thorlacius (1998) and Mulvey, Pauling, Britt and Morin (2007) for sample applications.

Towers Perrin has used this approach with considerable success in its models. Chapter 25 discusses two further scenario procedures, namely moment matching and by using a Wasserstein distance measure.

25
Using economic fundamentals to generate scenarios

Economic models are useful to generate scenarios and forecast the future

This third chapter on scenario generation introduces the vast potential of using economic fundamentals along with various scenario generation techniques to tilt the historical data into better future scenarios. Chapter 26 continues the theme of current market trends using scenarios.

We know from the theory of investment and gambling that to win we must have the mean right and not bet too much. So what we want is to use the tilted scenarios to determine when and if we have a mathematical edge and then develop our risk control so that we avoid large blowouts. These disasters occur when one overbets, does not truly diversify and a bad scenario occurs. So we especially want to avoid these bad scenarios.

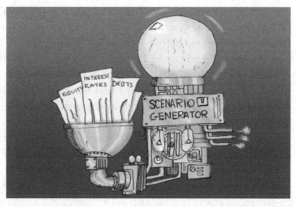

One way is to simply not play when the probability of a bad scenario is large. So one either exits positions or neutralizes in some way. We also must focus on what we can predict and what we cannot. In many cases, partial prediction, which leads to just a slight tilting of scenario probabilities, can be very valuable.

MODELS TO PREDICT RELATIVE AND ABSOLUTE ASSET PRICES

Let's start with ways to predicting relative value of stocks, country indices and end with large stock market crashes and their prediction and avoidance.

One of the most popular hedge fund strategies is termed statistical arbitrage. In its pure form, it is simply to estimate the best and the worst performing stocks over some period. One then forms various portfolios such as a long-short portfolio that is essentially market neutral with a portfolio beta of zero. If the predictions are good, then there should be steady profits and a good performance. Jacobs and Levy (1988) showed one way to do this by collecting monthly data and computing variables on 25 economic and industry specific variables. They did this for the US market with a large universe of high capitalized stocks. Since their firm now manages multibillions in assets, the approach can be successful. Commercial firms like BARRA and APT lease such models. But you can make your own as I did in 1989 in Japan for the 1000+ stocks on the Tokyo first section. This is described in Ziemba and Schwartz

(1991) and Schwartz and Ziemba (2000) but the general idea follows. The approach is straightforward but requires a lot of data collection and manipulation.

Figure 25.1 shows the best seven variables out of the 30 used as predictors in the model. The 30 were determined through discussions with my Yamaichi Research Institute colleagues and are similar to those used by Jacobs and Levy for the US. First one estimates the monthly model using data on the 30 factors for a reasonably long period, in my case 1979–1989 with some earlier data. The model is updated the model yearly. That is, data from year x to y is used to make a model for year $y + 1$. In year $y + 1$, as monthly data comes in, the forecasts are updated. The single best variable was future earnings relative to current price. We obtained three such forecasts for each stock of the 1000 plus stocks and averaged them. Averaging several forecasts leads to better future predictions. In sample, this single variable called EST-LACT (future earnings over current price), was worth about 10 % per year in advantage over the market index. Its relative, namely, current year's earnings over price to book, the familiar PE ratio was worth an additional 4 + % and was the sixth best variable. Small cap and price to book value, the famous Fama-French (1992) factors were the seventh and fourth best factors, respectively. These two factors were, of course, well-known before Fama-French and date at least to 1967 when Barr Rosenberg was discussing them when I was a PhD student at Berkeley.

Mean reversion, which has grown in popularity especially since Poterba-Summers (1988), shows up as the second and third best variables. They looked at indices. I found these mean reversions in 1989 for individual Japanese stocks. For similar in US stocks, see Jegadeesh and Titman (1993). The fifth best variable, R-MAX24, suggests that if a stock has fallen too much from its 24-month high, then it will have poor subsequent performance. The other 23 variables add to the predictive power of the model but these seven are very useful. Beta was not among the seven best predictive variables in Japan but was the eleventh best of the 30 variables.

Figure 25.1 shows the model in action out of sample for 1984 to 1989. Here the model was re-estimated yearly (initially up to December 1983) and monthly forecasts are made using new data. Portfolios of the top 50, 100, 200, . . ., 500 stocks are determined with monthly rebalancing assuming 1 % transactions costs. These portfolios beat the Topix (value weighted average of all 1000 plus stocks on Tokyo's first section) and the Nikkei (price weighted average of 225 major stocks) by a good measure. The small firm effect is shown by the difference between these indices and *All*, an equally weighted measure of all 1000+ stocks on the first section.

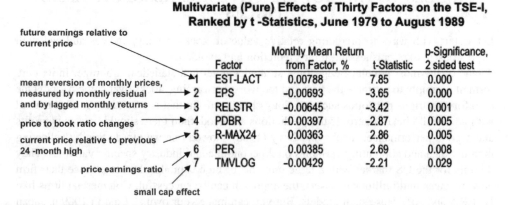

Multivariate (Pure) Effects of Thirty Factors on the TSE-I, Ranked by t -Statistics, June 1979 to August 1989

Factor	Monthly Mean Return from Factor, %	t-Statistic	p-Significance, 2 sided test
EST-LACT	0.00788	7.85	0.000
EPS	-0.00693	-3.65	0.000
RELSTR	-0.00645	-3.42	0.001
PDBR	-0.00397	-2.87	0.005
R-MAX24	0.00363	2.86	0.005
PER	0.00385	2.69	0.008
TMVLOG	-0.00429	-2.21	0.029

future earnings relative to current price

mean reversion of monthly prices, measured by monthly residual and by lagged monthly returns

price to book ratio changes

current price relative to previous 24 -month high

price earnings ratio

small cap effect

Figure 25.1   The seven best predictive variables. *Source*: Ziemba and Schwartz, 1991

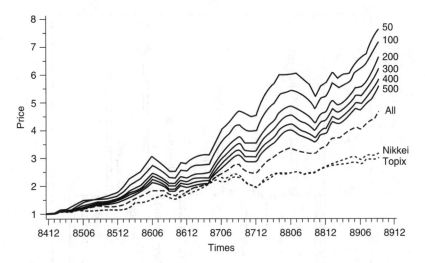

Figure 25.2   The 30 variable factor model predictions out of sample, 1984–1989. *Source*: Ziemba and Schwartz, 1991

The jig was up in Japan at the end of 1989 as discussed in Chapter 9. So what happened after? Actually all these variables work in reverse as well as forward. EST-LACT was still terrific in the decline when earnings were falling. A version of this model was used in the early 1990s by Buchanan, a London hedge fund, for buying cheap warrants and good stocks and selling short bad stocks. Do these models always work? They usually do. But when markets are taken over as they were in 1998/9 by only a few variables, then it was momentum and high cap, then they likely will fail as they did then. But you know that the market is not working right when it's dominated by only two variables that do not make full economic sense. In such cases when the script is not working watch out trouble is on the horizon.

Then, of course, we had the 2000–2002 crash. I discussed that in Chapter 23 so we update where the crash models were as of May 2005 later in this chapter.

How about ranking countries rather than individual stocks? Economist John Campbell of Harvard University and Arrowstreet Capital devised a simple model with three variables: short term momentum (over the past year), long term mean reversion (over the past 10 years) and value (measured by the country's dividend yield. These are the same variables we use in horseracing except they are called moving forward, bounce and value. Campbell's model is

$$b_1(return)_{-1} - b_2(10year\ cumulative\ return) + b_3(dividend\ yield)_{-1}.$$

As of March 2003, this led to the ranking over 1 and 10 years that Asia excluding Japan including New Zealand and Australia were the best countries; the US and Japan were average, and Finland was the worst. In general the predictions were accurate. The February 2005 predictions for major countries and emerging markets are shown in Figure 25.3. These are relative to the US which had an S&P500 dividend yield of 1.89 % in mid May 2005.

Let's now move to interest rates, the business cycle and stock market valuation and crashes. Figure 25.4 from Duke University finance professor Campbell Harvey shows that when the yield curve inverts, a recession almost always follows. Figure 25.5 shows real oil prices over time which are a factor here. The 2004–5 oil prices were very high in

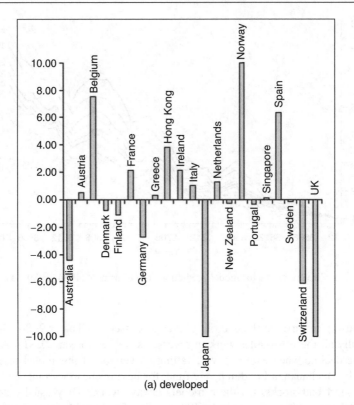

(a) developed

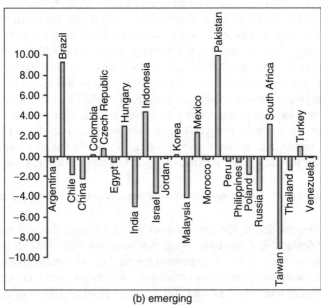

(b) emerging

Figure 25.3   February 2005 Active Country Weights (%). *Source*: Arrowstreet Journal, 2005

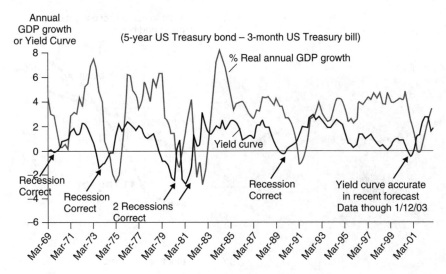

Figure 25.4 US yield curve inverts before the last six US recessions. *Source*: Harvey (2003)

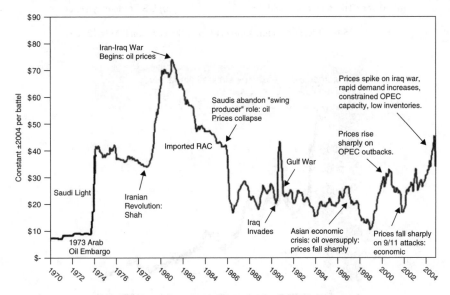

Figure 25.5 Major events and real world oil prices, 1970–2005 (prices adjusted by quarterly GDP deflator, 4Q 2004 dollars). *Source*: EIA

nominal terms but are way below the highest prices which occurred during the second oil crisis around 1980 during the Iran-Iraq war. That episode, as well as the first oil crisis in 1973–74, led to stock market declines.

In 2005 the yield curve has been flattened considerably as shown in Figure 25.6. Short term rates have moved in eight successive quarter point moves from 1 % to 3 %, see Figure 25.6a. The FED's statements indicate that these interest rate increases will continue on their *measured pace* at least for a while. A year ago 1-year T-bills were 1.63 %, now they are

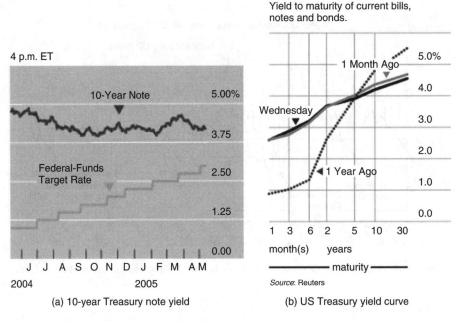

(a) 10-year Treasury note yield   (b) US Treasury yield curve

Figure 25.6   Treasury Yields. *Source*: Wall Street Journal, May 12, 2005

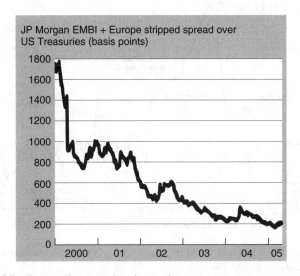

Figure 25.7   Eastern European bond spreads. *Source*: Financial Times, May 2, 2005

3.33 %. The spread between 10-year Treasury bonds and 1-year T-bills in May 2004 was $4.62 - 1.63 = 2.99\%$. In May 2005 it was $4.22 - 3.33 = 0.88\%$.

See Figure 25.6a for this convergence, Figure 25.6b for the flattening, and Figure 25.7 for how much the bond spreads for risky debt have narrowed since 2000.

Hence, possible danger is waiting in the wings. The best estimates of when this short term interest rate rise will stop are the Fed Funds futures contracts which are shown on

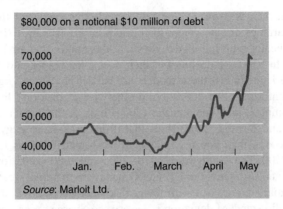

Figure 25.8 The Dow Jones investment grade CDX index. *Source*: Wall Street Journal, May 12, 2005

Bloomberg and the wagering on Fed increases at upcoming meetings of the FOMC on www.betair.com and www.tradesports.com and other betting exchanges. When and if the long rates will finally increase has been an open question since the 10-year rate bottomed at 3.11 % in June 2003. But Figure 25.8 indicates that the cost of protection against default on high grade company bonds is rising. Hence those on the long end of spreads like those in Figure 25.7, are taking a lot of risk. The year 2005 was also the first of a presidential election cycle and according to Hensel and Ziemba (2000) it is likely to have low stock market returns and so far it has since the S&P500 is negative through mid May. See the end of Chapter 23 for the S&P500 returns in 2004, to mid 2007. The returns in 2005 were low and predicted low because of the January barometer. A negative January, on average, predicts noise while a positive January predicts a good 11 months to come. When this book went to press in September 2007, the Fed had raised the Fed funds rate to 5.25 % and there is no recession yet even though many predict it. But a slowdown seems likely. The yield curve remains slightly inverted. The long, 10-year bond remains low in the 4.70 % range. Meanwhile, Princeton economist Ben Bernanke has replaced Alan Greenspan as chairman of the Federal Reserve System.

Why are short rates rising while long rates are dropping? This is a conundrum even to Fed Chairman Alan Greenspan. There seems to be a lack of concern for future inflation as predicted by spreads like those in Figures 25.6 and 25.7 and, more importantly, some of the main buyers of long term treasuries do not care what the yields are, as they simply have to put their excess dollars somewhere. These buyers are largely the central banks of Asia, especially China but also Japan, Korea, Taiwan and others who have large trade surpluses with the US. In June 2007 partly because of the Bear Stearns subprime loan hedge fund disaster the 10 year bond rose to the 5.3 % area and then fell to 4.67 % on August 3 as the US stock market indices hit new highs and then backed off violently 12 %.

I would like to end this chapter with a look at the current bond-stock yield differential, which I first used in Ziemba-Schwartz (1991). As discussed in Chapter 23, the bond-stock yield difference model, see also the academic papers of Berge and Ziemba (2006) and Koivu, Pennanen and Ziemba (2005) and the AIMR monograph Ziemba (2003), is very good at predicting large crashes. It correctly predicted the 1987 world wide crash in the US, Japan and elsewhere, the 1990 crash in Japan, the 2000 crash in the US and the 2002 crash (−22 % fall in the S&P500). Figure 12.1 which is based on KPZ's work is a special favorite of mine since it was one of the few models that predicted the 2002 fall which occurred because earnings dropped more than prices during late 2001 (EST-LACT at work again). The Fed indicator ratio log model goes into the danger zone in 1999 then is back to normal range after the 2000–1 decline but then goes even higher into the danger zone in late 2001. My experience is that these models are best at predicting large crashes, good at predicting subsequent rallies like 2003–4 and otherwise predict very little. See Berge and Ziemba (2006). Campbell and Vuolteenaho (2004) look at the effects of inflation in such models. But Berge and Ziemba (2006) show that if one uses the strategy: if the bond-stock indicator says to be out, then you go 100 % into cash and if it says to be in stocks you go 100 % into S&P500. The results from 1970–2005 and 1980–2005 for the five countries studied (the US, Japan, Germany, the UK and Canada) are that final wealth levels are about double a buy and hold strategy and with lower risk since about 20 % of the time one is in cash thus the portfolio standard deviation is less so the Sharpe ratios are higher.

For example, let's look at the US. Table 25.1 shows the nine 10 % plus corrections in the US from 1975–2005. Although the duration of the correction starting in January 1977 is longer than one year, it is considered a correction since the stock market dropped 11 % within ten months between January and October 1977. The same is true for the correction starting in April 2000 – the stock market dropped 23.9 % within the following twelve months.

Then Table 25.2 evaluates the performance of eight strategies for the US from 1975-2005 and 1980–2005. Here the mean excess return is the average monthly excess return of the strategy over the stock market. Terminal values refer to the gross performance of $ 100 invested using the strategy signals. Observe that the terminal wealth from all the strategies was about double the S&P500 buy and hold. Also since the strategies keep one out of the stock market about 12.63 to 19.35 % of the time, there is less risk. So the Sharpe ratios are about 50 % higher.

The strategies investigated are shown in Table 25.3. They use various years of data to obtain the extremes where one goes out of the stock market and then returns. the data can be based on the actual returns, called historical or based on a fitted normal distribution and the fractile rates for exits and entries. Results for Japan, Germany, the UK and Canada are in Berge and Ziemba (2006).

As of mid May the 10-year Treasury bond was 4.22 % and the 10-year Treasury bond was 4.49 % and the trailing PE ratio of the S&P500 was 19.71 %. So the model in difference

Table 25.1 Stock Market Corrections (10 % plus) in the US, 1975–2005. *Source*: Berge and Ziemba (2006)

Correction Number	Start Date	Duration (Months)	Decline (%)
1	July 1975	3	−11.8
2	January 1977	14	−15.2
3	April 1981	6	−11.6
4	December 1981	8	−11.1
5	September 1987	3	−29.4
6	June 1990	5	−14.1
7	July 1998	2	−14.7
8	April 2000	18	−31.2
9	April 2002	6	−29.1

Table 25.2 Evaluation of the Performance of the Strategies for the US. *Source*: Berge and Ziemba (2006)

Strategy	Number of Months in the Stock Market	Performance of the Strategies/the Stock Market Mean				
		Mean Log Return	Standard Deviation	Sharpe Ratio	Excess Return	Terminal Wealth
1	319 (85.75%)	0.01194	0.03933	0.17814	0.00162	8,480.41
2	300 (80.65%)	0.01255	0.03737	0.20378	0.00222	10,635.11
3	325 (87.37%)	0.01222	0.03936	0.18517	0.00190	9,420.42
4	314 (84.41%)	0.01246	0.03835	0.19632	0.00214	10,299.03
Stock Market (1975–2005)	372 (100%)	0.01032	0.04347	0.12401		4,649.75
5	273 (87.5%)	0.01254	0.03887	0.19773	0.00224	5,009.00
6	266 (85.26%)	0.01300	0.03835	0.21236	0.00270	5,781.16
7	260 (83.33%)	0.01215	0.03831	0.19039	0.00185	4,432.10
8	254 (81.41%)	0.01225	0.03785	0.19529	0.00195	4,569.44
Stock Market (1980–2005)	312 (100%)	0.01030	0.04389	0.12405		2,490.17

Table 25.3 Strategies Used to Evaluate the Predictive Ability of the BSEYD. *Source*: Berge and Ziemba (2006)

Strategy	Length of Interval (years)	Distribution Type	Fractile for exit Threshold level α_1	Fractile for entry Threshold level α_2
1	5	Historical	90	80
2	5	Historical	90	70
3	5	Normal	95	85
4	5	normal	95	75
5	10	historical	95	85
6	10	historical	95	75
7	10	normal	90	85
8	10	normal	90	80

form is $4.22 - 5.07 = -0.85$, using the more liquid 10-year bond. This is no where near the danger zone for a large crash which is about $+3.00$. In fact it is a very bullish signal despite the other weak aspects of the market. I also have a short term (2–3 month) crash model based on the relative put and call option prices and the message they send out regarding market sentiment. That model is based on S&P data from 1985–2002 and also called the July 2002 fall and another in mid 2003. Since then it has not signaled a crash and is still not now in mid May 2005, (nor as of June 29, 2007 when this book went to press). The bond-stock model has been out of the danger zone as well during these periods. Crashes, of course, can occur for other reasons than high interest rates relative to earnings or over confidence in option prices so in trading never overbet at any time. When the models indicate a crash is coming, do not bet at all or neutralize your positions in some way.

Chapter 26 continues the discussion of economic variables and scenario tilting.

Some mathematical approaches for scenario generation and reduction

Generating scenarios is a complex subject

Scenarios represent the set of possible future outcomes of the random parameters of the model at hand over the decision horizon. Since the number of scenarios can be very large, procedures to reduce their number while still retaining their representation of the future are of interest. So are ways to generate scenarios from given distributions. In this chapter, I discuss two basic mathematical approaches to accomplish this. Chapter 25 discussed how economic models, especially those relating to interest rates, earnings

and other key economic variables can be used to generate scenarios that tilt the past towards more likely futures. Chapter 27 discusses planning for disasters and then dealing with them. The first way is that scenarios can be generated by moment matching. The idea is that the reduced set of scenarios has the same moments as the original larger set of scenarios to some order. We used this idea in the five period Russell-Yasuda Kasai insurance model in 1989 which is discussed in Cariño, Myers and Ziemba (1998). See Ziemba (2007) for a survey of such models. Smith (1993), Keefer and Bodily (1993), Keefer (1994) have suggested such methods for static problems. Høyland and Wallace (HW) (2001) have expanded and refined the idea for multiperiod problems and they generate scenarios that match some moments of the true distribution. Typically it is the first four moments. Extensions of the HW work are in Høyland, Kaut and Wallace (2001) and Kouwenberg (1999).

MOMENT MATCHING

The procedure is easy to use and provides adequate scenarios. It does have its faults because the two distributions in Figure 26.1 have the same first four moments.[1] Such mathematical

---

[1] X is uniform on $[-\sqrt{3}, \sqrt{3}]$, and $Y = \sqrt[4]{\frac{3}{5}}I + \sqrt{1 - \sqrt{\frac{3}{5}}}Z$ where I is -1 or $+1$ with probability $\frac{1}{2}$ and Z is $N(0, 1)$. Then $E(x) = E(y) = 0$, $E(x^2) = E(y^2) = 1$, $E(x^3) = E(y^3) = 0$ and $E(x^4) = E(y^4) = \frac{9}{5}$. Hochreiter and Pflug (2003) derived this example using ideas from Heyde (1963) who showed that even infinite moment matching will not replicate all distributions.

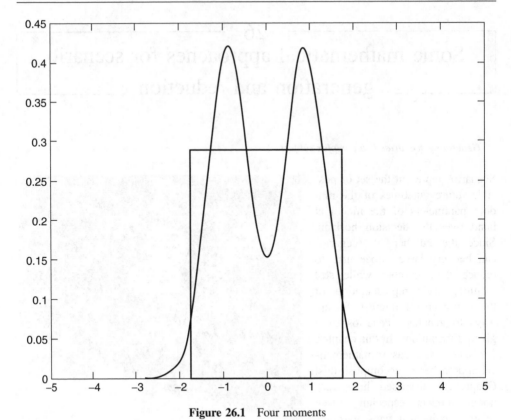

Figure 26.1 Four moments

mismatches aside, the HW approach is to find a set of discrete scenarios that best fits
the distributions first four moments minimizing least squares. The scenario tree consists of
realizations and their probabilities of all random parameters in all time periods.

The optimization problem is

$$\min_{x,p} \sum_{i \in Q} w_i \left(f_i(s, p) - Q_i \right)^2$$

$$\sum \lambda M = 1$$

$$\lambda \geqslant 0$$

where Q is the set of all specified statistical properties and Q_i the value of $i \in Q$, with
weight w_i, M is a matrix of zeros and ones, whose number of rows equals the length of
λ and whose number of columns equals the number of nodes in the scenario tree. Each
column in M provides a conditional distribution at a node in the scenario tree.

HW's examples, single and multiple period, consider four asset classes: cash, bonds,
domestic stocks and international stocks and the expectations are in terms of the interest
rate for cash and bonds and total returns for stocks. The decision maker must specify their
(subjective) expectations for the marginal distributions. This is a preferred way to solicit
experts' future views of key model parameters. Various methods exist for eliciting these

distributions. For calculations, HW use the NAG C library routine which, however, does not guarantee that the second derivative does not change sign.

Figure 26.2 shows fitted cumulative distribution functions for the four asset classes and their corresponding derived density functions (some with odd shapes) where the specified percentiles are denoted by triangles.

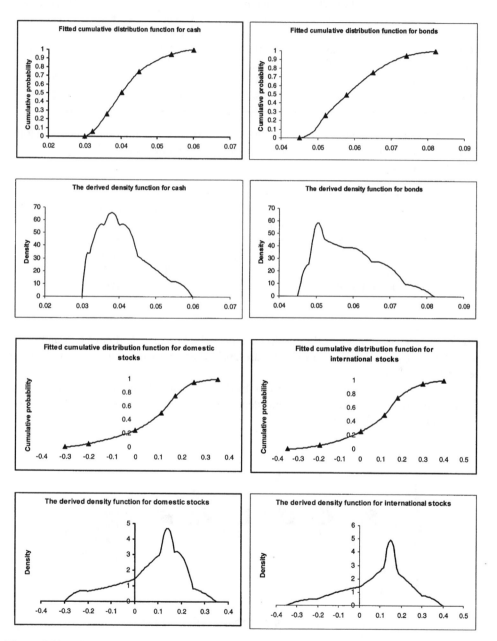

Figure 26.2 Fitted cumulative distribution functions and the derived density functions for the asset classes. *Source*: Hoyland and Wallace (2001)

The aim is to construct the return r and the probability p so that the statistical properties match those of the specified distribution. Once these are estimated the scenarios can be generated. The properties of the marginal distributions in the HW example are

	Expected value (%)	Standard deviation (%)	Skewness	Kurtosis	Worst-case event (%)
Cash	4.33	0.94	0.80	2.62	6.68
Bonds	5.91	0.82	0.49	2.39	7.96
Domestic stocks	7.61	13.38	−0.75	2.93	−25.84
International stocks	8.09	15.70	−0.74	2.97	−31.16

The normal distribution has a kurtosis of three. A kurtosis of less than three means that the distribution is less peaked around the mean than the normal distribution.

The correlations were:

	Cash	Bonds	Domestic Stocks	Intern'l Stocks
Cash	1	0.60	−0.20	−0.10
Bonds		1	−0.30	−0.20
Domestic stocks			1	0.60
International stocks				1

A set of six scenarios that exactly match the expected return, standard deviation and correlation data in these tables is shown in Figure 26.3 where the worst case event is given in the left most scenario.

Moving from static one-period scenarios to dynamic multiperiod scenarios has several added complexities such as intertemporal dependencies that need to be considered. These include volatility clumping and mean reversion.

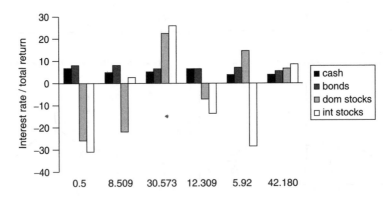

Figure 26.3 Six scenarios that match the expected return, standard deviation and correlation data of the HW example

Multiperiod scenario trees must either have independence across time or more likely have an intertemporal dependence structure. For example, HW assume that the volatility for asset class i in period $t > 1$ is

$$\sigma_{it} = c_i r_{i,t-1} - \bar{r}_{i,t-1} + (1 - c_i)\sigma_{Ait}$$

where $c_i \in [0, 1]$ is a volatility clumping parameter (the higher the more clumping), r_{it} is the realized return with expectation $\bar{r}_{it}$ and σ_{Ait} is the average standard deviation of asset i in period t. They model mean reversion of the two bond classes using $\bar{r}_{it} = MRF_i MRL_i + (1 - MRF_i)r_{i,t-1}$ where $MRF_i \in [0, 1]$ is the mean reversion factor (the higher the more mean reversion), MRL_i is the mean reversion level and r_{it} the interest rate for bond class i in period t. Mean reversion means that interest rates tend to revert to an average level. The assumption is that when interest rates are high, the economy slows down, and interest rates tend to fall and when interest rates are low, the economy improves and interest rates rise. Empirical studies, starting with Fischer Black in the 1970s show that the volatility for stocks increases after a large decrease in stock prices, but not after a large increase. Modeling this asymmetry is straightforward, but to simplify the presentation, HW assume equal volatility dependencies for all asset classes.

For stock, HW assume that there is a premium in terms of higher expected return which has associated with it more risk. The expected return is then $\bar{r}_{it} = r_{ft} + PR_t\sigma_{it}$ where r_{ft} is the risk free interest rate, σ_{it} is the standard deviation and RP_t is a risk premium constant for period t. For period 1, the assumptions are as above. For periods 2 and 3, the expected values and standard deviations are state dependent as modeled here. Other factors are assumed to be state independent and equal to the specifications in period 1. Correlations are as in period one for all three periods. These market expectations are summarized as follows

Asset class	Distribution property	(End of) Period 1	(End of) Period 2	(End of) Period 3
Cash – duration three months	expected value of spot rate	4.33 %	State dep	State dep
	standard deviation	0.94 %	State dep	State dep
	skewness	0.80	0.80	0.80
	kurtosis	2.62	2.62	2.62
	worst-case event	6.68 %	State dep	State dep
Bonds – duration six years	expected value spot rate	5.91 %	State dep	State dep
	standard deviation	0.82 %	State dep	State dep
	skewness	0.49	0.49	0.49
	kurtosis	2.39	2.39	2.39
	worst-case event	7.96 %	State dep	State dep
Domestic stocks	expected value total return	7.61 %	State dep	State dep
	standard deviation	13.38 %	State dep	State dep
	skewness	−0.75	−0.75	−0.75
	kurtosis	2.93	2.93	2.93
	worst-case event	−25.84 %	State dep	State dep
International stocks	expected value total return	8.09 %	State dep	State dep
	standard deviation return	15.70 %	State dep	State dep
	skewness	−0.74	−0.74	−0.74
	kurtosis	2.97	2.97	2.97
	worst-case event	−31.16 %	State dep	State dep

The risk premium $RP_t = 0.3$ for $t - 1, 2, 3$. The volatility clumping parameter $c_i = 0.3$ for all assets, the mean reversion factor $MRF_i = 0.2$ for all interest rate classes and the mean reversion level $MRL_i = 4.0\%$ and 5.8% for cash and bonds, respectively.

There are alternative ways of constructing the multiperiod trees. HW use a sequential procedure: (1) specify statistical properties for the first period and generate first-period outcomes; (2) for each generated first-period outcome, specify conditional distribution properties for the second period and generate conditional second-period outcomes. Continue specifying conditional distributions to generate consistent outcomes in all periods. This approach has numerical advantages from the decomposition into single-period trees. Each single-period optimization problem in nonconvex., However, by adjusting the number of outcomes and reoptimizing from alternative starting points, usually ensures that a perfect match is obtained for each of the generated single-period trees if one exists.

This sequential approach requires the distribution properties to be specified at each node in the tree. Hence, the approach does not control the statistical properties over all realizations in periods $t = 2, 3, \ldots$. An alternative is to construct the entire tree in one large optimization. This approach will render infeasible one period subtrees that lead to conditional multiperiod trees that do not have a full match. The drawback is a much more difficult optimization problem.

A three period scenario tree that has a perfect match with these specifications was generated in 63 seconds on a Sun Ultra Sparc 1 (each single period tree takes less than a second to construct).

The first two scenarios which have a perfect match are

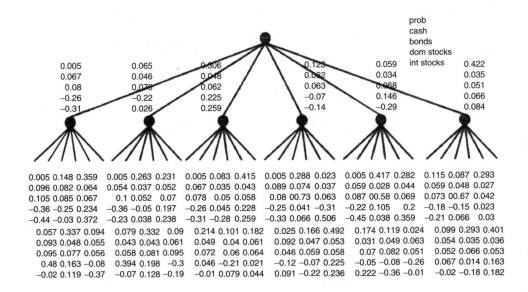

HW found that stability (the same objective value for different scenario trees) is improved by solving for larger scenario trees by aggregating several smaller scenario trees. See Høyland and Wallace (2001b) and Høyland, Kaut and Wallace (2001) for more discussion.

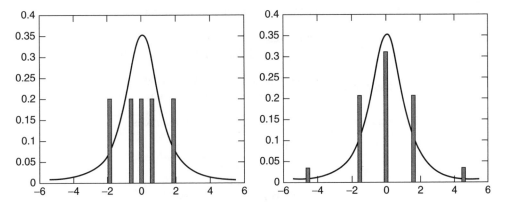

Figure 26.4 Approximation of a t-distribution with a Kolmogrov-Smirnov distance on the left and the Wasserstein distance measure on the right

THE WASSERSTEIN DISTANCE MINIMIZATION APPROACH

The second approach, due to Hochreiter and Pflug (HP) (2003), generates scenario trees using a multidimensional facility location problem that minimizes a Wasserstein distance measure from the true distribution. Moment matching can yield strange distributions. Hence they propose this alternative approach which approximates distributions with very few scenarios. The Kolmogarov-Smirnov (KS) distance approximations is an alternative approach but it does not take care of tails and higher moments. The HP method combines a good approximation of the moments and the tails. An example is the t-distribution with two degrees of freedom with density $(2+x^2)^{-\frac{3}{2}}$. This density is approximated in Figure 26.4 with the KS distance on the left and the Wasserstein distance on the right. The latter gives better approximations, the location of the minimum is closer to the true value and the mean is closer as well. Observe how few scenarios are used for the approximations. The KS distance is invariant with respect to monotone transformations of the x-axis and thus does not approximate the tails well like the Wasserstein distance.

The optimal approximation of a continuous distribution G by a distribution with mass points $z_1, \ldots, z_m$ with probabilities $p_1, \ldots, p_m$ using the KS distance is

$$z_i = G^{-1}\left(\frac{2i-1}{2m}\right), \quad p_i = \frac{1}{m}.$$

The Wasserstein distance is the solution of the non-convex program

$$\min\left\{\int \min|u - c_j|dG(u) : c_1, \ldots, c_m \in R\right\}.$$

The locations $c_i, \ldots, c_m$ then yield the probabilities

$$p_i = \int_{\{u:|u-c_i|=\min|u-c_j|\}} dG(u).$$

Figure 26.5 shows the scenario generation procedure. An example follows

for stocks
| which return | 1.19 | 1.05 | 0.92 |
| with probabilities | 0.23 | 0.48 | 0.29 |

and bonds
| which return | 1.055 | 1.04 | 1.03 |
| with probabilities | 0.22 | 0.52 | 0.26. |

The bond-stock correlation is -0.4 so the joint probability matrix is

	1.19	1.05	0.92
1.055	0.0154	0.2146	0
1.04	0	0.3054	0.1746
1.03	0.2046	0	0.0854

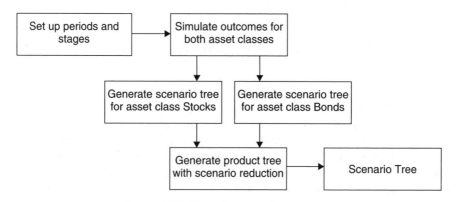

Figure 26.5   Scenario generation procedure

Scenario tree (stocks)			Scenario tree (bonds)		
1.049 (0.3223)	1.057 (0.532)	1.08 (0.524)	1.048 (0.2842)	1.052 (0.521)	1.054 (0.488)
		1.052 (0.476)			1.0505 (0.512)
	1.041 (0.468)	1.049 (0.511)		1.045 (0.479)	1.047 (0.503)
		1.032 (0.489)			1.0435 (0.497)
0.098 (0.368)	1.012 (0.502)	1.021 (0.494)	1.041 (0.4521)	1.0425 (0.5)	1.0435 (0.506)
		1.009 (0.506)			1.042 (0.494)
	0.991 (0.493)	0.997 (0.507)		1.04 (0.5)	1.0405 (0.49)
		0.981 (0.493)			1.039 (0.51)
0.959 (0.3097)	0.972 (0.481)	0.978 (0.512)	1.035 (0.2637)	1.038 (0.501)	1.039 (0.498)
		0.965 (0.488)			1.0365 (0.502)
	0.933 (0.519)	0.954 (0.47)		1.032 (0.499)	1.0345 (0.513)
		0.918 (0.53)			1.0305 (0.487)

Figure 26.6   Scenario tree for stocks and bonds

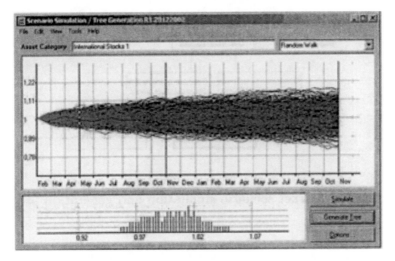

Figure 26.7   Scenario simulation

Combined scenario tree (stokcs and bonds)

1.049/1.048 (0.0956)	1.057/1.045 (0.5159)	1.08/1.0435 (0.4784)
		1.052/1.047 (0.5216)
	1.041/1.052 (0.4841)	1.049/1.0505 (0.4937)
		1.032/1.054 (0.5063)
1.049/1.035 (0.1974)	1.057/1.032 (0.529)	1.08/1.0305 (0.5278)
		1.052/1.0345 (0.4722)
	1.041/1.038 (0.471)	1.049/1.0365 (0.494)
		1.032/1.039 (0.506)
0.998/1.041 (0.4010)	1.012/1.04 (0.5262)	1.021/1.039 (0.4705)
		1.009/1.0405 (0.5295)
	0.991/1.0425 (0.4738)	0.997/1.042 (0.4902)
		0.981/1.0435 (0.5098)
0.959/1.048 (0.2171)	0.972/1.045 (0.5209)	0.978/1.0435 (0.4673)
		0.965/1.047 (0.5327)
	0.933/1.052 (0.4791)	0.954/1.505 (0.5241)
		0.918/1.054 (0.4759)
0.959/1.035 (0.0889)	0.972/1.032 (0.4802)	0.978/1.0305 (0.4799)
		0.965/1.0345 (0.5201)
	0.933/1.038 (0.5198)	0.954/1.0365 (0.5228)
		0.918/1.039 (0.4772)

Figure 26.8   Combined scenario tree for stocks and bonds

This yields the scenario trees in Figure 26.6 and 26.8 and the scenario simulation in Figure 26.7. In Chapter 25, I discussed how various economic models, especially those with interest rates, earnings, etc involved and expert judgment can be used to tilt existing scenarios, based on past data, towards more likely future scenarios. Chapter 27 discusses planning for disasters and dealing with them.

Minimizing the effects of disasters by planning ahead

Stochastic programming models allow one to plan now what to do if certain events occur

As I write this it is the fourth anniversary of September 11, 2001. Aside from the anniversary specials airing today, there is little in the news these days about Osama Bin Laden. The news today is about another crisis: how to recover from the huge disaster of hurricane Katrina's strike on the Gulf Coast two weeks ago. When CNN has broken away from Katrina coverage, it turns to the lingering instability in Iraq, which has

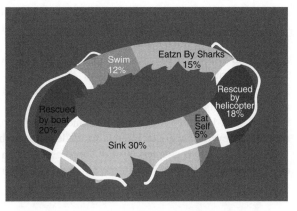

made some of our economic interactions more precarious and our future investments harder to predict. Neither of these reconstruction efforts are likely to be completed overnight and their effects are likely to reverberate through the US and global economies for a considerable period. The effects of Hurricane Katrina, like that of so many disasters and crises, are exacerbated by existing positions and any instabilities. It reminds us that we must choose our positions to hedge against anticipated as well as unanticipated risks.

As you read this, some time will have passed so we would like to draw some lessons from this crisis to show how to draw up scenarios and analysis that is useful for the future. The question is whether we have learned anything about risk and disaster preparedness since the 9/11 terrorist attacks? At first glance, it seems that there was a tremendous failure by the different levels of government in predicting the hurricane's effects and dealing with the crisis despite warnings, analyses and even mock emergency tests of preparedness. I do not want to engage in the blame game but rather to set out some aspects of the planning process to deal with such disasters and the economy and financial market impacts.

PLANNING IN ADVANCE: STAGE ONE OF A TWO PERIOD STOCHASTIC PROGRAM

It was well known that New Orleans, much of which is below sea level and includes a large lake, was extremely vulnerable to a huge hurricane. The fact that a big hurricane like Katrina could hit New Orleans as well as its potential aftermath were well known. For example a five part series published by the New Orleans newspaper *The Times Picayune*, June 23–27, 2003 included a scenario very similar to the August 2005 outcome. The series called *Washing Away* concluded that there was a disaster in waiting as the levees were not strong enough to withstand a category four hurricane. The Army Corps of Engineers had plans to upgrade the levies but funding was withheld.

The problem can be well modeled as a two stage stochastic program. Thus one should plan in advance against essentially all scenarios then if a bad scenario actually occurs one can optimally revise. It sounds simple but it provides a way to plan stage 1. How optimal was the crisis preparation? Stochastic programming computer codes and applications to many areas of finance, production, energy policy, etc. are detailed in Wallace and Ziemba (2005). In fact the evidence is that the planners in New Orleans did just that. They foresaw an event like Katrina and planned for it. The trouble was largely in the response by the various stakeholders.

Katrina was officially a category four hurricane when it hit just towards the outskirts of New Orleans. Earlier predictions feared that it might hit New Orleans as a category five storm. It first hit the Florida coast as a category one, then returned to sea gathering momentum and water for its strike on the Gulf Coast on August 30.

I got a brief glimpse of this act of nature. I was at the Saratoga (NY) racetrack on August 31 and witnessed the torrential rains for two plus hours under a tent there. For us it was no big deal and we could bet the simulcast at Del Mar and I could edit papers for the Asset-Liability Management Handbook (Zenios and Ziemba editors, 2006, 2007), which has several papers of interest to readers of this book including very good surveys of Kelly betting in two chapters by Ed Thorp and by Len MacLean and myself. This atypical downpour did give us an idea of the strength of the storm even more than a thousand miles away and more than a day after it hit New Orleans.

HOW MUCH HEDGING IS THERE AGAINST VARIOUS RISKS?

Figure 27.1 shows that as of August 2003, the world's top 500 companies as of August 2003 hedge most of their interest rate and currency risk but little of their commodity and equity risks.

Table 27.1 shows how much larger the predicted impact for Katrina was relative to previous large hurricanes in terms of damage. Insurance companies did predict some of these losses. The insurance companies (essentially put sellers) bear a substantial loss which is hard to estimate since water damage is not usually covered in policies and the coverage for other damage is unclear. However their loss is estimated to be about $ 25 billion of the up to $ 100 billion in total expected costs. Their decreased share is due in part to their greater scrutiny following the liabilities of 9/11 and the increase in hurricanes along the Gulf Coast and in Florida which drove the premiums up, tripling them is some parts of New

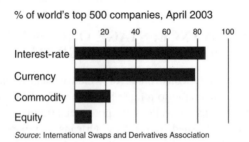

Source: International Swaps and Derivatives Association

Figure 27.1   Covered? Use of derivatives by type of risk

Table 27.1 Relative hurricane costs. *Source*: Action Economics

Hurricane	Category	Date	Damage (Bil. $)	Infl. Adj. Damage (Bil. $)
Katrina (LA, MS, AL)	4	8/05	$50.0E	$50.0E
Andrew (FL, LA)	5	8/92	$26.5	$34.1
Charley (FL)	4	8/04	$15.0	$15.3
Ivan (AL, FL)	3	9/04	$14.2	$14.5
Frances (FL)	2	9/04	$8.9	$9.1
Jeanne (FL)	3	9/04	$6.9	$7.0
Hugo (SC, GA, NC, VA)	4	9/89	$7.0	$10.0
Georges (FL, MS, AL)	2	9/98	$5.0	$5.8
Floyd (Mid-Atl., NE)	2	9/99	$4.5	$5.1
Fran (NC, SC, Mid-Atl.)	3	9/96	$3.2	$3.8
Opal (FL, AL)	3	10/95	$3.0	$3.6

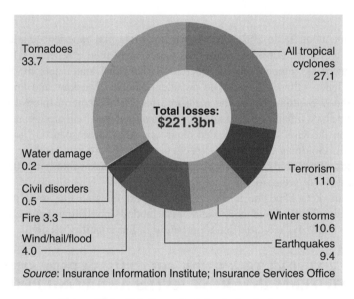

Tornadoes 33.7
All tropical cyclones 27.1
Water damage 0.2
Civil disorders 0.5
Fire 3.3
Wind/hail/flood 4.0
Terrorism 11.0
Winter storms 10.6
Earthquakes 9.4
Total losses: $221.3bn
Source: Insurance Information Institute; Insurance Services Office

Figure 27.2 Inflation adjusted catastrophe losses

Orleans and forced some to either self-insure or cobble together a mixed bag of policies. See Figure 27.2 for insurance losses from 1984–2004.

Despite the fact that almost everyone lost a lot, there were some redistribution effects and some short term winners such as:

1. Traders who bet on the overreaction of initial price moves and the subsequent drop and the eventual rise of oil prices, the euro, interest rates, S&P500, etc made considerable profits. See Table 27.2.
2. Construction companies who will be called on the rebuild and the various suppliers, this profit may not result until early 2006.
3. Gasoline companies who could take short term advantage of higher energy prices.

Table 27.2   Price overreaction evolution in several key financial markets around Katrina's hit on New Orleans

	August 29	August 30	Sept 9
10-year bond rate, %		4.01	4.12
Euro/dollar	122	125.51	124.19
Odds on a 0.25 % rise in short term interest rates on Betfair*	1.08	1.33	1.13
Dec Crude Oil	66.50	70.70	65.41
S&P500	1212.28	1208.41	1241.48

*Odds of 1+x means you bet 1 to either win x of lose 1.[1]

4. The 25 university students from Gulf area schools now temporarily attending Harvard and others at MIT, Brown and other top US universities. These students are recipients of the generosity of the colleges and the students already enrolled. Their lives are not on hold.

A few comments on Table 27.2. The 10-year bond rate first experienced a large drop then a gradual rise while the euro/dollar rate had a large rise then a reversal when the FED's interest rate increases moderated then increased. Hawkish statements by San Francisco Fed president Janet Yellen, Chicago Fed president Michael Moskow and Philadelphia Fed president Anthony Santomero that the measured pace of short term interest rate increases would continue since inflation uncertainty on the upside if anything are greater not less after Katrina's hit on the Gulf coast. Still Fed chairman Alan Greenspan did not usually raise rates in a crisis. Goldman Sachs thus expects a pause and no rate increase on September 20. But at odds of 4.7 (bid) to 7.4 (ask) on Betfair, the market thinks the 0.25% rise was by far the most likely scenario.

The equity markets liked the idea of lower interest rates so they rose throughout this period consistent with the bond-stock yield crash model's prediction that a crash from high interest rates is unlikely, see the discussion below in the volatility section.

SOME KEY MARKETS: CRUDE OIL, THE S&P500, SHORT AND LONG TERM INTEREST RATES AND BOND PRICES

Katrina was a classic case of the immediate overreaction of certain key commodities. Given the already significant price rises and instability of commodity prices, this crisis exacerbated the moves of these prices. There is a considerable academic finance literature on the controversial subject of over-reaction and under-reaction. It is an active and controversial subject. See papers of Richard Thaler, University of Chicago and Sheridan Titman, University of Texas, especially. Katrina was a classic case. As CNN reported the approaching storm, December crude exploded from the $66 per barrel area to peak around $71.70 on Globex on Sunday night August 28. By Monday morning before the US markets opened, it fell to the $70.40 area. A few hours later it fell to $68 only to return the next day to $70.70 and then in subsequent days, returned to pre Katrina levels. See Figures 27.3 and 27.4.

---

[1] Experience shows that the odds on the favorite shorten as one approaches the event. So 1.13 is much larger than 1.08 than one might think.

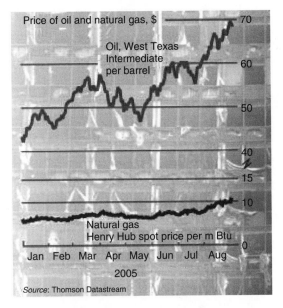

Figure 27.3   Crude oil prices

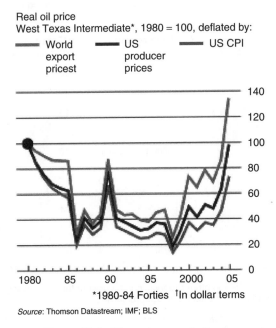

Figure 27.4   The real story of oil prices

Crude oil prices in September 2005 were more than 50 % above those a year earlier but well below the $ 90 inflation adjusted, in 2005 dollars, highs of the early 1980 s. The world-wide supply-demand graph shown in Figures 27.5 and 27.6 show why. Worldwide demand has caught up with supply hence any disturbance or uncertainty essentially anywhere in the

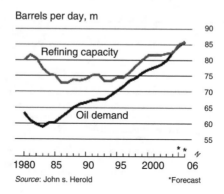

Figure 27.5   Worldwide refining capacity and oil demand is now essentially equal

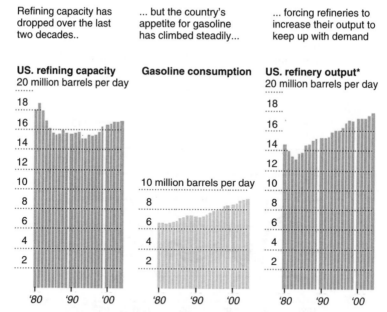

* Output of gasoline and other products can be greater than oil refining capacity because of additives introduced during processing.

Source: Energy Information Administration

Figure 27.6   Trying to keep up: there is a small amount of imported gasoline but the major imports are of crude oil to be refined

world would push up oil prices. Of course, early release of the strategic petroleum reserves and other emergency and humanitarian measures including increased production from OPEC, Canada, Mexico, etc which dampened the impact of Katrina on the price rise in the medium term. But it is clear that the case for higher prices is strong, especially since Saudi Arabia, Iran, Iraq and Venezuela, four of the top five oil producing countries, are potentially trouble spots. The market will likely continue to build in a cost premium due to this potential for instability.

VOLATILITY

The VIX index of CBOE, equity implied volatility, was little changed by the event. Volatility remains at historically low levels and was 13.52% on August 29, 13.65% on August 30 and then was basically flat, closing at 11.98% on September 9. See Figure 27.7. Since September is historically the worst stock market month, see for example, studies in Keim and Ziemba (2000), and there was a major catastrophe, this non event has to be attributed to

1. the lower interest rates of both the long 10-year bond and the lower odds of more FED short term hikes, especially the much lower odds of increases in the short term rate of 4.00 and 4.25, and
2. the fact that the bond stock yield difference model suggests that the odds of a large fall in the S&P500 are very low.

The calculation on September 9, 2005 was 4.09% for 10-year T-bonds or 4.40% for 30-year T-bonds minus the earnings/price ratio of 5.11 so the measure is <0. Historically for there to be trouble, this measure must be about 3; see Chapter 23. As well, the confidential sentiment model that I use for my own and client trading using option prices is also not close to the danger zone.

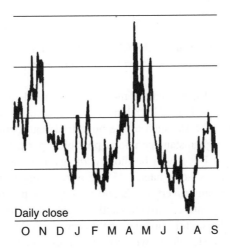

Daily close

O N D J F M A M J J A S

Figure 27.7   CBOE Volatility Index. *Source: Barron's*, September 9, 2005

FUTURE PROSPECTS AND THE 2006 OUTLOOK

It is too early to estimate accurately the impacts of Katrina. Some believe that the reconstruction effort will turn positive in 2007. However some like the Maxim group argue that:

> A major American city has been all but wiped off the map, taking the country's largest port with it. To put this into context, the costs for rebuilding New Orleans after Katrina will exceed those of rebuilding Chicago after the great fire, San Francisco after the 1906 earthquake and New York and DC after September 11th combined. And that's after adjusting for inflation.
>
> Despite what some of the more bullish pundits have been saying, the stimulus of rebuilding New Orleans will not outweigh the overall loss to the economy. If it did, we would level a different city each year and rebuild it from the ground up, shiny and new. But it doesn't, and so we don't.
> *Source*: Barrons, Friday, September 9, 2005.

I think this is overreaction and if so, relates not just to the crisis itself but it is exacerbating the pre-existing outflow of people and business from New Orleans, but costs of rebuilding are high. The success of Chicago and San Francisco after their disasters was partly due to the strategic role they played geographically and economically. New Orleans will only return to its place if those who have been displaced and others are convinced to return, rebuild and regenerate the city, something which the distrust of the government reaction may dampen. The city got a big psychological boost in 2006 from the excellent success of its NFL team the Saints and especially form the outstanding play of quarterback Drew Brees and rookie receiver and running back Reggie Bush.

LESSONS

> (Warren) Buffett, quoting Benjamin Graham, says: In the short term, the market is a voting machine. In the long-term, it's a weighting machine. That means it's cash flow in the long run that'll determine the value of a business.
> *Source*: Barron's, Friday, September 9, 2005

My Japanese factor model discussed in Chapter 25, indicates that Buffett is right: the best variable for predicting future stock prices is future earnings/price, a variable I called EST-LACT.

So I will go along with Warren and the models I have used since 1989. Watch the long bond rate and watch earnings. Figure 27.8 hints at some sectors to watch. There are several obstacles to this growth in the US such as the huge trade and current account deficits, the huge cost of the Iraq and Afghanistan operations, possible other crises such as one originating from hedge fund disasters. But it will be those earnings and interest rates that will likely prevail. Inverted yield curves, see Chapter 25, are also a danger as shown in Figure 27.9. Should the yield curve actually invert, the historical evidence predicts a recession. So even if the other measures are positive, extreme caution should be used. Up to early July 2007 when we went to press, the slightly inverted yield curve in 2006 and 2007 did not yet lead to a recession. But a 2007 slowdown with lower interest rates is the most likely current scenario. By June 2007 the inversion ended and the yield curve was upward sloping.

These steps outlined here show some of the ways actors (planners, insurance companies, short term investors) planned for and then reacted to government responses. They also provide a model for how investors and government actors could and do plan for and react

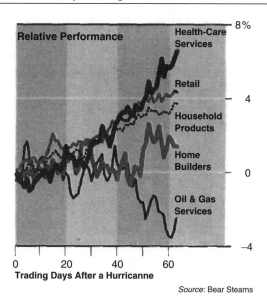

Figure 27.8 After the storm: sector performance, relative to the S&P500, after 13 previous hurricanes over the past 20 years. *Source*: *Barron's*, September 9, 2005

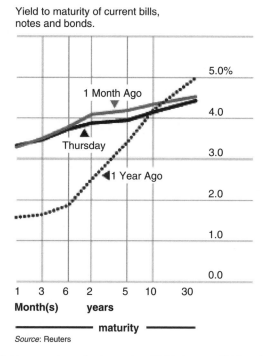

Figure 27.9 Yield curves in early September 2005, August 2005 and September 2004

to crises. However, in the case of Katrina, the focus on the relatively narrow vision of homeland security allowed the appropriation of resources away from natural disaster planning. Stochastic optimization and comparison to previous instability promoting crisis allows investors to assess their room for maneuver and we can at least draw lessons in the hope that we will not be doomed to repeat our mistakes.

Appendix
The great investors: some useful books

This appendix reviews the following three recent trade books.

1. William Poundstone (2006) *Fortune's Formula: The Untold Story of the Scientific System that Beat the Casinos and Wall Street*, Hill and Wang, New York, US$ 27, in hardback.
2. Nassim Nicholas Taleb (2005) *Fooled by Randomness: The Hidden Role of Chance in Life and Financial Markets* (Second Edition), Random House, New York, US$ 14.95 (but I got it for $ 10). It was named by Fortune 'one of the smartest books of all time'.
3. David F. Swensen (2005) *Unconventional Success: A Fundamental Approach to Personal Investment* was published by the Free Press and sells for US$ 27.50.

This section reviews these books is to ascertain what I learned from reading them and what the readers of this book might learn from them. It focusses on Poundstone's book with some thoughts about the other two.

WILLIAM POUNDSTONE

William Poundstone, a professional journalist, twice nominated for the Pulitzer prize, had endless discussions with major players related to the Kelly criterion, such as Ed Thorp, Tom Cover, Nils Hakansson, Harry Markowitz, Robert Merton, Paul Samuelson, and myself. He listened to us and on balance provides a good account of this approach for those not able to read the technical literature on the Kelly or capital growth criterion. In addition, there is fascinating discussion of the lives of the various players. The Kelly literature is well summarized by two long and very technical articles by Thorp (2006) and by MacLean and Ziemba (2006). Ziemba (2005) is an easier intuitive read for non-techies. The most advanced mathematical proofs with the weakest assumptions are in Algoet and Cover (1988). Thorp (2006) is a wonderful treatment of the theory and his experiences and MacLean and Ziemba (2006) adds the other literature and their research and experiences. While I have some quibbles with Poundstone's book as discussed below, I feel he did a very good job on a very tough assignment and the book is highly recommended, especially for the colorful stories and history related to the Kelly criterion development.

Poundstone starts out discussing the racetrack wire service and the early players in the development of modern gambling activities. Characters like those in the 1969 movie *The Sting* abound. This leads to the early work on blackjack by Ed Thorp and his involvement with the giant of information theory, Claude Shannon. The history of this era is told to a large extent as a bio of Thorp and Shannon. Since I have known Ed since the early 70 s, much but not all, of this section on his life is familiar to me but most of the Shannon discussion is new to me. It's a good read though for those who want to trace the difficulties and successes of the great thinker Thorp as he moves, to put it in his own words to me, from ***essentially zero wealth*** to a giant hundred million fortune. Throughout the book there is the tension between the academics who are efficient market types and those academics and others who feel that markets can be beaten. Unless you have experienced this pain as Thorp and I have, it is hard to have an appreciation of this. It is amazing that many who never trade at all think they are the experts and those who have made fortunes are thought to be simply lucky. In his next edition, Poundstone could use my breakdown of people into various stock market camps as discussed in Chapter 6.

I am especially interested in great investors in this book and Thorp is definitely one of them. Shannon, who I never met, was a giant of a thinker and inventor of gadgets and greatly influenced Kelly, Thorp and many others. Shannon's own portfolio of stocks and some IPOs made him very wealthy but the evidence Poundstone presents while impressive is sort of vague and does not really make the case. Shannon basically had just a few stocks with phenomenal returns but since the returns were high, around 28 % over many years, maybe he was a great investor. The volatility pumping on pages 202–204 is another early good idea he had. We stochastic programmers know that models that use information over time beat static models as fix mix; see Chapter 21. Thorp's Princeton-Newport and hedge funds record, with numerous hedged bets with advantage using mispricings and the constant search for new mispricings when current ones dried up, is more impressive.

The discussion of Shannon's life is interesting, especially the part of his transition from super productive researcher at Bell Labs to some sort of genius recluse at MIT. I was pleased that when he said he did not want to teach anymore they did not show him the door as most schools would. But MIT is smarter than most universities and has greater resources to do valuable things.

Logs abound in information theory and Kelly argued that maximizing the expected log of final wealth was a good idea. The idea of using log as a utility function was not new to Kelly and dates at least to Daniel Bernoulli in 1732. But Kelly, in an ad hoc math way, showed that it had good properties. Later Breiman (1960, 1961) cleaned up the math and showed the great long run properties:

1. Maximizing E log maximizes the rate of asset growth asymptotically, and
2. it minimizes the time to reach arbitrarily large goals.

This means that a log bettor, who is in competition with another bettor who bets differently infinitely often, will have arbitrarily more money than the other bettor as time goes to infinity. So the longer you play, the better log is, but we know from Chapter 4 that in the short run, log betting is extremely risky. Indeed the Ziemba-Hausch (1986) example discussed in Chapter 2 shows that you can make 700 bets on assets with a 14 % advantage, all independent, all with chance of winning of 0.19 to 0.57 and turn $ 1000 into $ 18. This is part of the Merton, Samuelson critique. Even if you play a long time and have a good advantage on every bet, you can still lose a lot. But, Kelly advocates like I am point to the great gains most of the time and the corrective action that you can take should you have a sequence of bad scenarios and the fact that in practice trading is financial engineering not pure financial economics. Even the great theorist Samuelson, a partner in the successful Commodities Corporation, does not appear to agree with this. See Samuelson (2006, 2007) and the response by Ziemba (2007) and especially by Thorp and Ziemba (2007).

Quibbles and minor errors – considerations for the revised edition

- Smarty Jones (page 69) was 4-1 not 5-1. The fair odds on Smarty were actually about 8-1. The $ 5 million which would be due Smarty if he won the Kentucky Derby (which he did) had to be hedged by Oaklawn Park which offered this bonus and the insurance companies including SCA which insured part of it. This hedging reduced Smarty's track odds to 4-1. It was not easy to hedge that bet especially as the Derby approached. Smarty Jones became America's horse just like Alysheba some years earlier. But both lost the Belmont; I think because of their high dosage. That is, their genetic heritage measured through key stallions called Chefs-de-race (see Bain et al, 2006) indicated that they did not have enough stamina to win the 1 1/2 mile Belmont. But the Kelly bet to place especially and show on Smarty that won was off the scale! Birdstone who won that Belmont was 30-1. Since he was the sole dual qualifier I felt his odds were more like 3-1.

- Man O'War (page 70) its edge/odds for bet here with Bernoulli ±1 bets. Man O'War lost one race to Upset so 100 % is not right. Man O'War once won a race by 100 lengths more than three times the margin Secretariat had in perhaps the greatest performance in history in the 1973 Belmont. If you want to visualize how great Man O'War was, go to the Kentucky horse park near Lexington and look at the stride of Secretariat and then look at John Henry's which is even longer. Then look at Man O'War's which is again a lot longer. Wow! This was the greatest racehorse of the 20th century. However, few horses ever have a 100 % chance of winning any race. Recall Barbaro's breakdown at the 2006 Preakness. On page 70, 99 % probability of winning yields 98 % Kelly bet (not 99 %) with Bernoulli ±1 bets. Northern Dancer, the greatest sire of the second half of the 20th century never was close to a 99 % chance of winning any of his races. 24 % on War Admiral – cannot tell as odds of winning not given, but it's not 24 %. On page 72, it's up to 30 % in exotics at some US tracks. Now large bettors have rebates so effective takes are about 10 % not 14–30 %. Japan's take is large but still some syndicates win well there. And that bastion of syndicates, Hong Kong, has high takes and no rebates until a new one was added in 2006 (if you bet 10 000 and lose you get a 10 % rebate).
- Buffett (page 124) acts as if he is a full Kelly bettor. Nice thing to add to the next edition. Ditto Keynes 80 % Kelly with $-w^{-0.25}$ in Ziemba (2003).
- Nobel Prize in Economics (page 127): it seems that recently they are going more to inefficient market research (Ackerlof, Spence, Smith, Stiglitz, even Engle and Granger) rather than efficient markets types such as Fama.
- Shannon (page 133) apparently he saw the Kelly formula as the mathematical essence (I would then add the word *risk*) arbitrage.
- Exotic bets (page 134) There are lots of exotic bets other than win, place and show. Infinite losses (page 144) for short calls not puts.
- Samuelson's critique (page 149) his JASA review was very unfair to Thorp and Thorp's later results verify this.
- Merton (page 162) – I thought Merton applied to 30 economics departments with only the one acceptance at MIT. Samuelson wanted a student with the *smoking gun* to find the *Black Scholes* formula. On page 163, Merton used the very advanced mathematical Ito calculus while Black-Scholes used the solved heat equation.
- Manny Ramirez (page 198) 0.349 is a bit high; even Ted Williams' was below this.
- Stocks (page 193) 20–30 stocks to cut portfolio risk in half is high. All you need is two independent assets. A: mean 1, var 1, B: mean 1, var 1 yields 1/2 A + 1/2 B: mean 1, var 1/2.
- Utility functions (page 212) the issue of when can you substitute utility function u_1 for u_2 and get correct results. The main result I know about is in Kallberg and Ziemba (1983). What you need is normal distributions (but symmetric will do the job) and the

same Rubinstein risk aversion measure. Rubinstein's measure is little known but it is optimal. Average Arrow-Pratt risk aversion works well empirically as a substitute. This idea is very powerful as it means that you can capture all concave utility functions with the average risk aversion index. You can just say $R_A = 4$ is pensions, $R_A = 8$ is very conservative and $R_A \approx 0$ is log. But this only works exactly with normal or symmetric assets.

- Airtight survival motive (page 213): my colleague Nils Hakansson's **airtight survival motive** is based on the idea that you cannot ever really lose all your money with a Kelly strategy. I rather prefer to adjust the Kelly fraction to stay above a wealth growth path. We are now implementing this in a London hedge fund where we use a convex penalty for movements below the wealth path. Getting anywhere near zero does not interest us, we want to stay above a nice path; see MacLean et al (2004) for a model of this. See Figure 5.1 for the idea.

- Pinball machine (page 214): this is ok but the Hausch-Ziemba simulation in Chapter 2 captures the issue better. I never liked those send 1000 letters, 500 say gains in January, 500 say it falls, 250 gains and 250 losses in February from the winners, etc – anti inefficient market arguments. They then conclude that a monkey could predict the monthly movements of the stock market over 12 months with probability (1/2)12. That's why they like index funds. Kelly people, of course, want superior returns.

- Error in JFQA, 1971 (page 218): Hakansson's error was a minor one and it did not affect the conclusions. Not infinitely often. An easy one for a non-mathematician to make (see Merton & Samuelson, 1974). A better solution is in Luenberger (1993). He shows that any investor with a long-term perspective, who cares only about the tail of the wealth sequence within a broad class of deterministic preferences, must trade off expected log and the variance of log.

- Geometric vs Arithmetic Means (page 220): I prefer my $100 \rightarrow 150$ (win 50 %) $\rightarrow 75$ (lost 50 %). The mean of zero is certainly not correct, and the -13.7% geometric mean captures this loss. Notice how winning and losing or losing then winning with Kelly yields a loss.

- *Non economists know nothing* (page 226): wow, what arrogance! Hakansson has PhD training in economics from UCLA as do I and other Kelly proponents. (I had five Nobels in economics as teachers in Berkeley and a few even smarter professors.) Kelly supporters also include Buffett even though he probably does not know it. But as a sometime insurance consultant for SCA a sports insurer, I know those Buffett bets have huge edges: lending the Williams company close to a billion at over 30+ % interest with good collateral is one example. Many $1 billion bets well diversifies Berkshire Hathaway. There is no LTCM overbetting there. Strategies like the one to stay above a wealth path like MacLean et al (2004) shown in Figure 5.1 help here as most of the growth is retained and with penalties you will be forced to be above the path almost all the time. I have been using this approach in ALM models since 1974; just have the penalties steeper and steeper, that is, convex. The calculations require accurate scenarios though so doing that will help in the analysis to avoid trouble.

- Poundstone is getting close to this on page 227 when he says **when the wager is too risky, the Kelly strategy stakes only a fraction of the bankroll in order to subdue the risk**. Here is would be better said as a lower Kelly fraction that will balance risk and return better using a calculation like that in MacLean et al (2004). Then he says **when an investment or trade carries no possibility of a total loss, the Kelly bettor may use** *leverage to achieve the maximal return*. Actually Hakansson and Miller (1975) proved that Kelly bettors never actually go bankrupt. Thus, even with bad scenarios there is something left.

- Violent Kelly wealth paths (page 228): yes, the full Kelly bettor will have a violent wealth path. That's why we use fractional strategies a lot, but not always, of course. One area that even our ad hoc method of calculating the fractional Kelly weights could be criticized is: what utility function is this equivalent to? My response is a modified log utility where penalties for losses are taken off.

  Unfortunately, I am part of this controversy with Merton and Samuelson who are advisors to my Handbook in Finance series. I think that the staying above a wealth path approach is a good compromise here. Then you get much smoother curves than that on page 228. Basically Thorp and Benter have a lot of this in their records. They are Kelly advocates but in actual bets, they likely frequently used fractional Kelly strategies, especially when parameters might be in error.

- Buffett and Kelly (page 230): re Buffett using Kelly-like strategies. I rather like Buffett's habit of making many large, at least by other peoples' standards, $ 1 billion bets with large advantages. When you have $ 140 billion, $ 1 billion is a small bet. But this does lead to some substantial losses – see Figures 7.1 and 7.2. I like the Hagstrom (2004) book and use it in my great investor lectures and courses but that analysis of Kelly and Buffett is anecdotal.

- Betting double Kelly (page 232): I like the discussion here but the graph is not in general symmetric; see MacLean, Ziemba and Blazenko (1992). Also see Markowitz's proof that twice the Kelly bet has a growth rate of zero (plus the risk free rate) at the end of Chapter 4 and Thorp (2006) who has a more general proof.

- Advice on Kelly (page 233): the statement by Thorp is a good way to think about risk-return tradeoffs:

  > Those individuals or institutions who are long term compounders should consider the possibility of using the Kelly criterion to asymptotically maximize the expected compound growth rate of their wealth. Investors with less tolerance for intermediate term risk may prefer to use a lesser fraction. Long term compounders ought to avoid using a greater fraction (*overbetting*). Therefore, to the extent that future probabilities are uncertain, long term compounders should further limit their investment fraction enough to prevent a significant risk of overbetting.

This brings one back to fractional Kelly strategies and how to compute then. The only real scientific paper on this is MacLean et al (2004) but even that can be criticized as it uses a Var approach. In actual implementations for hedge funds I use convex penalties.

- Probability of 29 % fall in the future on a single day is 1 in 10^{160} (page 236): maybe if you are a strict efficient market person. But my estimate after a week of $\pm 3 - 5$ % daily falls and smaller gains was more like 10 % for a giant fall and 50 % plus for a large fall. See the Friday before the October 1987 Wall Street Week interview with Marty Zweig. White as a sheet he said : 'I do not know if the Dow Jones average will fall 200 or 250 points on Monday but it's headed much lower'. It fell over 500 points from 2200 to 1700 area.

  Very few people in 2007 actually believe that each day's returns are completely independent of the past and drawn from an urn. Rubinstein well knows that much portfolio insurance, for example, was not executed by Friday's close so there had to be a lot of futures selling on Monday. While futures fell 29 %, the cash S&P500 only fell 22 %. So

I am most puzzled by his probability of a crash like that in 1987 of 1 in 10^{160}. My experience is that crashes usually occur after a period of high up and higher down volatility. In October 1987, the week before the crash, the market was up a lot, then down more in alternating days.

According to Poundstone, Rubinstein said

> So improbable is such an event that it would not be anticipated to occur even if the stock market were to last for 20 billion years, the upper end of the currently estimated duration of the universe. Indeed, such an event should not occur even if the stock market were to enjoy a rebirth for 20 billion years in each of 20 billion big bangs.

I will stick to my 10%. Rubinstein would do well to view the Zweig interview or read Taleb's books or Ziemba (2003) or this book.

- Risk arbitrage (page 241) is first mentioned here when it is all over the previous 240 pages.
- LTCM (page 284): LTCM used 'a sophisticated form of the industry standard Var'. A huge mistake! Var does not limit losses nor does it work in all scenarios. LTCM followed the recipe for disaster:

  1. overbet
  2. do not diversity in all scenarios

  and if a bad scenario hits you are wiped out, as they were. The scenario that hit them was *lack of confidence in financial assets*. This scenarios is sort of vague but it caused losses in all their trade areas. Multiple correlation scenario dependent matrices are needed or something equivalent; see Chapter 21 for more discussion.
- Mis-understanding Var (page 286): a Var report cannot address the question of what is the chance of losing everything? This needs to be fixed. It is known that LTCM did simulations and stress testing but with Var as your model, you are not well protected against bad scenarios.
- Shannon evidence (page 307): Poundstone is wearing me down. In the late 1950s through 1986 Shannon's return on his stock portfolio was about 28%. Pretty impressive!
- Factor models (page 308): in my factor model to rank the best to worst stocks on the Tokyo stock exchange; see Chapter 25, I found that future earnings/price was the best variable when averaged over three forecasting systems. It added a full 10%/year over the index. Also the usual PE ratio was in the top seven predictors. These models worked with stock prices rising in the 1980s and falling in the 1990s. Shannon seems to understand that earnings are crucial.
- The Shannon Portfolio (page 310): Teledyne (81% of portfolio) add Motorola (then over 90%) add Hewlett Packard (more than 98%). Little diversification. Shannon got good scenarios. I had a student at UBC who bought internet stocks in about 1996 for $2–3 per share. They went to $100 in 1999, then fell to $2–3 in 2001. He had a good scenario followed by a bad scenario. This does not mean that Shannon's gains were luck, but...Taleb might comment here.
- Haugen's crime (page 321): actually Jacobs and Levy (1988) is the original reference for the US. I redid this in Japan in 1989; see the discussion in Chapter 25 and the full paper by Schwartz and Ziemba (2000). Haugen discovered it much later. His real crime was not citing Jacobs and Levy and my work after I explained these things to him repeatedly.

This is typical sadly of modern academic finance. If it's not published in one of about five or perhaps 10 top journals, it does not exist! Haugen's work is solid and his factors are valuable. One thing he did differently than Jacobs and Levy, who have now a $20 billion plus firm, and I is the use of the same factors in all countries. I was surprised about this but his predictions seem to work.

- Sports betting (page 322): these behavioral factors probably are still not priced so now a non US person could bet them on Betfair or another betting exchange without going to a casino with better terms and do rather well.

- Complexity (page 324): complex means take account of your bet on the odds by using a nonlinear program with a non-convex (ratio) inside function. See the Hausch and Ziemba papers in Hausch et al (1994). My understanding is that it is 80 variables not 130.

- Shorting overpriced markets too soon (page 325): Woods is in good company. Soros funds lost $5 billion shorting the Nasdaq too soon. He also shorted the Nikkei in 1988, a year too early, well before the bond-stock model moved into the danger zone based on higher interest rates and higher price earnings ratios as prices rose.

- January (page 313): on the January effect in the futures markets, see Chapter 2 and the papers by Clark and Ziemba (1987) and Rendon and Ziemba (2007). I won on the Value Line/S&P trade (small-large cap) 14 straight years (1983/4 to 1997/8) till I taught it to Morgan Stanley with essentially infinite resources and decided to retire. Now there is little volume but the effect is still there.

  Roll made millions in a fund management company that priced factors and wrote one of the best early inefficient market papers on the January effect. I am puzzled why such a talented person and a data whiz could not win with anomalies (I taught with him at UCLA). I suspect it was easier to just manage large sums of money and collect fees rather than mess around with anomalies that seem to be there but change in various ways over time.

- Ooops, rethink this page (page 314): I disagree with the first paragraph. Factor models can be used by successful arbitragers and model crunching does add value. Also in the last paragraph I know that the Value Line usually works though not too well in 2006–7.

- Japanese warrants (page 318): see Shaw, Thorp and Ziemba (1995). This was my idea and execution, which I took to Thorp. Thorp and Shaw had major contributions to the analysis and Thorp won the over $1 million risk adjusted trading contest run by Barron's based on this trade. It's a long and interesting and successful story, which would add to the revised version. See Chapter 9 for a synopsis of the main points.

  Samuelson, whom I admire greatly and rate as the 20th century's greatest economist based on his own and his students' work as well as the contribution his ubiquitous textbook made to shaping an entire generation of economics students, wrote me a letter in 1988 regarding the Japanese stock market. By the way, I feel the most brilliant economist is Kenneth Arrow who has done seminal work and was unbelievable in seminars, even surpassing Samuelson, but he has had very few top students. Samuelson has trained Merton, Stiglitz, Shiller and many others. Anyway, Samuelson wrote that the Japanese stock market was held together with 'chewing gum'. He was right. It lost its stickiness. But I found, see Ziemba and Schwartz (1991) that it was economics that rules the Japanese market. Concepts such as anomalies in US markets were also found in Japan.

- Jim Simons of Renaissance: Jim Ax arranged for me to consult for a day on Kelly strategies in 1992. His $1.4 billion in fees in 2005 as the world's top hedge fund manager is very impressive as is his $1.6 billion 2006 paycheck which was the second highest.

So are the 5+44 fees and 60% gross, 30% net on $12 billion. I guess it is safe to say that he is another great investor and not into fully efficient markets.

NASSIM NICHOLAS TALEB

Nassim Nicholas Taleb, has a PhD in mathematics from the University of Paris (supervised by my colleague Professor Helyette Geman now at Birbeck College, University of London) and is co-presenter with Paul Wilmott of derivative courses based on many years of trading experience. Taleb is also now a professor at the University of Massachusetts in Amherst. I got my bachelor's degree in chemical engineering there, heard a great talk on operations research by University of Texas Professor Douglas Wilde who then headed to Stanford and I with great advice from Sidney Schloffer, my economics theory professor, headed to Berkeley, the then greatest university in the world. I have run out of space and time to say much but this is a must read and so is his new book on Black Swans. These are rare events that cannot be predicted that have a dramatic effect. He reminds you of fat tails and not to be overly impressed with winners and much more.

DAVID F. SWENSEN

As good as the Ford Foundation and the Harvard Endowment are, the Yale Endowment ranks right there at the top as we saw in Chapter 8. The endowment's chief investment officer is David F. Swensen, who also teaches at Yale. His earlier book, Swensen (2000), *Pioneering Portfolio Management: An Unconventional Approach to Institutional Investment* describes his approach and success at Yale. The current book is for individual investors and he argues against the use of active trading by profit-seeking mutual fund managers to produce satisfactory results for individual investors. He makes the case for exchange traded funds and index funds with low management fees. As an individual, it is hard to do what the professionals do but, of course, wealthy individuals can get results like the top professionals with hedge funds, private placements, real assets, etc. Swensen is a consultant to the Cambridge University Endowment. Cambridge and Oxford both did rather poorly during the 2000–3 stock market crash by listening too much to efficient market types and not enough to modelers like Swensen who is good at finding assets that go up in value especially through private placements and crash modelers like me whose signals kept investors out of that crash and the 22% fall in the S&P500 in 2002 early on. See Chapter 23 and also my AIMR monograph, *The Stochastic Programming Approach to Asset, Liability and Wealth Management*, 2003, especially Chapter 2 and appendix (thanks to Dr Alan King of IBM Research for the lovely review of this monograph in *Interfaces*, April 2005).

CLOSING THOUGHTS

I feel I have just scratched the surface of Poundstone's interesting book. This area of Kelly or capital growth is tremendously interesting and complex. Hence there was not much space for the other two excellent books. Chapter 8 discusses Swensen and Yale and other good university endowments.

POSTSCRIPT: THE RENAISSANCE MEDALLION FUND

The Medallion Fund uses mathematical ideas such as the Kelly criterion to run a superior hedge fund.[1] The staff of technical researchers and traders, working under mathematician James Simons, is constantly devising edges that they use to generate successful trades of various durations including many short term trades that enter and exit in seconds. The fund, whose size is in the $5–8 billion area, has very large fees (5% management and 44% incentive). Yearly fees are paid out so the fund does not grow much in size. Despite these fees and the large size of the fund, the net returns have been consistently outstanding, with a few small monthly losses and high positive monthly returns; see the histogram in Figure A1. Table A1 shows the monthly net returns from January 1993 to April 2005. There were only 17 monthly losses in 148 months and 3 losses in 49 quarters and no yearly losses in these 12+ years of trading in our data sample. The mean monthly, quarterly and yearly net returns, Sharpe and Symmetric Downside Sharpe ratios are shown in Table A2.[2]

We calculated the quarterly standard deviation for the DSSR by multiplying the monthly standard deviation by sqrt(3). The annual standard deviation for the DSSR was calculated by multiplying the quarterly standard deviation by 2 because there were no negative returns. All calculations use arithmetic means. We know from Ziemba (2005) that the results using geometric means will have essentially the same conclusions.

In Figure A3 we assumed that the fund had initial wealth of 100 dollars on Dec 31, 1992. Figures A2 and A3 show the monthly rates of return over time sorted in increasing order and the wealth graph over time assuming an initial wealth of 100 on December 31, 2002.

Medallion's outstanding yearly DSSR of 26.4 is the best we have seen even higher than Princeton Newport's 13.8 during 1969–1988. The yearly Sharpe of 1.68 is decent but not outstanding. The DSSR is needed to capture the true brilliance of this hedge fund.

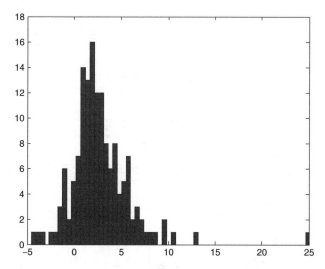

Figure A1   Histogram of monthly returns of the Medallion Fund, January 1993 to April 2005.

---

[1] WTZ is pleased to have had a minor role in teaching Simons about the Kelly criterion in 1992.

[2] Thanks to Ilkay Boduroglu for making these calculations. Recall that $DSSR = \frac{\overline{R}_p - R_f}{\sqrt{2}\sigma_{x-}}$, where $\sigma_{x-} = \frac{\sum_{t-1}^{T}(R_t - 0)^2}{T-1}$, so we forget about gains and only penalize losses then double that variance to get a full variance for all gains and losses.

Table A1 Net returns in percent of the Medallion Fund, January 1993 to April 2005, Yearly, Quarterly and Monthly

	1993	1994	1995	1996	1997	1998	1999	2000	2001	2002	2003	2004	2005
Annual													
	39.06	70.69	38.33	31.49	21.21	41.50	24.54	98.53	31.12	29.14	25.28	27.77	
Quarterly													
Q1	7.81	14.69	22.06	7.88	3.51	7.30	(0.25)	25.44	12.62	5.90	4.29	9.03	8.30
Q2	25.06	35.48	4.84	1.40	6.60	7.60	6.70	20.51	5.64	7.20	6.59	3.88	
Q3	4.04	11.19	3.62	10.82	8.37	9.69	6.88	8.58	7.60	8.91	8.77	5.71	
Q4	(0.86)	(1.20)	4.31	8.44	1.41	11.73	9.48	20.93	2.42	4.44	3.62	6.72	
Monthly													
January	1.27	4.68	7.4	3.25	1.16	5.02	3.79	10.5	4.67	1.65	2.07	3.76	2.26
February	3.08	5.16	7.54	1.67	2.03	1.96	−2.44	9.37	2.13	3.03	2.53	1.97	2.86
March	3.28	4.19	5.68	2.77	0.29	0.21	−1.49	3.8	5.36	1.12	−0.35	3.05	2.96
April	6.89	2.42	4.1	0.44	1.01	0.61	3.22	9.78	2.97	3.81	1.78	0.86	0.95
May	3.74	5.66	5.53	0.22	4.08	4.56	1.64	7.24	2.44	1.11	3.44	2.61	
June	12.78	25.19	−4.57	0.73	1.36	2.28	1.71	2.37	0.15	2.13	1.24	0.37	
July	3.15	6.59	−1.28	4.24	5.45	−1.1	4.39	5.97	1	5.92	1.98	2.2	
August	−0.67	7.96	5.91	2.97	1.9	4.31	1.22	3.52	3.05	1.68	2.38	2.08	
September	1.54	−3.38	−0.89	3.25	0.85	6.33	1.15	−1.02	3.38	1.13	4.18	1.33	
October	1.88	−2.05	0.3	6.37	−1.11	5.33	2.76	6.71	1.89	1.15	0.35	2.39	
November	−1.51	−0.74	2.45	5.93	−0.22	2.26	5.42	8.66	0.17	1.42	1.42	3.03	
December	−1.2	1.62	1.52	−3.74	2.77	3.73	1.06	4.3	0.35	1.81	1.81	1.16	

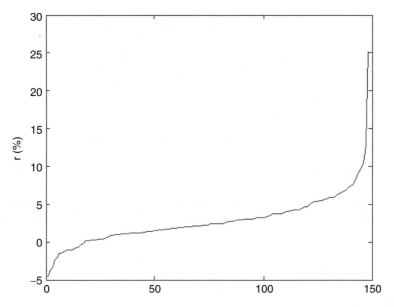

Figure A2   Monthly rates of return in increasing order, Medallion Fund, January 1993 to April 2005

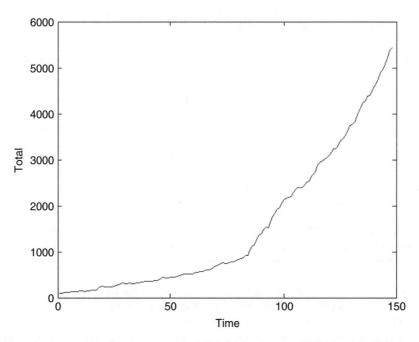

Figure A3   Wealth over time, Medallion Fund, January 1993 to April 2005

Table A2   Sharpe and Downside Symmetric Sharpe
Ratios for the Medallion Fund, January 1993 to April
2005

	Yearly	Quarterly	Monthly
SR	1.68	1.09	0.76
DSSR	26.4	11.6	2.20
Rate			

Table A3   Annualized T-bill interest rates in %, January 1993 to April 2005, Yearly, Quarterly and
Monthly

	1993	1994	1995	1996	1997	1998	1999	2000	2001	2002	2003	2004	2005
Annual													
	3.33	4.98	5.69	5.23	5.36	4.85	4.76	5.86	3.36	1.68	1.05	1.56	3.39
Quarterly													
Q1	2.99	3.27	5.77	4.94	5.06	5.07	4.41	5.53	4.85	1.71	1.14	0.90	2.56
Q2	2.98	4.05	5.61	5.04	5.08	5.00	4.43	5.75	3.70	1.71	1.05	1.06	
Q3	3.02	4.52	5.38	5.13	5.06	4.89	4.67	6.00	3.25	1.63	0.92	1.48	
Q4	3.08	5.31	5.28	4.97	5.08	2.30	5.05	6.03	1.93	1.36	0.91	2.01	
Monthly	1993	1994	1995	1996	1997	1998	1999	2000	2001	2002	2003	2004	2005
January	2.99	3.14	5.46	5.16	5.00	5.07	4.33	5.21	5.63	1.85	1.28	0.91	2.18
February	2.99	3.21	5.62	5.05	5.03	5.07	4.37	5.37	5.24	1.78	1.21	0.91	2.36
March	2.99	3.27	5.77	4.94	5.06	5.07	4.41	5.53	4.85	1.71	1.14	0.90	2.54
April	2.99	3.53	5.72	4.97	5.07	5.05	4.41	5.61	4.45	1.71	1.11	0.95	2.65
May	2.98	3.79	5.67	5.01	5.07	5.02	4.42	5.68	4.05	1.71	1.08	1.01	
June	2.98	4.05	5.61	5.04	5.08	5.00	4.43	5.75	3.66	1.71	1.05	1.06	
July	2.99	4.21	5.54	5.07	5.07	4.96	4.51	5.83	3.52	1.68	1.00	1.20	
August	3.00	4.36	5.46	5.10	5.07	4.92	4.59	5.92	3.39	1.66	0.96	1.34	
September	3.02	4.52	5.38	5.13	5.06	4.89	4.67	6.00	3.25	1.63	0.92	1.48	
October	3.04	4.78	5.34	5.08	5.07	4.69	4.80	6.01	2.81	1.54	0.92	1.66	
November	3.06	5.05	5.31	5.03	5.07	4.49	4.93	6.02	2.37	1.45	0.91	1.83	
December	3.08	5.31	5.28	4.97	5.08	4.30	5.05	6.03	1.93	1.36	0.91	2.01	

Jim Simon's Medallion fund is near or at the top of the worlds most successful hedge funds.
Indeed Simons' $1.4 billion in 2005 was the highest in the world for hedge fund managers
and his $1.6 billion in 2006 was second best. Since the fund is closed to all but about six
outside investors plus employees we watch with envy but Renaissance's new $100 billion
fund accepts qualified investors and other funds are planned.

Bibliography

Abaffy, J., M. Bertocchi, J. Dupačová, and V. Moriggia (2000) On generating scenarios for bond portfolios. *Bulletin of the Czech Econometric Society* (Feb), 3–27.

Ackermann, C., R. McEnally, and D. Ravenscraft (1999) The performance of hedge funds: Risk, return and incentives. *Journal of Finance* **54**, 833–874.

Agarwal, V., N. D. Daniel, and N. Y. Naik (2002) Determinants of money-flow and risk-taking behavior in the hedge fund industry. Working paper, London Business School.

Agarwal, V. and N. Y. Naik (1999) On taking the alternative route: Risks, rewards, style and performance persistence of hedge funds. *Journal of Alternative Investments* 2(4), 6–23.

Agarwal, V. and N. Y. Naik (2000) Multi-period performance persistence analysis of hedge funds. *Journal of Financial and Quantitative Analysis* **35**, 327–342.

Agarwal, V. and N. Y. Naik (2005) *Hedge funds*, Volume 1(2) of *Foundation and Trends in Finance*. NOW Publishers, Boston, MA.

Algoet, P. H. and T. Cover (1988) Asymptotic optimality and asymptotic equipartition properties of log-optimum investment. *Annals of Probability* 16(2), 876–898.

Ang, A., M. Rhodes-Kropf, and R. Zhao (2006) Do funds-of-funds deserve their fees-on-fees? Technical report, Columbia business School.

Arrowstreet (2005) Investment outlook. *Arrowstreet Journal* (February).

Aucamp, D. (1993) On the extensive number of plays to achieve superior performance with the geometric mean strategy. *Management Science* **39**, 1163–1172.

Aumann, R. J. (2005) War and peace. Nobel Lecture, December 8, 2005 and ETH, Zurich Lecture, November 20, 2006.

Bain, R., D. B. Hausch, and W. T. Ziemba (2006) An application of expert information to win betting on the Kentucky Derby, 1981-2001. *European Journal of Finance* **12**, 283–301.

Baquero, G. and M. Verbeek (2005) Survival, look-ahead bias and persistence in hedge fund performance. *Journal of Financial and Quantitative Analysis* **40**, 493–517.

Baquero, G. and M. Verbeek (2006) Do sophisticated investors believe in the law of small numbers? Technical report, Erasmus University Rotterdam.

Barclays Capital (2006) Icelandic Banks, 11 April.

Bawa, V. (1975) Optimal rules for ordering uncertain prospects. *Journal of Financial Economics* 2(March), 95–121.

Bawa, V. (1978) Safety first, stochastic dominance and optimal portfolio choice. *Journal of Finance and Quantitative Analysis* 13(June), 255–271.

Bawa, V. and E. Lindenberg (1977) Capital market equilibrium in a mean, lower partial moment framework. *Journal of Financial Economics* 5(Nov), 189–200.

BBC online (2007) http://news.bbc.co.uk/2/hi/business/3649187.stm.

Bell, R. M. and T. M. Cover (1980) Competitive optimality of logarithmic investment. *Math of Operations Research* **5**, 161–166.

Berge, K., G. Consigli, and W. T. Ziemba (2007) The predictive ability of the bond stock earnings yield differential. *Journal of Portfolio Management in press*.

Berge, K. and W. T. Ziemba (2006) The predictive ability of the bond stock earnings yield differential in worldwide equity markets, 1970-2005. Technical report, Sauder School of Business, University of British Columbia.

Berkelaar, A., H. Hoek, and A. Lucas (2002) Arbitrage and sampling uncertainty in financial stochastic programming models. Technical report, Erasmus University.

Bernanke, B. S. (2005) Comment. In B. S. Bernanke and M. Woodford (Eds.), *The Inflation-Targeting Debate*, pp. 293–998. University of Chicago Press, Chicago, IL.

Bicksler, J. L. and Thorp, E. O. (1973) The Capital Growth model: An Empirical Investigation. *Journal of Financial and Quantitative Analysis*, March, 273–287.

Birge, J. R. and F. Louveaux (1997) *Stochastic Programming*. Springer Verlag.

Black, R., E. Derman, and W. Toy (1990) A one-factor model of interest rates and its application to treasury bond options. *Financial Analysts Journal, Jan-Feb*, 33–39.

Blake, D., B. N. Lehmann, and A. .Timmermann (1999) Asset allocation dynamics and pension fund performance. *Journal of Business* **72**, 429–461.

Bloomberg (2006).

Blustein, P. (2005) *And the money kept flowing in (and out): Wall Street, the IMF and the Bankrupting of Argentina*. Public Affairs, New York.

Boender, G. C. E. (1997) A hybrid simulation/optimisation scenario model for asset liability management. *European Journal of Operational Research* **99**, 126–135.

Boender, G. C. E., P. van Aalst, and F. Heemskerk (1998) Modeling and management of assets and liabilities of pension plans in The Netherlands. In W. Ziemba and J. Mulvey (Eds.), *World Wide Asset and Liability Modeling*, pp. 561–580. Cambridge University Press.

Breiman, L. (1961) Optimal gambling system for favorable games. *Proceedings of the 4th Berkeley Symposium on Mathematical Statistics and Probability* **1**, 63–8.

Brinson, B., L. R. Hood, and G. L. Beebower (1986) Determinants of portfolio performance. *Financial Analysts Journal* **42**, 39–45.

Brown, S. J., W. N. Goetzman, and J. Park (2001) Careers and survival: Competition and risk in the hedge fund and CTA industry. *Journal of Finance* **56**, 1869–1886.

Brown, S. J., W. N. Goetzmann, and R. G. Ibbotson (1999) Offshore hedge funds: Survival and performance, 1989-95. *Journal of Business* **72**, 91–118.

Brown, S. J., W. N. Goetzmann, R. G. Ibbotson, and S. Ross (1992) Survivorship bias in performance studies. *Review of Financial Studies* **5**, 553–580.

Browne (1997) Survival and growth with a fixed liability: optimal portfolios in continuous time. *Math of Operations Research* **22**, 468–493.

Bruno, C. and D. Chudnovsky (Eds.) (2003) *Por que sucedió? : Las causas económicas de la reciente crisis argentina*. Argentina Editores, Buenos Aires.

Burton, J. (2007) Mapping the next China syndrome. www.marketwatch.com.

Burton, K. and J. Strasburg (2006) Amaranth plans to stay in business, Maounis says. Bloomberg News, 9/06.

Campbell, J. Y. and L. M. Viceira (2001) Who should buy long-term bonds? *American Economic Review* **91**, 99–127.

Campbell, J. Y. and T. Vuolteenaho (2004) Inflation illusion and stock prices? *American Economic Review* **94**, 19–23.

Cao, J., M. S. Ho, D. W. Jorgenson, R. Ruoen, L. Sun and X. Yue (2007) Industrial and aggregate measures of productivity growth in China, 1982–2000, Working paper, Harvard University (June 12).

Cariño, D., R. Myers, and W. T. Ziemba (1998) Concepts, technical issues and uses of the Russell-Yasuda Kasai financial planning model. *Operations Research* **46**, 450–462.

Cariño, D. and W. T. Ziemba (1998) Formulation of Russell-Yasuda Kasai financial planning model. *Operations Research* **46**, 433–449.

Cariño, D. R., T. Kent, D. H. Myers, C. Stacy, M. Sylvanus, A. L. Turner, K. Watanabe, and W. T. Ziemba (1994) The Russell-Yasuda Kasai model: An asset/liability model for a japanese insurance company using multistage stochastic programming. *Interfaces* **24**, 29–49.

Carpenter, J. (2000) Does option compensation increase managerial risk appetite? *Journal of Finance* **55**, 2311–2331.

Cecchetti, S. G. (2006) Measuring the macroeconomic risks posed by asset price booms. NBER Working Paper 12542, September.

Central Bank of Iceland (2005) Economy of Iceland (November).

Central Bank of Iceland (2006a). Financial Stability, Volume 2 (May).

Central Bank of Iceland (2006b). Monetary Bulletin, Volume 18:1 (March).

Central Bank of Iceland (2006) Statistical Year Book.

Cevik, S. (2007) Pegged Imbalances, Morgan Stanley May 31.

Chan, K. C., G. A. Karolyi, F. Longstaff, and A. B. Sanders (1992) An empirical comparison of alternative models of the short term interest rate. *Journal of Finance* **47**, 1209–1227.

Chan, K. L., K. C.Wei, and J. Wang (2003) Under pricing and long term performance of IPOs in China. *Journal of Corporate Finance*. **10**, 409–430

Chan, N., M. Getmansky, S. M. Haas, and A. W. Lo (2006) Systemic risk and hedge funds. *Economic Review 91*(4), 49–80.

Chopra, V. K. and W. T. Ziemba (1993) The effect of errors in mean, variance and co-variance estimates on optimal portfolio choice. *Journal of Portfolio Management* **19**, 6–11.

Chow, G. C. (2007) *China's Economic Transformation, Blackwell Publishers*. 2nd Edition.

Chow, G. C. and C. C. Lawler (2003) A time series analysis of the Shanghai and New York stock price indices. Mimeo, Princeton University Economics Department.

Chua, J. H. and R. S. Woodward (1983) J.M. Keynes' investment performance: a note. *Journal of Finance 38*(1), 232–235.

Clark, R. and W. T. Ziemba (1988) Playing the turn-of-the-year effect with index futures. *Operations Research XXXV*, 799–813.

Clifford, S. W., K. F. Kroner, and L. B. Siegel (2001) In pursuit of performance: the greatest return stories ever told. *Investment Insights, Barclays Global Investor 4*(1), 1–25.

Coleman, N. and C. Levin (2006) The role of market speculation in rising oil and gas prices: A need to put the cop back on the beat. U. S. Senate Permanent Subcommitee on Investigations, Committee on Homeland Security and Governmental Affairs, Staff Report, June 27.

Constantinides, G. M. (2002) Rational asset prices. *Journal of Finance* **57**, 1567–1591.

Crouhy, M., D. Galai, and R. Mark (2001) *Risk management*. McGraw Hill.

Crouhy, M., D. Galai, and R. Mark (2006) *The essentials of risk management*. McGraw Hill.

Davis, A. (2006) How giant bets on natural gas sank brash hedge-fund trader. *Wall Street Journal*, 9/19/06.

Davis, A., H. Sender, and G. Zuckerman (2006) What went wrong at Amaranth. *Wall Street Journal*, September 20.

Davis, A., G. Zuckerman, and H. Sender (2007) Hedge fund hardball: amid Amaranth's crisis, other players profited. *Wall Street Journal*, January 20.

Davis, N. (2003) Ned Davis Research Update on the S&P500.

DeBondt, W. F. M. and R. Thaler (1985) Does the stock market over react? *Journal of Finance* **40**, 793–805.

DeBondt, W. F. M. and R. Thaler (1987) Further evidence of investor over reaction and stock market seasonality. *Journal of Finance* **42**, 557–581.

Dempster, M. A. H., I. V. Evstigneev, and K. R. Schenk-Hoppé (2003) Exponential growth of fixed mix assets in stationary markets. *Finance and Stochastics 7*(2), 263–276.

Derman, E. (2006) *My life as a quant: reflections on physics and finance*. John Wiley & Sons Inc, Hoboken.

DeRosa, D. (2004) Yuan peg presents china with monetary dilemma. Bloomberg on-line, April 15.

Dimson, E., P. Marsh, and M. Staunton (2002) *Triumph of The Optimists: 101 Years of Global Investment Returns*. Princeton University Press, Princeton.

Dimson, E., P. Marsh, and M. Staunton (2006) *The Global Investment Returns Yearbook*. ABN-Ambro.

Duffie, D. and K. Singleton (2003) *Credit risk modeling*. Princeton University Press, Princeton.

Dunbar, N. (2000) *Inventing Money: The Story of Long Term Capital Management and the Legends Behind It*. John Wiley & Sons, Ltd, Chichester.

Dupačová, J., G. Consigli, and S. W. Wallace (2000) Scenarios for multistage stochastic programs. *Annals of Operations Research* **100**, 25–53.

Dybvig, P. H., H. K. Farnsworth, and J. N. Carpenter (2000) Portfolio performance and agency. Working paper, Washington University in Saint Louis.

Edwards, F. R. (1999) Hedge funds and the collapse of Long Term Capital Management. *Journal of Economic Perspectives* (Spring), 189–210.

Eklund, R. (2007) Predicting recessions with leading indicators: an application on the Icelandic edonomy. Technical Report 33, Central Bank of Iceland.

Embrechts, P. (2000) Actuarial versus financial pricing of insurance. *Journal of Risk Finance 1*(4), 17–26.

Embrechts, P., S. Resnick, and G. Samovodmitsky (1998) Living on the edge. *Risk 11*(1), 96–100.

Ethier, S. (1987) The proportional bettor's fortune. Proceedings 7th International Conference on Gambling and Risk Taking, Department of Economics, University of Nevada, Reno.

Ethier, S. and S. Tavaré (1983) The proportional bettor's return on investment. *Journal of Applied Probability* **20**, 563–573.

Fama, E. F. and K. R. French (1992) The cross-section of expected stock returns. *Journal of Finance* **47**, 427–265.

Figlewiski, S. (1989) What does an option pricing model tell us about option prices. *Financial Analysts Journal 45*(5), 12–15.

Figlewiski, S. (1994) How to lose money in derivatives. *Journal of Derivatives* (Winter), 75–82.

Finkelstein, M. and R. Whitley (1981) Optimal strategies for repeated games. *Advanced Applied Probability* **13**, 415–428.

Fischer, S. (2001) Exchange rate regimes: is the bipolar view correct? *Journal of Economic Perspectives 15*(2), 3–14.

Fishburn, P. C. (1977) Mean-risk analysis with risk associated with below target returns. *American Economic Review 76*(March), 116–126.

Fogel, R. W. (2005) Why China is likely to achieve its growth objectives, NBER WP 12122.

Fogel, R. W. (2007) Capitalism and democracy in 2040: forecasts and speculations, NBER 1314, June.

Forsyth, R. W. (2006) Generating returns isn't merely an academic question? *Wall Street Journal, September 29*.

Fung, W. and D. Hsieh (1997) Empirical characteristics of dynamic trading strategies: The case of hedge funds. *Review of Financial Studies* **10**, 275–302.

Fung, W. and D. Hsieh (2001) The risk in hedge fund strategies: Theory and evidence from trend followers. *Review of Financial Studies* **14**, 313–341.

Fung, W., D. A. Hsieh, N. Y. Naink, and T. Ramadorai (2006) Hedge funds: Performance, risk and capital formation. Technical report, London Business School.

Galiani, S., D. Heymann, and M. Tommasi (2003) Great expectations and hard times: The Argentine convertibility plan. *Economia 3*(2), 109–147.

Gallagher, S. and A. Markowska (2007) One conundrum answered, another one arises, *Societe Generale*, June 18.

Getmansky, M., A. W. Lo, and I. Makarov (2004) An econometric model of serial correlation and illiquidity in hedge fund returns. *Journal of Financial Economics* **74**, 529–609.

Geyer, A., W. Herold, K. Kontriner, and W. T. Ziemba (2002) The Innovest Austrian pension fund financial planning model InnoALM. Working paper, UBC.

Geyer, A. and W. T. Ziemba (2007) The Innovest Austrian pension fund planning model InnoALM. *Operations Research, forthcoming*.

Gibson, R. (Ed.) (2000) *Model Risk: Concepts, Calibration and Pricing*. Risk Books.

Gifford, H. and Fong (2005) *The world of hedge funds: characteristics and analysis*. World Scientific.

Glitnir (2006a). The Icelandic economy, June.

Glitnir (2006b). List of Available Funds, May.

Goetzmann, W., J. Ingersoll, M. Spiegel, and I. Welch (2002) Sharpening Sharpe ratios. Working paper, Yale School of Management.

Goetzmann, W. N., J. E. Ingersoll, and S. A. Ross (2003) High-water marks and hedge fund management contracts. *Journal of Finance 58*(4), 1685–1717.

Goetzmann, W. N., J. Ingersoll, Jr., and S. A. Ross (1998) High water marks. Working paper, Yale School of Management.

Gold, R. (2006) On a roller coaster, one energy firm tries hedging bets. *Wall Street Journal*, November 6, 2006.

Goldman, M. B. (1974) A negative report on the 'near optimality' of the max-expected log policy and applied to bounded utilities for long-lived programs. *Journal of Financial Economics* **1**, 97–103.

Gopinath, D. (2006) Niederhoffer, humbled by '97 blowup, posts 56 percent return. Bloomberg News, 05–31.

Green, S. (2007) The real deal on China's new mega fund, *Businessweek*, March 26.

Gregoriou, G. N. (Ed.) (2006) *Fund of Hedge Funds: Performance, Assessment, Diversification and Statistical Properties*. Elsevier.

Griffin, P. (1985) Different measures of win rates for optimal proportional betting. *Management Science* **30**, 1540–1547.

Guha, K. (2007) US way of Soverign Wealth Funds, *Financial Times*, June 20.

Hagstrom, R. G. (2004) *The Warren Buffett Way*. John Wiley & Sons, Inc, Hoboken.

Haitao, Z. and R. Ruoen (2007) International comparison of TFP level based on TT index between China and Japan, Working Paper, Beihang University (February 14).

Hakansson, N. H. (1971a). Capital growth theory and the mean-variance approach to portfolio selection. *Journal of Financial and Quantitative Analysis* **6**, 517–557.

Hakansson, N. H. (1971b). Multi-period mean-variance analysis: toward a general theory of portfolio choice. *Journal of Finance* **26**, 857–884.

Hakansson, N. H. and B. Miller (1975) Compound-return mean-variance efficient portfolios never risk ruin. *Management Science* **22**, 391–400.

Hakansson, N. H. and W. T. Ziemba (1995) Capital growth theory. In R. A. Jarrow, V. Maksimovic, and W. T. Ziemba (Eds.), *Finance Handbook*, pp. 123–44. North-Holland.

Harlow, W. V. (1991) Asset allocation in a downside-risk framework. *Financial Analysts Journal* (September-October), 28–40.

Harlow, W. V. and R. K. S. Rao (1989) Asset pricing in a generalized mean-lower partial moment framework: theory and evidence. *Journal of Financial and Quantitative Analysis* **24**(3), 285–311.

Harvey, C. (2003) Slides for talk. *Campus for Finance* (January).

Haug, E. (2006) *Derivatives Models on Models*. John Wiley & Sons, Ltd, Chickester.

Hausch, D. B., V. Lo, and W. T. Ziemba (Eds.) (1994) *Efficiency of Racetrack Betting Markets*. Academic Press, San Diego.

Heath, D., R. Jarrow, and A. Morton (1992) Bond pricing and the term structure of interest rates: a new methodology. *Econometrica* **60**.

Heinkel, R. and N. M. Stoughton (1994) The dynamics of portfolio management contracts. *Review of Financial Studies* **7**, 351–387.

Hensel, C. R., D. D. Ezra, and J. H. Ilkiw (1991) The importance of the asset allocation decision. *Financial Analysts Journal July/August*, 65–72.

Hensel, C. R. and W. T. Ziemba (1995) US small and large capitalized stocks, bonds and cash returns during Democratic and Republican administrations, 1928-1993. *Financial Analysts Journal* **51**(2), 61–69.

Hensel, C. R. and W. T. Ziemba (2000) How did Clinton stand up to history? US stock market returns and presidential party affiliations. In D. B. Keim and W. T. Ziemba (Eds.), *Security market imperfections in world wide equity markets*, pp. 203–217. Cambridge University Press.

Herbertsson, T. (2006) Collective pension arrangements: the case of ieland. paper prepared for the OECD.

Herbertsson, T. and G. Zoega (2006) On the fringe of Europe: Iceland's currency dilemma. CESifo Forum, 2 February.

Heyde (1963) *J. Royal Statistical Society B* **25**, 392.

Hilsenrath, J. E., K. A. J. Dunham, and T. Aeppel (2005) Katrina, fuel costs augur consumer-price climb. *The Wall Street Journal September 9*, A2.

Hochreiter, R. and G. C. Pflug (2003) Scenario generation for stochastic multi-stage decision processes as facility location problems. Technical report, Department of Statistics and Decision Support Systems, University of Vienna.

Høyland, K., M. Kaut, and S. W. Wallace (2001) A heuristic for generating scenario trees for multi-stage decision problems. Stochastic programming e-print series.

Høyland, K. and S. W. Wallace (2001) Generating scenario tress for multistage decision problems. *Management Science* **47**, 295–307.

Hua, J. and L. Jianxin (2007) Petro China to raise $6 billion on Shanghai Exchange, Reuters, June 20.

Ibbotson, R. and P. Chen (2003) Long-run stock returns: participating in the real economy. *Financial Analysts Journal* **59**, 88–98.

Ibison, D. (2006) An unhappy chain of events but nothing is broken. *Financial Times, July 21*.

IMF Staff Report (2006) Iceland-2006 Article IV Consultation, Concluding Statement, May 15.

Invest in Iceland Agency (2006) Financial System in Iceland.

Jacobs, B. I. and K. N. Levy (1988) Disentangling equity return regularities: new insights and investment opportunities. *Financial Analysts Journal* **44**, 18–43.

Jagannathan, R., A. Malakhov, and D. Novikov (2006) Do hot hands persist among hedge fund managers? an empirical evaluation. Technical report, Northwestern University.

Jamshidian, F. and Y. Zhu (1977) Scenario simulation: theory and methodology. *Finance and Stochastics* **1**, 43–76.

Jegadeesh, N. and S. Titman (1993a). Returns to buying winners and selling losers: Implications for stock market efficiency. *Journal of Finance* **48**, 65–91.

Jegadeesh, N. and S. Titman (1993b). Returns to buying winners and selling losers: Implications for stock market efficiency. *Journal of Finance* **48**, 65–91.

Jobst, N. J. and S. A. Zenios (2003) Tracking bond indices in an integrated market and credit risk environment. *Quantitative Finance* **3**(2), 117–135.

Jorion, P. (2000) Risk management lessons from Long-Term Capital Management. *European Financial Management* **6**, 277–300.

Jorion, P. (2007) *Value-at-Risk: The new benchmark for controlling market risk* (3 ed.). Irwin, Chicago.

Kaletsky, A. (2007) Beijing's shift to equities can move markets. Timesonline, February 12.

Kallberg, J. G., R. White, and W. T. Ziemba (1982) Short term financial planning under uncertainty. *Management Science XXVIII*, 670–682.

Kallberg, J. G. and W. T. Ziemba (1981) Remarks on optimal portfolio selection. In G. Bamberg and Opitz (Eds.), *Methods of Operations Research, Oelgeschlager*, Volume 44, pp. 507–520. Gunn and Hain.

Kallberg, J. G. and W. T. Ziemba (1983) Comparison of alternative utility functions in portfolio selection problems. *Management Science* **29**(11), 1257–1276.

Kallberg, J. G. and W. T. Ziemba (1984) Mis-specifications in portfolio selection problems. In G. Bamberg and K. Spremann (Eds.), *Risk and Capital*, pp. 74–87. Springer Verlag, New York.

Kaminsky, G. L., S. Lizondo, and C. Reinhart (1998) Leading indicators of currency crises. *IMF Staff Papers 45 (1), March*, p 1–48.

Kaupthing Bank (2006) Monthly Inflation Forecast, July 30.

Keefer, D. L. (1994) Certainty equivalents for three-point discrete-distribution approximations. *Management Science* **40**, 760–773.

Keefer, D. L. and S. E. Bodily (1983) Three-point approximations for continuous random variables. *Management Science* **29**, 595–609.

Keim, D. B. and W. T. Ziemba (Eds.) (2000) *Security Market Imperfections in World Wide Equity Markets*. Cambridge University Press.

Kelly, Jr., J. R. (1956) A new interpretation of information rate. *Bell System Technical Journal* **35**, 917–926.

Kelly, K., S. Ng and D. Reilly (2007) Two big funds at Bear Stearns face shutdown, Wall Street Journal, June 20.

Kingsland, L. (1982) Projecting the financial condition of a pension plan using plan simulation analysis. *Journal of Finance* **37**(2), 577–584.

Knight, J. and S. Satchell (2005) A re-examination of Sharpe's ratio for log-normal prices. *Applied Mathematical Finance* **12**(1), 87–100.

Koivu, M., T. Pennanen, and W. T. Ziemba (2005) Cointegration analysis of the Fed model. *Finance Research Letters* **2**, 248–259.

Koliman, J. (1998) The rise and fall of Victor Neiderhoffer. *Derivatives Strategy* **3**(1), 38–41.

Kouwenberg, R. (1999) Scenario generation and stochastic programming models for asset liability management. *European Journal of Operational Research* **134**, 51–64.

Kouwenberg, R. (2003) Do hedge funds add value to a passive portfolio: Correcting for non-normal returns and disappearing funds. *Journal of Asset Management* **3**, 361–382.

Kouwenberg, R. and S. A. Zenios (2006) Stochastic programming models for asset liability management. In S. A. Zenios and W. T. Ziemba (Eds.), *Handbook of asset and liability management*, Volume 1: Theory and Methodology of *Handbooks in Finance*. North Holland, 253–303.

Kouwenberg, R. and W. T. Ziemba (2007) Incentives and risk taking in hedge funds. *Journal of Banking and Finance (in press)*.

Kritzman, M. (1992) What practitioners need to know about currencies. *Financial Analysts Journal* (March-April), 27–30.

Kupiec, P. (1995) Techniques for verifying the accuracy of risk measurement models. *Journal of Derivatives* (December).

Kusy, M. I. and W. T. Ziemba (1986) A bank asset and liability management model. *Operations Research 34*(3), 356–376.

Kyle, A. S. and W. Xiong (2001) Contagion as a wealth effect. *Journal of Finance 56*(4), 1401–1440.

Ladman, P. (2006) Amaranth: the lawsuits. *Wall Street Journal*, October 20, 2006.

LaHart, J. (2006) Amaranth trader dreams of second act after loss. *Wall Street Journal*, October 28.

Lakonishok, J., A. Shleifer, and R. Vishny (1992) The structure and performance of the money management industry. *Brookings Papers on Economic Activity Microeconomics*, 229–91.

Latané, H. (1959) Criteria for choice among risky ventures. *Journal of Political Economy* **67**, 144–155.

Lawrence, R. Z. (2006) A US-Middle East Trade Agreement: A Circle of Opportunity? Working Paper: Peterson Institute for International Economics, November.

Liang, B. (1998) On the performance of hedge funds. *Financial Analysts Journal (July/August)*, 72–85.

Liu, J. and F. A. Longstaff (2000) Losing money on arbitrages: Optimal dynamic portfolio choice in markets with arbitrage opportunities. Working paper, UCLA.

Lo, A. (1999) The three p's of total risk management. *Financial Analysts Journal 55*(1), 13–26.

Lo, A. (2001) Risk management for hedge funds: introduction and overview. *Financial Analysts Journal 57*(6), 16–33.

Lo, A. W. (2002) The statistics of Sharpe ratios. *Financial Analysts Journal* **56**, 36–52.

Lo, C. (2007) Bond bear awakening, *Finance Asia*, June 20.

Lim, T., A. W. Lo, R. C. Merton and M. S. Scholes (2006) *The Derivatives Sourcebook*. NOW Publishers.

Locke, P. (2006) Natural gas price transparency and liquidity. Prepared for the Natural Gas Supply Association, Washington, D. C.

Loewenstein, M. and G. A. Willard (2000) Convergence trades and liquidity: A model of hedge funds. Working paper, Massachusetts Institute of Technology.

Luenberger, D. G. (1993) A preference foundation for log mean-variance criteria in portfolio choice problems. *Journal of Economic Dynamics and Control* **17**, 887–906.

Luenberger, D. G. (1998) *Investment Science*. Oxford University Press.

MacLean, L., R. Sanegre, Y. Zhao, and W. T. Ziemba (2004) Capital growth with security. *Journal of Economic Dynamics and Control 28*(4), 937–954.

MacLean, L. and W. T. Ziemba (1999) Growth versus security tradeoffs in dynamic investment analysis. *Annals of Operations Research* **85**, 193–227.

MacLean, L., W. T. Ziemba, and G. Blazenko (1992) Growth versus security in dynamic investment analysis. *Management Science* **38**, 1562–85.

MacLean, L., W. T. Ziemba, and Y. Li (2005) Time to wealth goals in capital accumulation and the optimal trade-off of growth versus security. *Quantitative Finance 5*(4), 343–357.

MacLean, L. C. and W. T. Ziemba (2006) Capital growth theory and practice. In S. A. Zenios and W. T. Ziemba (Eds.), *Handbook of asset and liability management*, Handbooks in Finance. North Holland.

Madisson, A. (1998) China's economic performance in the long run, OECD.

Maddision, A. (2005) Evidence submitted to the Select Committee on Economic Affairs, House of Lords, London for the inquiry into "Aspects of the economics of climate change."

Mahieu, R. and P. Schotman (1994) Neglected common factors in exchange rate volatility. *Journal of Empirical Finance 1*, 279–311.

Malkiel, B. G. and A. Saha (2005) Hedge funds: risk and return. *Financial Analysts Journal 61*(6), 80–88.

Manchester Trading, LLC (2006) MARHedge, San Francisco.

Mao, J. (1970) Models of capital budgeting, e-v vs. e-s. *Journal of Financial and Quantitative Analysis 5* (Jan), 657–675.

Maranjian, S. (2007) A market crash is coming. *The Motley Fool*, March 21.

Markowitz, H. M. (1959) *Portfolio Selection*. John Wiley & Sons, New York.

Markowitz, H. M. and A. F. Perold (1981) Portfolio analysis with factors and scenarios. *The Journal of Finance 36* (4), 871–877.

Martin, G. S. and J. Puthenpurackal (2007) Imitation is the sincerest form of flattery: Warren Buffett and Berkshire Hathaway. Working Paper: Texas A&M University.

Maug, E. and N. Naik (1995) Herding and delegated portfolio management: The impact of relative performance evaluation on asset allocation. Working paper, London Business School.

Mauldin, J. (2007) Be careful what you wish for, *John Mauldin's Weekly e-Letter*, June 15.

McCrary, S. A. (2006a). *Hedge Fund Course*. John Wiley & Sons, Inc, Hoboken.

McCrary, S. A. (2006b). *How to Create and Manage a Hedge Fund: A Professional's Guide*. John Wiley & Sons, Inc, Hoboken.

McGreggor, R., A. Bounds and E. Callan (2007) China cuts tax rebates to curb exports, *Financial Times*, June 19.

Mencions, J. (2007) Non-linear dependence and market timing ability in the hedge fund industry. Presentation, VIII Workshop on Quantitative Finance, University Ca''Foscari of Venice, January 25.

Merton, R. C. (1990) *Continuous-Time Finance*. Blackwell Publishers, Cambridge, Mass.

Merton, R. C. (2000a). Finance and the role of financial engineering in the 21st century. *Nikkei Market's Japan Investor's Watch, The Nikkei Weekly Asia Web Guide*.

Merton, R. C. (2000b). Future possibilities in finance theory and finance practice. In H. Geman, D. Madan, S. R. Pliska, and T. Vorst (Eds.), *Mathematical Finance: Bachelier Congress*, pp. 47–74. Springer.

Merton, R. C. and P. A. Samuelson (1974) Fallacy of the log-normal approximation to optimal portfolio decision-making over many periods. *Journal of Financial Economics* **1**, 67–94.

Miller, R. and A. Gehr (2005) Sample bias and Sharpe's performance measure: a note. *Journal of Financial and Quantitative Analysis* **13**, 943–946.

Mishkin, F. S. (1991) Asymmetric information and financial crises: a historical perspective. In R. G. Hubbard (Ed.), *Financial Markets and Financial Crises*, pp. 69–108. University of Chicago Press, Chicago, IL.

Mishkin, F. S. and T. Herbertsson (2006) Financial stability in iceland. Iceland Chamber of Commerce, May.

Modigliani, F. and R. A. Cohn (1979) Inflation, rational valuation and the market. *Financial Analysts Journal* **35**, 24–44.

Moffatt, C. (2006) Wall Street week 'hall of fame' inductee introduced to the George investment program class. thegeorginvestmentsview.

Mossin, J. (1968) Optimal multiperiod portfolio policies. *Journal of Business* **41**, 215–229.

Mulvey, J. M. (1996) Generating scenarios for the Towers Perrin investment system. *Interfaces* **26**, 1–13.

Mulvey, J. M. (2004) The role of hedge funds for long-term investors. *Journal of Financial Transformations*.

Mulvey, J. M. (2007) The role of alternative assets for optimal portfolio construction. Encyclopedia of Risk Assessment.

Mulvey, J. M., D. Darius, A. Ilhan, K. Simsek, and R. Sircar (2002) Trend following hedge funds and multi-period asset allocation. *Quantitative Finance fall*.

Mulvey, J. M. and B. Pauling (2002) Advantages of multi-period portfolio models. *Journal of Portfolio Management Winter*.

Mulvey, J. M., K. Simsek, and S. Kaul (2004) Evaluating trend-following commodity index for multi-period asset allocation. *Journal of Alternative Investments Summer*.

Mulvey, J. M. and A. Thompson (2006) Statistical learning theory in equity return forecasting. INFORMS Computer Society, 2005 Meeting and Publication, Annapolis, Maryland.

Mulvey, J. M. and A. E. Thorlacius (1998) The Towers Perrin global capital market scenario generation system. In W. T. Ziemba and J. M. Mulvey (Eds.), *World Wide Asset and Liability Management*, pp. 286–312. Cambridge University Press.

Mulvey, J. M., C. Ural, and Z. Zhang (2007) Optimizing performance for long-term investors: Wide diversification and overlay strategies. *Quantitative Finance*.

Mulvey, J. M., B. Pauling, S. Britt and F. Morin (2007) Dynamic financial analysis for multinational insurance companies. In W. T. Ziemba and S. A. Zenios (Eds.), *Handbook of Asset and Liability Management*, Vol. 2: Applications and Case Studies, North Holland, 543–590.

Mulvey, J. M., B. Pauling, S. Britt and F. Morin (2007) Dynamic financial analysis for multinational insurance companies in S. A. Zenios and W. T. Ziemba (Eds.), *Handbook of Asset and Liability Management*, Handbooks in Finance, pp. 385–428. North Holland.

Nelden (2006) *Hedge fund investment management*. Elsevier.

Nielson, L. T. and M. Vassalou (2004) Sharpe ratios and alphas in continuous time. *Journal of Financial and Quantitative Analysis 39*(1), 103–114.

Nordel, J. and V. Kristinsson (1996) Iceland, the Republic. Central Bank of Iceland.

Oxford Business Group (2006) Changing face of FDI. http://www.oxfordbusinessgroup.com/weekly01.asp?id=2422 .

Patrick, M. (2006) Man group fund looks to shut down. *Wall Street Journal*, November 28, 2006.

Pennanen, T. and M. Koivu (2002) Integration quadratures in discretization of stochastic programs. Stochastic programming e-print series.

Perlez, J. (2004) Across Asia, Beijing's star is in ascendance. *New York Times August 28*.

Perold, A. F. (1998) Long-Term Capital Management. Harvard Business School Case N9-200.

Poterba, J. M. and L. H. Summers (1988) Mean reversion in stock prices: evidence and implications. *Journal of Financial Economics* **22**, 27–59.

Rachev, Z. (Ed.) (2003) *Handbook of Heavy Tailed Distributions in Finance*. Handbooks in Finance Series, North Holland, www.elsevier.nl/homepage/sae/hf/menu.htm.

Rendon, J. and W. T. Ziemba (2007) Is the january effect still alive in the futures markets? *Finanzmarket and Portfolio Management, forthcoming*.

Reuters (2003, December). China fdi slump may signal fewer big deals.

Ritter, J. R. (1996) How I helped make Fischer Black wealthier. *Financial Management 25*(4), 104–107.

Ross, S. A. (1973) The economic theory of agency: The principal's problem. *American Economic Review* **63**, 134–139.

Ross, S. A. (1999) A billion dollars just isn't what it used to be. *Risk, (May)*, 64–66.

Roy, A. (1952) Safety first and the holding of assets. *Econometrica 20*(July), 431–449.

Ruoen, R. (1997) China's economic performance in an international perspective, OECD.

Ruoen, R. (1998) China's economic performance in international and long-term perspective. Working paper, Beihang University.

Ruoen, R. (2007) Private correspondence.

Ruoen, R. and S. L. Lin (2007) Total factor productivity growth in Chinese industries, 1981-2000 in D. W. Jorgenson, M. Kuroda and K. Motohashi (eds) *Productivity in Asia: economic growth and competitiveness*, Edward Elgar Publishing.

Samuelson, P. A. (1969) Lifetime portfolio selection by dynamic stochastic programming. *Review of Economics and Statistics* **51**, 239–246.

Samuelson, P. A. (1970) The fundamental approximation theorem of portfolio analysis in terms of means, variances, and higher moments. *Review of Economic Studies* **37**, 537–542.

Samuelson, P. A. (1971) The fallacy of maximizing the geometric mean in long sequences of investing or gambling. *Proceedings National Academy of Science* **68**, 2493–2496.

Samuelson, P. A. (2006) Letter to W. T. Ziemba, December 13.

Samuelson, P. A. (2007) Letter to W. T. Ziemba, May 7.

Schwartz, S. L. and W. T. Ziemba (2000) Predicting returns on the Tokyo stock exchange. In *Security Market Imperfections in World Wide Equity Markets*, pp. 492–511. Cambridge University Press.

Schwert, W. G. (2003) Anomalies and market efficiency. Handbooks in Economics 21, pp. 939–976. North Holland, Amsterdam.

Setser, B. and R. Ziemba (2006) Petrodollar Watch. Roubini Global Economics.

Sharpe, W. F. (1966) Mutual fund performance. *Journal of Business* **39**, 119–138.

Sharpe, W. F. (1994) The Sharpe ratio. *Journal of Portfolio Management 21*(1), 49–58.

Shaw, J., E. O. Thorp, and W. T. Ziemba (1995) Risk arbitrage in the Nikkei put warrant market, 1989-90. *Applied Mathematical Finance* **2**, 243–271.

Shiller, R. (2000) *Irrational exuberance*. Princeton University Press.

Shiller, R. J. (2006) Ivy league investors. Project Syndicate, www.project-syndicate.org/commentary/shiller-43/English.

Shleifer, A. (2000) *Inefficient markets: an introduction to behavorial finance*. Oxford University Press.

Siegel, J. J. (2002) *Stocks for the long run*. John Wiley & Sons, Inc, Hoboken.

Siegel, J. J. (2005) *The Future for Investors: Why the Tried and the True Triumph Over the Bold and the New*. Crown Business.

Siegel, L. B. (2003) *Benchmarks and investment management*. AIMR.

Siegel, L. B., K. F. Kroner, and S. W. Clifford (2001) The greatest return stories ever told. *The Journal of Investing* (Spring), 1–12.

Siegmann, A. and A. Lucas (2002) Explaining hedge fund investment styles by loss aversion. Working paper, Vrije Universiteit Amsterdam.

Sims, C. (1980) Macro-economics and reality. *Econometrica* **48**, 1–48.

Smith, J. E. (1993) Moment methods for decision analysis. *Management Science* **39**, 340–358.

Solnik, B., C. Boucrelle, and Y. Le Fur (1996) International market correlation and volatility. *Financial Analysts Journal* **52**, 17–34.

Sortino, F. A. and L. N. Price (1994) Performance measurement in a downside risk framework. *Journal of Investing* (Fall), 3(3), 59–65.

Sortino, F. A. and R. van der Meer (1991) Downside risk. *Journal of Portfolio Management* (Summer).

Spurgin, R. B. (2000) How to game your Sharpe ratio. *Journal of Alternative Investments* **4**(3), 38–46.

Standard and Poors (2006) Standard & Poor's revises republic of iceland outlook to negative on hard landing risk; ratings affirmed Standard & Poor's revises Republic of Iceland outlook to negative on hard landing risk; ratings affirmed, June 5.

Stanford Management Company (2006) Endowment asset allocation. www.stanfordmanage.org/smc.endowment.html.

Stone, D. and W. T. Ziemba (1993) Land and stock prices in Japan, *Journal of Economic Perspectives*, **7**(3), 149–165.

Studwell, J. (2003) *The China Dream: the Elusive Quest for the Greatest Untapped Market on Earth*. Profile Books, London.

Sun, Q., W. Tong, and J. Tong (2003) China share issue privatization: the extent of its success. *Journal of Financial Economics*, **70**(2), 183–222.

Swensen, D. F. (2000) *Unconventional Success: A Fundamental Approach to Personal Investment*. Free Press.

Swensen, D. F. (2005) *Pioneering Portfolio Management: An Unconventional Approach to Institutional Investment*. Free Press.

Tenebaum, E. (2004) Enemigos: Argentina y el FMI: la apasionante discusión entre un periodista y uno de los hombres clave del fondo en los noventa. Grupo editorial Norma, Buenos Aires.

Tett, G. (2006) Pension funds help derivatives market surge to $ 370,000 billion, Financial Times, November 19, 2006.

The Economist (2003) Fear of floating. July 10.

The Economist (2005) Counting the cost.

The Economist (2007) Even tigers get tired, Economist.com (May 23).

Thorp, E. O. and W. T. Ziemba (2007) Understanding the finite properties of the Kelly Capital growth criterion: response to Samuelson, mimeo.

Thomas, Jr., L. (2006) A $700 million hedge fund, down from $3 billion, says it will close. *Wall Street Journal*, October 31, 2006.

Thorp, E. O. (1962) *Beat the Dealer*. Random House, New York.

Thorp, E. O. (1966) *Beat the Dealer* (2 ed.). Vintage, New York.

Thorp, E. O. (1967) *Beat the Market*. Random House, New York.

Thorp, E. O. (1975) Portfolio choice and the Kelly criterion. In W. Ziemba and R. Vickson (Eds.), *Stochastic Optimization Models in Finance*. Academic Press, New York.

Thorp, E. O. (2006) The Kelly criterion in blackjack, sports betting and the stock market. In S. A. Zenios and W. T. Ziemba (Eds.), *Handbook of asset and liability management*, Volume I: Theory and Methodology Handbooks in Finance, pp. 385–428. North Holland.

Thorp, E. O. (2007) Private Correspondence.

Tian, L. (2000) State shareholding and the value of Chinese firms. Working paper, London Business School.

Till, H. (2006) EDHEC comments on the Amaranth case: early lessons from the debacle. Technical report, EDHEC.

Trigo, E., D. Chudnovsky, E. Cap, and A. López (2002) Los trangénicos en la agricultura argentina: Una historia con final abierto.

UN Conference on Trade and Development (2006) UNCTAD world investment report.

UniCredit Banca Mobliare (2004) Economic & market trends.

Valgreen, C. L. and R. Kallestrup (2006) Iceland: Geyser crisis. Danske Research, March 21.

Vasicek, O. A. (1977) An equilibrium characterization of the term structure. *Journal of Financial Economics 5(2)*, 177–88.

Wallace, S. W. and W. T. Ziemba (Eds.) (2005) *Applications of Stochastic Programming*. SIAM - Mathematical Programming Series on Optimization.

Wang, C. (2003) Ownership and operating performance of Chinese IPOs. Technical report, National University of Singapore.

Wang, C. (2004) Relative strength strategies in China's stock market: 1994-2000. *Pacific-Basin Finance Journal* 12, 159–177.

Wang, C. and S. Chin (2004) Profitability of return and volume-based investment strategies in China's stock market. *Pacific-Basin Finance Journal, forthcoming*.

Watts, J. (2006) China's powerhouse vision for 2050, The Guardian, February 10.

White, B. (2006) Amaranth chief defends policies. *Financial Times*, 9/ 3- 4/06.

Wikipedia (2006) Amaranth advisors. website.

Williams, J. B. (1936) Speculation and the carryover. *Quarterly Journal of Economics* 50, 436.

Wilson, D. and R. Purushothaman (2003) Dreaming with BRICs: The path to 2050, Global Economics Paper No 99, Goldman Sachs.

Winklevoss, H. E. (1982) PLASM: pension liability and asset simulation model. *Journal of Finance 37(2)*, 585–594.

Wise, C. and M. Pastor (2001) Argentina: From poster child to basket case. *Foreign Affairs November-December*.

World Bank (2007) Quarterly Report China. Beijing. May.

Xu, Y. and C. Wang (2004) What determines Chinese stock returns? Technical report, Shanghai Stock Exchange.

Yadav, V. (2007) The Political Economy of the Egyptian-Israeli QIZ Trade Agreement, *Middle East Review of International Affairs*, March.

Yale Endowment Committee (YEC) (2005, 2006). Annual reports, 2005, 2006.

Zakamouline, V. (2007) Generalized sharpe ratios and portfolio performance evaluation, mimeo, Agder University College, Norway.

Zellner, A. (1962) An efficient method of estimating seemingly unrelated regression models. *Journal of the American Statistical Association* 57, 348–368.

Zenios, S. A. and W. T. Ziemba (Eds.) (2006) *Handbook of Asset-Liability Management, Volume 1: Theory and Methodology*. North Holland.

Zenios, S. A. and W. T. Ziemba (Eds.) (2007) *Handbook of Asset-Liability Management, Volume 2: Applications and Case Studies*. North Holland.

Ziemba., R. E. S. (2003) Importing monetary stability? : An analysis of the dollarization trilemma. Unpublished MPhil Thesis, Oxford University.

Ziemba, R. E. S. (2005). Development implications of currency policies: Evidence from Egypt, Turkey and Argentina. working paper, September.

Ziemba, R. E. S. (2007) Adjusting to high oil prices: petrodollars and spending rises in the GCC, Iran and other oil exporters, RGE Monitor, July.

Ziemba, R. E. S. and W. T. Ziemba (2007) Rogue trading: can it be optimal? submitted, *American Economic Review*, 15 pp.

Ziemba, W. T. (1994) Investing in the turn of the year effect in the futures markets. *Interfaces 24(3)*, 46–61.

Ziemba, W. T. (1999)' The stochastic programming approach to hedge fund disaster prevention. Slides for a talk given at UNICOM Seminar, London, May.

Ziemba, W. T. (2003) *The stochastic programming approach to asset liability and wealth management.* AIMR, Charlottesville, VA.

Ziemba, W. T. (2005). The symmetric downside risk Sharpe ratio and the evaluation of great investors and speculators. *Journal of Portfolio Management Fall*, 108–122.

Ziemba, W. T., S. L. Brumelle, A. Gautier, and S. L. Schwartz (1986) *Dr. Z's 6/49 Lotto Guidebook.* Dr. Z Investments, San Luis Obispo, CA.

Ziemba, W. T. and D. B. Hausch (1986) *Betting at the Racetrack.* Dr. Z. Investments, San Luis Obispo, CA.

Ziemba, W. T. and J. M. Mulvey (Eds.) (1998) *World Wide Asset and Liability Modeling.* Cambridge University Press.

Ziemba, W. T. and S. L. Schwartz (1991) *Invest Japan.* Probus Professional Publishing, Chicago.

Ziemba, W. T. and S. L. Schwartz (1992) *Power Japan: How and why Japanese Economy Works.* Chicago, IL Probus Professional Publishing, Chicago.

Ziemba, W. T. (2007) The Kelly criterion and its variants: theory and practice in sports, lottery, futures and options trading, Mathematical Finance Seminar, April 6.

Index

Index compiled by Annette Musker